FROM
THE BLACK MOUNTAIN
TO WAZIRISTAN

BEING AN ACCOUNT OF THE BORDER COUNTRIES AND THE
MORE TURBULENT OF THE TRIBES CONTROLLED BY THE
NORTH-WEST FRONTIER PROVINCE, AND OF OUR MILITARY
RELATIONS WITH THEM IN THE PAST

BY

COLONEL H. C. WYLLY, C.B.

AUTHOR OF 'THE CAMPAIGN OF MAGENTA AND SOLFERINO'
'THE MILITARY MEMOIRS OF LIEUT.-GEN. SIR JOSEPH THACKWELL, G.C.B., K.H.'

WITH AN INTRODUCTION BY

LIEUT.-GEN. SIR HORACE L. SMITH DORRIEN

K.C.B., D.S.O., A.D.C. GEN.

MACMILLAN AND CO., LIMITED
ST. MARTIN'S STREET, LONDON
1912

TO

E. M. W.

PREFACE

THIS book is the outcome of my own experience of
the want of something of the kind in the early
autumn of 1897, when the Second Battalion of my
old Corps, the Sherwood Foresters, Nottinghamshire
and Derbyshire Regiment, then serving at Bareilly,
was ordered to join the Tirah Expeditionary Force.
The Battalion had then been in India for nearly
fifteen years, but only one or two of the officers, and
none of the other ranks, had ever been west of the
Indus, and few of us therefore knew anything of
the wild men against whom we were to fight, or of
the equally wild country in which the operations
were to be conducted.

The fault for such ignorance cannot fairly be said
to have been ours. There was at that time no single
book, generally procurable and of an up-to-date
character, describing the country immediately beyond
the North-West border, the men who inhabited it, and
the campaigns which, since the decline of the Sikh
power, have there become our natural and our
troublous inheritance. Paget and Mason's monu-
mental work, *Expeditions against the North-West
Frontier Tribes*, published in 1885, was wholly
admirable, but much of it was ancient history; it was

an enormous volume; it had for long been "confidential," and had never been placed on general sale. Mr. Oliver's most fascinating book, *Across the Border, or Pathan and Biluch*, had been published in 1890, but it contained little more than a general mention of certain campaigns. It was therefore almost inevitable that British officers—and especially those serving in India in British regiments—had no idea where, in regard to the Frontier, they could draw their knowledge or inspiration.

Even in the present day matters have not greatly improved. The cream has been drawn from Paget and Mason's book, it has been brought up-to-date, and re-christened *Frontier and Overseas Expeditions from India*; but the material is now contained in several large volumes, of which seven have already appeared, and it does not seem to be intended that these should be generally available, since each is labelled "For Official Use only."

It seemed then to me that there was room for a single volume, compiled from official and other sources, describing the more turbulent of the tribes beyond our Border, the countries they inhabit, and the campaigns which the Indian Government has undertaken against them during the last sixty-five years; and up to the time of completing the chapters which follow, I believe this to have been the first attempt which has been made to put such a record before the Army in one handy volume.

I wish to express my thanks to my old comrade, Sir Horace, for so kindly acceding to my request to write an introduction to my book; to my brother, Major Wylly, Librarian at the Royal United Service Institution, for much help in research; and to Mr. J. H. Harper, of the staff of the same Institution, for preparing nearly all the maps.

The appearance of this book has been delayed some four and a half months by the request of the Government of India that it should be submitted to Simla for scrutiny prior to publication; the delay is to be regretted, but it has admitted of advantage being taken of certain suggestions offered by the Indian authorities for adding to the instructional value of the work.

H. C. W.

March, 1912.

CONTENTS

Contents

CHAPTER IV

YUSAFZAIS AND GADUNS: OPERATIONS

CHAPTER V

AKOZAIS (SWAT)

CHAPTER VI

UTMAN KHELS

CHAPTER VII

CLANS OF BAJAUR AND DIR

Contents

CHAPTER VIII

CHITRALIS

CHAPTER IX

MOHMANDS

CHAPTER X

MOHMANDS: OPERATIONS

CHAPTER XI

AFRIDIS

CHAPTER XII

AFRIDIS: OPERATIONS

CHAPTER XIII

KHYBER PASS AFRIDIS: OPERATIONS

Contents

CHAPTER XVIII

WAZIRS: OPERATIONS

APPENDICES

LIST OF MAPS

INTRODUCTION

To do justice to an introduction to a book such as this, one requires to have first-hand knowledge of all the tribes on the Indian Frontier; but although I have served a good many years in India, and some six years altogether in peace and war on the Frontier itself, I cannot even pretend to possess the requisite knowledge to criticise this careful and complete work.

Colonel Wylly has done me the honour of asking me to godfather his book, I am sure more on account of our having been friends for some thirty-six years, than by reason of the outside chance of my being regarded as an authority on Indian Frontier inhabitants; added to which he is aware that I hold the view that no army should undertake a war without doing all in its power in peace time to become efficient up to the last button, and that one of the most important buttons is an accurate knowledge of the country and the people against whom a war may occur.

Let us suppose that our North-West Frontier were not, as it is, bristling with fine fighting races, but were merely an open coast-line with nothing beyond it but sea, and I ask in that case should we keep up an army in India of its present size? and I think all

will agree with me that we certainly should not.
The fair deduction then is that a very important
raison d'être for the army in India is the possibility
of having to suppress recalcitrant tribes on the North-
West Frontier.   It is therefore most important that
our soldiers should study their habits, countries,
armed forces, etc.

Now all that Colonel Wylly says in his preface
about the absence of conveniently small books which
will provide this information is perfectly true, and
the custom has been, when war against a tribe has
been imminent, for the Intelligence Department to
circulate in the army a *brochure* dealing with the
country and the people.   This was very useful, but
the fact that it was most necessary suggests that
opportunities were lacking for studying the question
thoroughly in the piping times of peace.

This book, *From the Black Mountain to Waziristan*, seems to provide the very want.

It is extremely well put together, the story of each
tribe being complete in itself, and with excellent
maps, and written in the easy, attractive style common
to all Colonel Wylly's books, is bound to appeal to all
who take an interest in this most important subject,
and I recommend it especially to the Army in India.

H. L. SMITH-DORRIEN,
Lt. General.

HARNHAM CLIFF, SALISBURY,
7th March, 1912.

CHAPTER I.

THE BORDERLAND.

THE whole of the country lying immediately to the west of the Punjab, and between it and the kingdom of Afghanistan, is held by the two great nations of Pathan and Baluch, the former lying to the north and the latter to the south of a line drawn from the western face of the Suleiman Mountains opposite Dera Ghazi Khan, almost due west to Quetta. The land, then, of the Pathans may be said to comprise the regions of the Sufed Koh and the Suleiman and adjacent mountains with their numerous offshoots; and their territory may be considered roughly to be enclosed by the River Indus on the east, by Afghanistan on the west, Baluchistan on the south, and on the north by Kashmir and the Kunar River—a veritable *tangle* of brown hills.

"It is a long strip of unutterably rugged country; stony barren heights, deep abrupt valleys seamed by occasional torrents; the farms represented by a patch of corn on a hillside or a scrap of cultivation on a narrow strip of alluvial soil alongside a mountain stream. No highways, save those made by us; the village roads—mere tracks straggling over hills

A

and among the roughest ravines—always difficult and often dangerous. The dwelling places, fortified towers or caves among the hills." The Pathan territories occupy many thousand square miles of mountainous country through which flow the Gomal, the Kurram, the Zhob, the Kabul and other smaller rivers with their tributaries, the principal tributaries of the Kabul River being the Chitral, the Bara, the Swat and the Kalpani. The rainfall in this region is scanty and uncertain, and agriculture can only properly be carried on in those tracts watered by these rivers.

The language of the Pathan is called Pushtu or Pukhtu, according as it is the softer Kandahari dialect or the hard guttural speech of the Peshawar Valley, the line which separates the two being the northern boundary of the Khattak tract in Kohat and the south-east corner of the Peshawar District. It is only since the fourteenth century that Pushtu has attained the dignity of a written language. And what of the men who speak it? What is a Pathan?

In India all Pushtu-speaking people come under this designation—a corruption of the word "Pukhtun" —the term being frequently used to denote equally the Pathan proper, the Afghan, the Tajik, the Hazara and the Ghilzai; but, strictly speaking, the title is not really applicable to any of the four last, who, though related to the true Pathan by historical, geographical and ethnological association, are none the less distinct peoples. There is great conflict of opinion as to the original stock from which the Pathans have sprung—

the traditions of the people themselves are conflicting, vague and misleading, but the Pathans believe that they are descended from Saul, the first King of the Jews. They speak of themselves as "Beni Israel," the children of Israel, and the greybeards of the Pathan tribes are fond of tracing their story back to Ibrahim, Isak and Yakub. However far-fetched and mainly traditionary the connection may be, there is, as discussed by Bellew, a savour of Israelitish custom and an often remarkable similarity of name still surviving—Amazites, Moabites and Hittites live again in Amazai, Muhibwal and Hotiwal, to be found on Mount Morah, the hill Pehor, and the plain of Galilee (Jalala); there is the valley of Sudum; the observance of the "Passover," offering sin and thank offerings, or driving off the scapegoat laden with the sins of the people—with many other religious and social observances which are Jewish rather than Islamic in their origin. It would seem that the Pathan race is closely allied to the Afghan on the one side, and, though perhaps not so closely, to certain tribes of Aryan Indians on the other. (The language is a mixture of partly Persian, partly Indian—Prakrit —origin.) The Pathan may be indeed described as an Indian Afghan, and the probabilities are that he represents an earlier eastern emigration of certain sections of the same tribes as have given birth to the Afghan; and from this point of view the Pathan and the Afghan are by origin one and the same. Whatever view is correct, there can be no doubt that the Pathan differs from the Afghan in the possession of

certain Indian affinities not present in the other.
Whether these are due to an admixture of Indian
blood, or whether they are merely the result of close
and prolonged political and social contact with India,
is a matter of no very particular importance.

Ibbetson favours the theory that the Pathans are in
the main a race of Indian extraction, that is, that the
Pathan stock is decidedly Indian despite the admixture of foreign blood. According to him, the true
Pathans are the modern representatives of an Aryan
Indian race called by Herodotus the Pactiyae, which
gave birth to many of the tribes represented to-day
in and on the borders of the Peshawar Valley.
According to this view the Pathans proper are those
Pathan tribes which have a decidedly Pactiyan stock,
in which the preponderating racial element is Indian ;
while the mixed Pactiyan and foreign tribes in which
the stock is not Indian, but Afghan, Turk or Scythian,
as the case may be, are Pathan by virtue of their
Pactiyan blood, as well as by their geographical
location, association, customs and language. But that
the stock is in the main Afghan rather than Indian,
seems borne out by the fact that from the earliest
times of which historical records exist, we find the
Pathan ever arrayed against and despising the Indian
—evincing an antagonism which is not merely
practical and political, but one of ideals and sentiment.
On the other hand, although the Pathan tribes have
had constant and bloody feuds with the Afghans, in
their brief periods of peace they display a marked
similarity of sentiment, ideals and aims, while the

mental characteristics of the Pathan also approximate much more closely to the Afghan than to those of any purely Indian tribe.

Of the other races and tribes to which the term Pathan is loosely applied, the *Ghilzais* are a race of mixed Turkish and Persian descent, which has now become assimilated with the Afghans by sentiment and association. The *Tajiks*, another to which the term Pathan is applied, are of pure Persian origin, and are believed to be the remnants of certain Persian tribes who once inhabited Afghanistan before the advent of the Afghans by whom they were subdued. The Tajiks still retain their Persian speech. The *Hazaras* are Persian-speaking Tartars who have long settled among the Afghans, but who hold among them a subordinate and dependent position.

The character of the Pathan is a favourite theme of disparagement amongst the frontier officials of the last half-century and more. In 1855, Mr. Temple, then Secretary to the Chief Commissioner of the Punjab, wrote thus of them: "Now these tribes are savages—noble savages perhaps—and not without some tincture of virtue and generosity, but still absolutely barbarians nevertheless. . . . They have nominally a religion, but Muhammadanism, as understood by them, is no better, or perhaps is actually worse, than the creeds of the wildest race on earth. In their eyes the one great commandment is blood for blood, and fire and sword for all infidels. . . . They are superstitious and priest-ridden. But the priests are as ignorant as they are bigoted, and use their

influence simply for preaching crusades against un-
believers, and inculcate the doctrine of rapine and
bloodshed against the defenceless people of the plain.
. . . They are a sensual race. They are very
avaricious; for gold they will do almost anything,
except betray a guest. They are thievish and predatory to the last degree. The Pathan mother offers
prayers that her son may be a successful robber.
They are utterly faithless to public engagements; it
would never even occur to their minds that an oath
on the Koran was binding, if against their own
interests. . . . They are fierce and bloodthirsty . . .
they are perpetually at war with each other. Every
tribe and section of a tribe has its internecine wars,
every family its hereditary blood-feuds, and every
individual his personal foes. There is hardly a man
whose hands are unstained. Every person counts up
his murders. Each tribe has a debtor and creditor
account with its neighbours, life for life. . . . They
consider retaliation and revenge to be the strongest of
all obligations. They possess gallantry and courage
themselves, and admire such qualities in others. . . .
To their minds hospitality is the first of virtues. Any
person who can make his way into their dwellings will
not only be safe, but will be kindly received. But as
soon as he has left the roof of his entertainer he
may be robbed and killed."

Mr. Ibbetson wrote of the Pathan in 1881: "The
true Pathan is perhaps the most barbaric of all the
races with which we are brought into contact in
the Punjab. . . . He is bloodthirsty, cruel and vindic-

tive in the highest degree; he does not know what truth or faith is, insomuch that the saying *Afghan be iman* (*i.e.* an Afghan is without conscience) has passed into a proverb among his neighbours; and though he is not without courage of a sort, and is often curiously reckless of his life, he would scorn to face an enemy whom he could stab from behind, or to meet him on equal terms if it were possible to take advantage of him, however meanly. It is easy to convict him out of his own mouth; here are some of his proverbs: 'a Pathan's enmity smoulders like a dung fire'; 'a cousin's tooth breaks upon a cousin';[1] 'keep a cousin poor but use him'; 'when he is little play with him; when he is grown up he is a cousin, fight him'; 'speak good words to an enemy very softly; gradually destroy him root and branch.' At the same time he has a code of honour which he strictly observes, and which he quotes with pride under the name of *Pukhtunwali*. It imposes on him three chief obligations—*Nanawatai*, or the right of asylum, which compels him to shelter and protect even an enemy who comes as a suppliant; *Badal*, or the necessity for revenge by retaliation; and *Mailmastai*, or openhanded hospitality to all who may demand it. And of these three perhaps the last is the greatest. And there is a charm about him, especially about the leading men, which almost makes one forget his treacherous nature. As the proverb says—'the Pathan is one moment a saint, and the next a devil.'

[1] It is significant that the Pushtu word *tarbur* means both cousin and enemy.

For centuries he has been, on our frontier at least, subject to no man. He leads a wild, free, active life in the rugged fastnesses of his mountains; and there is an air of masculine independence about him which is refreshing in a country like India. He is a bigot of the most fanatical type, exceedingly proud and extraordinarily superstitious." Holdich says of the Pathan that "he will shoot his own relations just as soon as the relations of his enemy—possibly sooner—and he will shoot them from behind. Yet the individual Pathan may be trusted to be true to his salt and to his engagements."

Of one Pathan tribe Macgregor said that "there is no doubt, like other Pathans, they would not shrink from any falsehood, however atrocious, to gain an end. Money could buy their services for the foulest deed; cruelty of the most revolting kind would mark their actions to a wounded or helpless foe, as much as cowardice would stamp them against determined resistance." While Mr. Elsmie has spoken as follows of his five years' experience as a Commissioner and Judge among the Pathans of the Peshawar border: "Crime of the worst conceivable kind is a matter of almost daily occurrence; murder in all its phases, unblushing assassination in broad daylight before a crowd of witnesses; the carefully planned secret murder of the sleeping victim at dead of night, murder by robbers, by rioters, by poisoners, by boys, and by women sword in hand. Blood always crying for blood, revenge looked upon as a virtue, the heritage of retribution passed on as a solemn duty from father to son. It would seem that the spirit of murder is latent in the heart of nearly every man in the valley." But, on the other hand, Oliver tells us in *Across the Border*, that the Pathan has sometimes been condemned in what appear too sweeping terms, and that "there is a sort of charm about the better sort that inclines many people to forget his treacherous nature, and even his 'vice is sometimes by action dignified.'"

Probably what Lieut. Enriquez says about these tribesmen in his *Pathan Borderland* describes them with, on the whole, more justice, if less vehemence, than have some of those other writers from whom quotations have here been made. "The Pathan," he says, "is not so black as he is painted. It should not be overlooked that most of the tribes have only been established three hundred years in their present territories, and that their habits are not really much worse than were those of the various English tribes during the first few centuries after their final settlement. The conditions of a feudal system, under which each baron lived in his own castle, and waged constant war with his neighbours over disputes relating to land and women, are simply being repeated again across our border. For stories of gross treachery, or cold-blooded murder and inter-family strife, we have only to turn back the pages of our own history book. In fact, it seems quite unfair to judge the Pathan according to twentieth century standards. For him it is still the tenth century. Moreover, it is ungenerous to assert that there are not many noble exceptions amongst them. . . . When you meet a Pathan, you meet a man like yourself. . . . He will never allow you to abuse him, but makes up for it amply by never making you wish to do so. There is perhaps no native of India who is less irritating to our nerves, and his ideas of tact seem to run on quite the same lines as our own. . . . He takes his independence for granted, and very seldom parades it in the garb of rudeness."

Take him for all in all, there is in the Pathan much to like, a good deal to respect and much to detest. He is very susceptible to the personal influence of Englishmen who are strong, resolute and fearless— men of the type of Nicholson, Abbott, Cavagnari, Battye and many others. In our service he has usually been a loyal and devoted sepoy, and no better instance of the loyalty of the Pathan soldier can be given than is furnished by that of the small body of Khyber Rifles in 1897, who, as Holdich has told us, "maintained British honour in the Khyber, while 9,500 British troops about the Peshawar frontier looked on."

The Pathan enlists freely into our service— there are at the present moment something like eleven thousand Pathans in the Indian Army, and probably the recruiting among the tribesmen was never brisker than during the few months immediately following the close of the operations in Tirah of 1897-98—and he will march anywhere and fight anyone against whom he may be led. Over and over again have Pathans fought in our ranks against their fellow-tribesmen and their own homes. Not only against fathers and brothers, but even against the still more potent religious appeals from the local Ghazis. One thing, however, the Pathan recruit does not give up, "but brings with him to his regiment, keeps through his service, must have leave to look after, will resign promotion to gratify, and looks forward to retiring to thoroughly enjoy— and that is—his cherished feud." If he has not got one when he joins, he may inherit one which may become just as binding, though it concerns people he has not seen for years, and hardly knew when he left home. In India the white man wants leave to get married, he is sick, he needs a change, or to avoid a bad station—for the Pathan soldier there is only one class of "urgent private affairs," but for this he must have leave. Everyone knows for what purpose he goes; it is the only reason when the refusal of leave would justify desertion. In many of the Punjab regiments which recruit Pathans there are cases of transfrontier soldiers who will serve together in all amity for years, but between whom is so bitter a feud that they must take their furlough at different times, since, if they went together, not all would come back.

As to the personal appearance of "the raw material," here is a picture drawn from life by Oliver: "The style of the Tribesman is a little after the manner of Rob Roy—'my foot is on my native heath,' and 'am I not a Pathan'? Even when he leaves his native heath behind, he takes his manners with him. He will come down, a stalwart, manly-looking ruffian, with frank and open manners, rather Jewish features, long hair plentifully oiled under a high turban, with a loose tunic, blue for choice—the better to hide the dirt—worn very long, baggy drawers, a *lungi* or sash across his shoulders, grass sandals, a sheep-skin coat with the hair inside, thickly populated, a long heavy knife, and a rifle, if he is allowed to carry either. He is certain to be filthy and he may be ragged, but he will saunter into a Viceregal *durbar* as proud as Lucifer, and with an air of unconcern a diplomatist might envy."

The Pathan tribes are partly agriculturists and partly nomads, but their migrations are on a small and restricted scale, being no more than annual moves within their own limits from one grazing ground to another, or from their homes among the hills to the warmer and lower valleys. Beyond and upon our frontier the Pathans live in fortified villages, to which are attached stone towers in commanding positions serving as watch towers and places of refuge for the inhabitants. A large number of the men of each tribe obtain their livelihood as petty merchants or traders, carrying goods in caravans between India, Afghanistan and Central Asia. These wandering traders are called *Powindahs*, a term derived from the Persian word *Parwindah*, which signifies a bale of goods. The villages are divided into several distinct allotments of sub-divisions called *Kandis*, according to the number of the sub-divisions of the tribe residing in it. Thus in each village each group of families which goes to form a *Khel*, or clan, has its own Kandi, at the head of which is a *Malik*, who acts as its judge, manager or administrator. In each Kandi, again, there is a *Jumaat*, or mosque, under a *Mullah*, or priest, and an assembly room, called *hujra*, where the residents meet to discuss their affairs, and where visitors and travellers are sheltered. At the head of each clan is a chief styled *Khan*, to whom the *Maliks* are subordinate, but the tribesmen being intensely independent and impatient of control, it is not surprising that neither Maliks nor Khans enjoy any real power. They may be said indeed to possess influence rather than power. All matters of general tribal interest are settled by the decision of a *jirgah* or council of Maliks and in this the real controlling authority resides, the Khan, or tribal chief, merely acting as president of the tribal jirgah, as their leader in time of war, and during peace as their accredited agent for inter-tribal communication. But among the Pathans there can be very little like ordered government, and as a matter of fact the several clans decide their disputes independently of any central controlling authority. The office of Malik and Khan is usually hereditary, but by no means always.

It is not very uncommon for families of one tribe or clan to quarrel with their brethren, and leaving their own tribe, to claim the protection of a neighbouring one. They then become *hamsayas*, or "dwellers beneath the shade," and secure protection in return for obedience. With the Pathans the action of this custom is chiefly confined to traders, menials and other dependents of foreign extraction, who are protected by, but not received into, the tribe.

The great majority of the Pathan tribes are Sunni[1] Muhammadans of a bigoted sort, the exception being the Turis and some of the Bangash and Orakzai clansmen, who are Shiahs. Of the different dignitaries of the Pathan Church there is no occasion here to speak further than to remark that the Mullah, to whom allusion has already been made, is the ordinary, hard working parish priest, whose duties are to attend to the services of the Church, teach the creed, and look after the schools. He is the most important factor in Pathan life and his influence is enormous, despite the fact, as Dr. Pennell points out, "that there is no priesthood in Islam," and that according to its tenets, there is no act of worship and no religious rite which may not, in the absence of a Mullah, be equally well performed by any pious layman. Since, however, "knowledge has been almost limited to the priestly class, it is only natural that in a village, where the Mullahs are almost the only men who can lay claim to anything more than the most rudimentary learning, they should have the people of the village entirely in their own control." The general security in which the Mullah lives is the best possible evidence of the deference accorded to his office. "He is almost the only man," says Oliver, "whose life is sacred from the casual bullet or the hasty knife, for whose blood the Pathan tariff does not provide a rate."

[1] The Sunnis represent the orthodox church of Islam, recognise no divine right of succession to the Caliphate, and claim for the "faithful" free choice in the selection of their spiritual leader ; the Shiahs, or sectarians, claim that the right of succession to Muhammad rests with his cousin Ali and Ali's descendants.

His flock is generally ignorant of everything connected with the Muhammadan religion beyond its most elementary doctrines. In matters of faith the Pathans confine themselves to the belief that there is a God, a prophet, a resurrection, and a day of judgment. They know there is a Koran, but are probably wholly ignorant of its contents. Their practice is un-Islamic. Though they repeat every day that there is one God only who is worthy of worship, they almost invariably prefer to worship some saint or tomb. Indeed, superstition is a more appropriate term for the ordinary belief of the people than the name of religion.

Since mention has above been made of the religious divisions of the tribesmen, I may perhaps briefly allude to their political factions, since reports from beyond the border make frequent mention of the feuds of Gar and Samil. In the fourteenth century a chief of the Bangash tribe, Ismail by name, had two sons, Gar and Samil, whose quarrels led to the tribe being split up into the two great factions which still exist under these names. Bangash or Bankash means "root-destroyer," and this was adopted or bestowed as the tribal name by reason of the enmity aroused between the rival factions. The distinction then established still remains, and affects almost all the surrounding tribes; and since some Sunnis by religion are Samil in politics, and some Shiahs are Gar, while sometimes both cases are reversed, it may easily be realised how prolific are the causes for private quarrels and tribal feuds beyond the Bloody Border.

Of so turbulent a race what Temple said about them

in 1855 might with almost equal truth have been repeated of them annually up to the present time : " They have kept up old quarrels, or picked new ones with our subjects in the plains and valleys near the frontier; they have descended from the hills and fought these battles out in our territory; they have plundered and burnt our villages and slain our subjects; they have committed minor robberies and isolated murders without number; they have often levied blackmail from our villages; they have intrigued with the disaffected everywhere and tempted our loyal subjects to rebel; and they have for ages regarded the plain as their preserve and its inhabitants as their game. When inclined for cruel sport they sally forth to rob and murder, and occasionally to take prisoners into captivity for ransom. They have fired upon our own troops, and even killed our officers in our own territories. They have given an asylum to every malcontent or proclaimed criminal who can escape from British justice. They traverse at will our territories, enter our villages, trade in our markets; but few British subjects, and no servant of the British Government, would dare to enter their country on any account whatever."

Since the 400 miles of our borderland, comprised in the stretch from Buner on the right to Waziristan on the left, is, as computed by the Commander-in-Chief in India in 1897, inhabited by 200,000 first-rate fighting men, of the quarrelsome character above described—every man at all times ready and eager for blood-letting—it would be as well now to recount the measures which the Government of India adopts for their restraint; to state the composition and general distribution of the instruments by means of which the peace of the frontier is more or less preserved; and to note the manner in which offences committed by independent tribes beyond the border are punished.

For the defence of the border, and to prevent the incursion of armed robbers, the system generally followed—with some recent modifications—has been the maintenance of a line of fortified posts along the frontier, garrisoned by regulars and militia. In the year 1884 there were fifty-four such posts situated in the Hazara, Yusafzai, Kohat, Bannu, Dera Ismail Khan, Dera Ghazi Khan and Rajanpur districts, and of these sixteen were held by the Punjab Frontier Force, twenty-six by militia, and the remainder by combined parties of both militia and regulars. In those days the Punjab Frontier Force was generally responsible—a responsibility which endured until 1903—for the military defence of the frontier, with the exception of the Peshawar district. The force was approximately 15,000 strong, and consisted of four regiments of cavalry, the Guides (cavalry and infantry), four mountain batteries, one garrison battery, and eleven infantry battalions, the whole commanded by a Brigadier-General. At that time it was immediately under the orders of the Lieutenant-Governor of the Punjab, but it was a few years later placed under the Commander-in-Chief in India. With the gradual extension of the frontier, and the general

B

forward movement made within recent years, it became apparent that the Punjab Frontier Force could
no longer remain a local and also a border force, and
that in any comprehensive scheme of frontier defence
other regiments of the Indian army must take their
share.   In 1903, then, the Punjab Frontier Force
was abolished.

Under Lord Curzon's rule in India a change was
inaugurated in the system of frontier defence.
Regular troops have been gradually withdrawn, as far
as possible, from advanced trans-frontier positions,
and have been concentrated in large centres within
easy reach.   Their places on the border have been
taken by various corps of militia, military police, and
levies raised locally ; communications have been improved; strategic railways have crept further forward ;
another bridge has been thrown across the Indus ;
and the frontier is now defended by the Peshawar
and Quetta divisions and the Kohat, Derajat and
Bannu brigades, moveable columns being held always
ready to move out at a moment's notice from
Peshawar, Kohat, Bannu and Dera Ismail Khan.
The general sphere of action prescribed for each of
these columns is as under :

Peshawar Column,	- -	The Khyber and the Malakand.
Kohat Column, -	- -	The Kurram.
Bannu Column,	-	The Tochi.
Dera Ismail Khan Column,		Waziristan.

It remains to note the manner in which offences
committed by independent tribes across the border
are punished.   The most simple way of dealing with

a refractory tribe, and in many cases the most
effectual, is to inflict a fine and demand compensation
for plundered property or for lives lost. When the
tribe is dependent upon trade with British territory,
or when a portion resides within British limits, or is
easily accessible from the plains to an attack by a
military force, the demand for payment of fine or
compensation is generally acceded to, and, being paid,
the tribe is again received into favour. Should the
demand be refused, hostages are demanded, or members of the tribe and their property found within
British territory are seized, until such time as the
compensation and fine are paid. Against some tribes,
as in the case of the Afridis of the Kohat Pass in
1876-77, a blockade is an effective measure of punishment. It can, however, only be employed against
such tribes as trade with British territory, and, while
it lasts, any member of the offending tribe found
within our border is at once seized and detained.
This means of punishment has often been found
effectual, and if effectual, it is preferable to a military
expedition, which often leaves behind it bitter
memories in the destruction of property and loss of
life. Last as a measure of punishment comes the
military expedition, which is only resorted to in
exceptional circumstances, and when every other
means of coercing a hostile tribe has failed.

The necessity, in certain circumstances, for military
expeditions has been admitted by the civil authorities of the Punjab in the following statement made
in 1864 by Mr. Davies, Secretary to the Punjab

Government: "The despatch of an expedition into the hills is always in the nature of a judicial act. It is the delivery of a sentence, and the infliction of a punishment for international offences. It is, as a rule, not in assertion of any disputed right, or in ultimate arbitration of any contested claim of its own, that the British Government resolves on such measures, but simply as the only means by which retribution can be obtained for acknowledged crimes by its neighbours, and by which justice can be satisfied or future outrages prevented. In the extreme cases in which expeditions are unavoidable, they are analogous to legal penalties for civil crime—evils in themselves inevitable from deficiencies of preventive police, but redeemed by their deterrent effects. Considerations of expense, of military risk, of possible losses, of incurring antagonism and combination against us on the part of the tribes, all weigh heavily against expeditions; and to set them aside, there must be irresistible obligation to protect and to vindicate the outraged rights of subjects whom we debar from the revenge and retaliation they formerly practised."

At the present moment rather over 9000 Pathans are serving in our militias, border military police and levies, while considerably more than 10,000 are in the ranks of the regular regiments of the Indian army; a certain number, too, are serving in the forces maintained by native chiefs. Considering the readiness with which the Pathan accepts military service, it cannot be said that these numbers are high, but the fact would seem to be that while some tribes are supplying us with more recruits than they can well afford, others have scarcely been drawn upon at all, and many races along the Pathan borderland remain still altogether unexploited.

[1] The North-West Frontier Province is, with the exception of Behar, Chota Nagpur and Orissa, the youngest of the provinces into which British India is divided, while in respect of population and extent of territory administered according to British law, it is also the smallest. It lies between the 31st and 36th degrees of latitude and the 69th and 74th degrees of longitude; its total length, as the crow flies, is over 400 miles, its average breadth is from 100 to 150 miles, the total area comprised within its limits being roughly 38,000 square miles. Only 13,000 square miles, however, are under full British law and administration, and 25,000 square miles are occupied by tribes who are under British political control, but who maintain their internal or municipal independence. The British territory part of the province is divided into the five districts of Hazara, Peshawar, Kohat, Bannu and Dera Ismail Khan, whose western boundary, known as the administrative border, is a sinuous line extending for some 600 miles. On the other side of this administrative or inner provincial border dwell the municipally independent tribes who

---

[1] For what follows I am indebted to a paper read by Mr. W. R. H. Merk, C.S.I., LL.D., at the Royal Society of Arts, and published in the Journal for June, 1911, on "the North-West Frontier Province of India." The North-West Frontier Province was formed on the 9th November, 1901.

are under the political control of the Chief Commissioner, a control which he exercises with the aid of
the officers in charge of the political agencies, viz.
Swat, Dir and Chitral, the Khyber, the Kurram, and
Northern and Southern Waziristan. These agencies
have been described as the tentacles of civilised order,
stretching into a mass of barbarism and savagery;
and the remainder of the space beyond the administrative border and as far as the "Durand line" or
"the outer provincial border," separating the British
and Afghan spheres of influence, is occupied by the
independent tribes. The length of this outer border
cannot be less than 800 miles.

The population of the five British districts is about
2,200,000, and of the outer portion of the province
probably a million and a half.

After the border war of 1897 a narrow gauge line
was laid from Nowshera, on the Kabul River, to the
foot of the Malakand; constructed in the first
instance for military reasons, it rapidly developed
into an important artery of commerce, justifying its
conversion from a narrow to a broad gauge. Another
railway which, in 1897, stopped on the left bank of
the Indus at Kushalgarh, now crosses the Indus
by a bridge, and has been extended via Kohat and
Hangu to Thal, at the southern end of the Kurram
Valley. A third line to the base of the hills is under
construction; it will be taken over the Indus at
Kalabagh and carried to Bannu. When the Thal
railway has been extended to the head of the Kurram
Valley; when a short line has been constructed in the

Hazara district; and when a lateral branch has been
provided from Bannu to Tank and Dera Ismail Khan,
the province will be fairly well equipped with railways of a distinct commercial and strategic value.

A perusal of the chapters which follow will probably
make it apparent that the general policy of the Government of India in regard to the frontier tribes is,
and has been—as well described by a former Chief
Commissioner of the North-West Frontier Province—
" a forward one only when necessity compels, and
stationary where circumstances permit."

CHAPTER II.

BLACK MOUNTAIN TRIBES.[1]

BEFORE describing the Black Mountain itself and the various tribes which inhabit its slopes, it may be as well to say something about the country which encompasses it on three sides and about the men who occupy it.

Allai is a valley bounded by Kohistan on the north and east, by the Bhogarmang Valley, Nandihar and Deshi on the south, and by the Indus on the west. The valley of Allai is divided from Kohistan on the north by a range of mountains rising to over 15,000 feet, and from Nandihar and Deshi by another range running from the British boundary to the Indus above Thakot. The average breadth of the Allai Valley is about twelve miles, and the total area about 200 square miles. Wheat, barley, Indian corn and rice are grown, and the mountain slopes at the eastern end are covered with forest.

The men of Allai are ever engaged in internal quarrels; blood feuds are rife, and often embroil the whole tribe. They are but little dependent on British territory; number some 9000 fighting men,

[1] See Map III.

indifferently armed; they have at times, although not of late years, given us some trouble, but have usually been coerced by means of a blockade, although a really effective one is not easy to enforce.

Nandihar is a valley lying to the south of Allai, and adjoining the British valleys of Bhogarmang and Konsh on the east. It is divided by a spur of the hills into two long narrow glens; the area of the valley is about ninety square miles, and its elevation is from four to five thousand feet. There are about a thousand fighting men; the people are perpetually at feud; the country is very easily accessible from British territory.

Tikari is a valley lying to the south of Nandihar, and between it and Agror in British territory. It is about eight miles long, four broad, and lies at an elevation of about 4500 feet. There are only some 400 fighting men. Supplies in Tikari are plentiful, with the exception of fuel, and water is abundant. The men of Tikari have not been troublesome neighbours.

Deshi is the name given to the country to the north of Agror, and lying to the west of Nandihar. It comprises a portion of the eastern slopes of the Black Mountain—a succession of bold, wooded spurs with intervening watercourses, on the banks of which are the villages. The fighting men number just over 700, indifferently armed. They are a united tribe, equally among themselves and when external danger threatens, but are easily accessible and exposed to attack, although not immediately on our border.

They gave us some trouble in 1868, but have been quiet since.

All the above-mentioned tribes are Swatis; none of them, except the men of Deshi, have a very high reputation for courage; they are all Sunni Muhammadans and very bigoted.

Tanawal, an independent State, is, roughly speaking, a square block of territory in the north-west corner of the Hazara district, south of the Black Mountain and Agror. It consists of 200 square miles of hilly country, held as a *jaghir* by the Nawab of Amb, a fort and village on the right bank of the Indus. Little is known of the origin of the Tanawalis.

We now come to the Yusafzai tribes inhabiting the slopes of the Black Mountain lying to the east of the Indus, and occupying the southern corner of the angle formed by that river and the British boundary. The total length of this mountain is about twenty-five to thirty miles, and its average height about 8000 feet above sea-level. It ascends from the Indus basin at its southern end near the village of Kiara, and so up to its watershed by Baradar; thence it runs north-east by north to the point on the crest known as Chitabat. From here the range runs due north, finally descending to the Indus by two large spurs, at the foot of the easternmost of which lies Thakot. The Indus, after passing Thakot, runs westward along the northern foot of the mountain till it washes the western of the two spurs above mentioned, when it takes a sharp bend to the south, and runs below and parallel to the western foot of the range.

The Black Mountain may be described as a long, narrow ridge with higher peaks at intervals, and occasional deep passes; the general outline of the crest is more rounded than sharp. From the sides numerous large spurs project, which are often precipitous and rocky, with deep, narrow glens or gorges lying between them, in which are some of the smaller villages of the tribes, the larger ones being, as a rule, situated on the banks of the Indus. The whole of the upper portion of the mountain is thickly wooded, with pine, oak, sycamore, horse-chestnut and wild cherry. The crest of the mountain is crossed by several passes. The mountain is bounded on the south by Tanawal; on the east by Agror, Pariari, and the Swati tribes of Tikari, Nandihar and Deshi; on the northern extremity lies the Indus and Thakot; and on the west, between the crest and the River Indus, the slopes are occupied by Yusafzai Pathans. These slopes fall steeply from the crest for some 2000 feet; then follows a zone of gentle, well-cultivated slopes; and then from 4000–5000 feet altitude the hill drops precipitously to the Indus. The actual Indus Valley here varies in width from a few hundred yards to nearly two miles, being narrowest at Kotkai and at its broadest at Palosi. It is crossed at about eleven different points by ferries, the boats holding from twenty to thirty passengers, but the inhabitants pass over the river almost everywhere on inflated skins.

There are many routes by which the mountain
can be ascended, and most of these have been used
by our troops in different expeditions : from British
territory all of them start from either Tanawal or
Agror.

The western face of the Black Mountain is inhabited by three clans :

        1. The Hassanzais.
        2. The Akazais.
        3. The Chagarzais.

On the eastern face are the Saiyids of Pariari,
besides the men of Deshi who have already been
described.

The Hassanzais are a division of the Isazai clan
of Yusafzai Pathans, and live on either side of the
Indus ; those cis-Indus occupy the most southern
portion of the western slopes of the Black Mountain,
while those trans-Indus live immediately opposite
to them. The former are bounded on the north
and east by the Akazais, on the west by the Indus,
and on the south the Hassanzai border adjoins the
territory of the Nawab of Amb. The Hassanzais
are divided into ten sub-divisions with a total fighting
strength of something under 2000 men, who are not,
however, specially noted for their bravery. In the
event of attack the Hassanzais could probably depend
for assistance upon two other divisions of Isazai
Yusafzais, the Akazais and the Mada Khels, of whom
the last named live on the right bank of the Indus.
Of the ten sub-divisions of the Hassanzais that known
as the Khan Khel is the most troublesome, so far

as we are concerned, but the whole clan is constantly engaged in internal feud.

During the days of the Sikh rule, the famous Sikh general, Hari Singh, with two regiments, made an expedition into the Hassanzai country via Darband and Baradar and burnt some of the villages.

The Akazais, like the Hassanzais, are the descendants of Isa, and are also a division of the Isazai clan of Yusafzais, inhabiting a portion of the crest and western slopes of the Black Mountain to the north of the Hassanzais, having on the east a part of Agror and the Pariari Saiyids, to the north the Chagarzais, and on the west the Indus. They have no territory trans-Indus, with the exception of part of one village which they share with the Hassanzais. Their chief villages are Kand, Bimbal and Biliani, the two first being nearest to the crest of the Black Mountain, and situated on flat, open ground, with difficult approaches. The Akazais are divided into four subdivisions, and can probably put some 1100 men in the field. Neither this clan nor the Hassanzais are dependent on British territory, but so far as the Akazais are concerned we possess the power to attack them, while we know all about the rich and accessible rice and wheat crops which they cultivate round the villages which they own, or in which they hold shares, in the Tikari Valley. During the Sikh rule, and up to 1868, the Akazais held the village of Shatut in the Agror Valley. It is only within the last twenty-five years or so that this clan has begun to give trouble.

The Chagarzais are a division of the Malizai clan of the Yusafzai Pathans, claiming to be descended from Chagar, the son of Mali, who was one of the sons of Yusaf. They occupy the country on either side of the river, those cis-Indus being located on the western slopes of the Black Mountain, to the north of the Akazais. They are divided into three sub-divisions, and could probably call together from both sides of the river some 4600 armed men—the larger body from across the Indus.

The southern boundary of the cis-Indus Chagarzais is contiguous with that of the Akazais, and follows the spur of the Black Mountain running from the Machai peak to the Indus bank—the southern face of the spur belonging to the Akazais and the northern to the Chagarzais. On the west and north the Indus forms the boundary, while on the east the Chagarzais are bounded by the country of the Deshiwals and of the Pariari Saiyids.

The Chagarzais are considered braver than the Hassanzais and Akazais, who would, however, probably unite with them if attacked, as would also contingents from Swat and Buner.

Little is definitely known about the communications in the interior of the country. The crest of the mountain and the Machai peak may be gained by advancing up the Kungali spur to Chitabat; but owing to the steep and rugged nature of the country, and the thick forest clothing the whole of the upper portion of the hill, an active enemy, well acquainted with the ground, would have every facility for annoy-

ing the troops and opposing the advance. About
three miles north of Machai is the high peak of
Ganthar, and the pass leading from Pariari to Pakban
—one of the principal villages—lies on the crest
between these two points. Here the ground is
broken and precipitous, flanked by thick pine forests,
and in all probability forms a strong position from
which the advance of a force moving from Machai upon
Ganthar could be disputed. From this point, which
lies in a deep hollow on the crest, the ascent to
Ganthar, though steep in places and everywhere
flanked by forest, is not of any great difficulty.
Beyond Ganthar the advance along the crest would
be easier.

The Chagarzais also are not in any way dependent
upon British territory. It is only since 1863 that
they have given us any trouble, and on the few
occasions when they have opposed us, their operations
have not been long protracted nor of a very serious
character.

Colonies of Saiyids, religious adventurers—theo-
retically those who are the direct descendants of
Ali, the son-in-law of the Prophet—occupy several
of the glens on the mountain itself, and have
caused much of the bloodshed and trouble which
have stained and disturbed these parts. In two
of these glens on the eastern slope of the Black
Mountain are the Pariari Saiyids. On the western
face, among the Hassanzais, are the Saiyids of Tilli;
one or two more such colonies are scattered through
the Chagarzai country; while a rather formidable

religious body, the Akhund Khels, holds the glens and spurs on the extreme north-west corner down to the Indus. Numerically all are more or less insignificant, but they exercise considerable influence.

Neither the extent nor the population of this Black Mountain country warrant its being ranked as of any exceptional importance. As Oliver reminds us, " the tribes are not numerous, nor particularly war-like, and most of them are miserably poor, but they, and the nests of fanatical hornets they shelter, have for long proved capable of inflicting an altogether disproportionate amount of annoyance."

OPERATIONS.

The first time the Hassanzai clan came into notice was on the occasion of the murder by them of two officers of the Indian Customs Department.

Shortly after the annexation of the Punjab a preventive line was established along the left bank of the Indus, so far as British jurisdiction extended, to prevent trans-Indus salt being smuggled into the Punjab. In 1851 this line was extended five miles beyond Torbela to a point on the Indus where the cis-Indus territory of the Nawab of Amb commenced. In November of that year two of our customs officials, visiting this portion of the border, were murdered by a band of armed Hassanzais, when actually within the bounds of the Nawab of Amb. The Nawab was at once called to account, and delivered up such Hassanzais as happened to be within his territory, for which act the Hassanzais made war upon him, laid waste his border villages, and seized two of his forts: upon this, British interference became necessary, and orders were issued for the assembly of a punitive force.

Expedition against the Black Mountain Hassanzais, 1852-53.—In December 1852 the troops, as enumerated below, were concentrated at Shergarh on the north-western border of the Hazara district under the command of Lieut.-Col. Mackeson,[1] C.B., Commissioner of Peshawar.

> Four guns, 5th Troop, 1st Brigade, H.A.
> Six guns, Mountain Train Battery.
> 16th Irregular Cavalry.[2]
> 7th Company Sappers and Miners.
> 3rd Native Infantry.[3]
> Kelat-i-Ghilzie Regiment.[4]
> Four Companies Corps of Guides.
> 1st Sikh Infantry.[5]
> 176 men Rawal Pindi Police.
> Two Regiments Kashmir Dogras.
> Levies (1760 men).

The force was divided into three columns with a reserve, occupying respectively Chatta, Shingli, Shoshni and Shergarh. The fort at Shingli, which was one of the two that had been captured by the Hassanzais from the Nawab of Amb, was recovered without loss, and while our troops were engaged in

---

[1] It is to be regretted that no "life" of this remarkable frontier official has ever appeared.

[2] Disbanded in 1861.

[3] Mutinied at Phillour in 1857.

[4] Now the 12th Pioneers.

[5] Now the 51st Sikhs.

making it defensible, the Hassanzais and Akazais occupied the crest of the Black Mountain, and advanced their picquets close up to Chatta. The authorities had forbidden the employment of the regular troops with the force on the top of the mountain at so late a season of the year, so that they were thereby restricted to the duties of a reserve at Shergarh—where, confined in a narrow valley and incumbered with all kinds of *impedimenta*, they were of little or no assistance to a force engaged in mountain warfare. Col. Mackeson consequently decided to move the reserve of regular troops round to the banks of the Indus, behind the Black Mountain, and thus to turn the position on the heights; and to let each column of attack trust to a small reserve of its own, and to the fort at Shergarh in the rear, if all were beaten back.

The regular troops accordingly marched on the 24th and 25th December from Shergarh to Darband, behind the screen formed by the irregular portion of the force at Chatta, Shingli and Shoshni. On the 27th, as the result of a reconnaissance, Col. Mackeson decided to alter his plans, and to place the main part of the regular troops at Baradar, with four companies in Chamberi, to make demonstrations on the heights in front of the last-named place—for to move them to the rear of the enemy's position would have involved them in difficult ground.

On the 29th, these dispositions having been completed, orders were issued for the advance of the remaining three columns, Panj Gali being named as their ultimate objective; in the event of a repulse they were to fall back either upon Chamberi or Baradar.

The right column, under Lieut.-Col. R. Napier, arrived, after a considerable amount of opposition, near the summit of the mountain at a point where a broad spur, forming the top of the range occupied by the Akazais, branched off at an elevation of some 9000 feet. By this ridge the enemy retired, and no further defence of the hill was made. Shortly before sunset the Guides, under Lieut. Hodson, arrived at the shoulder of the mountain above Panj Gali, which was still occupied by the tribesmen, but on the appearance of our troops they rapidly retreated, and the right column bivouacked here for the night.

The centre column, under Major J. Abbott, had ascended about halfway to Panj Gali when the troops suddenly came upon the main body of the Hassanzais, consisting of about 600 matchlock men, strongly posted upon a steep eminence in the centre of the main ravine. This position having been turned, the enemy fell back upon another equally strong at the head of the pass, but even after being joined by the left column under Captain Davidson, Lieut.-Col. Mackeson did not feel himself strong enough to attack, so awaited the appearance of Col. Napier's force in rear of the position, when the Hassanzais retreated, as already stated.

The left column was accompanied by Col. Mackeson, and marching by Agror and Pabal, was fired at from a hill overlooking Tilli, but the enemy were immediately dislodged and the column effected its junction with the centre one, as described, close to Panj Gali.

On the 30th the Hassanzai villages about here were destroyed, and the force moving on the next day to the Tilli plateau burnt all the villages between that place and Abu, while those along the Indus between Kotkai and Baradar were destroyed by the Nawab of Amb's men.

On the 2nd January the whole force retired to Baradar, being followed up by the enemy and their allies, and the expedition was at an end. The Hassanzais had made no submission, but it was considered that they had been sufficiently punished for the murder of the two British officers by the destruction of their villages and grain, and for some time after this lesson the Hassanzais remained fairly quiet, and the raids made by them in 1863 were directed chiefly against the Nawab of Amb's territory, and no doubt partook of the nature of reprisals for the assistance the Nawab had afforded us ten years earlier.

Our casualties in the 1853 expedition were about fifteen killed and wounded.

In November, 1867, it was determined to establish a body of police in the Agror Valley, and this was temporarily located in the village of Oghi until a fortified police post could be built. At daylight on the morning of the 30th July, 1868, this body of twenty-two policemen was attacked by some 500 men belonging to almost all the tribes, including the Pariari Saiyids, mentioned in this chapter. The enemy were driven off, but troops being called for from Abbottabad, a force composed of the Peshawar Mountain Battery and 350 of the 5th Gurkhas, under Lieut.-Col. Rothney, reached Oghi before midnight on the 31st, having marched forty-two miles in twenty-five hours, and here this force was joined on the 2nd August by the levies of the Nawab of Amb. It appearing that the attack had been instigated by the Khan of Agror, that chief was promptly arrested and sent in to Abbottabad.

During the next few days there were signs of serious unrest in the Agror Valley; the tribesmen refused to meet the Deputy-Commissioner, many villages were burnt by them, and on the 7th a general advance of the enemy took place, when all the neighbouring tribesmen joined them, while our own levies deserted in numbers to their homes. On the 12th, Col. Rothney, who had been reinforced, moved out from Oghi, and drove the enemy out of the Agror Valley. By this engagement, by the arrival of troops at Abbottabad, of further reinforcements at Oghi, and the presence of some Kashmir regiments in the Pakli Valley, the safety of the Hazara district was now secured, and Brig.-Gen. Wilde—who was now in command—only waited for more troops to carry out any punitive operations which might be ordered.

Up to this date twenty-one British villages had been burnt by the tribesmen, who had also caused us sixty-four casualties.

Expedition against the Black Mountain Tribes, 1868.—An expedition was now sanctioned, but in

view of the generally disturbed state of this portion
of the frontier, it was decided to draw the required
troops from cantonments further down country,
leaving the garrisons of Peshawar and of other border
posts as far as possible intact. Considering that
some regiments had come from as far south as Cawn-
pore, the concentration by the 24th September of the
following force at Agror, Darband and Abbottabad,
may be considered a very satisfactory piece of work :

At Agror :

 D. F. Royal Horse Artillery.
 E. 19th Royal Artillery.
 2. 24th Royal Artillery.
 Peshawar Mountain Battery.
 Hazara Mountain Battery.
 1st Battalion 6th Foot.
 1st Battalion 19th Foot.
 Guides Cavalry.
 16th Bengal Cavalry.[1]
 Det. Telegraph Sappers.
 1st Gurkhas.
 2nd Gurkhas.
 3rd Sikhs.[2]
 2nd Punjab Infantry.[3]
 4th Gurkhas.
 20th Punjab Native Infantry.[4]
 24th Punjab Native Infantry.[5]
 5th Gurkhas.

[1] Now the 16th Cavalry. [2] Now the 53rd Sikhs.
[3] Now the 56th Punjabi Rifles. [4] Now the 20th Punjabis.
[5] Now the 24th Punjabis.

At Abbottabad :

2nd and 7th Companies Sappers and Miners.

At Darband, in support of the Nawab of Amb :

38th Foot.

9th Bengal Cavalry.[1]

31st Punjab Native Infantry.[2]

This force was divided into two brigades, under Colonels Bright and Vaughan, the whole under command of Brigadier-General Wilde, C.B., C.S.I., and numbered some 9500 of all ranks. In addition, a contingent of 1200 troops was furnished by the Maharaja of Kashmir, but these, though present on the border, did not take any active part in the operations.

The overawing effect of the assembly of so large a force was immediately apparent in the petitions to be permitted to treat which now began to come in from the Swatis, the Hassanzais and the men of Tikari and Nandihar, and these were granted in the case of those clans which had not been specially hostile, or which it was considered particularly desirable to detach from the general coalition. The force which had been concentrated in Hazara had still, however, a sufficiently formidable task before it, having to deal with the Chagarzai and Akazai clans, with the Swatis of Deshi and Thakot, with the Pariari Saiyids, and not improbably with the Hindustani fanatics (of whom more will be said hereafter), and large bodies of trans-Indus Pathans.

[1] Now the 9th Hodson's Horse.   [2] Now the 31st Punjabis.

On the 3rd October the force moved out from the camp at Oghi; Brigadier-General Vaughan, with the Second Brigade, advancing by Bagrian, occupied with but insignificant opposition the Kiarkot Mountain, and closed up his brigade to Kilagai. Brigadier-General Bright at the same time advanced on Kungali and thence on Mana-ka-Dana, which he occupied after some little fighting, and which was found to form an excellent temporary base for operations against the Chitabat and Machai peaks. The Second Brigade was now ordered to support the further advance of the First, leaving the levies to move up the Barchar spur. On the next day—the 4th—the Chitabat position was carried with small loss—the road having, however, been found to be almost impracticable—and was put in a state of defence. The Second Brigade closed up this evening to Mana-ka-Dana. On the following day the First Brigade advanced against the enemy holding the Machai peak. This was naturally a very strong defensible position, the ascent being steep and rugged in the extreme, only to be climbed on a narrow front, as the ground on the left was precipitous, and on the right thickly wooded. The accurate and effective covering fire of the mountain batteries enabled the troops to capture the position with only eight casualties, the enemy not holding out to the last, but flying down the spurs into the Indus Valley.

Major-General Wilde was now in possession of the most commanding plateau of the range, he had ample supplies, his communications were secure, and he was able to inflict considerable damage on the mountain villages of the neighbouring Pathan tribes. Jirgahs of the clans now began to come in and make formal submission, and by the 12th the Machai peak was evacuated, the force finally reaching Oghi, via Tikari and Nandihar, on the 22nd October, with the objects of the expedition satisfactorily attained.

Our casualties totalled five killed and twenty-nine wounded.

Raids did not, however, entirely and immediately cease, and in the autumn of 1869 a force of some 700 men had to be moved out from Abbottabad to assist in the establishment of a blockade against the Hassanzais, Akazais and others who had raided into Agror. In April of the following year a party of Akazais attacked Barchar, and burnt Sambalbat and Bholu, despite the presence in the Agror valley of a small British garrison.

During the years 1871-75 offences continued to be committed on the Agror border by the tribesmen, and another expedition seemed inevitable, when, in September 1875, a settlement was arrived at, all the Black Mountain tribes agreeing in submitting to the British Government, and for some few years this part of the frontier was free from any serious trouble.

Up to 1884 there was no real cause for complaint; it had been found necessary in this year to blockade the Chagarzais, Akazais and Pariari Saiyids, and the same punishment was extended later to the Hassanzais; but it was not until June 1888 that a

serious outrage occurring on the Agror frontier necessitated the despatch of another expedition to the
Black Mountain. On the 18th of this month an
attack was made upon a small party of British troops
within British territory by Akazais, Hassanzais and
Pariari Saiyids, and two British officers and four men
were killed. Immediately upon this, large bodies of
these tribesmen assembled with the intention of
attacking Agror, but dispersed again without taking
any further offensive action ; the Indian Government
now once more took into consideration the question
of punitive measures against the Black Mountain
tribes, and on the 29th August an expedition was
decided upon.

Expedition against the Black Mountain Tribes,
1888.—The force was formed on the 7th September,
1888, and consisted of three mountain batteries, one
company sappers and miners, four battalions of
British, nine of Native infantry, with two battalions
of Kashmir infantry and the Khyber Rifles, and was
placed under command of Brigadier-General (temporary Major-General) J. McQueen, C.B., A.D.C.
The total strength was 9416 of all ranks, and the
force was organised in two brigades under Brigadier-
Generals Channer and Galbraith, each brigade being
sub-divided into two columns. There was further a
reserve composed of a regiment of cavalry and two
battalions of infantry. Headquarters and the first,
second and third columns were directed to concentrate at Oghi in the Agror valley by the 1st October,
and the fourth column at Darband on the Indus on

the same date; and the object of the expedition was stated to be the coercion into submission of the Akazais and the Khan Khel division of the Hassanzais, with the punishment of any clans or divisions which might assist these tribesmen in their opposition to our troops.

The following were the orders issued for the advance of the four columns:

No. 1 Column to move on the 4th to Mana-ka-Dana, and the following day to Chitabat, leaving a sufficient force at Mana-ka-Dana to protect its line of communications.

No. 2 Column to advance up the Barchar spur on the 4th, occupying Barchar; thence moving on the 5th to the crest of the ridge, one regiment being at once detached to the left to meet No. 3 Column.

No. 3 Column to advance up the Sambalbat spur to the village of the same name, which was to be occupied on the 4th. The advance to be continued to the crest on the 5th. The 24th Punjab Infantry and two guns Derajat Mountain Battery to move up the Chatta Spur, meeting the remainder of No. 3 Column on the morning of the 5th at the junction of the Sambalbat and Chatta spurs. The Khyber Rifles to advance up the Chajri spur between Nos. 2 and 3 Columns on the 5th.

No. 4 Column to advance on the 4th to the neighbourhood of Kotkai on the Indus.

The first three columns carried out their orders on the 4th and 5th, the 2nd and 3rd Columns practically unmolested, the 1st with but slight opposition, which chiefly took the form of firing into the bivouacs after nightfall; but the opposition experienced by the 4th, and more isolated, Column was of a considerably more serious character.

This column, under Colonel Crookshank, and accompanied by the Brigadier, crossed the frontier on the morning of the 4th and advanced to Bela on the Indus by a road which had been made practicable the previous day. The river bank was reached at 8 a.m., and a halt was made to allow the column to close up. On the advance being resumed, the village of Shingri was carried with but trifling opposition, but about a mile beyond large numbers of the enemy were found in occupation of a strong position about the villages of Towara and Kotkai, with both flanks held by skirmishers and even defended by guns. The flanks were turned by the 34th Pioneers and 4th Punjab Infantry,[1] but the advance was necessarily very slow, and the line was suddenly charged by a body of *ghazis* who had been concealed in a nullah on the left flank of the Royal Irish Regiment; they were, however, nearly all shot down before they arrived at close quarters. The enemy now began to break, and by 3.30 p.m. were in full retreat towards Kanar, when Kotkai was occupied.

On the 6th the other three columns were engaged

[1] Now the 57th Wilde's Rifles.

in collecting forage, improving their water supply, and in safeguarding their communications, and during the 7th they remained respectively at Chitabat, Nimal and Kain Gali.

From the 5th to the 10th October the 4th Column was engaged in reconnaissances to Kanar, Tilli, Kunari, Garhi and Ghazi Kot, and on the 13th the settlements and forts at Maidan, on the further bank of the Indus, of the Hindustani fanatics—many of whom had opposed us at Kotkai—were destroyed. These operations were nearly always opposed, but with the destruction of Maidan the active services of this column came to an end. Later on in the month a Hassanzai village on the right bank of the Indus was burnt, as were also Garhi, Bakrai and Kotkai, after which this clan sent in their jirgah, made submission and paid up their fine.

During this period the Agror Columns remained on the crest of the Black Mountain above the lands of the Hassanzais and Akazais, exploring the surrounding country and destroying villages of offending clans. These measures were successful; by the 19th the Akazai jirgah had come in and had unconditionally accepted our terms. The Hassanzais too, although they did not actually make submission until the 30th, had ceased to be actively hostile, and General McQueen was therefore now able to devote his attention to the coercing of the Pariari Saiyids and the Tikariwals. On the evening of the 20th October the Divisional Headquarters and No. 1 Column were at Mana-ka-Dana, No. 2 Column was in occupation of Chitabat, No. 3 was distributed between Karun, Akhund Baba, Nimal and Tilli, and No. 4 was at Ledh, Kanar, Kotkai, Shingri and Darband.

On a small force moving forward from Dilbori towards Chirmang, the Tikariwals at once came in and hurriedly paid up their fines, leaving now only the Pariari Saiyids to be dealt with; and on the 24th troops were sent into their country, Garhi was destroyed, Thakot was then entered, via Chanjal and Karg, without opposition, and preparations were now made for visiting Allai, the Khan of which had begged that his country should not be visited, but who had made no signs of submission. Allai was entered, via the Ghorapher Pass, by a force of six guns and some 2400 rifles under Brigadier-General Channer, divided into two columns. The ascent was found to be very difficult and precipitous, and the crest held in some force, but the enemy made no serious stand, and our casualties in the capture of the position were only one killed and one wounded. The crest of the Chaila Mountain was held during that night and the 2nd, and on the 3rd November the force marched to Pokal, the Khan's headquarters, destroyed it and returned to camp, having experienced some opposition in the advance and being persistently followed up in the retirement. Late this evening the Allai jirgah came in, followed on the next day by that of the Pariari Saiyids, and by the 13th the whole of the force had been withdrawn to British territory. The British casualties during the operations amounted to twenty-five killed and fifty-seven wounded.

The objects for which the expedition had been undertaken had been attained; the offending clans had met with severe punishment, and had made their submission; hostages had been given for future good behaviour; and some roads had been made, while a large extent of hitherto unknown country had been surveyed and mapped. For a year affairs on this border remained quiet, but the Government of India considered it necessary to take measures to secure its control over the clans and to make roads into their territories. To the construction of roads, however, the Hassanzais, Akazais and Pariari Saiyids made objections, and on Major-General Sir John McQueen moving a small force along the Border to prove our rights under the treaty which had been made, a considerable amount of opposition was shown by the clans immediately concerned, and the General withdrew his troops in accordance with his instructions, and to make way for a larger expedition now projected.

Expedition against the Hassanzais and Akazais, 1891.—The objects of these operations were to assert our right to move along the crest of the Black Mountain; to inflict punishment upon the clans which had recently shown hostility to the force under Sir John McQueen; and to occupy the country until complete submission had been made. In consequence of the experience gained in 1888 it was decided that Oghi, Tilli and Pabal Gali should be occupied, but that the advance should be made only by the Indus line, whence the Hassanzai and Akazai villages and lands could most easily be reached, and where the conditions of warfare would be more favourable to the British troops.

The force detailed was placed under command of Major-General W. K. Elles, C.B., and was directed to advance from Darband in two columns, one via Baradar and Pailam to Tilli, the other by the river via Kotkai and Kanar. The concentration was to be effected by the 1st March, 1891, as detailed below.

Left or River Column, at Darband :

> Three guns No. 1 M.B.R.A.
> Three guns Derajat Mountain Battery.
> 2nd Battalion Seaforth Highlanders.
> Headquarters Wing 32nd Pioneers.
> 37th Dogras.
> Guides Infantry.
> 4th Sikhs.[1]

Right or Tilli Column, at Darband :

> No. 9 M.B.R.A.
> 1st Battalion Royal Welsh Fusiliers.
> 11th Bengal Infantry.[2]
> Wing 32nd Pioneers.
> 2nd Battalion 5th Gurkhas.
> Khyber Rifles.

Divisional Troops at Darband :

> One squadron 11th Bengal Lancers and No. 4
> Company Bengal Sappers and Miners.

---

[1] Now the 54th Sikhs.   [2] Now the 11th Rajputs.

At Oghi :

> One squadron 11th Bengal Lancers.
> Three guns Derajat Mountain Battery.
> 28th Bengal Infantry.[1]

In Reserve at Rawal Pindi :

> One squadron 11th Bengal Lancers.
> 1st Battalion King's Royal Rifle Corps.
> 19th Bengal Infantry.[2]
> 27th Bengal Infantry.[3]

The weather was bad for some days after the concentration was effected, but good roads had been made to the frontier and to Bela, and both Phaldan and Bela had been occupied by our troops. General Elles proposed first to establish posts in Kanar and Tilli, and then with the Left or River Column to occupy the lower Hassanzai country on both banks and the Diliarai peninsula of the Akazais, while the Right Column, moving by Ril and Kungar, occupied the Khan Khel territory, and thus by degrees complete the occupation of the lands of both clans.

The advance commenced on the morning of the 12th, and Pailam and Kotkai were occupied by either column without any more opposition than was occasioned by some desultory firing at the River Column from across the Indus. On the next day the Right Column moved on to and halted at Tilli, while the River Column visited the Palosi plain and also Nadrai on the right bank, experiencing some

---

[1] Now 28th Punjabis.   [2] Now 19th Punjabis.
[3] Now 27th Punjabis.

D

opposition, but reconnoitring the road between Kotkai and Kanar. By the 15th it was reported that while the Hassanzais and Akazais were anxious to submit, other clans were gathering against us—mostly in the trans-Indus Chagarzai country.

About 3 a.m. on the 19th a weak company of the 4th Sikhs, providing an outpost at the small village of Ghazi Kot, on the left bank of the Indus, was heavily attacked by a large body of Hindustani fanatics. Reinforcements, however, furnished by the 4th Sikhs and 32nd Pioneers, were quickly on the scene, and the enemy were driven off with considerable loss. The following night there was a good deal of firing at Kanar; on the 21st the River Column had reached Palosi via Pirzada Bela; and the Right Column occupied Ril the same day, destroyed Seri on the next, and then returned to Tilli.

On the 23rd the establishment of a bridge at Bakrai was covered by a party of the 4th Sikhs, who were opposed by a large gathering of the enemy on the Diliarai Hill, overlooking Bakrai and about one mile to the north-west of that place. The enemy were driven off the hill, but on the Sikhs and Guides withdrawing to a position lower down, they were followed up so determinedly that Lieut.-Colonel Gaselee of the 4th Sikhs again advanced, and cleared and reoccupied the hill for the night. The fighting had been hand to hand, and the enemy—chiefly Chagarzais and Hindustanis—suffered rather heavily.

On the 24th Brigadier-General Hammond took a small force from Tilli to Palosi, and thence next day advanced up the Shal Nala against Darbanai—a village on a knoll jutting out from the main spur into the Indus Valley. The enemy were driven off this commanding position, and on the 27th General Hammond moved into lower Surmal and burnt some of the Chagarzai villages.

The gatherings of the tribesmen had now increased. There were a number of Bunerwals at Baio and in this neighbourhood, and in the Chagarzai country to the north there appeared to be a coalition of all the clans from Thakot to the Peshawar border—from Buner, Chamla, and from the Amazai and Gadun country. In consequence of these concentrations of clans, a regiment of cavalry and a battalion of infantry were ordered up from Nowshera to Mardan, and, with the troops already in garrison at the last-named place, were held in readiness for service against the Bunerwals; and the reserve brigade from Rawal Pindi was concentrated at Darband. At the same time representations were made to the Buner jirgah that we had no intention of invading either their country or that of the Chagarzais, but that they would be attacked if their forces did not disperse. These warnings had the desired effect, and the Bunerwals returned to their homes, while the lower Hassanzais had already made their submission. Towards the end of April the whole of the country of the Akazais, who still remained recalcitrant, was visited, and shortly after Darband was evacuated and the base transferred to Oghi; but it was not until a month later that the Akazai jirgah at last came in and tendered the unconditional submission of the tribe. The three Isazai divisions, with the Saiyids and Chagarzais of Pariari, consented to the perpetual banishment from their territories of a notorious disturber of the peace, one Hashim Ali, and promised generally to be of good behaviour and to exclude the Hindustani fanatics from their country.

Early in June the bulk of the troops composing the force returned to India, but some remained until the end of November in occupation of Seri and Oghi and of the crest of the Black Mountain.

In these operations—which cost us nine killed and thirty-nine wounded—we had a larger coalition against us than in any other expedition, with the exception of the Ambela outbreak of 1863 and the Pathan revolt of 1897.

In March 1892 the Hassanzais and Mada Khels broke the engagement into which they had entered with the British Government, by permitting Hashim Ali to return to their country and settle at Baio ; and accordingly in October a force of 6250 men and two guns, organised in two brigades, advanced from Darband under Major-General Sir William Lockhart. The Indus was crossed at Marer, and on the 6th October the two brigades advanced on Baio—the First Brigade from Wale and the Second Brigade from Manjakot. Baio was found deserted, and was destroyed, as was also Doba, a Mada Khel village. Demolitions were also carried out in Manja Kot, Karor, Garhi and Nawekili, and the force was back on the 11th October at Darband, where it was broken up. None of the tribesmen offered any resistance, and there were no casualties, but the troops suffered a good deal from fever and also from cholera.

Since this expedition the Black Mountain clans and their neighbours have given no serious trouble.

CHAPTER III.

YUSAFZAIS AND GADUNS.[1]

THE clansmen occupying the British border from the Black Mountain to the Utman Khel territory belong, with the exception of the Gaduns, to the important tribe of Yusafzai Pathans, of which the Hassanzais, Akazais and Chagarzais, already described, are also branches.

The Yusafzais inhabit the division of that name in the Peshawar district, as well as independent territory beyond the border. They are the descendants of the original Gandhari, who in ancient days occupied the Peshawar Valley, emigrating thence to the Helmand in the fifth century, and becoming fused with the Afghans of Ghor. In the fifteenth century, owing to pressure, the Yusafzais migrated with other tribes northwards to Kabul, and from thence in the sixteenth century into the Peshawar Valley, where they acquired the plain country north of the Kabul River and west of Mardan. Meanwhile, the Mohmands of the Ghoria Khel had followed the Yusafzais, and they in turn defeated the Dilazaks—whom the Yusafzais had already dispossessed of their lands—and forced them into the present Yusafzai plain, in the northeast corner of the Peshawar Valley. The Yusafzais

[1] See Map IV.

then, with the help of other tribes, drove the Dilazaks across the Indus into Hazara. The Yusafzais, with the Utman Khel and Tarkanris, now settled themselves in the Yusafzai plain, and during the next few years these three tribes made themselves masters of all the hill country along that border, from the Indus to the range separating the Bajaur and Kunar Valleys. In a later division of the country the Tarkanris took Bajaur; the Utman Khel the Swat Valley up to the junction of that river with the Panjkhora; while the Yusafzais occupied all the hills to the east as far as the Indus, including Lower Swat, Buner, Chamla and the Peshawar Valley east of Hastnagar and north of the Kabul River. At the present time the Yusafzais inhabit the north-east of the Peshawar district, or the Yusafzai plain, Swat, Buner, Panjkhora, and several strips of independent territory north and east of the Peshawar Valley. They have also considerable settlements to the east of the Indus as we have seen.

At the time of the final division of the country with the Tarkanris and the Utman Khels, the Yusafzais were divided into two great branches, the Mandanr and the Yusafzais, the whole race tracing its origin to Mandai, who had two sons, Yusaf and Umar. From Yusaf sprang the Yusafzais, and from a son of Umar called Mandan, the Mandanr took their name. On the occupation of this tract of country, an equal division of both plain and hill country was made between the Mandanr and the Yusafzais, but quarrels arising, the Yusafzais gradually became owners of the hill country, while the Mandanr were driven into the plains; it is thus actually the Mandanr who now occupy the so-called Yusafzai plain in the northeast of the Peshawar Valley, and who are generally known as Yusafzais, while the real Yusafzais, who dwell in the hill country, are usually called after the name of the territory they severally inhabit.

The Yusafzai is an agriculturist, generally a fine, well-limbed man, of good physique and appearance, with a great deal of race-pride, well-dressed and cheery, while his hospitality is proverbial. They have an established and recognised gentry, and all blue-blooded Yusafzais have a hereditary share in the land, their names appearing in the book of hereditary land-owners kept by the village *patwari*. The Yusafzai plain is very flat, and the soil, where properly irrigated, is very fertile, but the chief interest of this district lies in the numerous ruins of ancient Buddhist and Hindu cities, temples and inscriptions, scattered broadcast about the plain and the adjoining hills.

The Yusafzais may conveniently be divided into Cis- and Trans-frontier Yusafzais: under the former category come the

    (1) Mandanr,   (2) Sam Baizais,

while the following are the clans of trans-frontier Yusafzais :

(1) Akozais,	(6) Isazais,
(2) Amazais,	(7) Khudu Khel,
(3) Bunerwals,	(8) Nasozais,
(4) Chagarzais,	(9) Utmanzais.
(5) Chamlawals,	

First in order of the independent tribes on the British border between the Black Mountain and the Utman Khel territory, come the Mada Khel division of the Isazais and the Amazais, adjoining the lands of our feudatory the Nawab of Amb; to the south of the Amazais lie the Utmanzais, to their west the Gaduns, and beyond them the Khudu Khel. To the north of the Khudu Khel territory is the Chamla Valley, inhabited by members of different clans, and separated from Buner by the Guru range of mountains. Next come the Nurizai and Salarzai divisions of Buner, which march with our border. Between Buner and the Utman Khel limits is the district of Swat peopled by the Akozais, with the portion adjoining British territory inhabited by the Baizai and Ranizai tribesmen of Swat.

Something can here fittingly be mentioned with regard to the position of the Nawab of Amb on this border. His territory may be roughly described as a square block in the north-west corner of the Hazara district, separated on the west from the independent Pathan country by the Indus, and having the Black Mountain and Agror to the north. The Tanawal chief has also two or three villages beyond the Indus, and the largest of these is Amb. The Nawab holds his cis-Indus territory as a perpetual *jaghir* from the British Government, while his trans-Indus villages are independent. The existence of this little principality is, from its situation, in many ways convenient.

Cis-border Yusafzais. Mandanr.—These occupy the greater portion of the Yusafzai plain in the

north-eastern part of the Peshawar Valley, bounded on
the south by the Khattaks and the Kabul River, on
the west by Hastnagar and the Muhammadzais, and
on the east and north by the Indus River, and by the
Gaduns and the independent Yusafzai tribes. The
district is divided into two sub-divisions (*tehsils*),
Swabi and Mardan. The Mandanr are divided into
three divisions—the Usmanzai, Utmanzai and Razar
—of which the first named has its holdings in the
Mardan and the two latter in the Swabi tehsil. The
family in each of the three divisions, in which
the Khan-ship is hereditary, is known as the Khan
Khel, and these families have a higher social standing
than the others.

A number of other Pathans live among the Mandanr,
as do also many persons of Indian race, some of
them immigrants from the Punjab and Kashmir, and
some descendants of the original inhabitants of the
country. All these, however, speak Pushtu and
greatly resemble Pathans in appearance.

Sam Baizai.—These are a portion of the Baizai
division of the Akozai Yusafzais, who formerly occupied the whole of the northern portion of the Yusafzai
plain to the foot of the hills below the Morah Pass.
During the sixteenth century they called in the
Khattaks and Utman Khels to assist them against the
inroads of the Ranizais, and in return gave their allies
land in their country as tenants. In course of time
the new comers have practically ousted the Baizais,
who now possess but few villages of their own. In
regard to numbers they are an insignificant division.

Trans-border Yusafzais. Akozais.—These, which form the largest clan of trans-frontier Yusafzais, inhabit the whole of Swat proper, and will be found described in greater detail in Chapter V.

Amazais.—This people forms one of the two sub-divisions of the Usmanzai division of Mandanr Yusafzais, and is sub-divided into the Daulatzais and Ismailzais. The Amazai country is situated between that of the Chamlawals and Hassanzais on the north and west, the Mada Khel and Tinaolis on the east, and the Utmanzais, Gaduns, and Khudu Khel on the south. Within British territory the Daulatzai occupy the Sudum Valley, while the Ismailzai inhabit a strip of country in the Yusafzai sub-division of the Peshawar district, south of the Karamar range and east of the road from Mardan. The trans-frontier Amazais are divided into the Saiyid Khel and Mobarak Khel, two sub-divisions which are constantly at feud with one another. The Amazai country is divided into two by a northern spur from the Mahaban Mountain ; the villages lying to the east of this spur, and between it and the Indus, belong to the Saiyid Khel, and those to the west to both sub-divisions. The country is narrow, rough, well watered and wooded. The strength of the trans-frontier Amazais in fighting men is about 1500, and they have a high reputation for courage, but while a number of the cis-frontier men are en-listed, few come in for service from across the border.

The only occasion upon which we have come into direct conflict with the Amazais was in the Ambela campaign of 1863.

Bunerwals.—This clan inhabits the Buner Valley
—an irregular oval—which is bounded on the north-
west by Swat, on the north-east by the Puran Valley,
on the south-east by the Mada Khel and Amazai
territory, on the south by the Chamla Valley, and on
the south-west by Yusafzai.   It is a small mountain
valley, and the Morah Hills and Ilam Range divide
it from Swat, the Sinawar Range from Yusafzai, the
Guru Mountain from the Chamla Valley, and the
Duma Range from the Puran Valley.   The Buner
Valley is drained by the Barandu, a perennial stream
which joins the Indus above Mahabara ; the valley is
about thirty miles in length.   The term Bunerwals includes the Iliaszai division, occupying the north-western
portion of the country, and the Malizais, who inhabit
the south-eastern portion : these two divisions are
divided into seven sub-divisions.   The hereditary chiefs
of the tribe are the Khans of Dagar and Bagra, but
their influence is nominal, and the different clans are
entirely democratic.   Moreover, the Khan of Dagar
does not belong to any of the Buner clans, but his
family is recognised as the leading or Khan Khel
family.   The clan is neither so well armed nor so
adept at hill fighting as other trans-frontier tribes,
but can turn out some 6800 fighting men.   The few
who enlist with us—according to Enriquez just over
200—are well spoken of.   Their land is very fertile,
and the Bunerwals are purely agriculturists, the
men of good physique, dark and swarthy, and distinguishable by the dark blue clothes and pugarees
which they wear.

Although the Bunerwals have never been specially friendly with us, they have proved themselves on the whole most satisfactory neighbours. Though poor, they are not given to thieving; they discourage raiding into our territory; and though they will give an asylum to outlaws from our side of the border, they will not join with them in the commission of outrages. Oliver says of them that "there are in many ways few finer specimens of Pathans than the Bunerwals. Simple and temperate, they are content with the plain wholesome food, the produce of their own cattle and lands; courteous and hospitable to all who claim shelter, treachery to a stranger seeking refuge among them being considered the deepest reproach that could fall upon the clansmen, and such a case is almost unknown. Upright in their dealings, with enemies as well as with strangers, they have always been adverse to us, and though probably not anxious to begin the war, they were among our most determined enemies during the Ambela campaign. . . . Patriotic they certainly are, and in their way, which is a pastoral and agricultural one, industrious, though they hold all trade in the very lowest estimation; anything that savours of the shop or of trading is anathema to a Bunerwal. Therefore they are poor, but, for poor Pathans, have an exceptional regard for the law of *meum* and *tuum*. Their word, once given through the council of the tribe, may, according to Warburton, be depended on with almost certainty. Lastly, they are 'distinguished for their ignorance,' and ignorance being the 'mother of devotion,' they are deeply religious; greatly under the influence of the most bigoted of mullahs, saiyids, and pirs, and the many varieties of the priestly class, which is probably the most powerful and prosperous section of the community; while if there is any section whose heritage ought to be one of woe it is this, for it is from the priests most of the offences come throughout the whole of Yusafzai."

The winter climate in Buner is said to be very severe, snow falling thickly on the hills and lying in the valleys, while malaria makes the country unhealthy during the hot season.

Of the seven divisions into which the clan is divided, it will probably be sufficient briefly to notice the two which are nearest to British territory; these are the Salarzais and the Nurizais. The former are a powerful community, and could bring nearly 2000 men into the field; they have more intercourse with our subjects than any other section of the Bunerwals. The Nurizais are also a strong division, and of the two sub-divisions they contain, one is as favourably disposed towards the British as the other is inimical and troublesome. The Nurizais adjoin British territory to the south-east of the Salarzais, and are separated from the Chamla Valley by the Guru Range.

From Swat three passes lead into Buner, the Kalel, the Jowarai and the Karakar, and of these the last only is practicable for mule transport. On the east, the Indus being crossed at Mahabara, it is possible to enter Buner by the Barandu defile. From our territory two passes, both practicable for pack animals, lead into Buner—the Malandri Pass and the Ambela.

Chagarzais.—These have already been dealt with in Chapter II. under the Black Mountain tribes. They are divided into three divisions, and one only is located in Buner, living on the western slopes of the Duma Mountains. This division can turn out about one thousand fighting men.

Chamlawals.—These are the inhabitants of the small valley of Chamla, which lies to the south-east of Buner, and they are Mandanr Yusafzais. When the Yusaf and Mandan clans, after they had subjugated the country, began fighting among themselves, the Mandanr located their families in the Chamla Valley, and retained it at the conclusion of the struggle. The valley runs east and west, and is about seventeen miles long by two and a half broad. It is bounded on the north by Buner, south by the Khudu Khel country, east by the Amazai, and west by the British district of Rustam, in Yusafzai. The Chamlawals number about 1400 fighting men, but do not enjoy as such a very high reputation. They are divided into three divisions. The valley can be approached from the north from Buner by several passes, of which the easiest is said to be the Buner Pass, leading from Barkilai to Ambela; it leads through the Guru range, and is believed to be practicable for camels. From British territory it is entered by the Ambela, Sherdara and Narinji passes, and it is also approachable from the east and through the Khudu Khel country. Any trouble which the

Chamlawals may have given us in the past has usually been the result of tribal pressure.

Mada Khels.—This is a division of Isazai Yusafzais, of which the other two, the Akazais and Hassanzais, have already been described among the dwellers on the Black Mountain. The Mada Khel country is on the northern slopes of the Mahaban Mountain down to the right bank of the Indus, and is bounded on the north by the Hassanzais, on the east by the Indus, and on the south and west by the Tinaolis and Amazais. Settled in the country are a number of Dilazaks—the former occupiers of the Yusafzai country and now settled in Hazara—and Gujars, the descendants of the original Hindu population of the country. The Mada Khel have three sub-divisions, and are considered more enlightened than the other Isazai tribesmen. They can muster some 1500 men, very badly armed, and their young bloods do not readily enlist in the native army. Most of the villages are on the Mahaban Mountain, only two being on the banks of the Indus. The easiest approaches to Mada Khel territory pass through the Hassanzai country.

Khudu Khels.—These are a sub-division of the Saddozai division of the Utmanzai clan of the Mandanr Yusafzais. Their territory is bounded on the north by Chamla, on the west by Yusafzai, on the south by Utmanama, and on the east by the territory of the Gaduns and Amazai. Their country is about twenty-two miles long and about fifteen wide. The Khudu Khel contains two sections, is very much divided among its members, and could probably, if united, furnish some 1600 fighting men, of no particular value. Their country is very open to attack from British territory and to blockade, and for this reason the Khudu Khels have not given us any real trouble since 1847 and 1849, when a British force marched into their country and surprised their villages.

The Khudu Khel have settlements also in British territory in the Mardan district.

Nasozais.—This sub-division of the Iliaszai Yusafzais, though not included among the Bunerwals proper, is practically identical with them. It is located northeast of Buner in the Puran Valley on the eastern slopes of the Lilban Mountains, and is divided into two sections. The Nasozais can muster some 800 fighting men.

Utmanzais.—These are a clan of Mandanr Yusafzais. They inhabit both banks of the Indus, those on the right bank being independent and occupying a narrow strip of land between the river and the Gadun country, bounded on the north by the Tinaolis and on the south by the British. The Utmanzais on the left bank inhabit the Torbela-Khalsa tracts in British territory in the Hazara district. They contain four divisions and do not number more than 400 fighting men of good quality. About two-thirds of the original Utmanzai territory is now occupied by the Gaduns, who in old days were invited to cross the Indus as mercenaries, and were given in requital the lands they now hold on the western and southern slopes of the Mahaban Mountain.

E

This clan is more or less dependent upon us, and their territory can be reached by several routes.

Gaduns.—The origin of the tribe of Gaduns or Jaduns is not very clear, but they certainly have no connection with the Yusafzais among whom they dwell. They claim descent from the family of Ghurghusht, but are more probably of Rajput origin. Many of the descendants of Jadu, the founder of a Rajput dynasty, emigrated from Gujrat, some eleven hundred years before Christ, to the hills of Kabul and Kandahar. When they moved to the Mahaban range, the southern slopes of which some of them now occupy, is uncertain, but in the sixteenth century a portion of the tribe crossed the Indus into Hazara, where, about Sultanpur, Mansehra and Abbottabad, their descendants are still to be found. These have, however, lost all connection with their trans-frontier tribesmen, have even forgotten Pushtu, and are to all intents and purposes Punjabis.

"From opposite Torbela on the Indus, and from the boundary of our border on the right bank," says Oliver, "the Gadun country extends right up to the crest of the Mahaban Mountain, or rather that cluster of peaks and ranges which, rising 7000 feet from the Indus, extend back as a great spur of the Morah or Ilum. A thoroughly classic ground; 'the Great Forest' of the early Aryans; the 'Sinai' of Sanskrit, where Arjuna wrestled with God, and, like the Jewish Jacob, though defeated, still won his irresistible weapon, ground that, if not identical with Alexander's Aornos, is probably not very distant, that was famous for its numerous monasteries (Mahawana) when Hwen Tsang visited it in 630 A.D., and is studded with ruins to this day."

The tribe has three clans—the Salar, Mansur and Hassazai—of which the last is unrepresented among the trans-frontier Gaduns, while the other two are continually at feud. The trans-frontier clans contain about 2000 fighting men; they do not enlist freely nor are they much in request, being considered to be of smaller fighting value than other Pathans. The trans-Indus Gaduns are bounded on the east by the Utmanzais, on the north by the Amazais, on the west by the Khudu Khels, and on the south by British territory. The tribesmen are all cultivators or cattle-owners. They can be coerced by blockade or by means of an expedition, and their country could be overrun without other tribes being molested or too closely approached.

The Hindustani Fanatics.[1]—Something has already been mentioned about the colonies of religious adventurers which are found among the hills and valleys of this part of the border; and a more detailed description must now be given of the particular colony or colonies of Hindustani fanatics, who have been responsible for, and have taken so prominent a part in, most of the operations in which British troops have here been engaged.

It was in the year 1823 that one Saiyid Ahmad Shah, of Bareilly, a religious adventurer, made his

[1] For what follows, I am indebted to an article by Col. A. H. Mason in the Journal of the *United Service Institution of India* for 1890.

appearance on the Yusafzai frontier. He had been at
one time a friend of the notorious Amir Khan Pindari
—himself a Pathan born in Buner, who had fled before
James Skinner and his " Yellow Boys " from Bhurtpore
to the Himalayas. Saiyid Ahmad studied Arabic at
Delhi, and made a pilgrimage to Mecca via Calcutta,
and it was at this time that his doctrines gave him
an influence over Bengali Muhammadans, which led
them thenceforth to supply with recruits the colony
which he founded. His doctrines at that time, whatever they may have become thereafter, were those
of the Wahabi sect, and inculcated the original tenets
of Islam, repudiating commentaries on the Koran
and the adoration of relics. In 1823 then he appeared
upon the Yusafzai border of the Peshawar district
with some forty Hindustani followers, having arrived
there by way of Kandahar and Kabul.

At this time the Pathans of the frontier were
generally depressed by the crushing defeat which
they and the Peshawar Sirdars had sustained at the
hands of Ranjit Singh at the battle of Nowshera, so
that when the Saiyid began to preach a *jehad* many
people flocked to his standard, the number of his
Hindustani followers grew to 900, and the Peshawar
Sirdars also joined him. In the spring of 1827
Saiyid Ahmad proceeded to Nowshera with the intention of laying siege to Attock, but Ranjit Singh was
ready for him. The great Sikh general, Hari Singh,
with one army, awaited him on the Indus, while Budh
Singh, crossing the river with another, marched to
and entrenched himself at Saidu. Here Saiyid

Ahmad surrounded his force, and in time reduced
it to great straits, until Budh Singh, resolving to
fight, warned the Peshawar Sirdars of the approach
of another Sikh army under Ranjit Singh, and then
joined battle. The Sirdars fled, and the Musalmans
were routed with great slaughter. Saiyid Ahmad
escaped with a handful of followers via Lundkhwar to
Swat and thence to Buner, where the Saiyid was able
to persuade the Pathans that treachery alone had
been responsible for his defeat, and he was soon again
joined by thousands. He then went to Panjtar,
where he was cordially received by Fateh Khan, the
chief of the Khudu Khels, and his position thereby
greatly strengthened. Eventually he succeeded in
getting the whole of Yusafzai and Peshawar under
his control; he subdued the chiefs of Hund and Hoti;
levied tithes; defeated a Barakzai force which had
marched against him; took possession of Amb; and
finally, in 1829, he occupied Peshawar.

He had now come to the end of his tether; his
exactions had made him unpopular with his Pathan
following, and there was a general revolt against his
authority. The Sikhs organised expeditions against
him and his men, which, as Oliver says, "were exter-
minative rather than punitive. The villagers turned
out and hunted back the fugitives into the mountains, destroying them like wild beasts. The history
of the time is a record of the bitterest hatred. The
traditions tell of massacre without mercy. Hunter
quotes one instance in which the very land tenure
was a tenure by blood, certain village lands being

held by the Hindu borderer on payment to the Sikh grantees of an annual hundred heads of the Hassan Khel. The decline of Saiyid Ahmad's fame as an apostle came after his ill-advised effort to reform the Pathan marriage customs, which was really an attempt to provide wives for his own Hindustanis. Something like the Sicilian Vespers was repeated, the fiery cross was passed round the hills as the signal for the massacre of his agents, and in one hour—the hour of evening prayer—they were murdered by the tribesmen almost to a man."

With the men who were left, Saiyid Ahmad crossed the Indus and proceeded to Balakot, where the believers again rallied to him, and he gave battle once more to a Sikh army under Sher Singh. He was, however, signally defeated, he himself being slain, and, out of the 1600 Hindustanis who had taken the field with him, only 300 escaping to Sitana. This was a refuge for outlaws and for offenders of all kinds from Yusafzai and Hazara, and belonged to one Saiyid Akbar, who had been Ahmad's counsellor and treasurer. Here the Hindustanis established a colony and built a fort which they called Mandi.

CHAPTER IV.

YUSAFZAIS AND GADUNS: OPERATIONS.[1]

NONE of the dwellers in the territories described in the last chapter gave us any trouble during the first few years which followed upon the taking over of the frontier by the British. In 1853, however, it became necessary to punish the Hindustani fanatics, who had afforded some assistance to the Hassanzais during the expedition which the British Government undertook against them in the previous year, and who had seized the fort at Kotla on the right bank of the Indus, belonging to the Nawab of Amb. Early in January 1853, Lieutenant-Colonel Mackeson, C.B., moved the following force down to the Indus opposite Kotla:

> Two guns, Mountain Train Battery.
> 1st Sikh Infantry.
> 3rd Sikh Infantry.
> Two Dogra regiments of the Kashmir Army.
> Six Wallpieces.
> Six Zamburaks.

On the 6th the force was ferried across from Kirpilian in two large boats, and the Sikh regiments and mountain guns advanced, when the Hindustanis

<hr>

[1] See Map IV.

evacuated the fort and fled, being pursued and having considerable loss inflicted upon them by the Nawab of Amb's men. There was no more trouble in the Peshawar district until the year of the Mutiny, and it was then almost entirely due to the presence on the Yusafzai frontier of the Hindustani fanatics, who were supported by contributions of men and money from traitorous princes and private individuals in India.

The Yusafzai country was then controlled by the fort at Mardan, usually garrisoned by the Corps of Guides ; in the middle of May, however, this regiment had started upon its famous march to Delhi, and its place at Mardan had been taken by part of the 55th Native Infantry. On the night of the 21st May news reached General Cotton at Peshawar that some companies of the 55th, stationed at Nowshera, had mutinied, and that some of these had joined their comrades at Mardan. On the night of the 23rd a small force, accompanied by John Nicholson as political officer, quitted Peshawar for the purpose of disarming the 55th Native Infantry at Mardan. At sunrise on the 25th the disaffected regiment saw the column approaching Mardan ; "and then all but a hundred and twenty, who were restrained by the threats and persuasions of the officers, broke tumultuously from the fort, and fled. The column pressed on in pursuit ; but the mutineers were far ahead ; the ground was so heavy that the artillery could not get within range ; and the chase was all in vain until Nicholson, taking with him a few of the police sowars, dashed to the front and rode into the fugitive masses. Breaking before his charge, they scattered themselves over the country in sections and companies; but all day long he pursued them, hunted them out of the villages in which they sought for refuge, drove them over ridges, cut down their stragglers in ravines, and never rested till, having ridden over seventy miles, slain a hundred and twenty, and wounded between three and four hundred of the traitors, taken a hundred and fifty prisoners, and recovered two hundred and fifty stand of arms and the regimental Colours, he was forced by the approach of night to draw rein, while those who had escaped him fled across the border into the hills of Swat." [1]

The virtual ruler of Swat at that time was one whom Oliver has called " A Border Pope "—an aged priest, known as the Akhund, and he decided that these fugitives should not be accorded an asylum. They were accordingly guided to the Indus and put across the stream, whence they intended to endeavour to make their way to Kashmir. The majority of them succumbed, however, to the perils of the journey by way of Hazara or Kohistan, but a few took refuge in the country of the Khudu Khels, whose Khan was hostile to us, and in whose territory a settlement of Hindustanis had been established at a place called Mangal Thana, as a branch of the parent colony at Sitana. The presence of the Hindustanis was the cause of some trouble in July 1857 at Shekh Jana, and a fortnight later the fanatics, under the

[1] From *A History of the Indian Mutiny*, by T. Rice Holmes.

leadership of one Maulvi Inayat Ali Khan, crossed the border and raised the standard of religious war at a border village called Narinji, where some 650 desperadoes had collected. A small force was moved out from Mardan and Nowshera, and, marching at first in another direction so as to conceal the object of the expedition, arrived unexpectedly before Narinji. The position of the village was very strong, and in the days of Sikh rule it had more than once been unsuccessfully attacked, but under cover of the fire of the mountain guns, it was now speedily taken and destroyed. The enemy had lost very severely, and the retirement, which now took place, was quite unopposed. Our casualties had been five killed and twenty-one wounded.

The chief object of the operations—the capture of the Maulvi—had not, however, been attained ; cattle were raided from British territory ; and the enemy were being daily reinforced by men from Buner, Chamla and Swat. Major J. L. Vaughan, who had charge of the operations, now received additional troops from Peshawar, and early on the 1st August he left his camp at Shewa with the following force :

> 2 24-pounder Howitzers.
> 4 guns, Peshawar Mountain Train Battery.
> 50 bayonets, 27th Foot.
> 50 bayonets, 70th Foot.
> 50 bayonets, 87th Foot.
> 150 sabres, 2nd Punjab Cavalry.[1]
> 50 bayonets, 21st Native Infantry.[2]

[1] Now the 22nd Cavalry.　　[2] Now the 1st Brahmans.

400 bayonets, 5th Punjab Infantry.[1]
200 bayonets, 6th Punjab Infantry.[2]
150 bayonets, 16th Punjab Infantry.[3]
225 Mounted Levies and Police.
100 Foot Levies and Police.

Three hundred and fifty rifles were detached to take Narinji in flank and rear, and reached their position about half an hour after the main body had appeared in front of the village. The flanking party was vigorously opposed, but the frontal attack had a comparatively easy task, many of the defenders withdrawing early—among them being the Maulvi. The retreat was to some extent cut off, and many were killed, among the slain being several of the mutineers of the 55th Native Infantry. Our losses were only one killed and eight wounded.

The village was then completely destroyed and the troops retired.

The spirit of the people was not, however, by any means broken, for less than three months later the Assistant-Commissioner of Yusafzai, while encamped at Shekh Jana with a small escort, was attacked by the Hindustanis and Khudu Khels, assisted by the men of Shekh Jana and Narinji. The Assistant-Commissioner escaped with his life, but five of his party were killed, and the whole of his baggage was looted.

Expedition against the Hindustanis and Khudu Khels, 1858.—On the 22nd April, 1858, a force was

---

[1] Now the 58th Vaughan's Rifles.   [2] Now the 59th Scinde Rifles.
[3] Now the 24th Punjabis.

assembled, for the punishment of this outrage, on the left bank of the Kabul River opposite Nowshera. It numbered 4877 of all ranks, was commanded by Major-General Sir Sydney Cotton, K.C.B., and was divided into two brigades, respectively under Lieutenant-Colonel Renny and Major Alban, both of the 81st Foot, but before crossing the frontier, was divided into three columns as under :

FIRST COLUMN.

4 guns, Peshawar Light Field Battery.[1]
2 guns, Peshawar Mountain Train Battery.[2]
260 bayonets, 98th Foot.
100 sabres, 7th Irregular Cavalry.[3]
200 sabres, Guides Cavalry.
30 sabres, Peshawar Light Horse.[4]
100 bayonets, Sappers and Miners.
300 bayonets, 21st Native Infantry.[5]
300 bayonets, Guides Infantry.
400 bayonets, 9th Punjab Infantry.[6]
400 bayonets, 18th Punjab Infantry.[7]

[1] The Peshawar Light Field Battery was raised during the Mutiny from the Bengal Foot Artillery, horsed from the horses taken from the disbanded 5th Light Cavalry.

[2] Now the 23rd Peshawar Mountain Battery.

[3] Now the 5th Cavalry.

[4] Raised during the Mutiny from men of the 27th, 70th and 87th Foot : had a strength of ninety of all ranks, and was commanded by Captain Fane, 87th.

[5] Now the 1st Brahmans.   [6] Now the 21st Punjabis.

[7] Now the 26th Punjabis.

SECOND COLUMN.

200 bayonets, 81st Foot.

100 sabres, 18th Irregular Cavalry.[1]

47 bayonets, Sappers and Miners.

200 bayonets, Kelat-i-Ghilzie Regiment.

450 bayonets, 8th Punjab Infantry.[2]

THIRD COLUMN.

105 bayonets, 81st Foot.

10 bayonets, 98th Foot.

25 sabres, 7th Irregular Cavalry.

25 sabres, 18th Irregular Cavalry.[1]

60 sabres, Guides Cavalry.

254 bayonets, Kelat-i-Ghilzie Regiment.

155 bayonets. 21st Native Infantry.

76 bayonets, Guides Infantry.

54 bayonets, 8th Punjab Infantry.[2]

137 bayonets, 9th Punjab Infantry.

185 bayonets, 18th Punjab Infantry.

The force assembled at the frontier village of Salim Khan, which was made the base of operations, and on the 25th April the people of Totalai, who had long been oppressed by the chief of the Khudu Khels, now, encouraged by the proximity of the troops, made a rush upon Panjtar, intending to seize the chief, Mukarrab Khan, but he escaped to Chinglai, when his village was burnt before the troops arrived upon the scene. The first object of the expedition was thus unexpectedly and easily attained.

[1] Now the 8th Cavalry.   [2] Now the 20th Punjabis.

The following arrangements were now made : the First Column, under the Major-General commanding, marching by Chinglai, was to enter Khudu Khel territory by the Darhan Pass ; the Second Column was to move directly on Panjtar ; while the Third remained in charge of the camp at Salim Khan. The Darhan Pass was found to be a very narrow defile, about two miles in length, the passage of which might easily have been disputed ; no opposition was, however, encountered, and the troops reached Chinglai, which was destroyed under a slight and ineffectual fire from the enemy holding the heights. The column returned on the 27th to Salim Khan via Panjtar and the Jehangirra Darra. This route was found to form a very much more difficult approach to Chinglai than the Darhan Pass route, the track being chiefly through broken country, at one point passing through a rocky defile called Taralai—a very formidable obstacle if disputed. Although some of Mukarrab Khan's men, mounted and on foot, were seen, no attack was made upon the column. The Second Column had meanwhile thoroughly destroyed Panjtar and returned to Salim Khan.

The General now determined to attack a stronghold of the Khan's, called Mangal Thana, situated on one of the main spurs of the Mahaban Mountain. This place had also been the resort of Maulvi Inayat Ali Khan, who had so perseveringly endeavoured, at Narinji and other places, to raise Yusafzai in rebellion in 1857.

The force was again divided into three columns,

which were now, however, somewhat differently constituted—the First to act against Mangal Thana, the
Second to proceed as a support to Panjtar, the Third
remaining in reserve at Salim Khan.   On the 28th
April the First Column left camp while it was
moonlight; the ascent of the hills was found to be
very difficult, and it was necessary to leave half
the column at Dukarai.   No opposition was, however, met with, and Mangal Thana was found to be
abandoned.

Mangal Thana consisted of two villages, one above
the other, the upper containing the citadel of the
leader of the fanatics with enclosures for his followers,
and the whole surrounded by strong fortifications of
stones and timber.   The position was about 5000 feet
above sea-level, and the neighbourhood was densely
wooded.   The troops bivouacked here for the night,
blew up the fort next day, and returned on the 30th
to camp at Salim Khan.

The colony of fanatics at Sitana had now to be
dealt with, and accordingly, on the 2nd May, the force
marched to Khabal, about four miles from Sitana.
Between Amb, on the right bank of the Indus, and
our frontier village of Topi, is a narrow strip of land
forming part of the Utmanzai territory.   It contains,
in addition to the two or three small hamlets of Topi,
the villages of Upper and Lower Khabal (exactly
opposite Torbela), Upper and Lower Kai, and Lower
Sitana, Mandi and Upper Sitana.   The Utmanzais of
this strip had, previous to this date, had feuds with the
Saiyids and Hindustanis of Sitana, and consequently

welcomed our troops as allies against a common foe.

Early on the 4th May a force of five guns and 1050 rifles was sent to the left bank of the Indus, and advanced against the villages from the east; the main column moved against them from the south; while the men of our ally, the Nawab of Amb, occupied the hills to the north. On approaching Lower Sitana, two regiments were detached to move up the mountain in rear, the position was attacked in front, and the enemy were driven with considerable loss to their second position. Here they were met by one of the regiments coming up in their rear, and driven back on the bayonets of the troops in front. Hand-to-hand fighting now ensued until every Hindustani in the position was either killed or captured. Some Gadun allies of the fanatics made no stand, retiring precipitately. The enemy's position having been carried at all points and their villages destroyed, the force retired, being closely followed up. This was the first time the Enfield rifle had been used against the tribesmen, and the effectiveness of its fire made a great impression. Our losses had been six killed and twenty-nine wounded.

That night the force encamped on the Sitana Plain by the Indus bank, whence it proceeded next day to Khabal.

The Hindustanis, expelled from Sitana by the Utmanzais, had taken refuge with the Upper Gaduns, and to prevent the Utmanzais being compelled, on our retirement, to readmit them, the Gadun villages immediately on the Yusafzai border were surrounded by our troops, and coercive measures were threatened. This had an immediate effect, the Upper and Lower Gaduns sending in their representatives and binding themselves, equally with the Utmanzais, to expel and keep out the Saiyids and Hindustanis, and to resist any other tribe which should try to readmit them.

The force then marched back to Nowshera, where it was broken up.

The Hindustani fanatics, now ejected from Sitana, settled at Malka, on the north side of the Mahaban Mountain, but in 1861 they came down to a place called Siri, close to their old haunts, and began abducting Hindu traders from across the Hazara border. The only way whereby it seemed possible to check these crimes was to punish the tribes which allowed these robbers passage through their territories. The Utmanzais and Gaduns were accordingly placed under blockade, and towards the end of 1861 these came in, made submission, and again agreed to exclude the Hindustanis. For a brief period the kidnapping ceased ; then in the spring of 1863 came reports of two murders, followed in the summer by the news that the Hindustanis had suddenly re-occupied Sitana. Not only had the tribes above mentioned done nothing to prevent this, according to agreement, but some of the tribesmen had actually invited this occupation. A blockade of the Gaduns and Utmanzais was therefore reimposed, and a large number of troops and levies were disposed on either

r

bank of the Indus, while the 101st Fusiliers were
ordered up to Hazara.

The Hindustanis were now showing a very bitter
spirit against the British Government, their leaders
were preaching something of a *jehad*, and attacks on
our posts and villages were now projected or undertaken. Ou the night of the 3rd September a party
of Hindustanis attempted to attack the camp of the
Guides engaged on blockade duty at Topi, but were
driven off in panic ; the Hassanzais, instigated by the
Maulvi of Sitana, made an unprovoked attack upon
and destroyed several outlying villages in Amb territory ; later the same clan threatened Chamberi, and
attacked and killed several of the Amb levies on the
Black Mountain. By this time it seemed clear that
most of the Hazara tribes had now thrown in their
lot against the British, and an expedition against
them appeared inevitable ; it was therefore decided
that the force employed should be a large one, and
that Brigadier-General Sir Neville Chamberlain should
command it.

Two columns were to be employed, the one operating from the Peshawar Valley, the other from Hazara,
and the movements proposed for each were as under :
the Peshawar Column was to assemble at Nawa Kala
and Swabi, with the apparent intention of moving on
Mangal Thana, but when ready to move was to march
through the Ambela Pass, occupy Koga in the Chamla
Valley, and thence march on Sitana by Chirori ; the
Hazara Column remaining stationary at Darband to
overawe the riverain tribes and protect the Hazara

border. Additional troops were detailed to hold the line of the Indus, Hazara and Yusafzai at Darband, Torbela, Topi, Abbottabad, Rustam Bazar and Mardan. Hostilities were not anticipated from the Bunerwals, with whom we had no quarrel, and who were known to have no sympathy with the Hindustanis; but it was unfortunate that the absolute necessity for keeping the line of operations secret prevented the Bunerwals being informed that their frontier would be approached by our troops. Consequently they not unnaturally believed that an invasion of their country was intended, and eventually joined the coalition against us.

Ambela Expedition, 1863.—The preliminary arrangements for the expedition appear to have suffered to no inconsiderable extent from the fact that, in order not to alarm the frontier tribes, General Chamberlain had been asked not to join his command until the last moment. On the 19th October he wrote to his brother: "I never before had such trouble or things in so unsatisfactory a state. Carriage, supplies, grain-bags, all deficient. Some of our guns and the five and a half inch mortars have to be sent back as useless, after having taken the pick of men and animals to equip a half-inch battery of R.A. Our 1st L.F. batteries have to be stripped to make the Half Battery R.A. efficient." [1]

General Chamberlain reached Swabi on the 13th October, and marched on the 18th to the mouth of the Darhan Pass with the following troops :

[1] *Life of Field Marshal Sir Neville Chamberlain*, by G. W. Forrest.

Peshawar Mountain Train Battery.
Hazara Mountain Train Battery.[1]
1st Punjab Infantry.[2]
5th Gurkhas.

The other troops of the expeditionary force closed up at the same time to Nawa Kala from their camps in rear, and a proclamation was now issued to all the tribes concerned, stating the object of the operations and the reason for following this particular route. Then on the night of the 19th the following troops marched from Nawa Kala and joined at Parmalao the advanced column :

100 sabres, Guides Cavalry.
100 sabres, 11th Bengal Cavalry.[3]
Guides Infantry.
5th Punjab Infantry.
27th Punjab Native Infantry.[4]

The junction effected, the whole moved on, under Colonel Wilde, to the mouth of the Ambela Pass, which was reached at sunrise on the 20th.

On the 20th the pass was entered and traversed, the head of the pass being held by some 250 Bunerwals, who were, however, dislodged without any great difficulty, and Colonel Wilde's column encamped on and beyond the pass on tolerably open and level ground ; he posted picquets to hold the most important points, but was not strong enough to do more. The main column had left Nawa Kala

[1] Now the 24th Hazara Mountain Battery.
[2] Now the 55th Coke's Rifles.   [3] Now the 11th Lancers.
[4] Now the 27th Punjabis.

at 1 a.m. on the 20th October, and, after a short halt at Rustam, closed up to the rear of the advanced troops late in the afternoon. Both parties had found the road extraordinarily difficult; the track was tolerably good up to the village of Surkhabi, in our own territory, but thereafter deteriorated, in the pass often lying in the bed of a stream, and in other places being overgrown with jungle. In most parts it was possible to move only in single file; the rear guard did not get beyond Surkhabi; and though the ammunition mules managed, with difficulty, to keep up with their units, not a single baggage animal reached camp during the night of the 20th-21st, and only few had arrived there twenty-four hours later. It had been intended that Colonel Wilde should push forward the few cavalry with him, supported by the other arms, to reconnoitre the road down the further side of the pass and the head of the Chamla Valley, but in view of the difficulties of the road, it was deemed best to postpone any forward movement.

While halted on the pass, representatives came in from the people of Chamla and Buner expressing feelings of friendship, and no opposition seems therefore to have been anticipated from these tribes when the force again moved forward on the morning of the 22nd. To prevent any misunderstanding, a full explanation of our intentions was sent to the Buner maliks, and careful instructions were given to our reconnoitring party of cavalry and infantry, now sent on, to follow a road avoiding Buner territory as far as possible. The descent from the top of the

Kotal was found to be tolerably good going, and the rest of the pass was unoccupied by any of the tribesmen.

From the foot of the range on the northern side, two roads passed through the Chamla Valley; one skirted the village of Ambela and lay under the hills dividing Chamla from Buner on the north side of the valley, while the other went by Koga on the south; and as Ambela, though actually in Chamla, was regarded by the Bunerwals as one of their own villages, the advance guard was ordered to proceed by the Koga road so as to avoid all possibility of offence or misunderstanding.

Passing the kotal leading into Buner it was seen to be crowded by Bunerwals, but they did not come down into the valley, which appeared to be quite unoccupied. The reconnoitring party pushed on through Koga to Kuria and then returned towards the Ambela; by this time it was seen that numbers of Bunerwals had come down from the hills with the evident intention of cutting off the retreat of the party. The tribesmen were charged by the cavalry and driven back, and the infantry—the 20th Punjab Infantry[1] under Major Brownlow—then formed the rear-guard. Daylight had now gone, the enemy came on again and pressed the 20th very closely, rushing in among them sword in hand. As the retiring troops drew near camp, the picquets became engaged, and there was a general attack upon them in the front and on the flanks of the camp, which was kept up until midnight.

[1] Now the 20th Brownlow's Punjabis.

That the Bunerwals should thus have taken a
decidedly hostile part against us was very serious,
and our position now required to be strengthened and
the plan of operations to be changed. The line of
communications was secured by calling up additional
infantry and levies, but it was evident that the
Hindustani settlements on the Mahaban Mountain
could not now be reached by the Chamla Valley,
with a powerful and hostile tribe on the left flank
of the line of march.

On the 24th all sick, superfluous baggage and
spare transport were passed down the pass to the
rear, and the troops—on this date about 6000 in
number—were employed in improving the communications. The Bunerwals remained quiet, but it
was noticed that they were joined by large bodies of the
Hassanzais, Chagarzais, Mada Khels and Hindustanis.

Shortly after daylight next morning the enemy
were observed on a ridge opposite and close to the
advanced picquets of the right defence, and Major
Keyes, who was there in command, advanced and
dislodged them. He took up a position on a ridge
commanding the plain over which the enemy had
retired, and found he was then himself commanded, at
a range of 700 yards, from a conical hill on which
the tribesmen were collecting. He sent into camp
for reinforcements, but these did not reach him until
2 p.m., when the hill was attacked and captured. It
afterwards transpired that the enemy had intended
to attack both sides of the camp, but one force did
not come on.

The attention of the General commanding was now drawn to the left side of the camp, where was the Guru Mountain separating the Ambela Pass from Buner. The enemy had collected here in large bodies, and it was necessary to meet any attack from that quarter, and to provide for the security of a sick convoy which it was proposed to send to the rear. On the morning of the 26th, therefore, the left picquets, under Lieutenant-Colonel Vaughan, were reinforced with the following :

> Hazara Mountain Battery.
> 30 marksmen, 71st and 101st Regiments.
> 200 rifles, 71st Regiment.
> 5th Punjab Infantry.
> 6th Punjab Infantry.

These troops proceeded to the vicinity of the "Eagle's Nest" picquet, situated a full mile from the camp, and occupying the top of a very steep, rocky knoll rising out of the southern face of the mountain, and forming the apex of that portion overlooking the left side of the camp. This picquet had hitherto only been held during the day. Colonel Vaughan now placed the thirty marksmen with eighty men of the 20th Punjab Infantry in the "Eagle's Nest"—as many as it was capable of holding—and stationed another 120 men of the 3rd[1] and 20th Punjab Infantry among some large rocks at the base of the knoll. The rest of the force with Colonel Vaughan was disposed about a small underfeature, 400 yards west of the picquet.

[1] Disbanded in 1882.

On the crest of the hill opposite to and distant 500 yards from our picquet, was a breastwork occupied by about 2000 of the enemy, and shortly after noon these made two fierce assaults upon the "Eagle's Nest," and also attacked the rest of the troops immediately under Colonel Vaughan. All these attacks were gallantly repulsed, but our casualties were heavy, amounting to twenty-nine killed and ninety-two wounded; the enemy also lost seriously, and though no further attack was made, a heavy fire was kept up during the rest of the day. The picquet was not, as usual, withdrawn at sunset, and Colonel Vaughan's party maintained its positions all night; next day it was determined to hold permanently the "Eagle's Nest" with forty British and 300 Native soldiers, and another post on an adjoining height, called "Vaughan's Picquet," with the Hazara Mountain Battery, fifty British and 300 Native soldiers. Of the enemy's killed and wounded many were Hindustanis, and some were apparently exsoldiers of the late 55th Native Infantry.

News was now received that the Akhund of Swat, the Border Pope, had thrown in his lot with the Bunerwals, and had summoned also the people of Bajaur and Dir; Chamla sent its quota; the Utman Khels, Afridis from Lundkhwar, also took the field; and it was evident that there was now a general combination against us of almost all the tribes from the Indus to the boundary of Afghanistan. Old feuds seemed to be forgotten, for tribes and chiefs, usually bitter enemies, were now ready to fight side

by side against us ; and it was clear how greatly the
situation had changed for the worse since the force
had first entered the Ambela Pass. Then the troops
had merely to deal with the tribes on the Mahaban
Mountain, to expel the Hindustanis from that tract,
and march to its borders through a friendly, or at
least a not actively hostile, country. General Chamberlain recognised that it would be inadvisable to
make any advance, such as had been contemplated,
with his present force against so large a combination.
He therefore decided to remain on the defensive in
the position he now occupied, which was secure,
where at any rate his communications were safe-
guarded, and where supplies and reinforcements could
easily reach him, trusting that the discouragement of
repeated unsuccessful attacks would gradually weaken
the enemy's numbers and break up the coalition.

Between the 27th and 29th the force was strengthened by the arrival of two guns of the 3rd Punjab
Light Field Battery,[1] the 14th Sikhs, and the 4th
Gurkhas, but it was known that the tribesmen too
had received reinforcements, and that an attack was
shortly to be made upon the camp defences.

On the night of the 29th-30th the advanced picquets
of the right defence were furnished by the 1st Punjab
Infantry and a company of the Guides, under Major
Keyes. Above the main picquets and commanding
them was "the Crag"—a high rock, the ascent to
which was most precipitous, and the summit of which
was incapable of containing more than a very few

[1] Now the 22nd Derajat Mountain Battery.

men. Shortly before daybreak this position was
heavily attacked, and it soon became apparent that
its garrison was hard pressed. Reinforcements were
at once sent forward from the lower picquets, but,
before "the Crag" could be reached, the small garrison was overpowered and driven off the rock,
though the men held the ground lower down. Major
Keyes decided to hold his ground until daylight
among the rocks immediately below the summit and
sent for help. As day broke the picquets were here
reinforced by the 20th Punjab Infantry under Major
Brownlow, and this officer advanced by a ridge which
ran to the right of "the Crag" and threatened
the enemy in rear, while Major Keyes attacked in
front. The assault thus carried out and supported
was entirely successful; a hand-to-hand fight ensued
when the summit of the rock was reached, but the
enemy were driven out at the point of the bayonet
and the position was recovered. No sooner had "the
Crag" been recaptured than the right attack fell to
pieces and the tribesmen fled in panic. Lieutenants
Fosbery, 104th Fusiliers, and Pitcher, 1st Punjab
Infantry, were awarded the Victoria Cross for gallantry on this occasion.

While this attack on the right was in progress,
another by men from Swat was delivered on the front
of the camp, but this was easily repulsed; a demonstration was also made against the upper left flank
picquets. Our losses on this day amounted to fifty-
five killed and wounded, but those of the enemy
had been so heavy, and the effect of the defeat so

great, that many of the tribesmen returned to their homes.

The General commanding now decided to arrange for a new line of communications which should not be exposed to attack from the direction of the Guru Mountain. A line of road was therefore selected between the villages of Khanpur and Sherdara, and the base of operations was changed from Rustam to Parmalao. On the 28th October and 5th November the 7th Fusiliers, 93rd Highlanders, 23rd[1] and 24th[2] Punjab Native Infantry were ordered up to this frontier; a body of 275 police, horse and foot, was sent up to Nawa Kala to assist in the protection of the rearward communications; and later on 4200 camels and 2100 mules were collected at Nowshera, in view of the demand for pack transport which might have to be met when the force eventually moved forward. Working parties were also employed in making a road, to facilitate the forward march on Ambela, along the western slopes of the right ridge, and thus covered from any fire from the Guru Mountain. On the 6th November the operations on this road caused us considerable loss. The working parties had been sent forward as usual, covered by picquets beyond and above them, and all had gone well until the time came to withdraw. The working parties were successfully retired, but the forward covering parties seem to have, for some unknown reason, remained too long on their ground, and were surrounded by the enemy, who moved up in large numbers. The

[1] Now the 23rd Sikh Pioneers.   [2] Now the 24th Punjabis.

light was failing, and the enemy seem to have broken
in between some of the picquets : many of the covering party fought their way back to camp, but our
losses this day amounted to seventy-eight of all ranks
killed and wounded ; the bodies of some of the former
had temporarily to be left behind, but were recovered
next day.

On the 8th the new road to the rear was taken
into use, and a commencement was made in removing
supplies, etc., to the south side of the pass, where it
was proposed to form a new camp, thereby saving
much picquet duty and affording an actually stronger
position.

On the 11th the enemy ascended the hills about
Lalu, on our right front, in large numbers, evidently
with the intention of attacking the picquets on that
side of the camp. These were accordingly reinforced
and their defences strengthened. "The Crag" had
recently been much enlarged and improved, and was
now capable of accommodating a garrison of 160 men,
while it was supported by the mountain guns of the
Peshawar Battery from the main picquet. At 4 p.m.
on the 11th Major Brownlow assumed command of
"the Crag," having under him fifteen of the 101st
Fusiliers, thirty of the 14th Sikhs, and 115 of the
20th Punjab Native Infantry. Two of the four
mountain guns commanded the left shoulder of "the
Crag" hill and the front of the "Centre" picquet
below. The enemy occupied a position about half a
mile in length on a ridge facing and within 250 yards
of "the Crag" picquet. Between the two positions

was a hollow intersected by a ravine.   The right and
rear of "the Crag" were precipitous and practically
unassailable; the left face was the weak point, there
being cover for an attacker to within a few yards of
the position.   Anticipating an attack, every effort
was this day made to improve the defences.   About
10 p.m. the enemy moved down in large numbers to
the hollow in front of the picquet, and shortly after
made repeated desperate attacks until daybreak upon
the front and left of the picquet, but were beaten
back with loss, although at one time they nearly
penetrated the position at its left front angle; the
situation was saved by the gallantry and devotion of
Major Brownlow and five men of his regiment.   By
morning but very few of the enemy were anywhere
visible, and as Major Brownlow's men had been for
forty-eight hours on duty, they were relieved at 8 a.m.
on the 30th by ninety men of the 1st Punjab Infantry
under Lieutenant Davidson.

This officer soon after asked Major Keyes for reinforcements, as he did not consider his ninety men
sufficient garrison for the position, and thirty
additional men were sent him, all that could at the
moment be spared, as serious attacks were anticipated
upon other portions of the defence.   These reinforcements had only just reached "the Crag," when the
men of the picquet were seen to be vacating it and
rushing down the hill in confusion.   Major Keyes at
once proceeded to and occupied a breastwork on the
road between "the Crag" and the main picquet, and
there rallied the retreating men and checked the

advance of the enemy. Feeling the urgent need of the moral effect of a counter attack and the necessity for giving time for the arrival of support, he ordered an assault upon "the Crag." This, though bravely led and executed, was unsuccessful, owing to the paucity of men available, and the detachments fell back. The enemy occupying "the Crag" were now pouring a heavy fire into the camp, and its continued possession by them would render the lower picquets untenable. Lieutenant-Colonel Wilde, commanding the right defences, now asked for the 101st Regiment, and taking also three companies of the Guides, made for the advanced picquets, where the state of affairs was as follows : Major Ross, with some of the 14th Sikhs and men of other corps, was holding on halfway up "the Crag" hill, but unable to advance any further; parties of the enemy, attacking the lower picquets, were only kept back by the well-directed fire of the mountain guns; while the 1st, 20th, and two companies of the Guides with Major Keyes still held the breastwork, but could not hope to do so for long.

The 101st now at once advanced direct upon "the Crag," and never halted or broke until they had gallantly stormed the heights and secured the picquet, driving the enemy over the hills beyond, while the three companies of Guides swept the enemy from the right of the position. All opposition now ceased along the whole line, the enemy having lost very heavily, their casualties being 89 killed and 140 wounded. The defenders of "the Crag" seem to have been seized with an unaccountable panic, owing to the enemy concentrating a large force, unobserved, upon a weak picquet: Lieutenant Davidson was killed at his post.

During the next four or five days no attacks of a serious character were made by the enemy. Early on the morning of the 18th, the new camp being ready for occupation, the whole of the troops occupying the Guru Mountain were withdrawn, and the entire camp and troops transferred to the heights on the south of the pass, while steps were also taken to extend the position so as more effectually to command the water supply. Imagining from the evacuation of the Guru position that the force was retreating, the new left front of the camp was this day fiercely attacked, but the enemy were repulsed with heavy losses on both sides.

On the 20th November "the Crag" picquet was garrisoned by 100 bayonets from the 101st Fusiliers and an equal number from the 20th Punjab Native Infantry ; the "Water" picquet, within 450 yards of it, by 100 bayonets of the 71st Foot and 100 men of the 3rd Punjab Infantry. About 9 a.m. the enemy began to collect in large numbers near these picquets, principally threatening "the Crag," but were to some extent checked by the fire of the Peshawar mountain battery. Up to late in the afternoon the tribesmen had made no impression, though they had succeeded in establishing themselves within a few yards of the breastworks. About 3 p.m., however, the unaccountable conduct of an officer on the left of the picquet, who suddenly ordered the troops immediately under

his command to retire, gave the enemy possession
of the post—though not without a desperate resistance from the remainder of the garrison. On the fall
of "the Crag" being reported, General Chamberlain
ordered up the 71st Foot and the 5th Gurkhas to
retake it; the 71st stormed the position in front, the
Gurkhas and 5th Punjab Infantry attacking the lower
portion in flank, and the work was retaken without
much loss on our side. Among the wounded, however, was the General commanding, who had accompanied the storming party. Thus for the third time
was "the Crag" lost and won—a spot which, from
the heavy casualties there sustained on either side,
had become known in the country side as the *katlgar*,
or place of slaughter.

This action, despite the temporary success gained,
seemed to have a depressing effect on the enemy;
their numbers dwindled down, and from this date
until the 15th December they made no further attack
in any force. Sir Nevill Chamberlain's wound proving
more serious than was at first expected, he asked to
be relieved of the command, and on the 30th November his place was taken by Major-General Garvock.

Meanwhile the political officers had had some success in their attempts to detach certain clans from
the coalition. Two divisions of the Bunerwals had
thus seceded; 2000 Swatis had been induced to
return to their homes; one or two influential chiefs
had drawn off their followers; while amongst the men
who remained in the field a general mistrust prevailed.
The gathering, in fact, seemed to be only now held

together by the influence of the Akhund of Swat and
of the Maulvi. Still reinforcements reached the
tribesmen from Kunar and Bajaur, while our force
was strengthened by the arrival of the 7th Fusiliers,
the 93rd Highlanders, the 3rd Sikhs and 23rd Punjab
Native Infantry.

It was becoming increasingly evident that the
Buner and Chamla tribes were weary of the war, and
were beginning to realise that we had never harboured any idea of invading their country ; and on
the 10th December they sent a deputation into our
camp and agreed to accompany a force sent to destroy
the Hindustani settlement at Malka, and to expel the
Hindustanis from their country. On the 14th, however, they found themselves obliged to admit that
they had promised more than they could perform ;
that their proposals had been over-ruled ; and they
advised us that an attack would be made on the camp
on the 16th, and promised that, in the event of our
taking the initiative, they, the Bunerwals, would not
actively oppose us.

General Garvock accordingly determined to attack
the village of Lalu, where there was a force of about
4000 of the enemy, and for this purpose he moved
out on the 15th with some 4800 men, unencumbered
by tents or baggage, formed into two columns. The
first column assembled at the base of " the Crag "
picquet and drove the enemy before it to the " Conical " hill. The second column now emerged from the
camp, and deploying in prolongation of the line
formed by the other column, both prepared to assault

the "Conical" hill—a most formidable position, extraordinarily precipitous, rocky, and scarped by nature. Covered by the mountain guns, both columns descended the hill, crossed the valley, drove the enemy from the heights, and captured the position. Colonel Wilde secured the line of hills overlooking the Chamla Valley, while the rest of the force, pushing on after the enemy, captured the villages of Banda and Lalu. The enemy made a vigorous assault upon Colonel Wilde's position, but were driven off with great slaughter, and a desultory attack was also made upon the front and left of the camp, now held by some 3000 men under Colonel Vaughan. That night the first column occupied the ground it had gained about Lalu; Colonel Wilde that between the camp and "Conical" hill. Not a shot was fired that night. Early next morning the cavalry—some 400 sabres under Lieutenant-Colonel Probyn—were brought from camp, and the advance of the two columns was resumed, Colonel Wilde leading. Advancing across the valley towards the Buner Pass, as the column debouched into the open country the enemy appeared in great force on the hills covering the approach to Ambela—a well-chosen position, of great strength, and peculiarly capable of defence; but fearing that their left would be turned by the cavalry and the other column, the tribesmen abandoned the position and retreated slowly towards the pass leading to Buner. The force pressed on, captured and burnt the village of Ambela, and the first column endeavoured to cut off the enemy's retreat from the pass

towards which they were retiring. Here the tribesmen stood, and made a furious onset on the left of
the line, entangled in broken and wooded ground.
But the attackers were destroyed almost to a man,
and the force pushed forward into the pass, driving
the enemy before it. It was now getting late, there
was no wish to invade Buner, and the enemy further
was in great strength. General Garvock therefore
withdrew his troops, and bivouacked that night in
the vicinity of Ambela. During these two days the
tribesmen present in the field were estimated at
15,000, chiefly Hindustanis, Bajauris, and men from
Dir and Swat—none of the Bunerwals had taken any
prominent part in the fighting.

That night the men of Bajaur and Dir fled to their
homes, and the Swatis alone remained in the field ;
on the morning of the 17th the Buner jirgah came
once more into camp, actually *asking for orders*. It
was wisely decided to require the Bunerwals themselves to destroy Malka without any aid from our
troops, and to this the Buner jirgah unanimously
consented. Accordingly, on the 19th, a party of six
British officers, escorted by the Guides and accompanied by part of the Buner jirgah, left Ambela, and
marched through Chamla and Amazai territory—by
Kuria and Nagrai—to Malka, which was reached on
the 21st. On the following day the settlement was
burnt to the ground by the Bunerwals and Amazais,
and the party rejoined the force on the 23rd in the
Ambela Pass. During these four days matters once
or twice looked uncertain, and indeed threatening,

but throughout the Bunerwals maintained their reputation for keeping their engagements, while the sight
of so powerful a clan carrying out our orders upon
their own allies, afforded a salutary lesson to the
surrounding tribesmen.

General Garvock's force now began to withdraw to
the plains, and the whole had reached Nawa Kala by
Christmas Day. Our casualties during the whole
of these operations had been 238 killed and 670
wounded, while the estimated total loss of the enemy
was 3000.

During the next few years the behaviour of the
Bunerwals may, in comparison with that of many
other frontier tribes, be described as " good." Raids
were committed upon our border villages in 1868 and
1877, and in 1878 and 1879 there was a certain
amount of unrest in Buner, due to the inflammatory
preachings of certain mullahs. In 1884 renewed
outrages had to be punished by a blockade of the
Salarzai Bunerwals; and in 1887 a small column
composed of cavalry and infantry was sent to destroy
the village of Surai Malandri in punishment for the
incursions of raiding parties across the Malandri
Pass, but at the end of the year, the Bunerwals submitting, the long-continued blockade was removed.
During the Black Mountain expedition of 1888 the
Bunerwals evinced a disposition to take part against
us, but refrained from doing so; while in 1895 they
sent a contingent to help hold the passes against
General Low's force, but arriving too late for the
Malakand fighting, this party returned home again.

In 1897, however, the Bunerwals were well to the fore in much of the fighting at the Malakand and in Upper Swat, but when called to account at the end of 1897 they merely sent defiant answers to the ultimatum of the political officers, and it therefore became necessary to despatch an expedition into their country.

Expedition against the Bunerwals and Chamlawals, January 1898.—The Buner Field Force was placed under the command of Major-General Sir Bindon Blood, and the greater part of it concentrated at Sanghao : it was composed as under :

FIRST BRIGADE.

Brigadier-General Meiklejohn, C.B., C.M.G.

1st Battalion Royal West Kent Regiment.
16th Bengal Infantry.[1]
20th Punjab Infantry.
31st Punjab Infantry.

SECOND BRIGADE.

Brigadier-General Jeffreys, C.B.

1st Battalion The Buffs.
21st Punjab Infantry.[2]
Guides Infantry.

DIVISIONAL TROOPS.

10th Field Battery R.A.
No. 7 Mountain Battery R.A.
No. 8 Bengal Mountain Battery R.A.[3]
1 Squadron 10th Bengal Lancers.[4]

[1] Now the 16th Rajputs.   [2] Now the 21st Punjabis.
[3] Now the 28th Mountain Battery.
[4] Now the 10th Lancers (Hodson's Horse).

Guides Cavalry.

2nd Battalion Highland Light Infantry.

6 Companies 3rd Bombay Light Infantry.[1]

No. 4 Company Bengal Sappers and Miners.

No. 5 Company Madras Sappers and Miners.

Sir Bindon Blood, with the bulk of his troops at Sanghao, intended to force the Tanga Pass, about a mile to the northward, while a small column composed of the 31st Punjab Infantry, the Guides Infantry and a section of No. 4 Company Bengal Sappers and Miners, was to capture the Pirsai Pass, when the cavalry, moving from Rustam, was to cross over the Pirsai Pass and cut the enemy's line of retreat from the Tanga. This last-named pass was known to be held by about a thousand of the enemy, as were the Ambela and Malandri, but only forty or fifty men had collected for the defence of the Pirsai. The 2nd Brigade advanced on the morning of the 7th January and found the position defended by at least 2000 men, and from a parallel ridge facing the pass the Buffs and mountain guns opened fire at 1500 yards, under cover of which the rest of the troops pushed forward through the ravine, while the 20th Punjab Infantry had ascended a steep spur to the east, leading to a high peak overlooking the position. When the 20th were seen to be approaching their objective, the frontal attack commenced. The enemy, however, demoralised by the heavy gun and rifle fire, made no real stand, and, pressed by the 20th on their right, early began

[1] Now the 103rd Mahratta Light Infantry.

to abandon their position, and finally fled down the valley towards Kingargali and the hills beyond. Three battalions of the 1st Brigade pushed on to Kingargali, which was found deserted. Meanwhile the cavalry and infantry from Rustam and Pirsai had captured the Pirsai Pass without meeting with but slight resistance, and the cavalry pushed on up the narrow valley as far as Kuhai, returning to Chorbanda, two miles north of the pass, where the night was spent. On the 10th this column joined the 1st Brigade at Bampokha.

Two divisions of Bunerwals now at once came in and tendered their submission, but it was decided to visit the territory of every division, and General Meiklejohn's column accordingly marched to Jawar Bai, Hildai, Rega, where the house of the Mad Fakir (of whom more will be heard later) was destroyed, and Barkeli. The 2nd Brigade, which had returned to Sanghao after the capture of the Tanga Pass, entered Buner by the Ambela Pass and occupied Koga and Nawagai, the cavalry reconnoitring the Chamla Valley. These measures led to the prompt and complete submission of all divisions of the Bunerwals and of the men of Chamla, and the force was withdrawn by the Ambela Pass, and reached Mardan on the 20th January.

During the Ambela expedition of 1863 the behaviour of the Gadun tribe had not been uniformly satisfactory, and consequently on the break up of the force Colonel Wilde took a strong brigade into their country, visited Meni, and also Khabal in the territory of the Utmanzais, whose conduct had been of an equally hostile character. No opposition was experienced, but it was decided to require the two tribes to perform a similar service to that demanded of the Bunerwals, viz. to destroy a Hindustani fort and settlement called Mandi adjacent to Sitana. This was carried out and the force was then broken up; the effect of these measures was immediately apparent, for within the next few weeks the Mada Khels, the Amazais and the remaining sections of the Hassanzais all sent deputations to our political officers and made their submission. For some years, however, the Gaduns continued to give trouble, committing outrages of all kinds and raiding on the border. They were blockaded, coerced and fined, but continued to be troublesome; in 1897, too, they were implicated in the attacks on the Malakand and Chakdara posts, but in the end of that year they finally made submission and paid up the fines demanded of them.

This chapter commenced with some account of our dealings with the Hindustani fanatics, and may fittingly end with a few final words about them. Expelled in 1864 from Malka, they retreated into the Chagarzai country north of the Barandu River, but were not very comfortable there, their hosts frequently threatening them with expulsion. In 1868 they appear to have moved from their settlements in the Chagarzai territory to Bajkatta in Buner, and here in April they were joined by Feroz Shah, the son of the last king of Delhi. The presence

of the Hindustanis in Buner was abhorrent to the
Akhund, who induced his co-religionists to decide to
expel them. In consequence of this resolve, the
fanatics, now some 700 strong, hurriedly retreated
to Malka, where they commenced re-building their
houses. Some of them eventually got permission to
return to Buner, but, intriguing against the Akhund,
the order of expulsion was again put in force, and
they were hunted out of the country, suffering heavy
losses, and took refuge, first with the Chagarzais,
then at Palosi—moving again to Thakot, and eventually back again to the country of the Hassanzais
who rented them some land at Maidan near Palosi,
where they remained until 1888. After their dramatic
appearance at Kotkai in the Black Mountain operations of 1888, they resought an asylum among the
Chagarzais, but are now, to the number of 700,
living among the Amazais, neither occupying themselves greatly with local feuds nor being seriously
implicated in other disturbances. But of late years
there have not been wanting signs—faint, perhaps,
but discernible—of a slight revival of their former
activity.

CHAPTER V.

AKOZAIS. (SWAT.)[1]

THE district of Swat proper—as distinct from the tracts of country south of the Malakand and Morah Mountains, and inhabited by the same clans—comprises the valley of the Swat River, from its junction with the Panjkora northwards to the village of Ain, above which the country is known as Swat Kohistan. From Ain to the Landakai spur, five miles above Chakdara, the valley is called Bar, or Upper Swat, while Kuz, or Lower Swat, is the name given to the portion from Landakai downwards to the village of Kalangai. The valley is about seventy miles long and some twelve miles wide from crest to crest of its watersheds. The river, fed by glaciers and snow, begins to rise in the middle of April, and rapidly becomes unfordable, falling again in the middle of September, and being passable almost anywhere by midwinter. The climate is much the same as that of Buner, and the valley is unhealthy and malarious in summer.

Of the country of Swat, Oliver, in *Across the Border*, writes : " Its hill tops are clothed with rich forests, giving place to a variety of excellent fruit

[1] See Map IV.

trees in its well-watered valleys.   Its climate is temperate even in summer, and its capabilities great.
Many parts of it are known to be rich in ancient
remains; the frequent ruins in Swat and Bajaur
indicate the former presence of Greek, Buddhist and
Hindu, and innumerable inscribed tablets in Greek
and Pali—probably becoming fewer and less valuable
every year—only await scientific investigation to
throw much light on the ancient history of this part
of the world.... The river from which the district
takes its name, probably the Suastos of Arrian,
debouches on British territory near the fort of
Abazai, whence, up to its junction with the Panjkora
—the ancient Gauraios—it is a swift, deep torrent,
rushing between precipitous banks; the surrounding
hills impracticable for any except foot passengers, and
not easy for them, being in the hands of the Utman
Khels.... The whole valley is highly cultivated
and densely populated, each glen or gorge has its
village or hamlet, and the total population has
been estimated at not far short of 100,000 souls.
The fields are in terraces one above another, extensively irrigated by channels diverted from the
river or the torrents flowing into it. The course
of the river itself, working from side to side of
the valley, is marked by more numerous villages,
groves of trees, and almost unbroken cultivation.
The very burying-grounds, usually especially sacred
to Pathans, are regularly ploughed up, and the dead
buried in the fallow lands; hardly a single yard of
tillable ground is neglected. Wheat and most grains,

sugar-cane, lucerne, tobacco, and vegetables are extensively grown, and Upper Swat yields excellent fruits. In the hot weather, when a great portion of the valley can be irrigated, the lands everywhere near the river are a sheet of luxuriant rice, the steamy exhalations from which no doubt contribute largely to the unhealthiness of the valley. Picturesque it is in the extreme; the upper slopes of the mountains are well clothed with forests of pine and deodar; below lies a beautiful velvet-like turf, and again stretches of cultivation, dotted with houses—wretched hovels enough, but artistically half-hidden among rich clusters of plane or poplar; and bright clear streams everywhere rushing down to the brisk noisy Swat, dashing over its boulder-strewn bed, like a Scotch salmon river. All the same, the notorious insalubrity of the valley is a very serious drawback to all this beauty.... The men especially are weak, thin and feeble, hardly resembling Pathans in form or feature, and more like the Gujars of the Lower Punjab. The women, on the other hand, seem curiously much less affected, for they are described as stout and buxom, and though by no means good-looking, retain far more of the Pathan appearance. They have, moreover, entirely reversed the position of the sexes prevailing in ordinary Pathan communities. Not only do they go unveiled, and enjoy more liberty, but rule the men to a greater extent than is known among Pathans elsewhere. The men of the Swat Valley, are, in fact, credited with living to a great extent under petticoat government."

In character the people appear to differ but little from other Pathans. They possess all the vices common to that race, and are not behind them in pride, cupidity, revengefulness or treachery. In the last-named vice, indeed, they may indisputably be given the first place among Pathan tribes. At one time their courage was not held in very high esteem, but the fighting in 1895 and 1897 seems to prove that in this respect they have been by us and others curiously misjudged. Beyond a few individuals, however, none of the Swat tribes are represented in the Indian regular army, although some 400 are serving in the Dir and Swat levies; this service is popular with them, as it is close to their homes, and as they are generally prosperous, they prefer not to wander far afield in search of military service.

The Swat Valley, and those to the west and south-west of it, form classic ground, for it was through them that Alexander himself marched on his way to the invasion of India. It was in the winter of 327 B.C. that he left the city he had founded to the north of Kabul, and somewhere west of Jagdallak he divided his force into two parts. Hephæstion, with the heavy troops forming the main body, followed the direct route through the Khyber, marching on an ancient city, the capital of Gandhara, and to the north-east of Peshawar. Alexander, with the light troops, entered the Kunar Valley and crossed the Kunar watershed by the Spinasuka Pass, which leads direct from Pashat, the present capital of Kunar, into Bajaur, and there found himself close to Nawagai, the

present chief town of Bajaur.   Thence he passed over
the Gauraios or Panjkora River some few miles below
its junction with the Swat, and so came to the siege
and capture of Massaga, identified as Matkanai, near
the Malakand Pass, by which Alexander must have
crossed from the Swat Valley to the plain country
bordering the Indus.

The language spoken in Swat is Pushtu, except in
Swat Kohistan, where Torwali and Garhwi are used.

The best road into Swat from the south is over the
Malakand Pass; the Shakot, further to the east, is
shorter, but the ascent is steeper, while the Morah
Pass entrance is still more difficult.

The Government of Swat, like that of all Pathan
tribes, is an almost complete democracy.   The country
is split up into nearly as many factions as there are
villages.   Each sub-division of each division of each
clan has its separate quarrels, and supports its own
chief, who is generally at mortal feud with either his
own relations or his neighbours, and who is seldom
obeyed one instant longer than is convenient; so that
nothing short of pressing danger to the whole community from without could ever bring together all
the divisions into which Swat is separated.   But that
which could not be effected by ordinary means has,
in a measure, been brought about by the influence of
one individual, working on the religious feelings of a
mass of grossly ignorant and proportionately bigoted
people, such as are the inhabitants of Swat; this man
was the late Akhund of Swat.   The Akhund exerted
such a powerful influence, as already seen in the

Ambela campaign, not only over the district of Swat, but over the whole of the Yusafzai border, that an account of him somewhat in detail may not be out of place.

Abdul Ghafur, as was his original name, was born of poor and obscure parents, probably Gujars, at the village of Jabrai, in Upper Swat, and passed his early boyhood tending sheep and cattle. He was even then distinguished for his religious proclivities, and at the age of eighteen he decided to adopt the life of an ascetic, and proceeded to Barangola to learn to read and write, and master the rudiments of his religion. Thence, after a time, he set out as an "inquirer after wisdom," and at first took up his abode in or near a mosque about three miles from Mardan ; but moving on again after a stay of a few months, he became, at Tordhair, the disciple of a fakir who enjoyed in those parts a reputation for peculiar sanctity. Here the Akhund resolved to exchange the mosque for the hermitage, and became a recluse.

About the year 1816 he accordingly settled down, as a young man of barely twenty, to a life of the greatest austerity, at a lonely spot on the banks of the Indus, below the village of Beka, ten miles above Attock, where for twelve years he followed the *Nakshbandia* form of religious devotion—sitting silent and motionless, his head bowed on his chest, and his eyes fixed on the ground. His food was an inferior kind of millet moistened with water, and throughout his life—he died at the age of eighty-three—his diet was equally simple, milk being, however, subsequently substituted for water. His fame as a saint dates from his sojourn at Beka, and even to this day, in the most distant parts of Persia, he is still remembered as "the Hermit of Beka."

In an evil moment he unwisely allowed himself to be drawn into a quarrel between the Khan of Hund and Saiyid Ahmad of Bareilly, and found himself obliged to abandon his retreat at Beka, and wander forth unknown and of no account; but after some years he settled down in a ziarat at Ghulaman, in British Yusafzai, and recovering his old reputation for sanctity and piety, his advice and prayers were again in great request. Thence in time he removed to the village of Salim Khan, in the south-east of British Yusafzai and on the border of the Khudu Khels, and, being generally regarded as a saint, was given the title of Akhund by the learned Moslem doctors of the day.

On two occasions was the Akhund beguiled—possibly from some dread of loss of ascendancy among his co-religionists should he refuse—into taking up arms for "the Faith." In the year 1835, Dost Muhammad Khan, Amir of Kabul, invited him to join his force near Peshawar, with as large a body of his disciples as he could persuade to accompany him, and attack the camp of the Sikhs. This the Akhund did, and he and his following had some trifling success against the soldiers of the Khalsa. But the arrival of Ranjit Singh to command the Sikh armies in person was enough to send the Amir flying precipitately through the Khyber, and to scatter the Akhund's fanatical rabble in all directions. The Akhund himself made for Buner with a few followers, who quickly deserted him, and then, returning to his ascetic and secluded life, he settled for a time in Ranizai territory. From here he moved a few years later to the village of Saidu Mandz, in the Baizai district of Swat, where he lived surrounded by numerous disciples and visited by crowds of devotees. The Akhund gained such an ascendancy over the minds of his co-religionists that they believed all kinds of stories about him; that he was supplied by supernatural means with the necessities of life, and that every morning a sum of money, sufficient for his own needs and for the entertainment of the pilgrims who flocked to consult him, was found under his praying carpet. But most wonderful of all —he was never known to accept any present offered to him.

"His ascendancy over the Muhammadans of the Border and Eastern Afghanistan," says Oliver, "was as great as that of Loyola in Rome or Luther in Saxony; his edicts regarding religious customs and secular observances were as unquestioned as the Papal Bulls in Spain. When the chiefs of Swat recognised the possibility of British military operations extending to their valley and the necessity for federation, it was to the Akhund they turned to select them a king. His selection was a Saiyid of Sitana, who for some years carried on an organised government under the patronage of the Border Pope. Putting aside the incredulous stories about him as priest, his life seems to have been one of devotion, humility, abstinence and chastity; the doctrines he taught were as tolerant and liberal as those of his Wahabi opponents were intolerant and puritanical. Judged by the standard applied to other religious leaders, he used his influence, according to his lights, for good, supporting peace and morality, discouraging feuds, restraining the people from raiding and offences against their neighbours, and enforcing the precepts of Muhammadan law as far as ineradicable Pathan custom would permit him."

For many years after settling at Saidu Mandz, he held himself aloof from secular affairs, preached peace towards all men, and counselled the tribesmen to cultivate friendly relations with the British Government. In 1847 he did his best to prevent the Swatis from assisting the Baizais, whom we were engaged in punishing. When the mutineers of the 55th Native Infantry, flying from Mardan before Nicholson, crossed the boundary into Swat, he caused them to be deported beyond the Indus; and he supported our government so far as lay in his power during the anxious days of the Mutiny. He had always opposed the colonies of Hindustani fanatics, so that his conduct in 1863, when during the Ambela expedition he sided with them, seems difficult to explain. Colonel Reynell Taylor believed, and his belief was shared by those at the time best able to judge, that the Akhund had taken the line he did in fear that if he did not show sympathy with Buner on this occasion, his influence might pass to some more compliant leader.

The pressure brought to bear on him was practically irresistible; the adjurations of the Buner chiefs and people had been most passionate, all the mullahs of the country, with many of the women, having been deputed to beseech him to adopt their cause.

The expedition having come to an end, he went back to his former life, and never again took the field. He was then already seventy years of age, and thenceforth until his death in January, 1877, he did his best to hold in check the wild spirits of the border.

During his residence in Saidu Mandz the Akhund married a woman of a neighbouring village; she bore him two sons and a daughter. The elder of the sons was Abdul Manan, alias Mian Gul, who, after the death of the Akhund, became involved in a struggle for supremacy in Swat with the Khan of Dir, and in 1883, aided by the chief of Bajaur and the name of his father, he established himself for a brief period before his death. The younger son, Abdul Khalik, was, as his father before him, an ascetic and a hermit, but he had no influence whatever, and was unknown beyond the boundaries of his own valley.

"No Border Pontiff has yet arisen," writes the author of *Across the Border*, "who can successfully fill the chair of his eminence Abdul Ghafur, the Akhund of Swat."

The Akozais, the inhabitants of Swat, are separated into five divisions :

1. Baizai.   2. Ranizai.   3. Khadakzai.
4. Abazai.   5. Khwazozai.

The Baizais inhabit the country on the left bank of the Swat River from the borders of Kohistan as far as and including Thana; the division contains three sub-divisions, and of these certain sections live beyond the limits of the Swat Valley, in the Ghurban, Kana, Puran and Chakesar Valleys, the drainage of which finds its way into the Indus. In addition to the Baizai there are also the Sam, or lowland, Baizai, who occupy the land from our border to the foot of the hills below the Morah Pass. The villages in this territory formerly belonged to the Baizai maliks, and were occupied by their tenants and servants, but have now become independent.

The Ranizais occupy the left bank of the Swat River from the district of the most southerly sub-division of the Baizais at Thana to the Utman Khel boundary, which is about three miles above the junction of the Swat with the Panjkora. To the north their territory extends to the river, and includes the islands between the different channels, while the southern boundary is formed by the watershed of the hills on that side. The importance of the division lies mainly in their possession of the Malakand and Shakot Passes; the Digar Pass, which is further to the west, also leads into the Ranizai country, but the pass itself is partly in the hands of the Utman Khels.

Formerly the whole of the country from the hills to the British border, now held by the Sam Ranizais, belonged to the Ranizai division, as the people known as Sam Ranizais, and who are now independent, were originally servants and tenants of the Ranizais.

The Ranizais contain five sub-divisions, and their principal village is Aladand, at the mouth of the Shakot Pass.

The Khadakzais are on the right bank of the Swat River, extending from Abazai territory to the country of the Dusha Khel; the principal village is Barangola.

The Abazais inhabit a small valley on the right bank of the Swat River immediately below the Adinzai sub-division of the Khwazozais. Both the Abazais and the Khadakzais are insignificant divisions of the Akozai tribe, numbering between them no more than 750 fighting men, and within recent years these divisions and the Adinzai sub-division of the Khwazozai, which is stronger than the two combined, have been handed over to the Khan of Dir. The importance of the Adinzai sub-division consists in their possession of the village of Chakdara, where the river is bridged, and which is on the main route from India to Bajaur and Chitral. The Swat River runs here in six channels, covering about three-quarters of a mile of ground; the village is on a bank 60 feet high, and some 600 yards from the nearest branch of the river. An iron girder bridge crosses the river three-quarters of a mile below the village, and there is a fort on the right bank.

The Khwazozais are, next to the Baizais, the strongest division of the Swat clan; they are separated into five sub-divisions, and occupy the valley on the right bank of the river from Kohistan to Chakdara.

Besides the above five divisions of the Akozai clan,

mention must be made of some others who inhabit
territory adjacent to the country of Swat. The Dusha
Khels are Yusafzais, whose territory lies south of the
Talash Valley and east of the Panjkora, running down
in a narrow wedge between that river and the
Khadakzai country to the banks of the Swat River.
Their country is very mountainous, they themselves
are very independent in character, and bear a reputation for thieving. They have been handed over to
the Khan of Dir.

North of Swat proper, in Swat Kohistan, live
the *Torwals* and the *Garhwis*, and in the Panjkora
Kohistan are the *Bashkaris*. Little is known of
these tribes, but they are not Pathans, and are
probably the descendants of the races occupying Dir
and Swat prior to the arrival upon the scene of the
Pathans. The *Roganis*, *Katnis* and *Gurohs*, who are
supposed to be of Kafir descent, are also located in
Dir.

OPERATIONS.

Up to the year 1895 the only Akozais of Swat with
whom the British had had any dealings were the
Baizais and Ranizais, who inhabited the country south
of the Morah Mountain.

Operations against the Baizais, 1847.—The first
time we came in contact with these people was in
October 1847, when Major George Lawrence, then
holding the Peshawar Valley for the Sikhs, was fired
on by the men of the Baizai village of Babuzai, and,
obtaining no satisfaction for the outrage, he determined to attack the village. This was awkwardly

placed; a direct attack was inadvisable, for Babuzai was situated at the further extremity of a *cul-de-sac*, 500 yards long and 300 yards broad, formed by two short, steep and rugged spurs from the lofty ridge of hills dividing Lundkhwar from Sudum.   Only the year previously the village had repulsed a superior force under the Sikh Sirdar, Sher Singh.   The force under Major Lawrence was composed of a brigade of all arms belonging to the Sikh Durbar, aided by the newly-raised Corps of Guides.   It was discovered that the heights above the village could be gained, and Major Lawrence accordingly sent some levies of the Sudum chief, with thirty bayonets of the Guides, to ascend the heights by night and co-operate at day-break with the main frontal attack.   Early on the 11th Major Lawrence advanced, but one of his columns was at first driven back; the rear attack being now seen descending on the village, a general assault was ordered, and Babuzai was carried and burnt.   It being ascertained that men from Palai, in Sam Baizai, had assisted in the defence of Babuzai, Major Lawrence moved thither on the 14th, inflicted some loss on the enemy, destroyed the village and retired.

Our casualties had been only one killed and thirteen wounded, and the moral effect of these operations was such that a few days after ten villages made their submission, several of which had never before tendered allegiance either to the Durani or to the Sikh rulers.

Two years after these events the Peshawar Valley

was annexed, and then and thereafter the Swatis proved themselves bad neighbours. Plunderers and marauders, mounted and on foot, issued from Swat, passed through Ranizai, and raided into our territory. They kidnapped almost all classes except Pathans; and Swat became an Alsatia where evilly-disposed persons, criminals of all shades, and people hostile to the British Government were readily granted help, asylum and countenance.

In October 1849 it was reported that the whole of the Utman Khel villages of Sam Baizai had refused to pay revenue or to receive the native revenue collector, and that the people were all preparing for war. The Deputy-Commissioner of Peshawar urged that a military force should be sent into the country, pointing out that, whereas the Sikhs collected their annual revenue under the cover of a considerable military force, none of our troops had ever been seen near this part of our border, and the hill tribes therefore imagined we had either no force to employ, or were afraid to entangle it in those fastnesses.

Expedition against the Sam Baizais, 1849.—An expedition was sanctioned and a force as below detailed, and, under command of Lieutenant-Colonel Bradshaw, C.B., 60th Rifles, left Peshawar on the 3rd December, 1849 :

> 2nd Troop, 2nd Brigade Horse Artillery.
> 200 bayonets, 60th Rifles.
> 300 bayonets, 61st Foot.
> 13th Irregular Cavalry.[1]

[1] Mutinied in 1857.

A Company Bombay Sappers and Miners.

3rd Bombay Native Infantry,
strengthened later by the Corps of Guides and 100
bayonets, 1st Punjab Infantry.

On the 11th December Colonel Bradshaw moved
with his whole force against the village of Sanghao.
This was situated in a very strong position, but,
attacked in front and on both flanks, it was soon
carried, the enemy effecting their retirement by a
path up the height in rear of the village, which
had not been noticed. The enemy were here very
numerous, having been largely reinforced from Buner.
Their loss was considerable ; our casualties amounted
to four killed and eighteen wounded.

On the 13th December the force marched to a
position at the mouth of the Bazdara Valley, near the
villages of Palai, and of Zormandai and Sher Khana
in Sam Baizai. The enemy were here in great force ;
5000 of them occupied a hill to the right of and
commanding Palai, while hills to the right and rear
of the other villages were held by large bodies. They
were also in strength in the valley in front of Palai,
their right and left resting on the hills which enclosed
it. The hill to the right of Palai was first stormed and
captured, when the left was also turned, and the force
swept up the valley, carrying and destroying the
villages and driving off the enemy. Colonel Bradshaw then withdrew unmolested from the valley.
Our losses were three killed and twenty-two wounded.
The enemy had been in great strength—the local
fighting men having been assisted by people from

Swat proper numbering 5000 to 6000—and it was afterwards known that reinforcements of 15,000 were hastening to the scene when news of the defeat reaching them caused them to turn back.

This expedition did not have the effect of causing outrage and trouble to cease; raids continued by the tribesmen either upon one another or upon our subjects; in 1855 and 1857 disputes were constant, while during the Ambela expedition the inhabitants of British Baizai flocked in numbers to assist the Bunerwals, and gave a good deal of trouble by cutting up stragglers between the British position and the rear. The suggestion that a punitive force should be sent against them was made, but was negatived. After the close of the campaign, however, the tribal maliks were sent for and a fine of Rs. 2500 was imposed upon them.

The effect of this measure was, temporarily at any rate, to check outrage in our territory, while it seems to have led to disagreement, feud and fighting among the tribesmen themselves. Serious fights took place between the men of different villages, the aid of villages within and without our border was invited and accorded, and a regular warfare, disturbing the whole of that portion of the frontier, went on for some time. Heavy fines inflicted in 1865 did something to remedy the disturbed state of affairs, but in the following year quarrels broke out afresh, and it became evident that this lawlessness must be suppressed lest other districts should be affected. It was therefore determined to move out a force, the object of whose employment was merely to destroy certain refractory and aggressive villages, but which at the same time had to be strong enough to resist any combination of tribes which might be brought against it. On the 15th January, 1866, then, a force of 4000 men with twelve guns was assembled at Nowshera, under the command of Brigadier-General Dunsford, C.B., and moved out to Mardan. Here it was found that the approach of a punitive force had of itself been sufficient to cause some of the villages to come to terms; the troops then marched on, destroyed the villages of Sanghao, Mian Khan aud Barmul, and the inhabitants of these were forced to rebuild upon other and less inaccessible sites. After this there was an occasional recrudescence of trouble, but finally the people of Baizai, realising how easily they could be reached and punished, made overtures to the Assist-ant-Commissioner of Yusafzai, concluded satisfactory arrangements for the settlement of all outstanding claims, and for some years they gave us small cause of complaint.

Colonel Bradshaw's operations in 1849 against the Sam Baizais had opened the eyes of the Swat chiefs to the possibility of their own valley being one day visited by us, and they became alarmed. It was agreed to combine for defensive purposes under some one responsible chief, and to nominate a king of Swat. There were naturally many claimants for the appointment, and the selection seemed likely to lead to so serious a broil as actually to defeat the union which it was proposed to establish. Finally the Akhund of

Swat suggested the election of Saiyid Akbar of
Sitana, a former follower and functionary of the famous
Hindustani fanatic, Saiyid Ahmad of Bareilly, and
he was accordingly installed. He appears to have
marked his accession by the creation of a standing
army, and eventually managed to collect a force of
800 mounted men, 3000 footmen and five or six
guns. Towards the end of 1861 the Swatis began to
move large bodies of armed men to the foot of the
Morah Mountain and into Sam Ranizai for the purpose of creating disaffection on our border; and on
the 6th March, 1862, a party of 180 horsemen, under
Mukaram Khan, formerly of the Peshawar police,
made a sudden attack by night upon thirty sabres
of the Guides cavalry escorting a Survey Party, and
who were stationed at the British village of Gujar
Garhi. The Guides, under Ressaldar Fateh Khan, re-
pelled the attack with great gallantry, inflicting a loss
at least equal to that they themselves experienced.

Expedition against the Ranizais, 1852.—It being
evident that this party had passed through and had
probably been harboured in the Sam Ranizai territory,
it was determined to punish them as a tribe. A force
was accordingly got together under the command of
Brigadier Sir Colin Campbell, K.C.B., and marched
on the 11th March, 1852, from Peshawar towards
Tangi. It was composed as follows :

1st Troop 1st Brigade, Horse Artillery.
600 bayonets, 32nd Foot.
15th Irregular Cavalry.[1]

[1] Disbanded in 1861 as the 16th.

Wing, 29th Native Infantry.[1]
66th Gurkha Regiment.[2]

The force had reached Turangzai when, on the 14th, the Sam Ranizais sent in offering to submit to any terms imposed, but this was evidently no more than a *ruse* to gain time, for the maliks shortly after declared they would oppose us and were expecting assistance from Swat. The delay, however, had also favoured the British, since it enabled two heavy howitzers with elephant draught to join Sir Colin from Peshawar. The force now marched on, and arrived on the 21st at our frontier village of Sherghar, about eight miles from Shakot.

The maliks now and again on the 22nd, while the force was marching to Shakot, made offers of submission; they were told that the advance would continue into the Ranizai valley, but that if all our terms were accepted no damage would be done to either villages or crops. Eventually, after much shilly-shallying, the Ranizai maliks tendered full submission, and conducted the force as far as Dargai, close to the foot of the Malakand Pass. The general encamped that night at Sherghar, returning Peshawarwards on the 23rd.

In the following month some Ranizais were implicated in an attack by the Utman Khels on the village of Charsada, in Hastnagar,[3] and while the fine imposed upon the tribe in March had not yet been liquidated, they now refused payment

[1] Mutinied in 1857.   [2] Now the 1st Gurkha Rifles.
[3] For particulars see Chapter VI.

and repudiated the hostages who had been taken for its settlement. Further coercion now, therefore, became necessary, and on the 15th May, a force, as detailed below and numbering 3270 of all arms, was assembled at Sherghar under Sir Colin Campbell:

> Six guns, 1st Troop 1st Brigade, Horse Artillery.
> Two guns, No. 19 Light Field Battery.
> 32nd Foot.
> 2nd Irregular Cavalry.[1]
> Guides Cavalry.
> 1st Punjab Cavalry.[2]
> 2nd Company Sappers and Miners.
> 28th Native Infantry.[3]
> 66th Gurkha Regiment.
> 1st Punjab Infantry.

From reports received it was evident that considerable numbers were flocking from Swat and other parts to Shakot to defend the Ranizai Valley, and that many ghazis had come over the passes to fight against us.

On the 18th the force moved on to Shakot, situated between a very deep and narrow nullah on the east and some hills on the west, and here it was seen that the enemy were in strength, holding a position about a mile and a half long on the edge of the nullah. The Horse Artillery guns shelled the centre of the position with great accuracy, but the enemy stood firmly, availing themselves of the broken ground for

[1] Now the 2nd Lancers (Gardner's Horse).
[2] Now the 21st Cavalry (Daly's Horse).
[3] Mutinied at Shahjahanpur in 1857.

cover. The Guides and Gurkhas now stormed the
nullah, covered by the guns and supported by the
1st Punjab Infantry and the Light Company of
the 32nd. A heavy fire and stern resistance were
encountered, the tribesmen charging into the midst
of the Gurkhas and fighting hand-to-hand. The
guns were advanced closer, and the enemy at last
broke, some ascending the hills in rear of Shakot and
others making for the Malakand Pass. In their
retreat the enemy lost heavily, both from the fire of
the guns and the sabres of the cavalry. Our casualties only amounted to eleven killed and twenty-nine
wounded.

In addition to the armed villagers, about 4000
infantry and 500 mounted men, all from Swat, had
opposed us, while the King and the Akhund had
watched the fight from the crest of the Malakand
Pass.

Shakot and Dargai were now completely destroyed,
and the troops returned to Sherghar on the following
day. On the 20th the whole of the Ranizai Valley
was traversed, and eight villages and much grain were
destroyed, no opposition being met with. On the
22nd a strong force of all arms visited and burnt the
village of Hiro Shah, nine miles distant, being followed, on retirement, by a matchlock fire until quite
clear of the hills and ravines, but no casualties were
sustained. The force then marched back through
Lundkhwar to Gujar Garhi, where it was broken up,
and before the end of the next month the Ranizais
had tendered unconditional submission.

It was very evident that Swat was the fountain-head of all this offending, and there were at this time some thoughts of despatching an expedition thither via the Malakand Pass. The idea was, however, eventually abandoned, and the necessity for an expedition did not again arise, for the Swatis seemed to realise how heavy had been the punishment inflicted on the Ranizais, and dreaded similar operations in their own valley. They abstained, therefore, from annoyance, and for some time at least the Peshawar districts enjoyed immunity from marauding, either instigated or perpetrated by men from Swat. Strangely enough, the troubles of the Mutiny year were not taken advantage of by the leaders in Swat. The King died on the very day that the first news of the outbreak at Meerut reached Peshawar, and the Akhund took no action inimical to British authority—on the contrary, as has been already stated, he deported the mutineers of the 55th Native Infantry who sought an asylum in Swat. In 1863, however, he adopted a different line ; but thereafter he invariably advised his people to behave as good neighbours, to meet our just demands, and comply with our terms. When he died he left two rival factions in his country ; one was headed by Sherdil Khan, chief of the Ranizais ; the other by Abdul Manan, *alias* Mian Gul, the eldest son of the Akhund.

With the death of the Akhund in 1877 the Ranizais again began to give trouble on our border, and the villagers of Shakot acquired a bad name for harbouring outlaws and disregarding the orders of our frontier

I

officials. This state of things could not be permitted
to continue, and on the 13th March, 1878, Colonel
R. Campbell left Mardan to punish the men of Shakot,
accompanied by the Hazara Mountain Battery, 249
sabres and 428 bayonets of the Corps of Guides, arriving unsuspected, within two miles of Shakot, at 2 a.m.
on the 14th. Two companies of infantry were sent
to seize a small detached hill commanding the village
on the north-west, and when, at daybreak, the remainder of the force advanced, the headmen of
Shakot, seeing the hopelessness of resistance, came
forward and made an unconditional surrender, no
shot having been fired on either side. All our demands were at once agreed to without demur,
thirty-three hostages were selected, and no attempt
to assist Shakot was made by any of the neighbouring villages, whose headmen now arrived to pay their
respects. The troops remained in occupation of the
village until 10 a.m., when the retirement commenced,
and Mardan was reached the same evening, the men
having marched nearly fifty miles in twenty-four
hours.

In this same year the two sons of the late Akhund
endeavoured to preach a *jehad*, but the movement
was an utter failure. In 1880 Sherdil Khan died,
and the chief political power in Swat passed to
Rahmatulla Khan, the chief of Dir, who remained
passive when, during the Afghan War, the Mohmand
mullahs tried to stir up the tribes of Dir and Swat to
attack our communications near Jalalabad. In 1883
a desultory contest was carried on between Mian Gul

and the Khan of Dir for supremacy in Swat, but in
March 1884 these two came to terms. During the
next six years, however, the Swat Valley was greatly
disturbed, and its people divided into factions, by the
ambitions of Umra Khan of Jandol, of whom more
will be said later. Abdul Manan, otherwise Mian
Gul, the Akhund's eldest son, died in 1887, and was
succeeded by his brother, Abdul Khalik, and the
political trouble was increased by the fact that Mian
Gul had left two young sons, who had also supporters.
In all these questions the Indian Government did not
meddle, but since the easiest way to our outposts in
Chitral led by Swat, it was impossible to permit
any other Power to acquire an influence over these
countries, and by the Durand Mission our claims to
include Swat, Dir and Bajaur within our sphere of
influence were pressed, and in some degree admitted.

In 1890 Umra Khan expelled and dispossessed the
Khan of Dir, and in 1893 he attacked the Dusha
Khel and drove out the Khan of Aladand, putting in
a nominee of his own. In the same year the last
surviving son of the Akhund died, and the succession,
though temporarily in abeyance, was recognised in a
son, Saiyid Badshah, of the elder Mian Gul. Then,
for the next two years, there was continual internal
fighting in Swat, but, so far as the Indian Government was concerned, it appeared that while the Khans
were anxious to be loyal, the priesthood was persistently preaching against us.

Prior to the year 1895 no British troops had ever
entered the Swat Valley, and the events which led to

this forward policy, with the operations which resulted, will be found described in Chapter VII.

The Swatis opposed us in that year on the Malakand, but quiet and friendly feelings were soon restored, and on the withdrawal of our force they seemed to acquiesce in the establishment of our posts on the Malakand at the entrance to their valley, and at Chakdara where their river was bridged. When Umra Khan fled from Swat, the Khan of Dir returned, reassumed possession of his original territory, and became heir to that of his immediate predecessor; but his rule was not altogether acceptable or popular. There was a good deal of friction and constant faction fights; the Khan interfered perhaps rather more than was wise, and his subjects made constant appeals to the British Political Agent at the Malakand. So far as our presence in the country was concerned, no resentment was shown, and the annual reliefs of the Chitral garrison were carried out in 1896 and 1897 without a shot being fired in Swat.

Early in 1897 the Swatis, like all Pathans along the border, had been influenced and disquieted by the preachings of the Hadda Mullah and others in Dir and Swat, but no serious trouble was anticipated until, about July, there appeared in Lower Swat a Buner Mullah, afterwards known as "the Mad Fakir." Regarded everywhere at first as an irresponsible lunatic, his preachings soon attracted earnest attention and large audiences, but no actual disturbance was expected to result.

Attacks on the Malakand and Chakdara, July

1897.—Late on the 26th July, however, disquieting
rumours as to the success of the Mad Fakir's teaching
reached the Political Agent; later still it was reported
that this pestilent priest had reached Aladand with a
large gathering, and it was arranged to send out a
column to seize the Amandara Pass, about a third of
the way to Chakdara, while the Guides at Mardan
were asked by telegram to reinforce the Malakand
garrison as soon as possible. Two reports now came
in from the Swat Valley close upon one another.
The first was from Chakdara, stating that the Fakir
with his following had already passed Khar village
on his way to the Malakand ; the second was brought
in person by a Jemadar of Levies, who announced
that the Fakir was now close at hand with a gathering
of armed men swelled by every village through which
he had come.

The troops of the Malakand Brigade were under
the command of Colonel Meiklejohn, C.B., C.M.G.,
and occupied a rather extended position. To the
south-west of the Kotal and, in a direct line some 500
yards from it, was a fort garrisoned by 200 men of
the 24th Punjab Infantry. North of the Kotal, in a
hollow known as " the Crater," were located six companies each of the 24th Punjab Infantry and 45th
Sikhs, and No. 5 Company Madras Sappers and
Miners, with the Engineer Park and Commissariat
Stores. On the high ground on either side of " the
Crater" were picquets, and to the front, closing in
the camping grounds, was an isolated conical hill,
called " Gibraltar," also held by a picquet. On either

flank of "Gibraltar" a road wound down to the valley; that to the west led to a second camp—North Camp—situated on flat open ground within a breast-work, while the eastern road led down to the valley, and, passing through the Amandara defile, ran on to Chakdara and Chitral.   North Camp was held by one squadron 11th Bengal Lancers (less twenty sabres at Chakdara), No. 8 Bengal Mountain Battery, and six companies, 31st Punjab Infantry; Chakdara, at the bridge-head of the Swat River crossing, had a garrison of twenty sabres of the 11th Bengal Lancers, and 180 men of the 45th Sikhs; while at Dargai, at the southern foot of the Malakand Pass, were 200 rifles of the 31st Punjab Infantry.

At 10 p.m., on receipt of the news brought by the Levy Jemadar, the "alarm" was sounded, and the troops had barely reached their posts when the attack opened. A party of the 45th Sikhs seized the gorge, through which the old Buddhist road descends from the Kotal, just in time to check a rush of tribesmen; but the enemy succeeding in occupying the high ground on either side of the gorge, the Sikhs fell back to a more commanding position in rear, where they withstood all attacks until 2 a.m., at which hour the enemy here beat a retreat.   Meanwhile large numbers had advanced along the main road, drove in the picquets, rushed the *serai* held by levies, attacked the bazar, and some forced their way into the Commissariat enclosure.   They twice charged the position in the centre of the camp held by the Sappers and Miners, and passed the abatis enclosing it, capturing a quan-

tity of ammunition. A reinforcement of 100 men
was sent for to the fort to reinforce the defenders of
"the Crater" Camp, who were hard pressed, but at
4.30 a.m. on the 27th the enemy drew off. Our
casualties during the night had been one officer and
twenty-two men killed, five officers (two of whom
died) and thirty-one men wounded.

The troops in the North Camp had not been
seriously attacked, and were ordered to move out in
pursuit, but, having arrived near Khar village, were
recalled, as a large hostile force was seen on the hills
and in the valley beyond. The squadron of the 11th
Bengal Lancers, however, pushing on, reached Chakdara with two men and some horses wounded. This
day North Camp was evacuated, and the troops concentrated in the Malakand position ; the withdrawal,
which was effected before dark, was rather harassed
by the enemy. Colonel Meiklejohn had received a
further welcome reinforcement before night in the
arrival of the Guides from Mardan, the magnificent
infantry of this corps covering the thirty-two miles
in seventeen and a half hours. The reinforcement
numbered 160 sabres and 300 rifles, of which latter
fifty had remained at Dargai to strengthen that
post.

Again on this night was an attack made, commencing at 8.30 and continuing until daylight, the centre
and right being most closely pressed. The enemy
were, however, everywhere repulsed with loss, while
our casualties numbered eleven killed and forty-six
wounded. Throughout the 28th the enemy maintained

a fire on the camp, and attacked again at night with great energy, but the troops had been employed during daylight in improving the defences, and the attack was more easily repulsed and without incurring so many casualties—two killed and sixteen wounded during this night. On the 29th the position was further improved, the front cleared, and arrangements made for lighting up the ground over which the tribesmen must advance.

Chakdara signalled that it was successfully holding out, and the reinforcements ordered by the military authorities were beginning to arrive. A squadron 11th Bengal Lancers came in escorting ammunition, and in the evening the 35th Sikhs and 38th Dogras reached Dargai, the first-named regiment having lost twenty-one men from heat apoplexy on its march from Nowshera.

Again, on the night of the 29th-30th, was the attack renewed, chiefly against the flanks, but was everywhere repulsed with great loss, and the same may be said of the following night, when the attack, though repeated, seemed to have lost something of its energy and fire. On these two nights our losses were one man killed and nineteen wounded. On the 31st reinforcements, amounting to over 700, reached the Malakand position, and that night the usual attack was not delivered.

On the 1st August Colonel Meiklejohn made an attempt at the relief of Chakdara, but the start was rather delayed, and the enemy showed themselves in such strength that the orders had to be cancelled.

On this date Major-General Sir Bindon Blood, having been appointed to command a newly organised Malakand Field Force, arrived in the position, and approved of a strong force moving out at daybreak on the 2nd to effect the relief of Chakdara. The relieving force, under Colonel Meiklejohn, was stoutly opposed all the way, but the determination of the enemy only made their losses the heavier, the cavalry getting among them with their lances and the Sikhs with the bayonet. As the force drew near, the enemy surrounding the fort began to withdraw, their retirement being hastened by a vigorous *sortie* by the garrison. The relieving column had five men killed and twenty-eight wounded, while the casualties of the Chakdara garrison only amounted to three killed and nine wounded during their six days' close investment, standing continually to their posts by day and night.

That day the villages of Aladand and Thana were visited, no opposition being met with, and Colonel Meiklejohn's column marched to and remained in camp at Amandara in preparation for the reconstitution of the field force.

Operations of the Malakand Field Force, 1897.— To punish all the attacks above described, the Government of India sanctioned the despatch of a force, to be known as the Malakand Field Force, to concentrate, the First Brigade at Amandara, the Second at Khar and Malakand, the Reserve at Rawal Pindi and Mardan.

FIRST BRIGADE.

Brigadier-General Meiklejohn, C.B., C.M.G.

1st Battalion Royal West Kent Regiment.
24th Punjab Infantry.
31st Punjab Infantry.
45th Sikhs.

SECOND BRIGADE.

Brigadier-General P. D. Jeffreys, C.B.

1st Battalion the Buffs.
35th Sikhs.
38th Dogras.
Guides Infantry.

DIVISIONAL TROOPS.

One squadron 10th Bengal Lancers.
11th Bengal Lancers.
Guides Cavalry.
No. 1 M.B.R.A.
No. 7 M.B.R.A.
No. 8 Bengal Mountain Battery.
22nd Punjab Infantry.
Two companies 21st Punjab Infantry.
No. 4 Company Bengal Sappers and Miners.
No. 5 Company Madras Sappers and Miners.

THIRD (RESERVE) BRIGADE.

Brigadier-General J. H. Wodehouse, C.B., C.M.G.

1st Battalion Royal West Surrey Regiment.
2nd Battalion Highland Light Infantry.
6 companies 21st Punjab Infantry.

39th Garhwal Rifles.

No. 10 F.B.R.A.

No. 3 Company Bombay Sappers and Miners.

By this time some idea could be formed of the extent of the rising and how far the neighbouring tribes were infected by the spirit of unrest which had been aroused. It was known that a division of the Bunerwals, the Utman Khels, the inhabitants of Lower Swat, and certain numbers of Upper Swatis had taken part in the attacks upon the Malakand position ; not to mention the Dusha Khels, certain divisions of the Khwazozais, and other sub-divisions, whose names would only be worth repeating as showing how general was the rising among the local clans. But the tribes further north did not seem to have been infected with any excitement or restlessness; communication between Gilgit and Chitral was still open. The Indus-Kohistan, the Mohmand country, the Khyber, Kohat and Kurram, all then appeared to be undisturbed; the Nawab of Dir reported that the Bajauris had remained tranquil, as had also the tribes on the Peshawar border. The only disquieting frontier news to hand at this time was to the effect that a number of mullahs, with a following of fanatical tribesmen, had left Ningrahar and the neighbourhood of Jalalabad to join either the Hadda Mullah or the Mad Fakir. The bulk of the attacking force had been furnished by the men of Lower Swat, hitherto, and with some reason, despised as fighting men. Thus the Khan of Aladand, whose conduct had been exemplary since the Chitral Campaign, whose people

were largely employed as levies, and who himself
drew a subsidy from Government, was among those
killed in one of the attacks.   Thana lost nearly all its
young men, and men of other villages, who for the
last two years had regularly furnished supplies, turned
out for this "Holy War" in obedience to the exhor-
tations of the Mad Fakir.

The concentration of the troops composing the
Malakand Field Force was completed on the 8th
August; and already on the next day and on the
12th certain Ranizai and Khwazozai jirgahs came in
to sue for peace, their submission being accepted on
payment of heavy fines, surrender of arms, and promise
of future good behaviour and non-molestation of the
troops.

On the 16th Sir Bindon Blood, leaving his Reserve
Brigade at Mardan and Rustam to observe the Buner
passes, advanced by the left bank of the river towards
Upper Swat, bivouacking at Thana, and sending forward to Landakai his cavalry, who reported that the
enemy were holding the hills above the village in
strength.   The position at Landakai was naturally a
very strong one, and was occupied by some 3000
tribesmen behind *sangars* on a steep rocky spur
running down to the water's edge from the mountains
on the south.   This spur commanded the approach
by a gorge, the road through which only permitted of an advance in single file; but further to
the west another ridge came down from a height
overlooking the Landakai spur and ended at the
village of Jalala.   The few tribesmen holding Jalala

were early dispossessed, and the ridge being then
seized by the West Kent Regiment, it was occupied
as an artillery position by a field and mountain
battery, and a heavy fire was opened from here upon
the Landakai spur.

The rest of the infantry, with another mountain
battery, moved to the right along the rear of this
position, and occupied a spur commanding the enemy's
left flank. The tribesmen, prevented from reinforcing
this flank by the heavy infantry and gun fire from the
Jalala spur, began to waver and then to fall back.
Many escaped by the Morah Pass, and those who
held on to the position were driven from their
sangars by the advance of the whole of the infantry,
who pursued them to Kota, the cavalry following as
far up the valley as Abuwa, on the Barikot road, and
doing considerable execution. Our losses this day
were light—two killed and nine wounded. On the
two following days the force moved on by Ghalegai
to Mingaora, encountering no opposition, and finding
the inhabitants ready enough to tender their submission and furnish supplies. From Mingaora, where
the force remained some days, reconnaissances were
sent out in all directions, the country was as far as
possible disarmed, and the terms of submission were
enforced. By the 22nd August jirgahs, representing
all the Upper Swat clans, had agreed to unconditional
surrender, and the force then commenced to withdraw, reaching Khar and the Malakand on the 27th.

While the Headquarters and the First Brigade had
been operating in Upper Swat, the Second Brigade had

remained at Khar to overawe the people of Lower Swat, pushing reconnaissances in all directions, the inhabitants remaining perfectly submissive. There had been some idea of employing this Brigade for the punishment of the Bunerwals and Utman Khels, implicated in the recent rising, but by this time the frontier generally was in a blaze, and it was decided that two of Sir Bindon's brigades should be sent through Dir and Bajaur in order to co-operate with the Mohmand Field Force from Nawagai : these operations, in which the Second and Reserve (Third) Brigade were employed—the First Brigade remaining in occupation of Swat—will be found described in Chapter VII.

Since this year there has been no further outbreak of fanaticism and no other trouble in Swat, and the prosperity of the country has made very real progress.

CHAPTER VI.

UTMAN KHELS.[1]

THE trans-frontier portion of this tribe occupies the country between the Rud River on the north, the Panjkora and Swat Rivers on the east and south-east, and the Ambahar River on the south and south-west: their neighbours being the Bajauris on the north, the Akozai Yusafzais or Swatis on the east, and the Mohmands on the west; while the Peshawar district is the southern boundary. The country is a network of low hills and nullahs, and is generally unfertile and unproductive. The cis-frontier people of the tribe own certain lands in the northern portion of the Yusafzai Plain, originally bestowed upon them by the Baizais, when these, some time in the sixteenth century, were being pressed by the Ranizais. In the course of time the Baizais have practically been pushed from their own country by the Utman Khels. The Utman Khels hold the villages situated on the spur running down from the Pajja and Morah Ranges, and also the villages of Shamozai and Matta, on the north-west slopes of the Ganga Ghar Mountain.

The Utman Khel are said to be Sarbani Pathans of

[1] See Maps V. and VI.

the Kodai Karlanri branch, who moved eastwards with
the Yusafzais when these migrated from their earlier
homes north-west of the Suleiman range, occupying
their present territory simultaneously with the Yusafzai
conquest of Swat. They are a hardy set of mountaineers, of good physique, hardworking, many of
them eking out a scanty livelihood as labourers about
Peshawar; "often," so Oliver tells us, "naked from
the waist up—a custom opposed to Pathan ideas—
but not very civilised. They live in small groups of
houses, rather than villages, stuck on the mountain
side, secure in their inaccessibility." There are no
chiefs of any importance among them, and they are a
very democratic people. They are estimated to number
some 9,000 fighting men, poorly armed. The trans-
frontier Utman Khels have always held themselves
rather aloof, and few of them enlist with us; but the
cis-frontier men have lately taken more freely to
service in the levies, and even in the Indian army,
and are said to make excellent soldiers.

Their country lies on both banks of the Swat River
until the limits of the Mohmand territory are reached,
and here the river bends to the south and forms the
boundary between the two tribes. The country is
throughout very difficult, there are few roads passable
by any but a pedestrian, and the only means of crossing the Swat—here rushing a deep swift torrent
between steep cliff-like banks—is afforded by a few
rope bridges. To the north of the river are a number
of valleys between spurs running out from the Koh-i-
Mohr. To the south and south-east of this mountain

are the important divisions of Barang and Ambahar;
to the north-east lies Arang; and south of the Swat
River, and between it and British territory, is the
narrow hilly tract of Laman or Daman, traversed by
the Sulala Range.

The tribe is divided into eight main clans as
under :

1. Ismailzai.	5. Gurai.
2. Mandal.	6. Peghozai.
3. Alizai.	7. Bimarai.
4. Matakai.	8. Sinazai.

The Ismailzai is by far the largest and most
important clan, and occupies the right bank of the
Swat River and the northern slopes of the Koh-i-Mohr.
The three last-named clans of the tribe live in Totai
on the left bank of the Swat below its junction with
the Panjkora, within Sam Ranizai limits, and separated
from the Laman by the Jhindai Valley. The Laman
accommodates a number of other tribes besides the
Utman Khel.

The roads leading from our territory into the Utman
Khel country are all difficult, but there is a good road
from Matta, on the Mohmand border, through Pandiali
to Ambahar. The dwellers in Laman can be easily
coerced, but in their time, and particularly during the
first years of British occupation of the frontier country,
they have given a great deal of trouble, raiding the
border and sheltering outlaws.

The Utman Khels are quite a distinct people, being
unconnected with any of the Pathan races which

surround them—whether Mohmands, Bajauris, or Yusafzais; they have more than once waged war with the Mohmands, but consider themselves to be on specially friendly terms with the Shinwaris.

OPERATIONS.

In the middle of the last century the favourite raiding ground of the restless spirits of the Utman Khels was the Hastnagar division. Early in 1852, they permitted one Ajun Khan, a notoriously disaffected man, to take up his residence in Utman Khel villages to the north of the district, and here he gathered together a band of adventurers like himself to raid upon our border. Finally in April, Ajun Khan collected some 200 mounted men, attacked Charsada, the headquarters of the division, plundered the treasury and slew some of our officials. On the following day he occupied Abazai, and then visited Pranghar and Nawedand, where he took up his quarters. Within a week, however, Sir Colin Campbell was moving troops out against him from Peshawar.

Expedition against the Independent Utman Khels, 1852.—Sir Colin Campbell established his headquarters at Abazai and there concentrated the following force :

First Troop, 1st Brigade Horse Artillery.
Two 8-inch howitzers, 4th Battalion Artillery.
300 bayonets, 32nd Foot.
One squadron 2nd Irregular Cavalry.
One squadron Guides Cavalry.
2nd Company Sappers and Miners.

300 bayonets, 28th Native Infantry.
300 bayonets, 66th Gurkhas.
Guides Infantry.

On the 11th May the force moved out and destroyed Nawedand, experiencing some slight opposition, and while the operations were in progress Sir Colin was joined by the 1st Punjab Infantry under Captain Coke, and by two squadrons of the 1st Punjab Cavalry under Lieutenant Hughes. These regiments had left Kohat at 2 a.m. on the 8th and reached Peshawar, forty miles distant, the same day; there was a delay in crossing the Kabul River owing to the bridge of boats having been swept away, but by the evening of the 10th Coke's party was across, arriving at Abazai at daybreak with a two hours' halt *en route*. Finding at Abazai that Sir Colin had left to attack Nawedand, Coke again pushed on, took part in the attack, and returned with the force to Abazai, having thus covered another forty miles, or a total of eighty since 2 a.m. on the 8th.

On the 12th General Campbell moved about seven miles to Gandera, and on the 13th he attacked, carried and destroyed Pranghar, the stronghold of the Utman Khels, who were in considerable strength and held out gallantly against the fire of our ten guns. The force then withdrew.

At the end of this year the fort of Abazai was erected for the better security of this part of the border.

After this expedition, the conduct of the Independent Utman Khels—as distinguished from the Utman

Khels of Sam Baizai—was uniformly good, and for more than twenty years the Indian Government had no grounds for any complaint against them. On the 9th December, 1876, however, an offence of the very gravest description was committed by this tribe, chiefly by men from Ambahar and the Laman; a number of them, instigated by persons of influence in British territory, attacking a body of unarmed coolies engaged in the preliminary operations connected with the canal about to be taken from the Swat River near Abazai. It appears that the party, consisting of a hundred men, surrounded the tents in which the coolies were sleeping about 2 a.m.; then, at a given signal, having cut through the ropes of the tents, threw them down and butchered the helpless, struggling inmates through the tent-cloth. The camp was then robbed of almost everything it contained, some of the dead and wounded being stripped of the very clothes on their backs. Of the sixty-five coolies, six were killed and twenty-seven wounded, some dangerously. Having plundered the camp, the raiders effected their escape to the hills before any assistance could reach the spot from Fort Abazai; but all the neighbouring headmen, suspected of complicity, were apprehended and sent into Peshawar.

It seems probable that this raid would never have taken place if proper steps had been taken for the protection of the men employed on the canal works— a project, and the taking up land for which, known to have aroused suspicion and dislike; and it cannot be denied that sufficient precautions were not taken by the responsible officers to prevent an attack of this kind, when the work was being carried on so near the border. It could not, however, have well been anticipated that a Muhammadan tribe would, without provocation and with no quarrel with the British Government, attack and kill an unarmed body of their co-religionists—a dastardly outrage, which brought down upon the perpetrators the virtual excommunication of the aged Akhund of Swat.

Operations against the Independent Utman Khels, 1878.—In consequence of this affair, the Utman Khels were, as a tribe, excluded from British territory, but at the time it was not possible to take more active measures against them. At the beginning of 1878, however, it was proposed to Government that an attempt should be made to surprise the village of Sapri, where dwelt the man who had been the leader of the party concerned in the attack on the coolie camp; for it was felt that while he was at large and unpunished, any really satisfactory settlement with the tribe would be practically impossible; his village, moreover, was close to our border. The proposal was sanctioned, and at 7 p.m. on the 14th February, 1878, Captain Wigram Battye,[1] accompanied by Captain Cavagnari,[2] marched from Mardan with 264 sabres and twelve bayonets of the Guides, the infantry mounted on mules.

The party moved by the main Tangi-Abazai road

[1] Afterwards killed at Fatehabad during the Afghan War.

[2] Afterwards killed in the attack on the British Residency at Kabul.

for some distance, but on arrival near Tangi, the column turned off to the north, crossed the line of the Swat Canal, and arriving within two miles of Abazai, left the horses there under a small escort. The troops had marched thirty-two miles, making a long detour so as to avoid villages whence news of the movement might have been conveyed across the border. Moving on, the Swat River was struck, and its left bank ascended for about four miles to Mada Baba Ziarat, where a mountain torrent joins the river; and climbing a rough path by the side of this torrent, the kotal leading to the village of Sapri was soon reached. It was still dark, but from here Captain Battye sent a small party on to a spur commanding the village, and especially the towers of the man particularly wanted for the outrage near Abazai. With daylight the village was rushed, the tribesmen being taken completely by surprise, and Mian Rakan-ud-din, the leader, was shot down. Some of his immediate attendants surrendered, and others bolted to the hills above the village, whence they kept up a desultory fire on the troops. But Captain Battye was able to withdraw his party to Fort Abazai without further molestation. Our casualties were eight wounded.

As a result of this measure some of the Utman Khel villages showed themselves most anxious to effect a satisfactory settlement with Government; others, how-ever—those of Zirak and Pakhai—remained recusant, and consequently, while the submission of the repentant villages was accepted, it was decided to coerce

the remainder. On the 20th March, therefore, Lieutenant-Colonel Jenkins left Mardan for the Utman
Khel border with a force composed of four guns of
the Hazara Mountain Battery, 245 sabres and 453
bayonets of the Guides. The Zirak villages were
first dealt with. The force entered the hills as day
was breaking, and experienced no opposition at the
first village, Tarakai, but moving on from here entered
a valley formed by the Sulala range of hills and
divided into two parts by the Tor Tam hill; on the
near side of this hill were the remaining Zirak villages,
and on the other were those of Pakhai. The first
village was found to be deserted, but our troops were
fired on from the others; the enemy were, however,
easily dispersed and the remaining Zirak villages
cleared. Leaving now the Guides cavalry in occupation, Colonel Jenkins secured possession of the Tor Tam
hill with the infantry and guns without any serious
opposition, and thence had the Pakhai villages at his
mercy. The Zirak and Pakhai headmen were now
called upon to submit, which they did after the usual
hesitation, and agreed to pay the fines demanded of
them. The force then withdrew from the valley
unmolested, and bivouacked that night at the Jhinda
outpost of the Swat canal works, having marched
over forty miles since noon of the previous day.
Mardan was again reached on the 22nd.

During 1882 there was a slight revival of trouble
in connection with the canal works, but thenceforward
the Utman Khels gave us no cause for complaint
until 1895, when some divisions opposed General

Low's advance [1] at the passage of the Swat River; they also shared in other attacks upon us during the operations of that spring, but no punitive measures were taken against them for these signs of hostility. In 1897 again large numbers of Utman Khels took part in the attacks on the Malakand; some assisted their old enemies the Mohmands in the fighting about Shabkadar; and others again of the divisions which live on the further bank of the Swat River helped in the assaults on Chakdara, and later tried to seize the bridge over the Panjkora, but were forestalled by General Meiklejohn.

The trans-frontier Utman Khels thereafter only broke out once, joining the Mamunds in the attack on General Jeffreys' camp described in Chapter VII., but, on the whole, they remained quiet while our troops were in Bajaur, and even helped to keep open the lines of communications where these passed near their border.

Expedition against the Utman Khels, 1897.—As stated in Chapter V., General Blood had intended sending a brigade from Lower Swat into the Utman Khel country, but at the moment the services of the troops were required elsewhere, and operations against the Utman Khels had to be postponed. For the time, therefore, Government contented itself with imposing terms upon such clans as had shown themselves hostile, and demanding the submission of the whole tribe. By the close of the year, however, the Utman Khel generally had evinced no inclination to comply

[1] See Chapter VII.

with our terms, and on the 22nd November, therefore, a small force was collected to compel submission.
It was concentrated near Dargai, at the southern foot
of the Malakand Pass, and was placed under the
command of Colonel A. J. F. Reid; it was composed
as under:

> One squadron, 10th Bengal Lancers.
> No. 8 Bengal Mountain Battery.
> No. 5 Company Madras Sappers and Miners.
> 1st Battalion The Buffs.
> 21st Punjab Infantry.
> 35th Sikhs.

In addition to the above, the 16th Bengal Infantry
was sent to Abazai to protect the head of the Swat
River canal, and to help the local political officers in
dealing with the Utman Khels of the Laman. The
initial destination of the force was the Totai Valley,
and on the 23rd Colonel Reid marched to Hariankot
at the foot of the pass leading to Kot, which was
reached next day. The road over the pass, although
it had been improved by working parties, was found
very difficult for laden camels. On the west side of
the pass the valley widens considerably, and is highly
cultivated. The villagers of Lower Totai showed
every sign of wishing to be friendly, and many
jirgahs came in asking for terms. All the clans
accepted our terms without hesitation, except the
Agra jirgah, and the force accordingly arranged to
march into that valley. Two routes were reconnoitred from Kot, but that via Silai Patai was
eventually adopted, although it required much work

to make it passable. The villagers along the route
proved very submissive, bringing in supplies, and the
Agra jirgah met Colonel Reid on their boundary to
tender submission.   On the 27th the troops marched
to Bargholai along a very difficult track through a
narrow gorge.   The Agra Valley was thoroughly explored, reconnaissances were pushed forward to the
passes, and much useful survey work was done.   All
the representatives of the Utman Khel had now submitted except the Kanauri Ismailzai, so a small column
was detailed to visit the Kanauri villages, which lay
high up in the hills above Kot, to the west of Colonel
Reid's camp.   The road was very bad and steep, but
half-way there the jirgah was met hurrying down to
submit.

By the 4th December all the clans had complied
with our terms, and the troops were withdrawn to
Hariankot and the column broken up.

Since that date this tribe has given no serious
trouble to the British Government.

CHAPTER VII.

THE CLANS OF BAJAUR AND DIR.[1]

THE inhabitants of both these countries are mainly Yusafzais—Tarkanri or Tarklanri Yusafzais in Bajaur, and Akozai Yusafzais in Dir.

Bajaur is bounded on the north by Dir, and on the east by Dir and Swat, on the south-east and south by the Utman Khel country, on the south again for a short distance by the Mohmands, and on the west by Afghanistan. It is an extremely mountainous country, watered by the Rud River, and including within its area the valleys of the Rud, of Babukarra, Watelai and Chaharmung.

The Bajauris or Tarkanris are Sarbani Pathans of the Khakhai Khel branch and representatives of the ancient Gandhari, with whom they returned from Kabul in the fifteenth century to the Peshawar Valley, and a hundred years later subjugated and dispossessed the Gujars, then in occupation of Bajaur. "In 1504," we are reminded by Oliver, "the Emperor Baber acquired the sovereignty of Kabul and Ghazni, and in the following year made an extensive frontier tour, coming by the Khyber Pass to Peshawar, going

[1] See Maps IV. and V.

along the whole border, and returning by the Sakhi
Sarwar Pass and the Bori Valley to Ghazni.   At this
period the Pathan settlers are described as pretty well
established in Laghman, Peshawar, Swat and Bajaur ;
though some of the original occupants still struggled
for independence under their hereditary chiefs.   During
the next twenty-five years the Mogul Baber undertook
many forays—for most of them could not be called
anything else—to punish the hill Pathans, or to
protect his own subjects, dispersing the men, carrying
off the women and cattle ; but, as a rule, the tribes
were even then fully able to hold their own.   Guided
by the Dilazaks, he marched against Bajaur, carried
the fortress of the original Sultan by escalade, using
the new matchlocks, which greatly astonished the
enemy, the net result being to extend the power of
the Tarklanris."

The Tarkanris have three main divisions :

    1. Ismailzai.

    2. Isozai.

    3. Mamunds,

and of the different valleys into which Bajaur is split
up, the Maidan Valley is occupied by the Ismailzai,
the Baraul and Jandol Valleys by the Isozai, and the
valleys of Babukarra, Chaharmung and Watelai by
the Mamunds, who also own a good deal of land
across the border in Afghanistan.   Some six or seven
alien tribes also live among the Bajauris—chiefly in
the Jandol and Maidan Valleys.   Originally Jandol
belonged to Bajaur, but it has within recent years
come under the political control of Dir, whose ruler,

however, has little or no authority over the people of the Jandol Valley.

The Maidan Valley is about ten miles long, rich and fertile and well cultivated, watered by the Maidan or Kunai River. The Jandol Valley, whose northern and southern boundaries are the Janbatai Range and the Rud River, has a total area of some 144 square miles, being about fourteen miles long, with a breadth ranging from six to ten miles, and is also rich and well cultivated. The Baraul Valley is divided into an upper and a lower, the upper including the Janbatai district, and good crops are raised here, and iron of excellent quality is exported. The Babukarra Valley is about fifteen miles long, with an average width of five or six miles; the range of the Hindu Raj divides it from Asmar on the north, on the east the Takwara spur separates it from Jandol, on the west is the Mamund or Watelai Valley, while to the south, on the right bank of the Bajaur River, is the country of the Utman Khel. The Chaharmung Valley lies between the Mamund country on the north-east and the Kamangara Valley on the south-west. The Watelai Valley, occupied by the Mamunds, the most important section of the Tarkanris or Bajauris, lies between the valleys of Chaharmung and Babukarra; it is about thirteen miles in length, with a maximum breadth of ten miles, and is well cultivated, but has no main river of any importance running through it, and the bed of the valley is much cut up by deep nullahs. The Mamunds are probably the most warlike of the Tarkanris, and can put

12,000 men in the field, all well armed as frontier tribesmen go.

The position of the Khan of Nawagai requires some explanation. He is the hereditary chief of a branch of the Salarzai sub-division of the Mamunds, and also of all the Tarkanris, but his authority has of late years very greatly diminished, although he is still by no means without influence, even far beyond the borders of his own Khanate. His actual territory is an irregular tract of country on the left bank of the Rud River, together with the district of Surkamar; part of his country was encroached upon some years ago by the Mohmands, and he has never been sufficiently powerful to regain permanent possession of it.

The country known as Dir comprises roughly the whole area drained by the Panjkora River and its affluents, as far south as its junction with the Rud River of Bajaur. The Upper Panjkora Valley is known as the Panjkora Kohistan, and is divided into two parts called Bashkar and Sheringal. The principal subsidiary valleys of Dir are the Kashkar or Dir, the Baraul and the Maidan on the west, and the Ushiri and Talash Valleys on the east. The northern limit of Dir is the crest of the mountain range which divides it from Chitral and Yasin; the Durand line is the boundary on the west; on the east it is bounded by Kohistan, and on the south by the valley of Upper Swat and by Bajaur. From the mass of mountains to the north three giant spurs or ranges run down towards the south. The easternmost of these, forming the watershed between the Swat and the Indus

Rivers, runs first due south and then west to the Malakand. The central forms the watershed between the Panjkora and Swat. The westernmost range is a continuation of the Hindu Raj, runs south-westerly, and forms the watershed between the Panjkora and Rud Rivers on the one side and the Kunar on the other. The most important pass which crosses it is the Lowari or Laorai (10,250 feet), open for convoys from April to November; it carries the main road from India to Chitral.

The four sections of the Malizai sub-division of the Khwazozai-Akozais resident in Dir are :

1. Painda Khel.   3. Nusrudin Khel.
2. Sultan Khel.   4. Ausa Khel.

On the Panjkora River, commencing from the north, in the Kashkar Valley, in which the village of Dir is situated, is the Akhund Khel sub-section of the Painda Khel Malizais, to which the Khan of Dir belongs. Below these again, on the left bank of the river, are more of the Painda Khel, and on the right bank the Sultan Khel; and, still further down, the Sultan Khel, Nusrudin Khel and Ausa Khel on both banks of the river.

The route to Chitral from the Swat Valley leads through this country. Leaving the Swat River at Chakdara, the road turns abruptly to the west and enters the Uch Valley, passing by the Katgola Pass (3000 feet) into the Talash Valley, where, as Bellew tells us and as later travellers have confirmed, there are extensive ruins of massive fortifications on the south side of the valley and nine or ten miles from the Panjkora, covering the hills for a distance of several miles. From here the ascent is very steep to the summit of the Kamrani Pass, to the northeast of which, in a valley, lies Mundah, the stronghold of Mian Gul Jan, the quarrelsome younger brother of the Khan of Dir. The descent from the kotal to Sado or Khungai is very steep. Turning to the right from Sado, the road passes up the Panjkora Valley, the river being crossed on the fourth march from Sado at Chutiatun, whence, a few miles further along the right bank of the Dir stream, Dir itself is reached. "Here," writes Enriquez, "situated on a low hill is the stronghold of the Khan. The fort has three towers, each surmounted with a loopholed fighting top. . . . The vale of Dir is well cultivated and numbers of chenars are scattered about it, so that its greenness is refreshing after the wearying aridity of the Panjkora. The little town of Dir occupies a steep khud abreast of the fort. Its crazy huts are built one above the other, so that the roof of one forms the promenade or front garden of the one above." Then on up the Dir Valley, via Mirga, to the Lowari Pass and Chitral. An alternative route, branching off from Sado, runs westward for some way and then, turning northward again, ascends the bed of the Jandol River to the Janbatai Pass (7212 feet) ; after crossing this the road leads along the Baraul Valley to Chutiatun and Dir, where it joins the first mentioned road.

The people of Dir and Bajaur are all Sunni Muhammadans, intensely bigoted, but superstitious rather

than religious. Their country is very much priest-
ridden, and the people are unusually susceptible to
the influence of the mullahs, who are able to excite
them to fanaticism more easily and to a greater
degree than among other Pathans. The fighting men
in Dir and Bajaur number probably not less than
80,000; they, and more particularly the men of Dir,
have a very strong sense of discipline; and in the
event of a general fanatical rising the combination
of tribes which could be formed would be by no
means one to be despised, since they would probably
receive material assistance, if not indeed open and
active help, from Swat, from the Utman Khels, and
very possibly from the men of Buner.

OPERATIONS.

It will be convenient here to give some account
of Umra Khan of Jandol, whose usurpations were
responsible for the formation of the Chitral Relief
Expedition, the operations of which, in the countries
of Dir and Bajaur, are about to be described.

Umra Khan was a younger son of the Khan of
Jandol, and a grandson of the Chief of Bajaur who
took up arms against us during the Ambela campaign. He quarrelled with his father and was expelled
from the country; but returning in 1878 he killed
his elder brother, and later, as the result of a year's
successful fighting, he made himself master of Jandol,
and eventually brought under his control a tract of
country extending from the Dir-Chitral border in the
north to the Swat River in the south, and including

L

the whole of Dir, the greater part of Bajaur and a portion of Swat. In 1891 and 1892 the Kabul Government undertook certain operations, which were not particularly successful, to check Umra Khan's aggressions, and up to the latter year he seems to have been friendly inclined towards the British. In 1892, however, when he was being somewhat pressed, both by the Afghans from without and by rebels within his kingdom, an appeal which he made to the Government of India for assistance in the form of arms and ammunition was refused; and in 1893, as a result of the Durand Mission to Kabul, the territory of Asmar, which he had coveted and seized, and whence he had been driven, was handed over to Afghanistan. All this gave great offence to Umra Khan, and it was shortly after these events that he mixed himself in Chitral affairs—described in their proper place—leading to the despatch of the Chitral Relief Force in 1895 and the resultant operations in Dir and Bajaur.

Chitral Relief Expedition, 1895.—It had been intended to mobilise the First Division as being nearest to the scene of operations; but some of the units of which it was composed were then on service in Waziristan, while the nature of the country to be operated in precluded the employment of others. The force was ultimately composed as hereunder detailed, was placed under the command of Lieutenant-General Sir R. Low, K.C.B., and its base was fixed at Nowshera.

FIRST BRIGADE.

Brigadier-General Kinloch, C.B.
1st Battalion Bedfordshire Regiment.
1st Battalion King's Royal Rifles.
15th Sikhs.
37th Dogras.

SECOND BRIGADE.

Brigadier-General Waterfield.
2nd Battalion K.O.S. Borderers.
1st Battalion Gordon Highlanders.
4th Sikhs.
Guides Infantry.

THIRD BRIGADE.

Brigadier-General Gatacre, D.S.O.
1st Battalion The Buffs.
2nd Battalion Seaforth Highlanders.
25th Punjab Infantry.[1]
2nd Battalion 4th Gurkhas.

DIVISIONAL TROOPS.

11th Bengal Lancers.
Guides Cavalry.
13th Bengal Infantry.[2]
23rd Pioneers.
15th Field Battery R.A.
No. 8 M.B. Royal Artillery.
4 guns, No. 2 Derajat Mountain Battery.
No. 1 Company Bengal Sappers and Miners.
No. 4 Company Bengal Sappers and Miners.
No. 6 Company Bengal Sappers and Miners.

[1] Now the 25th Punjabis.   [2] Now the 13th Rajputs.

RESERVE BRIGADE.

Major-General Channer, V.C., C.B.

No. 7 Bengal Mountain Battery.[1]
3rd Battalion Rifle Brigade.
26th Punjab Infantry.[2]
2nd Battalion 1st Gurkhas.
2nd Battalion 3rd Gurkhas.

LINES OF COMMUNICATION TROOPS.

1st Battalion East Lancashire Regiment.
29th Punjab Infantry.[3]
30th Punjab Infantry.[4]
No. 4 Hazara Mountain Battery.

MOVEABLE COLUMN (ABBOTTABAD).

No. 8 Bengal Mountain Battery.
2nd Battalion 2nd Gurkhas.
2nd Battalion 5th Gurkhas.

Railway concentration commenced on the 26th
March, and in seven days the force was concentrated at Hoti Mardan and Nowshera.   A proclamation
was published to the tribes through whose territory it
would be necessary for the force to pass, announcing
that the quarrel of the British Government was only
with Umra Khan of Jandol, and stating that there
was no intention of permanently occupying the tribal
country, or of interfering with the independence of
its inhabitants.   In reply, the Sam Ranizais consented
to our passage through their territory, while some of

---

[1] Now the 27th Mountain Battery.   [2] Now the 26th Punjabis.
[3] Now the 29th Punjabis.   [4] Now the 30th Punjabis.

the headmen in Lower Swat tried to adopt an attitude of armed neutrality, and the Upper Swatis failed to combine against us. The Khan of Nawagai promised to do his best to keep Bajaur quiet, and the maliks among the Bunerwals, Utman Khels and Mohmands seemed anxious to keep their people out of the quarrel.

On the 1st April the First Brigade moved to Lundkwar, the Second and Third to Jalala, the General intending to advance into Swat by the Shakot and Malakand Passes. During this day, however, the report of the friendly or neutral intentions of the border tribes was seriously discounted by the receipt of information that large bodies of tribesmen were holding not only these two passes, but also the Morah, which, by reason of its propinquity to Buner, there had been no intention of using. It appearing that of the three the Malakand was the least strongly occupied, Sir Robert Low decided to force the Malakand, making a feint with his cavalry towards the Shakot. He therefore concentrated all three brigades at Dargai, at the southern foot of the Malakand, early on the morning of the 2nd April.

Leaving Dargai, the track took for some way a north-easterly direction up the gradually narrowing valley; it then turned north-west and, leaving the bed of the valley, zigzagged up to the crest, whence two paths led into the Swat Valley. The kotal itself is some 2850 feet above sea-level, but on the left of the position precipitous hills rise to a height of over 400 feet, while on the right the crest of the range slopes steeply up to three tall peaks. The whole of the ridge, with the heights on either flank, formed a position not less than two miles long and was held in strength.

The Second Brigade was sent forward early on the 3rd to force the pass, it being the intention of the general commanding that the position once taken, the First Brigade, which alone was entirely supplied with mule transport, should then be pushed on to the Swat River. Of the Second Brigade, the 4th Sikhs and Guides Infantry ascended parallel spurs on the west of the valley, intending to turn the position from this flank; while the remaining battalions, covered by the fire of three mountain batteries, advanced directly upon the Pass. The infantry on the flank were, however, very stubbornly opposed, while the actual ascent was most difficult, and the general commanding the Second Brigade, seeing that the advance would be greatly delayed, sent forward his remaining battalions to the frontal attack, which the First Brigade was now called upon to support. The infantry, during their advance, captured sangar after sangar, and moving forward very steadily, the position was finally carried, after some five hours' fighting, at the point of the bayonet, the 4th Sikhs and Guides running in on the enemy's right at the same time. Two regiments of the First Brigade pressed the pursuit of the retreating enemy as far as Khar, where they bivouacked; the 4th Sikhs occupied the vicinity of the crest; and the remainder of the Second Brigade withdrew to Dargai.

It was estimated that we had been opposed by about 12,000 men, of whom probably a third pos-

sessed firearms; their losses, mainly by reason of
their holding the position to the last, were heavy;
our casualties were 11 killed and 51 wounded.

During the advance, our troops fortunately came
upon the remains of an old disused Buddhist road, well
built and skilfully aligned, and which two days' work
rendered fit for camel transport, thus greatly facili-
tating the passage of supplies.

Early on the afternoon of the 4th, the First Brigade
advanced into the Swat Valley, the Second Brigade
taking its place on the Malakand, and the Third remaining at Dargai. The leading brigade was opposed,
and even attacked, with great boldness, by large
numbers of tribesmen falling back from the Shakot
and Morah Passes, but these lost severely from the
fire of our infantry and the sabres of the Guides
Cavalry, who made a fine charge over bad ground.

The First Brigade halted at Khar, where that of
General Waterfield joined it, and whence reconnaissances moved up the Swat Valley. Opportunity was
further taken of the halt to open communications with
the head men of many of the neighbouring villages,
and also with the former Khan of Dir, whom Umra
Khan had dispossessed of his country; and by these
measures our troops were assured an unopposed
passage through the Baraul and Dir Valleys, and of
the neutrality of some of the more powerful of the
clans of Upper Swat and Bajaur.

On the 6th, it being reported that a large body of
Umra Khan's personal followers, under command of
his brother, had occupied Chakdara and the fort and

village of Ramora, about two miles further up the Swat River, five squadrons of cavalry, supported by other arms from the Second Brigade, were ordered to cross the Swat River early next morning and reconnoitre towards Uch, opportunity being at the same time taken to destroy the fort at Ramora. These parties, and another sent out to search for a suitable site for a bridge over the Swat River, were opposed by some 4500 men who lost very severely, especially at the hands of the cavalry, who pursued as far as the Katgola Pass, about 7½ miles distant. Chakdara was then occupied and a bridge constructed.

It was now determined that the First Brigade should remain in occupation of the Swat Valley, and it accordingly handed over all its mule transport to the two other brigades—the Second taking up the lead and crossing the Swat River, while the Third advanced to Khar; and on the same day, the 8th, the cavalry reconnoitred the Talash Valley as far as Shamshikhan, and the Adinzai Valley up to the foot of the Laram Pass, which was reported impracticable for transport. On the 9th the cavalry reconnoitred up to Sado on the Panjkora River, which can be approached by two roads, that to the west by the Shigu Kas being just passable, while that by the Kamrani Pass (3300 feet) was unfit for transport. Next day the advanced troops reached Sado, and the cavalry reconnoitred for some distance up the Rud River, being fired on near Kotkai by a small body of the enemy; the Second Brigade marched to Gumbat and part of the Third closed up to Uch.

At this period, in view of the possibility of trouble in the Buner and Mohmand countries, the Reserve Brigade was moved up to Mardan from Rawal Pindi, and a second reserve brigade was mobilised, but the units composing it were not required to leave their garrisons; they were No. 1 Mountain Battery R.A., 2nd Battalion Oxfordshire Light Infantry, 28th Punjab Infantry, and 39th Garhwal Rifles.

The Panjkora River had been rising every day, and by the 11th April had become quite unfordable, and, while bridging materials were being collected, the Second Brigade was closed up to Sado and Khungai, the Third being distributed between Gumbat and Chakdara. By the night of the 12th the bridge was ready for foot traffic, the river showed no signs of further rising, and six companies of the Guides crossed to the right bank, where they formed an entrenched position to serve as a bridge-head, commanded at short range from the high ground of the left bank. Here the Guides were conveniently placed to carry out the orders they were to execute on the following morning, viz. to march down the right bank of the river and destroy certain villages whence the convoys had been persistently annoyed. It had been intended to support the Guides by passing over other troops, and another company of the Guides was later able to cross; but during the night of the 12th-13th the river suddenly rose, bringing down large masses of timber and practically breaking up the newly-completed bridge.

At 6 a.m. Lieutenant-Colonel Battye took five

companies up the Rud River, leaving two companies
to hold the bridge-head, and marched up the left
bank to Subhan Killa, whence parties were detached
to the east to burn three villages.   Re-concentrating
then at Subhan Killa, the Rud or Jandol River was
crossed and the heights on the right bank of the
Panjkora were ascended, from whence other villages
were destroyed.   About noon large parties of the
enemy appeared to be advancing, and on Colonel
Battye signalling this information to Headquarters at
Sado, he was directed to fall back on the bridge-head,
where the high bank was lined by troops of the
Second Brigade to cover the retirement.   As usual
on the frontier, the retirement had no sooner commenced than it was hotly pressed, and it was perhaps
not begun quite so soon as it might have been, or as
was under the circumstances advisable, owing to the
fact that it was impossible for the commander with
the main body of the Guides infantry to be certain
whether the detached parties had, or had not, complied
with the order to fall back.   The conduct of the retirement, made practically under the eyes of the whole
of the Second Brigade, was, as recorded by General
Low and as endorsed by all who saw it, "a splendid
performance."   Very deliberately the different companies retired, fiercely assailed on all sides, yet coolly
firing by word of command, and relinquishing quietly
and almost imperceptibly one position only to take
up another a few yards back.   Twice did the Guides
fix bayonets to meet the onrush, expected but never
actually made.   Shortly before recrossing the Jandol

River near its junction with the Panjkora, Colonel Battye fell mortally wounded, the command devolving on Captain Campbell.

The bridge-head was reached just before dark, and the enemy kept up a fire till nearly 11 a.m. The Guides were reinforced by two Maxims and a company of the 4th Sikhs sent across the river on rafts, while support was also afforded by five companies of infantry on the left bank and a mountain battery, whose firing of star shell probably prevented any attempt to rush the post. By early morning of the 14th the tribal gathering—chiefly Utman Khels and men from Mundah—had dispersed, having experienced very heavy losses. On this day the Third Brigade moved up to Sado, and six more companies of the 4th Sikhs were sent over on rafts to the Guides entrenchment; but the continued rapid rise of the river made bridge construction at this spot impossible, and eventually a suspension bridge was thrown across a gorge two miles lower down the river, being completed by the evening of the 16th.

On this date the rain, which had been falling heavily for some days, ceased, and the river began to subside. The Third Brigade was now ordered to lead, and crossed to the right bank on the 17th, the Second Brigade moving over next day. General Gatacre advanced up the Jandol Valley, experiencing some opposition about Manugai, and finally bivouacked at Ghobani, where early next morning the Second Brigade joined him. An hour later the combined force advanced on Mundah and Miankilai, which were

found deserted, and the cavalry pushed a reconnaissance to the foot of the Janbatai Pass, finding the
people generally friendly.

From here it was decided to despatch a small flying
column to Chitral, and a mountain battery, with two
infantry battalions and half a company of Sappers
from the Third Brigade, marched on that afternoon
to Barwa and on the 19th to the Janbatai Pass.

Bandai was reached by General Gatacre's advance
column on the 20th, and here he received news that
the Chitral garrison was in great straits, and therefore he proposed to General Low that he should be
permitted to push on with 500 men; this suggestion
was approved, and, pressing forward, General Gatacre
was in Dir on the 22nd.

In the meantime the situation had undergone some
change. Umra Khan had fled to the Asmar border,
and thence to Kabul, leaving the resettlement of his
territory to the British; the left flank of our line of
advance was in a measure menaced by the presence of
the Utman Khel, Nawagai and Mamund tribesmen;
while intelligence, received on the 21st, that the siege
of Chitral had been abandoned, obviated the need
for any forced march to its relief such as had been
arranged.

From Dir to Ashreth in Chitral territory via the
Lowari Pass was twenty-three miles, and the whole
of General Gatacre's column, in spite of the extraordinary difficulties of the road, was concentrated at
Ashreth by the 30th April, and was ordered to halt
there for the present. On the 10th May the 1st Bat-

talion the Buffs, the Derajat Mountain Battery, and the 4th Company Bengal Sappers and Miners were led by General Gatacre to Chitral, where the Gilgit Column had arrived on the 20th April, and with this the object of the expedition may be said to have been accomplished; Umra Khan, who had actually originated all the trouble, had fled the country, while on the 27th April Sher Afzul, the late claimant to the Mehtarship of Chitral, had been brought into our camp at Dir, having been captured in Bashkar by some of the Khan of Dir's levies.

On the 10th May the troops hitherto serving on the lines of communication were formed into a Fourth Brigade of the Chitral Relief Force, under Brigadier-General Hammond, V.C., C.B., D.S.O., A.D.C., and it was not until the middle of August that some of the troops—mostly of the Fourth Brigade—commenced their return march to India. On the 4th September the Third Brigade ceased to exist; on the 28th General Low's Headquarters demobilised at Nowshera; and about the same date Brigadier-General Waterfield assumed command of the Malakand Brigade and of all troops remaining beyond the frontier.

On the final withdrawal of the force it was found that while regular troops must continue to be maintained on the Malakand Pass, at Chakdara, and in Chitral territory, it would be possible to keep open the Nowshera-Chitral road by peaceful means, its security from the Swat River to the borders of Chitral territory being maintained by levies, and the route adopted being via Panjkora and Dir.

During this expedition the troops under Lieutenant-General Sir Robert Low had sustained a loss in action of twenty-one killed and 101 wounded; but in addition, and in consequence of fanatical attacks, further casualties were experienced, altogether two soldiers and forty-nine followers having been killed, and three soldiers and forty-seven followers wounded, between the middle of April and the date of the final withdrawal of the force.

After our troops had returned to India the condition of affairs in Bajaur and Dir was generally satisfactory, and the arrangements for the maintenance of the road promised to work well. There was a certain amount of local unrest, as was only perhaps to be expected; but both in 1896 and 1897 the Chitral reliefs marched by the Malakand-Chitral road without experiencing any interference whatever on the part of the tribesmen. At various times both the Khan of Dir and the Khan of Nawagai attempted to extend their influence by force of arms, the one in Jandol, the other in the Babukarra Valley, but both showed themselves ready to yield to the pacificatory influence of the political agent for Dir and Swat. There were rumours also that Umra Khan contemplated revisiting this part of the frontier, but he ultimately decided to return to Kabul.

The whole country had been so recently pacified that it was hardly to be hoped that it would remain quiescent during the disturbances of the year 1897. The Mullahs, always opposed to the establishment of any civilising influence tending to weaken or destroy their supremacy over their peoples, had been busy preaching against the British, and it was known that they were doing their utmost to form a hostile combination of the clans against us; while other outside influences, which need not here be particularly specified, were also known to be in action. The Khans of Dir and Nawagai behaved very well under difficult circumstances, and seem to have done their best to check and stifle sedition, but proved in the end unable altogether to restrain the fanaticism of their followers. When the "Mad Mullah" actually arrived in Swat from Buner in July, 1897, the Khan of Dir was away in Kohistan, but even had he been present it seems improbable that he would have had sufficient influence or power to stem the outbreak, culminating in the attacks upon the Malakand and Chakdara positions described in Chapter V. But on his return to Swat, and when the tide had turned in our favour, both he and the Khan of Nawagai did what in them lay to assist the British Government, by reopening communications and by holding the important river crossings on the Chitral road.

Operations of the Malakand Field Force in Dir and Bajaur in 1897.—The attacks on the Malakand and on the Chakdara post, with the composition and early operations of the Malakand Field Force, under Major-General Sir Bindon Blood, have already been described in Chapter V. These operations commenced with the subjection and punishment of the people of Lower and Upper Swat. It had been proposed to deal next with the Utman Khels, but more

important events then transpiring, obliged the post-
ponement of the coercion of this tribe; and the news
that the forces of the Hadda Mullah, signally defeated
on the 9th August by the troops from Peshawar,
were advancing into Dir, caused the recall of General
Blood's Second Brigade from Utman Khel territory,
and the move of his Third Brigade to Uch in the
Adinzai Valley. The Mullah's gathering now dispersed, and General Blood was directed to co-operate
with General Elles in the punishment of the Mohmands, by moving with two brigades through Bajaur
via Sado and Nawagai. At Nawagai our troops would
be in rear of the Mohmands, who had never before
been attacked from the north, and from this place a
caravan route leads due south to the Peshawar border,
passing Lokerai in the Bohai Valley, where are many
Mohmand villages.

On the 4th and 5th September General Wodehouse
moved his brigade—now somewhat reconstructed—
hurriedly from Uch to Sado, and was only just in
time to prevent the seizure of the Panjkora Bridge
by the Bajauris and Utman Khels, who had now
made up their minds to oppose us. The First
Brigade (Meiklejohn) was now left to hold the Swat
Valley and our communications up to Sado; the
Second (Jeffreys) marched from Chakdara, via Sarai,
the Panjkora and Kotkai to Ghosam, where it arrived
on the 9th; while by the 11th the Third Brigade
(Wodehouse) was concentrated at Shakrata, equi-
distant from Mundah and Barwa, cavalry reconnaissances being pushed forward to the Batai and

Shinai passes. On the 12th the Second Brigade was at Khar,[1] and the Third at Shamshak in the Watelai Valley, where the camp was fired into during the night.

Sir Bindon Blood had now intended to co-operate with General Elles, and for this purpose he himself moved on the 14th with the Third Brigade to Nawagai, while General Jeffreys seized the Rambat Pass, bivouacking on the Chaharmung stream near Inayat Kila, an Utman Khel village. Here a determined attack was made upon the Second Brigade camp at night by Mamunds and Utman Khels, who were unusually well armed and, creeping along the broken ground, were able to gain positions near the camp from which they maintained a very galling fire for nearly six hours, almost without intermission. Our casualties were seven killed (three British officers) and ten wounded, and the losses among the transport were serious, amounting to nearly a hundred. When daylight appeared the cavalry were sent after the retreating enemy and accounted for many of them.

The idea of joining the Third Brigade at Nawagai had now to be given up in favour of punitive operations in the Mamund country, and co-operation with General Elles was for the present impossible; the First Brigade was therefore ordered to move up to the Panjkora, the Third remaining entrenched at Nawagai. Here, on the night of the 19th and 20th determined attacks were made upon the camp,

[1] Not to be confused with the village of the same name in Lower Swat.

M

chiefly by the Hadda Mullah's men from the Bedmanai Pass; they were beaten off without much
difficulty, but some of them were shot down within
ten yards of the entrenchment; we had one man
killed and thirty-one wounded, among the latter
being General Wodehouse. On the 22nd Sir Bindon
Blood proceeded to the Mamund Valley to rejoin
General Jeffreys; the Third Brigade on the same date
being attached to the force under General Elles for
completion of the operations against the Mohmands.

In the meantime the Second Brigade under General
Jeffreys had been engaged in further fighting. On
the 16th the troops marched up the Watelai Valley
in three small columns, directed respectively on
Badalai, Badan and Agra, and experienced in the
operations which resulted the heaviest loss which
British troops have suffered in frontier warfare, in
a single day's fighting, since the Ambela campaign.
The right column destroyed some villages and then,
finding a considerable force of the enemy occupying
a strong position from which it seemed impossible to
dislodge them without guns, returned to camp. The
remaining two columns moved up the valley, the
enemy retiring before them; when, however, it
became necessary for the troops to halt to await
the return of a party which had been detached,
the enemy began to press forward in considerable
numbers, inflicting some loss upon two companies
of the 35th Sikhs, which were falling back upon their
supports. The pressure was, however, temporarily
relieved by an opportune charge of a squadron of the

11th Bengal Lancers under Captain Cole. The two
columns commenced their withdrawal to camp at
Inayat Kila about 3 p.m. A flanking party of two
companies of the 35th Sikhs had not received the
order to retire, but when the party commenced to
do so, it withdrew in a direction rather diverging
from the general line of retreat. These companies
were assailed by the enemy on all sides, and did
not extricate themselves, assisted finally by the
Guides, until they had suffered over forty casualties.
As the whole force continued its retirement darkness
came on, accompanied by a heavy thunderstorm, and
the General, considering it would be difficult to reach
camp that night and anxious about his flanking
parties, decided to occupy some villages till morning.
The orders failed, however, to reach all the units;
some pushed on to camp; but about dusk General
Jeffreys found himself with no troops at his immediate
disposal, except four guns of No. 8 Bengal Mountain
Battery, a small party of Sappers, and a few men of
the Buffs and 35th Sikhs, who had become separated
from their companies in the dark. With these the
General decided to occupy a hamlet called Bilot,
about 3½ miles from camp. Part of this village was
burning and half was in possession of the enemy,
who had been following up closely, and the party
with the General was only able to occupy and
entrench one angle of the hamlet. Fighting was
kept up at the closest possible quarters, and with
heavy losses on both sides, until the arrival, about
midnight, of four companies of the 35th Sikhs, with

whose assistance the enemy were easily driven off, the rest of the night passing quietly.

The casualties during this day's fighting amounted to 38 killed and 116 wounded, including three followers.

During the next few days the Second Brigade was busily employed in destroying villages and removing grain-stores—always under fire, while the retirement to camp was invariably closely pressed. On the 23rd the Mamunds professed to be disheartened at their losses and anxious to make terms; but it seems probable that all they wished was to gain breathing time, for the negotiations came to nothing, and operations were accordingly resumed on the 29th September when many towers were demolished. The wounded were sent down to the Panjkora, and the heavy casualties in transport animals were made good.

On the 30th September the brigade attacked the villages of Agra and Gat, and severe fighting ensued, the enemy in great numbers occupying a position of considerable strength. More than once the Mamunds had to be driven from their sangars at the point of the bayonet, and, although the object of the operations was effected and the retirement was satisfactorily carried out, the want of more troops—for the brigade was by now greatly weakened—was much felt; on this day the casualties numbered twelve killed and forty-nine wounded, while throughout the losses in officers had been out of all proportion. Sir Bindon Blood now reinforced the troops in the Mamund country by bringing up another squadron of the Guides Cavalry, the 10th Field Battery, No. 8 Bengal Mountain Battery, the 2nd Battalion Highland Light Infantry, four companies of the 24th Punjab Infantry, and No. 5 Company Madras Sappers and Miners.

On the 3rd October the Second Brigade, with two mountain batteries, attacked and destroyed the village of Badalai, experiencing small opposition until the retirement commenced, when the enemy came on with great boldness, and to the number of between two and three thousand.

There was now a very large body of troops at Inayat Kila, and the Mamunds began clearly to recognise the hopelessness of prolonging the resistance. They accordingly opened negotiations through the Khan of Nawagai, their jirgah finally coming in on the 11th October and agreeing to all our terms. The operations against the Mamunds, who had shown fighting qualities of a high order, now came to an end, and the troops were withdrawn from the Watelai Valley. During the period from the 14th September to the 11th October, our casualties totalled 61 killed and 218 wounded.

On his way back to the Malakand, Sir Bindon Blood halted in the Salarzai Valley and easily forced that section of the Tarkanris to submit, while the Babukarra Valley was thoroughly explored. The last of the troops crossed the Panjkora on the 23rd, and four days later the whole force returned to the Swat Valley.

Since the conclusion of the operations just described,

the clans of Dir and Bajaur have given no trouble to the British Government; but the efforts which the ambitions of the local khans cause them to make in order to add to their territories, and the constant intrigues of pretenders and other claimants, combine with the natural pugnacity of the Pathan to cause some occasional anxiety as to the continued security of our communications with Chitral.

CHAPTER VIII.

CHITRALIS.[1]

CHITRAL is the largest and the most important state
on the northern part of the north-western frontier.
It lies immediately to the west of Gilgit, while
on the other side it is divided by the Hindu
Kush from the province of Kafiristan—transferred
to the dominions of Afghanistan during the latter
part of the reign of the late Amir Abdurrahman
Khan. South of Gilgit the Shandur spur and
the watershed between the Chitral and Panjkora
Rivers divide the country from Yasin, Kohistan and
Dir; it is bordered on the north by the Hindu Kush;
while to the south the watershed of the Arnawai
Stream forms the boundary between Chitral and the
districts of Dir and Asmar. It is an especially mountainous country, "composed partly of gigantic snowy
peaks, mostly of barren rocky mountains, and, in a
very small degree, of cultivated land. The valleys
are narrow and confined, the main ones in their
inhabited portions running from 5000 to 8000 feet
above sea level. It is only in them that any cultivation at all is found, and even then it is not carried on

[1] See Map V.

very extensively.... But the whole food production is small, and barely suffices for the people of the country, leaving little to spare for outsiders. The climate varies according to the height of the valley. In the lower parts, at about 5000 feet above sea level, it ranges from 12° or 15° in winter to 100° in summer, and higher up, at 8000 feet, it would vary from 5° or so below zero to about 90° in summer." [1]

Sir George Robertson, in his *Chitral*, says that " food is so scarce that a fat man has never yet been seen in the country ; even the upper classes look underfed, and the most effective of bribes is a full meal. The hill tracks, which form the main lines of communication, are seldom easy ; they are often difficult, sometimes dangerous."

The country is watered by the river which goes in its northern course indifferently by the names of the Yarkhun, the Mastuj or the Chitral River, and which, flowing from a glacier of the Hindu Kush, runs south-westerly to Asmar, where it becomes known as the Kunar River, and falls into the Kabul River near Jalalabad. During its course it receives the drainage of numerous valleys on either side, and is spanned by many rope bridges, by several untrustworthy native-built bridges, usually constructed on a rough cantilever principle, and by good suspension bridges at important crossings, such as Chitral, Mastuj, Drosh and other places. "Even when the rivers are moderately placid and shallow, the fords,"

[1] Sir Francis Younghusband in the *Journal of the Society of Arts*, April 1895.

Sir George Robertson tells us, "are always bad, because of the boulders and stones in their beds; they are frequently devious also; and, consequently, always require a guide. It is dangerous to miss the proper line, for then one is liable to be carried into deep, heavy water, or to find oneself in a quicksand." [1]

There are two main routes from Chitral to India: that which has been followed in the preceding chapter, from Chitral over the Lowari Pass, through Dir and Swat, and across the Malakand to railhead at Dargai; and another from Chitral across the Shandur Pass to the Gilgit road, and thence through Kashmir and the Jhelum Valley to the rail at Rawal Pindi. Those passes leading to the north or to the west are for the most part very difficult; some are impracticable for pack animals, some are only passable at all during certain brief seasons of the year; others again could only be crossed by a lightly equipped force of selected troops under unusually favourable circumstances. The Baroghil Pass (12,460 feet), which leads out of the Yarkhun Valley into Wakhan, is practicable for laden animals during eight months of the year, and climbs over what Holdich calls "the comparatively easy slopes of the flat-backed Hindu Kush." Many passes, but all more or less difficult, lead from Chitral into Kafiristan, while that leading from Chitral to Upper Badakshan—the Dorah Pass (14,800 feet)—is much trodden, and is used by laden animals as a commercial link between the Kunar Valley and Badakshan. It is

[1] *Chitral, the Story of a Minor Siege.*

open from July to September, and has been crossed as late as early in November.

Chitral is an important state by reason of its situation at the extremity of the country over which the Government of India exerts its influence. Sir Francis Younghusband has described this state as "one of the chinks in the wall of defence. Not a very large one, but certainly capable of being made into a considerable one if we do not look after it, and in time; for not only is there a chink just here, but the wall is thinner too. Practicable roads across the mountains, especially those by the Baroghil and Dorah passes, lead into Chitral; while the width of the mountains from the plains on the south to the plains on the north, as the crow flies, is 400 miles by the Pamirs and Gilgit, but through Chitral only 200. So Chitral is a place to be looked after and efficiently guarded."

Gilgit and Chitral seemed to the Government of India to afford good watch-towers whence the country south of the Hindu Kush might be guarded and controlled, since the northern passes provide a difficult but by no means impracticable route for the incursion of a hostile force large enough to cause trouble, or at least excitement, upon this portion of the Border. But our occupation of Chitral is not universally approved. Sir Thomas Holdich [1] has said that "the retention of Chitral may well be regarded as a doubtful advantage. . . . As an outpost to keep watch and ward for an advance from the north, Chitral is useless,

---

[1] *The Indian Borderland.*

for no serious menace is possible from the north. As a safeguard otherwise, it is hard to say from what it will protect us. It is in short the outcome of political, not of military, strategy. As a political centre it must be remembered that it possesses an outlook westwards over the hills and valleys through which the Amir's great commercial roads have been projected, as well as northwards to the Hindu Kush passes. But it is at best an expensive and burdensome outpost, and is, on the whole, the least satisfactory of all the forward positions that we have recently occupied."

Elsewhere,[1] however, Sir Thomas Holdich seems in some degree to qualify these opinions. Writing of these northern mountain approaches to India, he says, " We cannot altogether leave them alone. They have to be watched by the official guardians of our frontier, and all the gathered threads of them converging on Leh or Gilgit must be held by hands that are alert and strong. It is just as dangerous an error to regard such approaches to India as negligible quantities in the military and political field of Indian defence, as to take a serious view of their practicability for purposes of invasion. . . . The Dorah Pass . . . is the one gateway which is normally open from year to year, and its existence renders necessary an advanced watchtower at Chitral."

The country is divided into the nine districts of Laspur, Mastuj, Torikho, Mulrikho, Kosht, Owir, Khuzara, Chitral and Drosh. The population totals something over seventy thousand, and the fighting

[1] *The Gates of India.*

strength is estimated at six thousand men, armed for the most part with matchlocks of local manufacture or imported from Badakshan. There are also in the country under a thousand Sniders and muzzle-loading Enfield rifles, presented at different times to the Mehtar or ruler by the Indian Government.

The Chitralis are the only non-Pathan tribe described in this book and are a mixed race of Aryan type, of whose origin little is known : the language of the country is Chitrali, and Persian is also spoken by some of the upper classes. The people are all Muhammadans, mostly Sunnis, but by no means of a particularly strict or fanatical type ; and while the priests have a certain amount of influence, they are unable to work their flocks up into any high degree of religious frenzy as is possible with certain Pathans. The people of Chitral are splendid mountaineers with great powers of endurance, and have fought well on occasion. Sir George Robertson has thus described their characteristics : [1] " There are few more treacherous people than the Chitralis, and they have a wonderful capacity for cold-blooded cruelty ; yet none are kinder to little children, or have stronger affection for blood or foster-relations when cupidity or jealousy do not intervene. All have pleasant manners and engaging light-heartedness, free from all trace of boisterous behaviour, a great fondness for music, dancing and singing, a passion for simple-minded ostentation, and an instinctive yearning for softness and luxury, which is the mainspring of their intense cupidity and avarice.

[1] *Chitral, the Story of a Minor Siege.*

No race is more untruthful, or has greater power of keeping a collective secret. Their vanity is easily injured, they are revengeful and venal, but they are charmingly picturesque and admirable companions. Perhaps the most convenient trait they possess, as far as we are concerned, is a complete absence of religious fanaticism. . . . Sensuality of the grossest kind, murder, abominable cruelty, treachery or violent death, are never long absent from the thoughts of a people than whom none in the world are of simpler, gentler appearance."

The early history of Chitral is a record of intrigue, civil war and assassination—"a monotonous tale of murder and perfidy—the slaying of brother by brother, of son by father," and each successive Mehtar appears to have waded to the throne through seas of blood. The founder of the Chitral Royal Family was Shah Katur, whose descendants, dividing into two branches, parcelled the mountainous country from Kafiristan to Gilgit between them—the Khushwakt branch ruling the eastern portion, while the Katur branch governed in the west, or Lower Chitral. At the time of the British occupation of the Punjab, one Gauhar Aman reigned in the Khushwakt district, while Shah Afzul II. ruled in Lower Chitral. About 1854 the Kashmir State, having long suffered from the encroachments of the ruler of Upper Chitral, appealed to Shah Afzul for assistance, and he, induced thereto far more by hatred of his kinsman than by any wish to oblige the Kashmir authorities, seized, in 1855, Mastuj, then the headquarters of the Khushwaktia chief. Possession was, however, regained in the year following, but the place was again captured by the Chitralis in 1857.

In this year Shah Afzul II. died quietly in his bed —the demise of a ruler from natural causes was almost unprecedented in this country—and was succeeded by his second son, Aman-ul-Mulk, known as "the great Mehtar." In 1860 the eastern chief also died, being succeeded in the Mehtarship of Khushwaktia by Mir Wali, who was deposed and slain by his own brother; while in 1880 Aman-ul-Mulk invaded and possessed himself of the eastern portion of Chitral, uniting the whole country under his sovereignty. Not long after this, during the viceroyalty of Lord Lytton, it was decided that the policy of the Government of India should be so extended as to control the external affairs of Chitral in a direction friendly to our interests; so as to secure an effective guardianship over the northern passes, and to keep watch over what goes on beyond them. To initiate and carry out this policy, Major Biddulph was sent to Gilgit in 1877 and spent some years there, succeeding in entering into relations with Aman-ul-Mulk, then Mehtar of Chitral. No very definite arrangement was come to at this time, the position was considered rather too isolated, and Major Biddulph was withdrawn. Then in 1885 Lord Dufferin despatched the late General Sir William Lockhart at the head of an important mission, to enter into more definite and closer relations with the Mehtar of Chitral, and to report upon the defences of the country. Colonel Lockhart, as he then was, spent more than a year in Chitral; he wintered at Gilgit, traversed the State of Hunza, crossed the Hindu Kush, passed through Wakhan down the southern-most branch of the Oxus, and travelled over Chitral territory from one end of the country to the other. Similar visits were paid to Chitral by Colonel Durand in 1888 and 1889, and in this latter year the Agency at Gilgit, withdrawn in 1881, was re-established, and certain allowances, doubled in 1891, were granted to the Mehtar, Aman-ul-Mulk.

In the following year the thirty-two years' reign of "the great Mehtar" came to an end, he dying suddenly of heart failure while in *durbar*. His eldest son, Nizam-ul-Mulk, was away in Yasin at the time, and the second brother, Afzul-ul-Mulk, seized the fort at Chitral with its arsenal and treasure, and sent off urgent demands to the Agent at Gilgit that he might at once be recognized as Mehtar. Nothing was to be feared from Nizam, who was no fighter and fled to Gilgit, leaving Afzul to return triumphant to Chitral. Afzul had, however, apparently overlooked or disregarded the fact that there was another candidate for the Mehtarship in one Sher Afzul, fourth son of Shah Afzul II., and consequently a younger brother of Aman-ul-Mulk and uncle to Afzul-ul-Mulk. Sher Afzul seems to have left Kabul, where he had been living, directly he heard of his brother's death, crossed the Dorah Pass from Badakshan at the head of a handful of followers, and, marching rapidly, surprised the fort at Chitral, Afzul-ul-Mulk being shot down in the ensuing *mêlée*.

Sher Afzul, who seemed to have many adherents in the country, was now proclaimed Mehtar, but his reign was a very short one. Nizam-ul-Mulk, plucking up courage, determined to proceed to Chitral and turn out the new pretender. He was joined by a Hunza chief of considerable military capacity and force of character, while his advance appears to have been preceded by extravagant rumours that his candidature was supported by the British authorities; and Sher Afzul then, losing heart, fled back to Kabul by way of the Kunar Valley.

Nizam-ul-Mulk was now formally recognised as Mehtar by the British Government, and two of the political officers of the Gilgit Agency visited the new ruler in Chitral and promised him that, under certain conditions, the same allowances and support would be given to him as had been afforded to his father, Aman-ul-Mulk. So far as could be seen, it appeared that the new ruler was in the way to be fairly well established on the throne.

It is now necessary to revert to Umra Khan of Jandol, of whom some mention has already been made in the last chapter, and whose actions and aggressions were largely responsible for the troubles which now arose upon this part of the frontier.

At the end of 1894 the situation here was as follows: Umra Khan had at last made friends with his old enemy, the Khan of Nawagai; he had established his authority over a considerable portion of Swat, the greater part of Bajaur, and the whole of Dir; while he had possessed himself of the strip

of country known as Narsat, hitherto claimed alike
by Chitral, Dir and Asmar. He had attacked some
villages in the Bashgul Valley, claimed by Chitral;
had commenced to build forts at Arnawai and Birkot,
in the Kunar Valley; and had encroached upon
Chitral territory, and demanded the payment of
tribute from Chitral villages. The ex-Khan of Dir
was at this time a refugee in Upper Swat. Nizam-
ul-Mulk was proving himself a fairly efficient and
popular, though not a strong, ruler; Sher Afzul was
believed to be safely interned at Kabul; and Nizam's
younger brother, Amir-ul-Mulk, who had at first fled
from Chitral, had now returned there and been well
received by the new Mehtar.

On the 1st January, 1895, Nizam-ul-Mulk was shot
dead while out hawking by one of the servants,
and at the instigation, of Amir-ul-Mulk, who at once
caused himself to be proclaimed Mehtar, but his
recognition was delayed for reference to Simla. There
can be little doubt that this fresh murder was the
outcome of a conspiracy between Amir-ul-Mulk, Sher
Afzul and Umra Khan, and that the object was to
remove Nizam and cause him to be temporarily succeeded by Amir, who was then to resign in favour of
Sher Afzul. Umra Khan was to be called in merely
to help the furtherance of the schemes of the other
two : but Umra Khan had his own personal interests
to consult, and on hearing news of the murder he at
once crossed the Lowari Pass with between 3000 and
4000 men, and occupied the southern Chitral Valley.
He sent on letters stating that he had come to wage

a holy war against the Kafirs of the Bashgul Valley, that he had no hostile designs against Chitral, and that if Amir-ul-Mulk did not join and help him he must take the consequences. Umra Khan now advanced on Kila Drosh, twenty-five miles below Chitral fort.

At this date there were rather over 3000 troops garrisoning posts in the Upper Indus, Gilgit and Chitral Valleys, and of these roughly one-third were regular troops of the Indian Army, the remainder belonging to regiments of the Kashmir Durbar. When the murder of Nizam took place, Lieutenant Gurdon was in political charge at Chitral, accompanied by no more than eight men of the 14th Sikhs, drawn from a detachment of 103 posted at Mastuj under Lieutenant Harley. There were no other troops of any kind in Chitral, and the nearest garrison was at Gupis, far on the eastern side of the Shandur Pass. The nearest regular troops were ninety-nine men of the 14th Sikhs at Gilgit, while the 32nd Pioneers, rather over 800 strong, were employed on the Bunji-Chilas road. Gurdon at once drew upon Mastuj for fifty Sikhs of its garrison, and these reached him unhindered and unmolested on the 7th January. In anticipation of possible trouble, the following moves then took place: Mastuj was reinforced by 100 men of the 4th Kashmir Rifles from Gupis, 200 men of the same regiment moved up to Ghizr, while Gupis was strengthened by 150 men of the 6th Kashmir Light Infantry from Gilgit.

Shortly before this Surgeon-Major Robertson—now

Sir George Robertson—had relieved Colonel Bruce
in charge of the Gilgit Agency, and he now at once
left for Chitral, taking with him some of the 4th
Kashmir Rifles under Captain Townsend, Central
India Horse, and the remainder of the 14th Sikhs
from Mastuj—100 in all. Before he reached there,
however, the Chitralis, who had at first evinced some
intention of opposing Umra Khan, had been driven
from a position they had taken up in front of Kila
Drosh ; while a fortnight later—on the 9th February
—the fort of Drosh was surrendered, without any
pretence of resistance, to Umra Khan, with all its
rifles and stores. About the 18th the situation,
already sufficiently complicated, was rendered even
more so by the news that Sher Afzul, probably the
most generally popular of all the claimants to the
throne, had arrived at Drosh.   He was at once joined
by some of the lower class Chitralis, and by the end
of February nearly all the Adamzadas (members of
clans descended from the founder of the ruling family)
had also gone over to him.   On the 1st March the
British Agent withdrew his escort—now numbering
100 of the 14th Sikhs and 320 of the 4th Kashmir
Rifles—into the fort at Chitral ; and on the following
day in *durbar*, it being patent that Amir-ul-Mulk,
listening to the promptings of ill-advisers, had been
intriguing with Umra Khan, Amir was placed under
surveillance, and his young brother, Shuja-ul-Mulk,
was formally recognised as Mehtar, subject to the
approval of the Government of India.

The number of followers with which Umra Khan

had entered Chitral territory had been gradually
increasing, as his star appeared to be in the ascendant,
and his total strength was now estimated at between
5000 and 8000 men. On the afternoon of the 3rd
March Sher Afzul reached the neighbourhood of
Chitral at the head of an armed force, and took up a
position in some villages about two miles to the
south-west of the fort. At 4.15 two hundred men of
the Kashmir Rifles were sent out, under Captains
Campbell, Townsend and Baird, to check the enemy's
advance.

Captain Campbell proposed to attack the position
in front, while fifty men under Captain Baird made a
flank attack along some high ground to the west.
The enemy were found to be well armed and strongly
posted; the Kashmir troops were met with a very
heavy fire, and the attempts to carry the position by
assault failed. It was rapidly getting dark, and
Captain Campbell commenced to retire, being followed
up closely by the enemy. The main body sustained
heavy losses, but gained the fort under cover of the
fire of a party of the 14th Sikhs; Captain Baird's
detachment became, however, isolated, Baird himself
was mortally wounded, being carried back by Surgeon
Captain Whitchurch, and this party only made its
way back to the fort after desperate fighting, in which
several were killed and many wounded. On this day,
out of 150 men actually engaged, twenty-five were
killed and thirty wounded. Captain Campbell was
severely wounded, and the command of the troops in
Chitral fort now devolved upon Captain Townsend.

On this day the siege of Chitral fort may be said to have commenced, and for many weeks no news of the garrison reached the outer world.

Events on the Chitral-Gilgit Line.—We may now conveniently describe the events which took place on the line of communications between Chitral and Mastuj, and all that befell the small bodies of reinforcing troops and the convoys, which were struggling westward through a very difficult and actively hostile country.

On the 26th February the following instructions had issued from the British Agent: "Lieutenant Edwardes, commanding at Ghizr, to hand over that garrison to Lieutenant Gough, and to come on to Chitral, there to take command of the Puniali levies which had been ordered up from Gilgit; Lieutenant Moberley, commanding at Mastuj, was directed to order Lieutenant Fowler, R.E. (expected shortly to reach Mastuj with a party of Bengal Sappers and Miners), to continue his march to Chitral; and to send on a supply of Snider ammunition to Chitral by a suitable escort making ordinary marches." These two last-mentioned orders were received at Mastuj on the 28th February, and on the following day the ammunition was sent off to Chitral under escort of forty of the Kashmir Rifles. On the 2nd March, however, disquieting news reaching Mastuj as to the state of affairs on the road, Lieutenant Moberley was in doubt as to whether he should not recall the ammunition escort, but it was ultimately permitted to proceed. On this date Captain Ross was expected at Laspur with 100 of the 14th Sikhs, and Lieutenant Moberley wrote asking him to come straight through to Mastuj in a single stage; this Captain Ross did, reaching Mastuj on the 3rd.

He marched on again the following day to support the ammunition escort, which had been obliged to halt at Buni owing to the onward road having been broken down; and on the 5th the force at Buni was further strengthened by the arrival there of twenty men of the Bengal Sappers and Miners, accompanied by Lieutenants Fowler and Edwardes.

The possibility of the road being designedly broken had been foreseen by the British Agent, who had caused certain orders to be issued to meet such an eventuality; but as these never reached Lieutenant Moberley, to whom they had been addressed at Mastuj, it seems unnecessary here to recapitulate them.

On the 5th March Captain Ross returned with his Sikhs to Mastuj, while on the next day the combined detachment—two British officers, twenty Bengal Sappers and forty of the 4th Kashmir Rifles—marched on to Reshun, a large, straggling village situated on a sloping plain on the left bank of the Chitral River. Here news came in of fighting at Chitral, but the night passed quietly, and at noon on the 7th the two officers, with the twenty sappers, ten rifles and a number of coolies, moved off to repair a break reported about three miles distant. Reaching a narrow defile near Parpish, sangars were noticed on the high cliffs; these were at once occupied by the tribesmen, firing became general, four of the little party were hit, one being killed, and a retirement on Reshun was now ordered.

Eight more men were hit during this retirement. On arrival at an entrenchment which had been thrown up by the rest of the party near the village, the position was found too exposed, and a cluster of houses—affording better cover—was seized, and the work of improving the defences was at once proceeded with.

A fierce but unsuccessful attack was made just before dawn, and firing was kept up during the 8th from a large number of Martini and Snider rifles; at the end of the day the total losses of the defence—including the casualties near Parpish—amounted to seven killed or died of wounds and sixteen wounded. For the next five days the little garrison defended its post with conspicuous gallantry against heavy odds and repeated attacks from the enemy, who had succeeded in establishing themselves under cover close up to the walls. Lieutenant Fowler specially distinguished himself in making several successful sorties to obtain water. On the 13th the enemy opened negotiations, stating that all fighting at Chitral had ceased, and that Sher Afzul was engaged in friendly correspondence with the British Government. By the 15th, it seeming that matters were in course of arrangement, the two officers were persuaded to leave their defences, and were then treacherously seized, while the Chitralis succeeded in rushing the defences. Lieutenants Edwardes and Fowler were now taken in charge by some of Umra Khan's men, and proceeding by Chitral and Drosh to Jandol, were eventually released and sent in to Sir Robert Low's camp at Sado in April.

When, on the 6th March, Lieutenant Edwardes heard of the gathering below Reshun, he had at once sent back news to Mastuj, where it arrived the same evening, and Captain Ross thereupon started next morning with his party—two British officers, one native officer and ninety-three of other ranks—to bring Lieutenant Edwardes' detachment back to Buni. Reaching Buni late on the night of the 7th, he there left his native officer with thirty-three rank and file, and pushed on next morning for Reshun with the remainder of his party. At 1 p.m. the Koragh Defile was reached ; as described by Robertson, " the defile is the result of the river cutting its winding course through terrible cliffs. A goat, scuttling along the high ridges, might start a thunderous avalanche of boulders down the unstable slopes. At the lower end of this frightful gorge the pathway begins to ascend from the river above some caves, and then zigzags upwards. There the 'point' of the advance guard was fired upon, and hundreds of men disclosed themselves and set the very hillsides rolling down." The small party were in a trap. Several men were at once hit, and Captain Ross then decided to occupy some caves in the river bank. He made several attempts to scale the cliffs and to force his way back to Buni, but was everywhere met by a heavy fire from both banks of the river, and by a deadly hail of rocks from the cliffs above. Captain

Ross was killed, and eventually his subaltern, Lieutenant Jones, with only fourteen men, ten of the party being wounded, reached Buni on the evening of the 10th. Here he occupied a house and held it until the 17th, when Lieutenant Moberley marched out from Mastuj with 150 men of the Kashmir troops, and relieved and brought in the remnants of Captain Ross' party.

From the 22nd March until the 9th April Mastuj was invested by the enemy, but on this latter date they began to retire owing to the advance of the Gilgit column under Lieutenant-Colonel Kelly. The Mastuj garrison had only one man wounded.

Advance of the Gilgit Column.—During the first week in March reports of the serious state of affairs in the Chitral Valley began to reach Gilgit, whence a few days later the Assistant British Agent sent down a request to Lieutenant-Colonel Kelly to bring to Gilgit a wing of the 32nd Pioneers, then engaged in road-making between Bunji and Chilas. In peace time this officer commanded no more than his own regiment, but on hostilities occurring he automatically became the military head of the whole district, and all military responsibility rested on him alone. The message reached Colonel Kelly on the 14th, and by the 22nd the wing (strength 403) had arrived at Gilgit; on the same day Colonel Kelly was informed by telegraph from the Adjutant General that he was in military command in the Gilgit Agency, and was also Chief Political Officer so long as communications with Chitral were interrupted; in regard to operations he was to use his own judgment but was to run no unnecessary risks. He was also informed of the advance of a relief force via Swat about the 1st April. Lieutenant-Colonel Kelly now issued the following orders: 200 men to start early on the 23rd for Chitral, followed on the next day by the remainder of the wing, accompanied by two guns of No. 1 Kashmir Mountain Battery. Of the other half battalion 200 were called up to Gilgit from the Indus Valley, while the remainder of the regiment (242) was to proceed to Chilas.

At this time the various happenings on the Gilgit-Chitral road were known, except that no tidings had come in of the disaster to the party under Lieutenant Edwardes. Colonel Kelly's command now extended from Astor to Chitral, and contained, exclusive of the troops in the Mastuj and Chitral districts, four mountain guns, 845 of the 32nd Pioneers, about 1250 Rifles of the Kashmir Infantry, and 160 Kashmir Sappers. But in deciding upon the numbers of which the Relief Column was to be composed, with which he intended to force his way to Chitral, it was necessary also to provide for the safety of Gilgit and for keeping open the line of communications. There was nothing to be feared from the people of Hunza and Nagar, whose chiefs at once furnished 1000 men for employment as levies; but the people of Chilas required watching, though apparently submissive, while those of Yasin were sure to be in sympathy with their near neighbours of Chitral. From Gilgit to Chitral was 220 miles, and between the two posts

was the Shandur Pass (12,250 feet), at this season
deep in snow. As far as Gupis there was a made
mule road, but thence forward the road was a mere
track; while throughout its length there were many
places where it might be easily blocked, and where
an enemy might take up an almost impregnable
position. The supply question was further one of
great anxiety, especially should the country prove
hostile, but it was known that reserve supplies were
stored at Gupis, Ghizr and Mastuj. Bearing all these
points in mind, Lieutenant-Colonel Kelly decided to
limit the strength of the Relief Column to 400 men of
the 32nd Pioneers, two guns of the Kashmir Mountain
Battery, 40 Kashmir Sappers and 100 of the Hunza
and Nagar levies. The column started in two parties.
As far as Gupis, which was reached on the 26th and
27th, mule transport was used, but this was here
exchanged for coolies and ponies; owing, however,
to desertions among the coolies the loads had to be
reduced—there were no tents and each man had
an allowance of 15 lbs. of baggage—while only six
days' supplies could be taken with the column.

Ghizr was reached on the 30th and 31st March,
and the march to the Shandur Pass was commenced.
The snow was now so deep that the battery mules
and the ponies could not proceed; Colonel Kelly
therefore withdrew 200 of his men under Captain
Borradaile to Teru and returned himself with the
rest of the column to Ghizr where the supply
question did not present such difficulties. Borradaile
was next day to attempt to cross the Shandur Pass,

reach and entrench himself at Laspur, return the
transport, and try and open communications with
Mastuj.

Snow fell heavily during the next twenty-four
hours and no start could be made until 11 a.m. on
the 3rd, by which time the guns and a detachment
of the Kashmir Rifles had joined Borradaile. The
pass was crossed under extraordinary difficulties, the
infantry reaching Laspur on the night of the 4th,
and the guns and Kashmir Infantry the following
afternoon. A reconnaissance on the 6th revealed the
presence in the neighbourhood of the enemy, who were
reported also to be entrenched near the Chakalwat
defile some thirteen miles further on. On this day
Colonel Kelly arrived with fifty Nagar levies, and
next day fifty Puniali levies also came in. Some
idea of the severity of the climate may be gathered
from the fact that among the troops there were
sixty-three cases of snow blindness and forty-three
of frost-bite.

The second part of the column, delayed at Ghizr,
was unable to reach Laspur until the 9th, but Colonel
Kelly, considering it inadvisable to wait, pushed on
to Gasht with the remainder of his party, and after
reconnoitring the enemy's position, determined to
attack. The enemy's position was naturally very
strong and the sangars well placed; these blocked
the valley on either side of the river and were
continued up to the snow line, while the right of
the position was further protected by a mass of fallen
snow descending into the water. On the 9th Colonel

Kelly advanced towards the enemy's position at
Chakalwat; the Hunza levies were sent up the
heights on one side to get above and fire into the
sangars; while the Puniali men ascended on the
other flank to drive the enemy from their stone shoots
on the slopes above the river.

The force deployed on a gentle slope facing the
right-hand sangars, and the two guns opened fire at
800 yards range. This shell-fire and the volleys of
the infantry cleared the enemy out of the right
sangar, while the Hunza levies had already driven
them from those higher up. The next line of sangars
was attacked in the same manner, and the enemy now
began to give way and were soon in full flight, having
lost between fifty and sixty killed. Our casualties
were only four men wounded.

Colonel Kelly now moved on to Mastuj, where the
rest of his column closed up on the 11th, and the
three days spent here were occupied in the collection
of transport and supplies and in pushing out reconnaissances. These disclosed the presence of the enemy
in a strong and well-fortified position, where the
Chitral River Valley is cleft by a deep ravine known
as the Nisa Gol, 200 or 300 feet deep, with precipitous
sides. The defence was prepared on much the same
lines as at Chakalwat, but the sangars were of better
construction, being provided with head cover, while
their front was covered by the precipices of the
Nisa Gol.

It was decided to attack on the 13th and to try
and turn the enemy's left. Colonel Kelly pursued

the same tactics as in the earlier action, bringing his artillery fire to bear on the sangars while keeping up a heavy rifle fire, his levies climbing the precipitous hillsides and turning the flank. The guns silenced sangar after sangar, gradually moving in closer; a place was discovered where the ravine could be crossed, and a party reached the opposite side just as the levies had turned the position. The enemy now evacuated their defences and fled, fired on by the guns and the infantry. Our loss was seven killed and thirteen wounded.

There was no further opposition to the advance of the Gilgit column, beyond such as was experienced from broken bridges and roads, and on the 20th April Colonel Kelly's force marched into Chitral and joined the garrison.

The Siege of Chitral Fort.—This commenced, as has been said, on the 3rd March, after the action of that date wherein the British troops had suffered many casualties; and when, in consequence of Captain Campbell having been severely wounded, the command of the troops devolved upon Captain Townsend. The garrison of the fort consisted of six British officers, of whom five only were fit for duty, ninety-nine men of the 14th Sikhs, and 301 of all ranks of the 4th Kashmir Rifles. There were in addition fifty-two Chitralis—men whose loyalty was at best dubious—and eighty-five followers. The supplies, on half-rations, could be made to last two and a half months, while of ammunition there were 300 rounds per Martini-Henri rifle of the Sikhs and 280 rounds per

Snider of the Kashmir troops. The fort was about seventy yards square with a tower at each corner, and a fifth guarded the path to the river; the walls of the fort were some twenty-five feet in height and from eight to ten feet thick; it was practically commanded on all sides, and surrounded on three by houses, walls, and all kinds of cover. The number of British officers was so small and the Kashmir troops, who composed three-fourths of the fort-garrison, were so shaken by their losses on the 3rd, that Captain Townsend resolved to remain as far as possible on the defensive. He confined his energies, therefore, to devising measures of defence, to the provision of cover within and the demolition of cover without the walls, to arranging a system for quickly extinguishing fires, and to providing as far as possible for proper sanitation.

The garrison was therefore engaged in real fighting on two occasions only during the forty-eight days that the siege lasted, and the losses incurred in the passive defence of the fort were not heavy; there was, however, much sickness, and at the end of the first week only eighty Sikhs and 240 of the Kashmir Rifles remained fit for duty. From the 16th to the 23rd there was a truce, during which Sher Afzul did his best to persuade the British Agent to agree to withdraw the garrison to Mastuj, or to India by way of Jandol. During the suspension of hostilities Captain Townsend effected many improvements in the defences. The guard duties were very heavy, half the effectives being on duty at a time, and the defenders were harassed day and night by a desultory rifle fire.

On the 7th, under cover of a heavy rifle fire, a party of the enemy crept up to the tower at the south-eastern corner and managed to set it on fire. A strong wind was blowing, and for some time matters looked very serious, as the tower, being largely composed of wood, burned fiercely. No sooner did the fire seem to be mastered than it blazed up again; the enemy, occupying the high ground, were able to fire upon men going in and out of the tower with water and earth; the British Agent and a Sikh soldier were here wounded, while a sentry of the Kashmir Rifles was killed. On the 10th an attack was made on the water-way, and on the morning of the 17th the enemy could distinctly be heard at work upon a mine, leading to the same tower as that attacked on the 7th. It was clear that the entrance of the mine was in a summer-house about a hundred and fifty feet from the tower, and which there had been no time to demolish; while from the distinctness with which the sound of digging could be heard, the mine had evidently reached within a few feet of the base of the tower. It was decided to make a sortie, carry the summer-house where it was thought the mine-shaft would be found, and destroy the mine, since matters had gone too far to counter-mine.

For this duty forty men of the 14th Sikhs, with their *jemadar*, and sixty of the Kashmir Rifles, with a native officer, were placed under command of Lieu-

tenant H. K. Harley, 14th Sikhs, with orders to leave
the fort at 4 p.m. by the east gate, rush the summer-
house, and hold it on the enemy's side, while the rest
of the party destroyed or blew in the mine gallery.
The summer-house was taken with a loss of two men
killed, the defenders—some thirty Pathans—bolting
to the cover of a wall and opening fire from thence
upon Harley's party. Leaving some men to keep
these in check, Harley led the remainder to the mine
shaft, just outside the summer-house. Thirty-five
Chitralis, armed with swords, came out and were
at once bayoneted. Harley now cleared the mine,
arranged powder and fuse, but it was untamped and
the charge exploded prematurely; none the less the
effect was excellent, the mine being burst open right
up to the foot of the tower, and lying exposed like
a trench. Two prisoners were brought in, two of the
enemy were killed in the mine by the explosion,
two Pathans were shot in the summer-house, and
many of the enemy were shot down by the covering
fire from the walls of the fort. Harley's party had
eight men killed and thirteen wounded.

The enemy now seemed to have made their last
effort; they had learnt that the defenders were still
able to assume a vigorous offensive, and they knew
that help was drawing nearer from the direction of
Gilgit. On the night of the 18th-19th the investing
force quietly withdrew and abandoned the siege;
Sher Afzul and the Jandol chiefs fled that night to
Bashkar and Asmar, and on the afternoon of the 20th
the Gilgit force marched in.

During the siege the loss of the garrison of Chitral fort amounted, exclusive of the casualties on the 3rd March, to seventeen killed and thirty-two wounded.

CHAPTER IX.

MOHMANDS.[1]

THE Mohmands are divided into two main branches, the trans-frontier or Bar (hill) Mohmands and the cis-frontier or Kuz (plain) Mohmands, and both belong to the Ghoria Khel branch of the Afghans, who, when driven from their holdings on the head waters of the Tarnak and Arghastan Rivers by the Tarin Afghans, emigrated eastwards, at the commencement of the fifteenth century, by way of Ghazni, Kabul and Ningrahar. The Bar Mohmands separated from those of the Kuz branch at Dakka, the latter going to the Peshawar Valley, while the former made for the original Gandhar and took possession of the hills which they still occupy. Thus separated, the two branches have long since lost touch with each other.

Speaking generally, the country of the trans-frontier Mohmands extends from a little south of the Kabul River, on the line Girdi Kats to Fort Michni on the south, to Bajaur on the north. On the east it is coterminous with the Peshawar district from Gandi, three miles north of Jamrud, to Fort Abazai, and

[1] See Map VI.

along the right bank of the Swat River about twelve
miles above Abazai. On the west it is bounded by
the Kabul Tsappar Range and by the Kunar River,
which constitute the dividing line between the Mohmands under British and Afghan spheres of influence,
for by the Durand Agreement of 1893 the Mohmand
country, which from the days of Ahmad Shah had
been more or less subject to the Kabul rulers, was
divided between the British and the Afghan Governments. The settlements of the cis-frontier Mohmands
lie immediately south of Peshawar, and are bounded
on the north by the Bara River, on the west and
south by the Aka Khel and Adam Khel Afridis, and
on the east by the Khattaks, their country being
some twenty miles long by twelve miles broad. The
greater portion of this is irrigated by the Bara River,
is very productive, and its inhabitants for the most
part fairly well to do.

In regard to the circumstances attending the
partition of the Mohmand country, the author of
Afghanistan wrote as follows in the *United Service
Magazine* of April, 1908 : " At the period of the
Durand Mission the Government of India laid claim to
the entire region—Bulund Khel, Mohmandstan, Asmar
and Yaghistan, the latter embracing Chitral, Bajaur,
Swat, Buner, Dir, Chilas and Waziristan. The Amir
put forward a demand for Chageh in Baluchistan and
the Asmar Valley, which he had previously occupied,
and objected to the British pretensions. In point of
fact, the rights of the Government of India had
been already established by conquest and by moral

superiority, since this zone, the home of border
ruffians, had always required the watchful initiative
of a strong Government.... Ultimately, after long
discussion, the negotiations concluded, when it was
revealed that at needless sacrifice the Asmar Valley,
commanding the approach to the Pamir-Chitral region
and south-eastern Afghanistan, and of great importance to strategic considerations on the Indian frontier,
had been surrendered to the Amir, the Birmal tract
separated from Waziristan, and an ethnic absurdity
perpetrated where the Mohmands' country had been
divided by the watershed of the Kunar and Panjkora
Rivers."

On the 12th June, 1894, Mr. Udny, the Commissioner of Peshawar, who had been nominated as
chief of the Mohmand Boundary Delimitation Commission, issued a proclamation to "all Bajauri,
Mohmand and other tribes inhabiting the country
towards the Indian Empire from the Kabul River to
the southern limit of Chitral," giving what he called
"a brief sketch of the boundary." He stated that
"whereas the kingdom of Great Britain has agreed
that his Highness the Amir should retain in his
possession the country of Asmar on the north of
Chanak, situated on the Kunar River, or the River of
Kashkar, the boundary demarcation will commence
from Chanak in a south-westerly direction up to
Kunar, and at a distance of a few English miles from
the bank of the Kunar River towards Bajaur. From
Kunar the boundary line goes southwards, and, taking
a bend, ascends the hills close to Satala Sar, which

hills divide the watershed between the Kunar and
Panjkora rivers. From Satala Sar the boundary
passes over the crest of the hill, on one side of which
the waters flowing from the Dag Hills fall into the
Panjkora River, whilst the waters on the other
side passing through the Satala Valley, fall into the
Kabul River. And in the centre of this hill lies the
kotal of Satala. The extreme end of the boundary
touches the Kabul River, in the vicinity of Palosi.
From a review of the above details, you will understand that, in addition to the countries watered by
the Kunar River which lie towards the limits of the
Indian dominions, his Highness the Amir has agreed
not to interfere in all that country, the eastern waters
of which fall into the Panjkora River, nor to interfere
or stretch his hand in that quarter of the Mohmand
country, the waters of which fall into the Kabul
River below Palosi."

When, however, Mr. Udny met in August at
Jalalabad the Sipah Salar, Ghulam Haidar, the Amir's
representative, it seemed that the Amir intended to
repudiate the Durand Agreement, so far as it concerned
the Mohmand and Bajaur country; the proposed
partition of Mohmand spheres of influence was
rejected, it appearing that the Sipah Salar, on behalf
of his master, claimed to exercise jurisdiction over the
Mohmands right down to the Peshawar Valley. A
solution of the difficulty was, however, found, and
Colonel Sir T. Holdich has something to tell us about
it in his *Indian Borderland*, where he writes : " It
was impossible to give any effect to the agreement

of 1893 without clearly ascertaining whether the
geographical conditions of the country admitted of a
direct interpretation. For the most part they did
not. The boundary of the agreement was partly a
geographical impossibility, but for a great part there
was no obstruction in the way of carrying out its
intention, except a new and varied interpretation
which the Amir put upon the text of it. ... A
boundary was found between Afghanistan and the
independent tribes to the east, from the Hindu Kush
to a point in the Kunar Valley from whence it
diverged to Lundi Kotal; and although at that point
it had to be temporarily abandoned, and has remained
undemarcated, enough was secured to lead up to a
better geographical knowledge of the whole position,
on the basis of which it was possible to effect a
subsequent agreement which has rendered actual
demarcation through the Mohmand country unnecessary," in spite of the fact that no part of the boundary
defined south of the Hindu Kush was the actual
boundary of the agreement.

Of the Kunar River and Valley Holdich has a good
deal to say, both in *The Gates of India* and in *The
Indian Borderland*. In the former book he writes
that it was in the Kunar Valley that Alexander the
Great "found and defeated the chief of the Aspasians.
The Kunar River is by far the most important of the
northern tributaries of the Kabul. It rises under
the Pamirs, and is otherwise known as the Chitral
River. The Kunar Valley is amongst the most lovely
of the many lovely valleys of Afghanistan. Flanked

by the snowy-capped mountains of Kashmund on the
west, and the long level water-parting which divides
it from Bajaur and the Panjkora drainage on the east,
it appears, as one enters it from Jalalabad, to be
hemmed in and constricted. The gates of it are
indeed somewhat narrow, but it widens out northward, where the ridges of the lofty Kashmund tail off
into low altitudes of sweeping foothills a few miles
above the entrance, and here offer opportunity for an
easy pass across the divide from the west into the
valley. This is a link in the oldest and probably the
best-trodden route from Kabul to the Punjab, and it
has no part with the Khyber. It links together these
northern valleys of Laghman, Kundar and Lundai (*i.e.*
the Panjkora and Swat united) by a road north of the
Kabul, finally passing southwards into the plains
chequered by the river network above Peshawar.
The lower Kunar Valley in the early autumn is
passing beautiful. Down the tawny plain and backed
by purple hills the river winds its way, reflecting the
azure sky with pure turquoise colour—the opaque
blue of silted water—blinking and winking with tiny
sun shafts, and running emerald green at the edges.
... The clustering villages are thick in some parts—
so thick that they jostle each other continuously....
Higher up the river the valley closes until, long
before Chitral is reached, it narrows exceedingly.
Here, in the north, the northern winds rage down the
funnel with bitter fury and make life burdensome.
The villages take to the hill slopes or cluster in patches
on the terraces at their feet."

In *The Indian Borderland* we are told that " the
Kunar River rises in a blue lake called Gaz Kul, or
Karumbar, under the southern slopes of the Hindu
Kush. This, at least, is one of its sources. Many a
mighty glacier standing about the head of the Yarkhun
River offers its contributions. The Yarkhun flows
past the foot of the Baroghil Pass, over pebble and
boulder-covered flats, and through terrific gorges,
with here and there the snout of a glacier protruding
(or even temporarily blocking the valley) till it reaches
Mastuj. From this point you may call it the Chitral
River, or Kashkar, for it now flows past Chitral, and
through the district known to hill people as Kashkar.
It does not become the Kunar till it reaches the
neighbourhood of the ancient kingdom of Kunar,
which occupies the last fifty miles of its course before
it joins the Kabul River. . . . The Kunar Valley and
the Valley of the Bashgul, or Arnawai, together lead
up to the Mandal and Dorah passes, either one of
which is the gateway to the rich valleys of eastern
Badakshan, and opens up a direct line to Jalalabad
from the Oxus, which does not touch Kabul at all.
These passes are high (14,000 feet to 15,000 feet),
difficult, and very much more buried under snow than
those further west ; but a well-constructed road across
them would still be a passable trade route for many
months in the year ; and would offer a far more direct
connection between the Oxus regions and India than
any which now exist."

" Asmar is the most unattractive corner of the
Kunar district. A narrow, three-cornered patch of

dusty valley, over which the wind comes dancing and sweeping from all sides at once, with the river running deep in a rocky gorge below; steep pine-clad hills to the west, and more reasonable slopes to the east, amongst which there winds up one of the chief routes into Bajaur... such is the general view of Asmar."

The aspect of the Mohmand hills is exceedingly dreary, and the eye is everywhere met by dry ravines between long rows of rocky hills and crags, scantily clothed with coarse grass, scrub and the dwarf palm. In summer the want of water is greatly felt, and the desert tracts radiate an intolerable heat; this, coupled with the unhealthiness of the river lowlands, probably accounts for the inferior physique of the Mohmands as compared with their Afridi and Shinwari neighbours. The want of water is especially felt in the Gandab district, which with the Shilman and Pandiali are the largest valleys in the Mohmand country, and the entrances to which are covered by the respective forts of Shabkadar, Michni, and Abazai. The villages, or rather fort clusters, are scattered along the valleys wherever a spring, or proximity of water to the surface, encourages cultivation, but in some cases the drinking water has to be brought from great distances, and is either obtained from springs whose supply is uncertain or from small tanks made to retain the rain water. The women are employed in the laborious task of bringing the water from these places for the use of the village.

The crops in the Mohmand hills are almost entirely dependent on the winter and autumn rains, and should

these fail there is considerable distress. Even in
ordinary times the country cannot support the surplus
population, which has for years past been steadily
emigrating to the Peshawar district. The products
of the Mohmand country are few and rude; a little
grain, firewood, grass, charcoal, ropes and mats, honey
and cattle from the Baizai hills—these are the chief
exports. But through the Mohmand country come
Indiawards the wood rafts from Chitral, Kunar and
Laghman on the Kabul River, and from Dir and Swat;
wax, hides, ghi and rice from Kunar; and the iron of
Bajaur in lumps and bars. The imports are salt, cloth,
paper, soap, tea, indigo, sugar, grain, tobacco, needles,
scissors and other manufactures of civilisation, purchased by the Mohmands for themselves and their
northern neighbours. The through trade, therefore,
is considerable, and it is with transit dues levied on
trade, and the profits earned as carriers of goods to
and from the trade centres of Peshawar, Jalalabad,
Pesh - Bolak, Lalpura and Shabkadar, that the
Mohmands supplement the scanty returns of their
barren soil. In the hot weather trade is brisk on the
Kabul River, upon which wood rafts, or merchandise
carried on inflated skins, are floated down to British
territory.

There are numerous roads through the Mohmand
country, as the hills, though rugged and rocky, are
nowhere impassable. The most important perhaps of
these are the roads from Peshawar to Dakka, one from
Shahgai via Tartara in the Mullagori country and the
Shilman Valley, and the other from Fort Michni across

the Kabul River by the Shanilo ferry into the Shilman Valley; in old days these were important trade routes. The other roads of importance from British territory are one from Shabkadar to the Gandab Valley, and another from Matta, a few miles north of Shabkadar, over the Inzarai Pass into the Pandiali Valley; this is comparatively easy and is known as the Alikandi route.

Of the Gandab Valley, Lieutenant Enriquez says that "it is certainly a hopeless wilderness. Mile after mile the scenery offers nothing but dreary boulder-strewn mountains. The streams in summer disappear under ground and only rise to the surface at intervals. The purity of the water is not above suspicion.[1] In the deeper pools there are quantities of little fish which can be caught in a sheet, and which make a very tolerable substitute for white-bait. Smalls eels are also quite common and can be hooked. The hardy pink oleander thrives in the ravines, and lends the only touch of colour to the desolate landscape. In June the climate of the Gandab Valley is detestable. The excessive heat is intensified by radiation. The narrow glen acts as a funnel for the scorching wind, which blows hard for days on end. No tent can stand against the storm, and I have seen half a camp collapse when struck by a sudden blast. Dust and even small pebbles are blown about with great violence."

Oliver says of the Mohmands that "in physique, though there are among them fine men, they are as a rule inferior to many of the surrounding Pathans;

---

[1] The word "Gandab" signifies bad water.

and though they have on occasions fought well against
us, their courage is decidedly open to suspicion. They
have plenty of pride and haughtiness, sufficient reputation for cruelty and treachery, and like other Pathans
a good deal to say about their honour; the value of
which may, perhaps, be best judged by the frontier
proverb concerning them, to the effect that 'you
have only to put a rupee in your eye, and you may
look at any Mohmand, man or woman.' They are on
fairly good terms with their neighbours of Bajaur and
Kunar, have usually avoided collisions with the
Afridis, though between them and the Shinwaris a
guerilla war has lasted for centuries; the belt of
desert from Lundi Kotal to Pesh-Bolak bearing witness
to the destruction caused by raid and counter-raid.
Private blood-feuds are common, and the tariff for
injuries runs rather low. In many other social and
domestic customs,"—and in dress and language, it
might also be added—" they resemble the Yusafzais;
but they have no *hujras*—an institution which to the
Pathan 'young blood,' corresponds to the English
notion of a club—the want of which, in a Pathan's
opinion, is to stamp a tribe as little better than
savages. They differ, moreover, conspicuously in
having a more aristocratic tribal constitution, in that
they have hereditary chiefs or Khans,[1] drawn from
the old families, who from ancient times have supplied leaders—the most important being the Khan of
Lalpura in the east, and the Baizai Khan of Goshta
in the west."

[1] Usually termed " Arbaba."

The cis-frontier or Kuz Mohmands are divided into five main clans:

1. Kayakzai.   3. Dawezai.   5. Sirgani.
2. Musazai.   4. Matanni.

These are represented by some 500 men in the regular army and levies, and of these branches of the Mohmand family, who settled in the south-west corner of the Peshawar Valley when their progenitors finally ousted the Dilazaks, it may be said that they have been for so long separated from their cousins of the hills as to have become practically an altogether separate tribe.

Of the independent, Bar or hill, Mohmands there are four main clans:

1. Tarakzai.   3. Baizai.
2. Halimzai.   4. Khwaezai.

The *Tarakzais* inhabit the hills north and west of Michni adjoining the British border—the Burhan Khel and Isa Khel divisions of the clan living in Pandiali, and the Morcha Khel divisions having settlements on either bank of the Kabul River round Lalpura and Dakka. A small proportion of the Tarakzais live in Loi Shilman, and some are also settled in British territory in the *Doaba*, the triangular piece of country between the junction of the Kabul and Swat Rivers. The chiefs of the Tarakzais are the Khans of Lalpura and Pandiali.

The *Halimzais* were originally considered to be a branch of the Tarakzais, but they have so grown in numbers and importance as to be now looked upon as a separate clan. They live in the Gandab Valley and in Kamali, and have also a colony in Loi Shilman.

The *Baizais* are the most powerful clan of the Mohmands, and inhabit the more westerly portion of the tribal country. They are bounded on the north and west by the Kunar River, south by the Kabul River, south-east by the Khwaezais, and east by the Safis and the territory of the Khan of Nawagai. They also extend into Afghanistan. The chief of the Baizai clan is the Khan of Goshta.

The *Khwaezai* settlements stretch from the west, from the north of the Kabul River near Lalpura, across the Bohai Dag as far as the Kamali limits of the Halimzais to the east.

Of the independent Mohmands very few enlist in the Indian Army, but there are a good many in the regiments of the Amir of Afghanistan and in the contingents of the local Khans. The physique of the tribe is generally good, and a rough estimate of the fighting strength of the Bar Mohmands places it at 19,000 men, of whom the Baizais supply almost half. They have gained for themselves of more recent years a reputation as brave fighters as well as troublesome raiders, but are thoroughly mistrusted and detested by their neighbours, who accuse them of the grossest treachery. The Mohmands, moreover, are very vindictive, frequently exhuming and burning the bodies of enemies, even of their own faith ; they often, too, refuse permission to relatives to remove their dead for proper burial after a war. At one time the Mohmand fighting men did not possess many modern rifles, but latterly it is said that they have received several large consignments of arms from the Persian Gulf via Kabul, and have also purchased numbers of rifles from the Adam Khel factories in the Kohat Pass.

To be considered in connection with the independent Mohmands are three affiliated clans living on the northern outskirts of the Mohmand country, and also three vassal clans.

The three first mentioned are the *Dawezais*, of whom some live permanently in the Upper Ambahar Valley and others leave their families in the winter in Ningrahar, migrating during the summer to the neighbourhood of the Unai Pass and the Upper Helmand River; the *Utmanzais*, who live in Bar and Kuz Yakhdand; and the *Kukkozais*, whose settlements are in Ningrahar.

The three vassal clans are the *Mullagoris*, the *Safis*, and the *Shilmanis*.

The *Mullagoris* are a people of doubtful origin, it being open to conjecture whether they are of Dilazak, Durani or Ghilzai stock. They are not acknowledged as being connected with any of the neighbouring tribes. The bulk of the clan is situated to the north of the Khyber Pass, extending from the Dabbar Pass on the west to the Peshawar district on the east, the Kabul River being their northern boundary. Their neighbours on the west are the Shilmanis, on the north the Tarakzai Mohmands, and on the south the Kuki Khel Afridis, with whom, as well as with other Afridis, they are at feud. They have other settlements at Sapri in the Mohmand Hills, in the Sisobi

Glen, on the western slopes of the Pandperi Range, and along the banks of the Kunar River. Those of the clan who are settled about the Khyber go in the summer to Kambela, which lies below Mutlani Sar to the west. The Khyber Mullagoris are very united, have a good reputation for courage, and enlist freely in the Khyber Rifles.

The *Safis* or *Kandaharis* are supposed to be descendants of the original Gandhari of the country included between the Indus and Kunar Rivers, and which is bounded on the north by the Koh-i-Mor Range, and on the south by the Kabul River. Of these a great number emigrated in the fifth and sixth centuries to the valley of the Helmand, being driven out by Jat and other Scythic tribes from across the Hindu Kush. "In appearance often florid," says Oliver, "with light eyes and hair, speaking a language only distantly related to the Pushtu of the Mohmands, whose dialect has much in common with that spoken in Kabul, both they and the Dehgans of the Laghman Valley are either directly descended from, or largely admixed with, the Kafirs, and are comparatively recent converts to Islamism. In Baber's time they were still called Kafirs; in Nadir's —Safis, a name which Masson suggests they may have acquired by becoming 'pure' in comparison to the adjoining 'impure' idolaters." They are very bigoted and are fanatical, but make good soldiers. The main portion of them live in a wide valley, called Sur Kamar, which divides the Baizai country from that of the Dawezai and Utmanzai Mohmands. It is bounded on the north and east by the Sarlarra Range and Utmanzai country, on the south by the Darwazgai Range, and on the west by the Amrohi Range. They hold their valley by favour of the Mohmands, but are really dependents of the Khan of Nawagai.

The *Shilmanis* look upon the trans-frontier Mohmands as their parent stock, but their origin is rather doubtful—it has been stated to be Turk or Indian, and the latter seems the more probable. Their ancient home appears to have been in Shilman on the banks of the Kurram River, whence they migrated to the Tartara Mountain north of the Khyber, and to Hastnagar during the fifteenth century. At the end of the same century the Yusafzais drove the Hastnagar section into Swat, since which time they have sought the protection of the Mohmands, who had also taken possession of the country north of the Kabul River, and thus have become affiliated with them. The tract of country occupied by the Shilmanis is to the north of the Loargai plain and between it and the Kabul River, being bounded on the east by the Dabbar Hill, and on the west by the Shilman Gakhe. It is divided into four portions: 1, the Kam Shilman Valley; 2, the Prang Darra Glen; 3, the Loi Shilman Valley; and 4, from Shinpokh to the mouth of the Kam Shilman Glen along the right bank of the Kabul River. The tribes bordering this tract of country are the Mullagoris on the east, the Shinwaris on the south, and the Mohmands on the west and north.

About one-tenth of the Shilmani fighting men take service in the Khyber Rifles.

CHAPTER X.

MOHMANDS: OPERATIONS.[1]

THE British Government first came into contact with the Mohmands during the Afghan War of 1838-42, at which time one Saadat Khan was Chief of Lalpura. On the news of the approach of the British army, Turabaz Khan, his cousin and enemy, immediately started off to meet the army of the Indus at Jhelum. Saadat Khan thereupon espoused the cause of the Barakzais, and Turabaz Khan was installed as Khan of Lalpura by Colonel Wade, and seems to have done loyal service for Mackeson while we held Afghanistan. After the disasters at Kabul the whole country rose, and Turabaz Khan, at risk to himself, saved an English lady and her child from the Pesh-Bolak garrison, and took them down the river on a raft to Peshawar. The officers of the *Jazailchis* stationed at Pesh-Bolak escaped over the Tartara hills, and Turabaz Khan himself took refuge in British territory. He returned with General Pollock's force, but was ousted by Saadat Khan on the withdrawal of our troops. He subsequently made his peace with the Amir and received a *jaghir*, or grant of land, in Kama.

[1] See Map VI.

During the early years of British rule in the Peshawar Valley, the Mohmands gave more trouble than almost any other tribe.

The Michni Mohmands, after annexation, were allowed to hold a fief from the British Government in the Doaba, of which they collected the revenue. A portion of the lands they cultivated themselves, farming out the remainder to other tribes of the plains as tenants. Many of their clansmen dwelt in the plains of Michni, and some in the neighbouring hills, and they traded largely in the Peshawar Valley. The Halimzai Mohmands also held Panjpao in British Doaba as a fief, chiefly cultivated by tenants. A few of their men lived in the plains, but the majority in the hills, and these also traded in the valley. The Pandiali Mohmands at a former period had held a similar jaghir in the Doaba, but not since British rule. They had few relations either with the Government or the people of the Peshawar Valley, and inhabited a very strong locality in the hills. These fiefs had originally been granted to the Mohmands by former governments, as blackmail to buy off depredations.

The first inroad of the Mohmands occurred in December, 1850, in an unprovoked attack on the village of Shabkadar, organised by Fateh Khan, a son of Saadat Khan, who at that time was still the chief of Lalpura, and who was naturally not well disposed towards us, and was doing his best to incite the tribe to hostilities. In the following year a number of outrages were committed : two attacks

were made upon Matta in March and April by the
chief of Pandiali; other minor depredations succeeded
in July, headed by a leading man from Panjpao; and
in October the Michni Mohmands made so serious an
attack upon British villages, that later in the month
the Supreme Government directed that the Mohmand
fiefs in the Doaba should be confiscated, our border
posts strengthened, and that punitive operations should
be undertaken against the offenders.

Operations against the Mohmands in 1851-52.—
Accordingly on the 25th October of this year, a force
numbering 1593 of all ranks marched out from Peshawar towards the Mohmand frontier.   It was under the
command of Brigadier Sir Colin Campbell, K.C.B., and
was composed as under :

> Det. 3rd Company 1st Battalion Artillery.[1]
> No. 17 Light Field Battery.[1]
> Two companies 61st Foot.
> Two companies 98th Foot.
> 2nd Irregular Cavalry.
> 2nd Company Sappers and Miners.
> 66th Gurkha Regiment.
> Wing 71st Native Infantry.[2]

The force moved, unopposed, to the village of Dab,
via Mian Khel, and here the hamlets were destroyed,
Shabkadar and Matta were reinforced, and a position
was taken up to cover the erection of a fort at Michni.
In the meantime several outrages had been committed
in Peshawar, instigated by Saadat Khan, then at the

[1] Ceased to exist after the Mutiny.
[2] Mutinied at Lucknow in 1857.

head of a small armed force in the Tartara Hills ; and it seeming likely that he meditated an attack upon some of our frontier villages, measures were taken by Sir Colin for their protection, and for that of the bridge of boats over the Kabul River forming his communications with Peshawar.

Saadat Khan continued very active ; he busied himself in endeavouring to unite the Mohmands ; on the 26th he had moved to Gandab, twenty miles north-west of Shabkadar, and here on the 30th he was joined by the Chief of Bajaur with a large following. On the 28th and 29th the Mohmands attacked two of our villages, burnt another, and finally, on the 7th December, Saadat Khan suddenly moved out of a gorge in the hills to the right front of camp, and took up a position with 4000 footmen and a small body of horse. At the same time the hills to the westward, near Dab, had been strongly occupied by the enemy, while a party of 200 came down to the left bank of the Kabul River immediately in rear of the camp. Seeing the force thus displayed, the Brigadier directed that a troop of Horse Artillery and six companies of the 53rd Regiment should at once move out from Peshawar to the bridge of boats on the Kabul River.

On the 8th December the Mohmands, to the number of 3000 or 4000, under Saadat Khan, advanced upon Matta, but were driven off, and all this day the tribesmen were reported to be collecting in great strength in Pandiali, under the Chief of Bajaur, and Sir Colin accordingly sent in to Peshawar for reinforcements; and their arrival, after a forced march, the 53rd having covered forty-two miles in thirty hours, undoubtedly prevented an attack upon the camp near Dab. The British force was now far too strong for the Mohmands, whose gathering broke up, Saadat Khan returning to Lalpura. Desultory operations continued for some few more weeks, but finally the force was recalled to Peshawar on the 14th February.

On the 30th March news was received at Fort Shabkadar that the Mohmands were collecting in the high ground in front to the number of between 400 and 500, and troops were moved out from the post, causing the enemy's retreat to the hills. It was known that Saadat Khan was making great efforts to unite the various clans in view of again attempting the recovery of the lands we had annexed; and finally, on the 15th April, the Mohmands debouched from the hills, in numbers not less than 6000 matchlock men with some eighty horsemen, and moved along the foot of the hills in front of Shabkadar, taking the direction of Matta. Sir Colin Campbell had himself gone out to Shabkadar, where he had gathered some 600 troops, and he speedily issued from the fort with two Horse Artillery guns and 266 sabres of the 7th Light Cavalry [1] and 15th Irregular Cavalry,[1] and dispersed the enemy, causing them considerable loss.

In the month of July following this affair, the Michni and Panjpao Mohmands, exiled from house and lands and cut off from trade, tendered their sub-

[1] Mutinied in 1857.

mission and prayed for the restoration of their fiefs, which were handed back on payment of a nominal annual tribute. The Panjpao or Halimzai Mohmands gave no further cause for dissatisfaction, but the men of Michni fell into arrears in the payment of their tribute, and their Chief, when invited into Peshawar to make an explanation, fled instead to the hills. It was therefore necessary to attach the property of the tribesmen to the extent of the amount of tribute and, further, to inflict and recover a fine. To assist the civil authorities in enforcing these measures a small force of all arms proceeded to Michni, a company of infantry was sent to Mian Khel, and patrols so arranged as to seize all cattle moving off to the hills. It was proposed to transfer the Michni jaghir to some of our own subjects, but it was obvious that these could not hold the lands and be responsible for the revenue, unless they were secured from all chance of raids from the independent border villages beyond Michni. It was therefore resolved to destroy the three villages particularly concerned, and to prevent their being ever reoccupied; for such measures it was necessary to obtain the assistance of a military force strong enough to meet any resistance the Mohmands of that part of the border might make.

Operations against the Michni Mohmands in 1854. —For this purpose, while the garrisons of the forts and posts at Abazai, Shabkadar, Mian Khel and Michni were strengthened, a force as below enumerated was concentrated at Michni, under command of Colonel Cotton, 22nd Foot :

Two guns 1st Troop 3rd Brigade Horse Artillery.

2nd Company 2nd Battalion Artillery with Mountain Train Battery (4 howitzers and 4 guns).

Two companies 22nd Foot.

2nd Company Sappers and Miners.

One squadron 10th Light Cavalry.[1]

One squadron 1st Irregular Cavalry.[2]

Three companies 1st Native Infantry.[3]

9th Native Infantry.[4]

1st Sikh Infantry.

The advance commenced on the 31st August along the left bank of the Kabul River in the direction of Shahmansur Khel, which was captured after some opposition. While the destruction of the village and the removal of grain stores was in progress, the heights above had to be seized and held, and the troops engaged on this duty were exposed to an unceasing and galling fire, and suffered several casualties, but the subsequent retirement to camp was practically unmolested. On the 2nd September Colonel Cotton again moved out, and destroyed the villages of Dab and Sadin, when the troops returned to Peshawar, and the well-affected among the Michni Mohmands paid up their share of the tribute due.

After this the Mohmands continued to commit outrages, issuing in large bodies from the hills and harrying the border, and between March, 1855, and July, 1857, no fewer than thirty-six serious raids,

[1] Mutinied in 1857.   [2] Now the 1st Lancers (Skinner's Horse).
[3] Mutinied in 1857.   [4] Mutinied in 1857.

having plunder and murder for their objects, were
committed by the Mohmands of Pandiali. The Commissioner, Colonel Edwardes, had been supported by
the Chief Commissioner, Sir John Lawrence, in recom-
mending punitive operations in the Pandiali Valley,
but the Government were unwilling to undertake
them at the time, and when the Mutiny broke out
in 1857 our attention was at once more pressingly
directed to other quarters.

During this period the Mohmands failed, by any
concerted action, to avail themselves of an unusually
favourable opportunity of increasing their annoyance,
but raids and outrages did not cease, while there were
no troops available on the frontier to move out against
them. From the beginning of September 1857 to
March 1860, thirty-nine serious outrages were committed by members of this tribe. Within five years
eighty-five raids had been conducted by parties of an
average strength of seventy-five men, in which fourteen British subjects had been killed, twenty-seven
wounded, and fifty-five carried off, while over 1200
head of cattle had been plundered. This was exclusive
of forty minor raids in which thirty-five British subjects had been killed or wounded and 267 head of
cattle driven away, but though an expedition was
urged by the local authorities, the Government still
refused to sanction one. At last, about the end of
March 1860, Nauroz Khan, an adopted son of Saadat
Khan of Lalpura, sent in seeking for peace, and finally
it was agreed that bygones should be bygones, that
the Chief of Lalpura should be responsible for the

future peace of the frontier, that there should be something of a general amnesty, and that the blockade of the country should be raised.

Soon after this the Khans of Lalpura and Pandiali came into Peshawar in person and made their submission to the Commissioner. For three years there was peace on the border, the Mohmands desisting from troubling until the Ambela expedition in 1863, described in Chapter IV., when the emissaries of the Akhund of Swat were sent all over the hills bordering the Peshawar Valley, but were successful in exciting disturbances among the Mohmands only. Sultan Muhammad Khan, another son of Saadat Khan, Chief of Lalpura, owned the Akhund's religious supremacy, and was, moreover, ill-disposed towards the British. Collecting a body of Mohmands, joined by a miscellaneous rabble of Safis, Bajauris and the like, he came down to our frontier on the 5th December, 1863, at the head of some 500 men. The officer commanding Fort Shabkadar at once turned out with fifty-five sabres and ninety-six bayonets, and drove the enemy back beyond our frontier, inflicting some loss. The Shabkadar garrison was reinforced from Peshawar, and the Mohmands again advancing on the 7th from the shelter of the hills, were again forced to retire. Nauroz Khan now, however, joined his brother, and, supported by the priesthood, the two managed, by the beginning of the new year, to collect a miscellaneous assemblage of close upon 6000 armed men— mostly Mohmands and mainly represented by men from the Halimzai and Khwaezai clans—and with these it was now proposed to meet the British troops stationed at Shabkadar.

This force had recently been very considerably strengthened, and now numbered some 1800 of all ranks, with three Horse Artillery guns, under Colonel Macdonnell, C.B.

On the morning of the 2nd January, 1864, the enemy made their appearance, debouching from a gorge north-west of Shabkadar, and formed up in something of the appearance of a crescent. The action which resulted was on our side almost entirely confined to the cavalry and guns. The British commander succeeded to some extent in drawing the enemy into the plain, where they were repeatedly charged by the cavalry and finally driven beyond the border, having sustained about eighty casualties.

The effects of this check were felt throughout the Mohmand country, at least 1000 men departing next morning to their homes, while in a few days the gathering completely dispersed.

The Amir Sher Ali Khan now took the Mohmands in hand, ejecting and imprisoning Saadat Khan and his son, Nauroz Khan, and replacing the former in the chieftainship by a son of his ancient rival, Turabaz Khan. Eventually, however, Nauroz Khan came to his own again, returning from Afghanistan in 1870 and assuming the Khan-ship.

During the years immediately following the operations near Shabkadar in 1864, the Mohmand border was not disturbed by anything more than isolated outrages—sufficiently serious though these were ; and

it was not until the invasion of Afghanistan in 1878
that the independent Mohmands began again to be
really troublesome.   At this time a grandson of
Saadat Khan was Chief of Lalpura, and he sent a
Mohmand contingent to co-operate with the Amir's
troops at Ali Musjid.   These, however, fled without
firing a shot, and the Khan then came in and tendered
his submission to Sir S. Browne at Dakka. The Khan
of Goshta refused to come in, and it was believed to
be at his instigation that a raid was made by hill
Mohmands on the village of Sarai, on the left bank of
the Kabul River, in the Kama district.   A small
column was sent out from Jalalabad, and some of the
ringleaders were captured.

On the 6th February a mixed force of 12,000
Mohmands and Bajauris made an attack upon the
village of a friendly chief, one Azim Khan, who had
been placed by us in charge of the two districts of
Goshta and Chardeh.   On the next day General
Macpherson, V.C., C.B., took out a small force of
some 900 cavalry and infantry from Jalalabad, intending to act in combination with another body moving
from Basawal by Chardeh upon Goshta, and which
was to intercept the Mohmands in their retirement;
but the enemy having received notice of the proposed operations, retreated hurriedly to the hills,
and the two columns returned to their respective
stations.

Affair at Kam Dakka in 1879.—After this some
of the Tarakzais and Halimzais were implicated in an
attack upon a surveyor's party near Michni, for which

the divisions concerned were fined ; and then in April of this year there was a more serious gathering of Mohmands brought together by a notorious mullah, for the purpose of raiding into British territory or making attacks on our posts in the Khyber. On the night of the 20th April between 200 and 300 Khwaezai and Halimzai Mohmands began to cross the Kabul River from Palosi to Shinpokh—from the left to the right bank. The Khan of Lalpura sent the news in to Dakka that a large body of Mohmands was within three miles of that place and had already engaged his outposts. He asked for help, as he expected a night attack. Arrangements were made for rendering such assistance as could be afforded, but no attack was delivered. The officer commanding at Dakka moved out on the 21st with a small mixed force, found the Kam Dakka Pass clear, and also that the village of that name, on the right bank of the Kabul River and seven miles east of Dakka, was unoccupied by the enemy. It was reported here that the Mohmands were in great strength in the vicinity of the north bank, and the villagers appeared alarmed and seemed unwilling that Major Barnes' force should be with-drawn. The troops, however, returned the same day, unopposed, to Dakka, but on arrival here it was decided to send infantry to Kam Dakka, and 130 rifles of the Mhairwara Battalion[1] started thither at 5 p.m., reaching the village at 11.15 p.m. This detachment, commanded by Captain O'Moore Creagh, was to protect Kam Dakka from an attack from the

[1] Now the 44th Merwara Infantry.

north bank of the river, and was to hold the village
for three days.

The villagers, however, appeared unwilling to be
compromised by harbouring British troops, said they
were quite capable of taking care of themselves,
objected to the troops entering their village, and
seemed, in fact, anything but friendly.

Early next morning Captain O'Moore Creagh took
up a position partially covering the village, and then,
finding crowds of Mohmands crossing the river and
threatening his flank, he withdrew to a better position
near a graveyard and on the river bank, where he
hastily threw up an entrenchment. He had by this
time been reinforced by thirty-six rifles of his regiment
from Dakka. Scarcely had this entrenchment been
completed, about 9 a.m., and followers and baggage
animals been brought under cover, water stored, etc.,
when the enemy came down from the hills and completely surrounded the detachment. They persistently
attacked from 9 a.m. to 3 p.m., frequently getting to
the closest quarters, and having to be repulsed with
the bayonet. The ammunition now began to run low,
the enemy had closed in all round to within sixty to
a hundred yards, and the situation became most
critical, when it was relieved by the opportune
approach of reinforcements.

These had been sent off from Dakka and Lundi
Kotal so soon as the situation at Kam Dakka had
become known at divisional headquarters. Under
cover of the fire of the reinforcing troops, and some
dashing charges by a troop of the 10th Bengal

Cavalry, the Mhairwara detachment was withdrawn from the entrenchment, and the retirement on Dakka was commenced. This was reached about 8.30 p.m., the enemy pressing the rearguard closely, but being unable, owing to the darkness, to cause more than a very few casualties. A strong force of all arms moved out on the next day to Kam Dakka, but few of the enemy were met with.

In April, 1879, the same month as the Kam Dakka affair above related, Muhammad Sadik Khan, the eldest son of Nauroz Khan, who was with the British force at Gandamak, fled from the camp and joined the Amir Yakub Khan—whose mother was a sister of Nauroz Khan—and, as soon as our troops left Dakka in June, 1879, he was appointed Khan of Lalpura in the place of the Khan installed in 1875. When the second invasion of Afghanistan took place, the Khan of Lalpura hesitated for some days as to what action he should take, but at length appeared at Dakka, and for two months all went well at Lalpura and also at Goshta.

Action on the Gara Heights, January 1880.— The journey of the Amir Yakub Khan to India gave the first shock to the Mohmands, and further agitation was produced by the news of the fighting at Kabul. The mullahs began to arouse the fanaticism of the tribesmen, and the Khans of Lalpura and Goshta placed themselves at the head of the movement and collected large numbers of men at Palosi and Rena. On the 11th January the Mohmands began to pass the river, and three days later about

5400 men under the Khan of Lalpura had crossed and taken up a strong position on the Gara Heights, about two miles from Fort Dakka and between that place and Kam Dakka. Fortunately, this move had been anticipated, and nearly all the officers at Fort Dakka had made themselves thoroughly familiar with the features of the position. Arrangements were now made to attack the enemy on the Gara Heights in front from Dakka, while another column from Lundi Kotal attacked them in flank and rear, so that, beset on three sides and with the unfordable Kabul River on the other, escape would be impossible and destruction almost certain.

On the 15th the Dakka Column moved out and was drawn up in position facing the Gara Heights by 11 a.m. It was commanded by Colonel Boisragon, 30th Punjab Native Infantry, and was composed as under :

Four guns I Bty. C. Bde. Royal Horse Artillery.
94 sabres 6th Dragoon Guards.
50 sabres 17th Bengal Cavalry.[1]
110 bayonets 1st Battalion 25th Foot.
100 bayonets 8th Native Infantry.[2]
500 bayonets 30th Punjab Native Infantry.

It had been arranged that the force from Lundi Kotal should start six hours previously, and it was hoped that by this time it was in a position to enable it to cut off the enemy's retreat. The Dakka force advanced to the attack covered by the fire of the four

[1] Now the 17th Cavalry. [2] Now the 8th Rajputs.

guns, and the heights were taken without any very serious opposition, the enemy evacuating one position after another, until, utterly routed, they fled down the reverse slopes towards Kam Dakka. As soon as the guns of the Lundi Kotal column were heard, about 5 p.m., Colonel Boisragon pressed on and joined hands with Brigadier-General Doran, commanding the troops from Lundi Kotal, in Kam Dakka. In the meantime the enemy had made good their escape, either towards Rena or across the river.

Brigadier-General Doran had left Lundi Kotal at 4.30 a.m. with the undermentioned troops :

Two guns 11-9th Royal Artillery.

20 sabres 17th Bengal Cavalry.

200 bayonets 5th Fusiliers.

200 bayonets 25th Foot.

30 bayonets Madras Sappers and Miners.

300 bayonets 1st Madras Native Infantry.[1]

200 bayonets 4th Madras Native Infantry.[2]

300 bayonets 31st Punjab Native Infantry.

Progress, via the Inzari Kandao, was very slow, the troops could move only in single file, the battery mules could hardly be got along, some baggage animals fell over the precipices and were lost, and the rear-guard was sixty-seven hours in covering seventeen miles. The gorge of the Shilman Gakhe was forced after but a feeble resistance, and eventually Brigadier-General Doran was able to join Colonel Boisragon as already related ; but all the baggage of the Lundi Kotal column, owing to the extraordinary

---

[1] Now the 61st Pioneers.   [2] Now the 64th Pioneers.

difficulties of the road, did not reach the bivouac until the morning of the 18th. Meanwhile, on the 16th January, 500 men had been passed over the river on rafts and destroyed the village of Rena, whereafter the columns returned unmolested to Dakka and Lundi Kotal.

The operations, though a failure in regard to combination, had not been without effect; the tribesmen had suffered a severe defeat and had sustained many casualties; and nearly all the clans having been represented in the force opposed to us, the moral effect of the defeat was felt throughout the tribe, and for some months the Mohmands remained quiet. The success of Ayub Khan at Kandahar excited a rising which collapsed on the news of his subsequent defeat, and during the next sixteen years or more there was no recrudescence of large-scale trouble among the Mohmands on our border.

The difficulty of restraining and punishing the Mohmands had for years been intensified by the doubts which existed as to the respective spheres of influence of the British and Kabul Governments; it had been hoped that the Durand Agreement of 1893 had helped to smooth these difficulties away; but the Agreement, although apparently concurred in by the Amir, did not commend itself to his judgment on reconsideration, so far at least as the partition of control over the Mohmands was concerned. At last in 1896 the Government of India, with a view of terminating a state of indecision which had become intolerable, resolved to make an attempt to bring certain of the

Mohmand clans more immediately under British control. The efforts made in this direction were so far successful that, despite certain hostile influences— religious and political—the Halimzais, Tarakzais, Utmanzais, Dawezais, and also the Pandiali sections, were held to be henceforth in British territory, and seemed themselves cordially to concur when the new arrangement was announced to them.

When the frontier disturbances commenced in 1897 the above-named clans evinced no disposition to take part, although the Hadda Mullah, an especially notorious agitator, himself lived in the Mohmand country and had acquired a commanding influence over the clans, with some of whom he was said to have helped to defend the Malakand in 1895; and when in July the rising occurred among the men of Swat, some of the leading Mohmands among our new subjects offered their assistance to the representatives of the British Government.

Eventually the Hadda Mullah succeeded in stirring up the tribesmen, who, while unwilling to assist their co-religionists in Swat, had no objection to raid in the vicinity of their own border; and accordingly by the 7th August information had reached the authorities at Peshawar that some 3000 Mohmands were marching from Gandab to attack Shabkadar. The General Officer commanding at Peshawar proposed reinforcing Fort Shabkadar with regular troops, but this proposal was negatived by the Commissioner, who was in hopes that the Halimzais, who had so recently accepted our protection, would be able and willing to prevent the advance of the raiders.

It was, however, speedily apparent that measures so heroic were quite beyond the power of the Halimzais; they temporised, they gave information of the hostile movement, but they did not oppose the forces of the Hadda Mullah; and eventually, as was almost to be expected, many of the Halimzai fighting men enlisted under his banners.

On the afternoon of the 7th August the attack was delivered, both the fort of Shabkadar and the neighbouring village of Shankargarh being the objects of the assaults of the tribesmen, who, to the number of nearly 5000, now descended from the hills. The village was burned, but the attack on the fort was easily beaten off, and by next morning many of the enemy had retired whence they came. The news of the projected attack had reached Peshawar on the night of the 7th, and about midnight a force as under started for Shabkadar under Lieutenant-Colonel Woon, 20th Punjab Infantry :

> Four guns 51st Field Artillery.
> Two squadrons 13th Bengal Lancers.
> Two companies Somerset Light Infantry.
> 20th Punjab Infantry.

The cavalry went on in advance and reached Shabkadar early on the morning of the 8th, but the guns and infantry were much delayed in crossing the Kabul River, then in flood, by the ferry at Hajizai, and did not reach the scene of action until some hours later. With the troops available, Lieutenant-Colonel Woon moved out against the enemy, but finding them in considerable strength and occupying a favourable position, he decided against attacking, and withdrew to the fort. Early on the 9th the Shabkadar troops again advanced to the attack; the enemy, who had been reinforced during the night, had now taken up a line about two miles in length, occupied by some 6000 men, whose right rested on the higher hills; their centre extended across the low hills; while the left stretched into the cultivated ground in the plain itself. Colonel Woon began his attack in front with the infantry, intending to turn the enemy's left with the cavalry and artillery, but he could effect little or no impression on the Mohmand position, and the enemy now making a determined attempt to turn our left, Colonel Woon began to withdraw towards the fort to avoid being completely enveloped.

At this moment Brigadier-General Elles arrived upon the scene from Peshawar, and finding that most of the enemy had hurried down from the high ground and were engaged with our infantry in the open, he directed the two squadrons of the 13th Bengal Lancers to charge from right to left along the whole line of tribesmen. Charging down upon the left rear, the squadrons rode down the whole line, clearing the front; the infantry then again advanced, the Mohmands were driven back and pursued to the high ground, and in a short time not a man of them was to be seen.

Our loss was nine killed and sixty-five wounded, while among the enemy more than 200 were killed and many wounded.

The gathering seems to have been representative of almost every tribe living north of the Kabul River and between our border and that of Afghanistan, from the banks of the Swat, Panjkora and Kunar Rivers, with perhaps the single exception of the Tarakzais.

A cavalry reconnaissance was made next day, the 10th, some miles up the Gandab Valley without seeing anything of the enemy; but as the gathering, so far from having dispersed, was reported as intending to return to the attack after replenishment of ammunition and supplies, the troops at Shabkadar were made up to 2500 men, a bridge of boats was substituted for the ferry at Hajizai, telegraphic communication was established between Peshawar and Shabkadar, and fresh troops were sent up to fill the gaps in the Peshawar garrison.

While the necessity for the early chastisement of the Mohmands was recognised by the Indian Government, it was considered that, in view of the generally disturbed state of the north-west frontier, the moment was not propitious for such action, and consequently it was decided merely to concentrate two strong moveable columns, the one at Peshawar and the other at Shabkadar, ready for eventualities.

Expedition against the Mohmands, 1897.—Signs of restlessness were now being daily reported from the Afridi and Orakzai country, and finally, on the 23rd and 24th August, the smouldering embers of fanaticism in this direction burst suddenly into flames, and the Khyber forts were attacked as described in Chapter XIII.   The Hadda Mullah was once again rumoured to have taken the field with 4000 Baizai Mohmands, intending another attack upon Shabkadar; his other plan of attacking Dir, in retaliation for the friendly attitude towards us of the Khan of that country, having come to naught by reason of operations which have been elsewhere described. In consequence of these reports the Government now, during the first week in September, sanctioned extensive punitive operations against the various tribes on the Peshawar border, and decided that the Mohmands should be the first tribe to be taken in hand. Everything pointed to the operations being short and decisive, as two powerful bodies were about to move into the Mohmand country from opposite directions. Sir Bindon Blood was to act from the north and east, while Brigadier-General Elles (with the rank of Major-General), with two brigades under Brigadier-Generals Westmacott and Macgregor, would move from Shabkadar.

1ST (WESTMACOTT'S) BRIGADE.

1st Battalion Somerset Light Infantry.
20th Punjab Infantry.
2nd Battalion 1st Gurkhas.

2ND (MACGREGOR'S) BRIGADE.

2nd Battalion Oxfordshire Light Infantry.
9th Gurkhas.
37th Dogras.

DIVISIONAL TROOPS.

13th Bengal Lancers.
No. 3 Mountain Battery R.A.
No. 5 Mountain Battery R.A.

28th Bombay Pioneers.[1]

Patiala Regiment, Imperial Service Troops.

Nabha Regiment, Imperial Service Troops.

Two Maxim guns, Devonshire Regiment.

Marching out of Shabkadar on the 15th September, General Elles reached Ghalanai next day with the 1st Brigade, the 2nd Brigade getting no further than Dand, as the road, especially over the Kharappa Pass, required much work on it to make it practicable for baggage animals. On the 17th a small force under General Westmacott moved on to Katsai, two and a half miles south of the Nahaki Pass, which was reconnoitred and reported very difficult. On this day communication was established with Sir Bindon Blood, and measures were concerted for the attack on the Bedmanai Pass which the Hadda Mullah was said to be holding with a large force; the Gandab Halimzais came in at Nahaki and agreed to comply with our terms. On the 19th Westmacott's Brigade was concentrated at Nahaki, and that of General Macgregor began to close up from Dand to Ghalanai.

On the 21st September General Elles with the 1st Brigade arrived at Lakarai, where General Blood was met; and on the day following General Elles moved his force on to Khazina, where he was joined by the 3rd Brigade of the Malakand Field Force, placed at his disposal by General Blood, to enable him to deal with the gathering at the Bedmanai Pass and to clear the Mitai and Suran Valleys. The Nahaki Pass, dominating the whole of this part of the Mohmand

[1] Now the 128th Pioneers.

country, was now held by troops of Macgregor's brigade.

The Bedmanai Pass lies some five miles west-south-west of Khazina. The track leading thence to the pass runs along the bed of a broad dry nullah, and about a mile and a half further on, a narrow gap, between the Gharibai Hill and the northern end of a spur jutting out from the Yari Sar Mountain, gives entrance to a broad valley. Crossing this, four small villages are passed, and the path winds upwards along the nullah through a narrow gorge, until the summit of the pass, commanded from the highest point of Yari Sar, is reached.

On the morning of the 23rd the troops moved forward and, after some opposition, carried the Bed-manai Pass, the capture of which, contrary to expecta-tion, proved tolerably easy of accomplishment, as not more than 700 or 800 Mohmands, chiefly Baizais, were present. As to the actual assault, the 20th Punjab Infantry led and were opposed on every ridge, and the men of this regiment particularly distinguished themselves in clearing the heights, well supported by the fire of the guns and Maxims. The attached brigade meanwhile moved in support of General Westmacott up the centre and guarding the right flank, and was only slightly engaged, our casualties totalling no more than four. This easy victory was attributable to the heavy losses which the men led by the Hadda Mullah, had already experienced in their attack upon General Blood before described. That, their real effort, had failed, and they had very little heart for

further fighting; also General Elles had previously so
disposed his cavalry as to prevent any help reaching
the defenders of the Bedmanai Pass from the Mitai
and Suran Valleys.

During the two following days these valleys were
visited and towers were destroyed. The attached
brigade now left to join the Tirah Expeditionary
Force, marching via Nahaki and Gandab to Peshawar; and General Elles prepared to move on Jarobi,
where, in the most rugged and inaccessible part of
the Baizai Mohmand country, a glen at the head of
the Shindarra Valley, was the home of the Hadda
Mullah. The road thither was found to be very
difficult, but the opposition was not formidable, only
some nineteen casualties being experienced.

During the next few days the troops were employed
in marching through the Bohai Dag and adjacent
valleys, demolishing the defences of the Baizai Mohmands and exacting submission. The opposition here
was rather more formidable but was easily broken
down. The clans now began to give in: the
Khwaezai, Halimzai, Utmanzai, Dawezai jirgahs
arrived asking for terms, the acceptance of which
was expedited by the troops continuing to visit the
· uttermost parts of the country; and by the 3rd
October all our claims had been met and the force
returned to Peshawar, where, on the 7th, it was
broken up.

The objects of the expedition had been accomplished. All concerned in the raid on Shabkadar
had been punished; the Hadda Mullah had been

discredited, his dwelling destroyed and he himself driven into Afghan territory; and the Mohmand country had been traversed from end to end.

That these operations did not, however, immediately initiate a period of absolute quiet on the Border, goes without saying. There were outbreaks and raids upon villages close to our frontier and within the territories of tribes which had come under our protection; and it was very apparent that the Indian Government could exercise but little more than a nominal authority over any of the clans of the Mohmand tribe. Still, some advance had been made, and when in 1906 an extension of the railway was commenced from Peshawar to the Afghan frontier through Shilman, the Mohmands did not offer any really serious opposition to the undertaking.[1]

In March, 1908, three rather serious raids were carried out in our territory by Mohmand tribesmen —at the village of Marozai, six miles north-east of Shankargarh (Shabkadar); at Mirzadhar, two miles from Marozai; and at Chikkar, nine miles south-east of Shankargarh.

All three raids were believed to be the work of men of the Mohmand gathering which collected at the end of the Zakha Khel expedition, as mentioned in Chapter XIII.; in consequence of these outrages the posts at Abazai and Shabkadar were strengthened. Early in April, however, the mullahs began to preach against the British in Ningrahar, and within a few

[1] The permanent way and girders of this Loi-Shilman extension of the N.W. Railway were removed in the winter of 1911-12.

days had succeeded in collecting a large following
of Mohmands with the reported object of attacking
Shabkadar. The movement spread, villagers in masses
joined the force, and by the 17th it was computed
that some 5000 men, including 2000 Afghans, were
gathered together under Hazrat Mullah in Kamali,
to the north-west of Halimzai territory. It is not
surprising under the circumstances that the Chief
Commissioner, North-West Frontier Province, detected
danger of a fanatical outbreak.

Within four days the numbers of the Mohmand
lashkar had increased to 10,000 men, our post at
Matta was fired into, and on the 21st General
Anderson, with two guns and 1000 bayonets, moved
out from Peshawar, to which place troops were sent
forward from Nowshera. At Matta and Shabkadar,
and towards the Mohmands generally, General Willcocks, commanding at Peshawar, occupied, according
to instructions, a purely defensive advanced position,
the object being to prevent any collision and to offer
no possible ground for Mohmand attack. It was, however, abundantly clear that the fanatical feeling against
us was spreading, that *ghaza* was being preached,
and that men were flocking to the standards of the
mullahs from Bajaur, Utman Khel territory, Asmar,
Kohistan and Kunar, while grain, ammunition and
money were being sent down to the Mohmands from
Ningrahar.

On the 23rd considerable bodies of the enemy occupied the foothills just across our border opposite Abazai,
and General Willcocks accordingly, considering that

the Mohmands probably intended assuming the offensive, ordered up additional troops from Peshawar to Shabkadar, and with their arrival he had, on the line Abazai-Shabkadar-Michni, 2700 infantry, 520 sabres and twelve guns.

Expedition against the Mohmands, 1908.—The authorities at home and at Simla now concurred in thinking that no good purpose was likely to be served by the maintenance of the mere defensive, and that it would probably be a safer policy to advance and disperse the gathering before it became larger and led to a big fanatical outbreak. The immediate mobilisation of two brigades with divisional troops and a reserve was ordered. General Willcocks was placed in command, and directed to cross the border and assume the offensive. The force was thus composed :

FIRST BRIGADE.

Brigadier-General Anderson.

1st Battalion Northumberland Fusiliers.
53rd Sikhs.
57th Wilde's Rifles.
59th Scinde Rifles.

SECOND BRIGADE.

Major-General Barrett.

1st Battalion Seaforth Highlanders.
Guides Infantry.
28th Punjabis.
55th Coke's Rifles.

RESERVE BRIGADE.

Major-General Ramsay.

1st Battalion Royal Munster Fusiliers.
21st Punjabis.
22nd Punjabis.
40th Pathans.

This brigade to proceed to Peshawar.

DIVISIONAL TROOPS.

21st Cavalry.
No. 8. M.B.R.G.A.
23rd Peshawar Mountain Battery.
28th Mountain Battery.
No. 6 Company Sappers and Miners.
No. 1 Company Sappers and Miners.
34th Sikh Pioneers.

The troops being for the most part all on the spot, in consequence of the conclusion, then just arrived at, of the Zakha Khel expedition, no time was lost, and on the 24th April an advance was made with all troops available at Shabkadar and Matta, when the enemy's positions to the west of these posts were attacked and captured. A heavy blow was inflicted on the Mohmands, and a reconnaissance, carried out on the following day, found no signs of them about their former positions or in the Gandab Valley. It was, however, very clear that the rising was not crushed; the mullahs were doing their best to enlist recruits in Dir and Swat, and an attempt was also being made to induce the Zakha Khels to join, so far,

however, without success; but there seemed small
doubt that all branches of the Mohmands were represented in the recent actions with our columns from
Matta and Shabkadar. For some few days after the
dispersal of the gathering in front of Shabkadar, the
British troops remained inactive, in order to see
whether the assembly of the tribal jirgah, which had
been arranged for, would enable General Willcocks to
arrive at reasonable terms.

It had been hoped that the disinclination shown by
the tribes of Dir, Swat, Bajaur and the Bazar Valley
to make common cause with the Mohmands, and the
difficulty of keeping the lashkar in the field, would
have led to the gradual dispersal of the whole gathering, especially in view of the projected meeting of the
jirgah on the 4th May.

On the 2nd May, however, the Viceroy telegraphed
to the India Office explaining that the centre of unrest
had now shifted to the Khyber, where for some time
past at Pesh-Bolak one Sufi Sahib, a noted firebrand,
had been collecting a force of Afghans. This army,
whose numbers were estimated at anything between
13,000 and 20,000 men, had already passed Lundi
Khana, and was believed to intend an attack on the
fortified serai at Lundi Kotal that evening, and possibly also on Ali Musjid and the fort at Chora belonging to the Malikdin Khel chief, who had often proved
himself our friend.

In consequence of the threatening aspect of affairs
troops were despatched to Jamrud with a view to
rendering assistance, and the Mohmand Field Force

was directed to remain strictly on the defensive. The General Officer left in command was further instructed, when the jirgah assembled, to observe a temporising policy, encouraging attendance and requiring an explanation of past conduct, but neither announcing terms nor making any definite communication. Recognising also that the greater danger was now threatening from the Khyber, the larger part of the force present under General Willcocks at Shabkadar and Peshawar was drawn to the pass.

The Reserve Brigade, under General Ramsay, reached Lundi Kotal on the 3rd May, while that under General Barrett marched to Ali Musjid; General Anderson remained at Shabkadar with his brigade in observation of the Mohmands.

On the night of the 2nd May repeated efforts had been made by the Khyber gathering (which appeared to be entirely composed of Afghans, no Afridis having joined it), to capture our post of Michni Kandao, which was ably defended by Subadar Tor Khan of the Khyber Rifles. Lundi Kotal was also fired into, and several attempts made to burn the serai, but these were all beaten off, although firing took place daily. On the 4th General Willcocks felt himself strong enough to attack, and moved out from Lundi Kotal in two columns against the enemy, who occupied the Shinwari villages about 4000 yards to the west. One column consisted of Ramsay's infantry brigade, with the 80th Battery R.F.A. and the 28th Mountain Battery, while the other was under

R

Colonel Roos-Keppel, and was composed of fifty dismounted men 19th Lancers, two companies 21st Punjabis, and 500 of the Khyber Rifles. The enemy were driven from their sangars and the shelter of the villages, and, having suffered severely, disappeared over the Afghan boundary. It being apparent that nothing further was to be apprehended on this part of the frontier, the troops left Lundi Kotal on the 7th, and were back in Peshawar on the 8th and 9th, having left behind two mountain guns at Lundi Kotal and the 54th Sikhs at Jamrud.

During the absence of the force all had remained quiet on the Mohmand-Peshawar border from Michni to Abazai, but there were signs of a general disinclination to send tribal representatives to a jirgah; and finally, on the 9th May—by which date the limit of time allowed had expired—news arrived of the refusal of some maliks to come in, and of the receipt of insulting messages from others. It was therefore decided, on the 10th May, to send troops into the Mohmand country, and the advance commenced accordingly on the 13th.

In the meantime cases of cholera had occurred among the troops, and certain changes became inevitable in the composition of the Mohmand Field Force. In the 1st Brigade the 22nd Punjabis replaced the 1st Battalion Northumberland Fusiliers; in the 2nd Brigade the 54th Sikhs replaced the Guides Infantry, relegated, with the 21st Punjabis, to the lines of communication beyond Shabkadar; while in the 3rd Brigade the 1st Battalion West Yorkshire

Regiment and the 19th Punjabis replaced the Munster
Fusiliers and the 22nd Punjabis.

Nahaki was occupied on the 14th by part of the
1st Brigade without opposition, but a reconnaissance
made to the Khapakh Pass was fired on, and it was
found to be held in strength. Both brigades closed
up on the 16th at Nahaki, and while here the camp
of the 1st Brigade was attacked in a most determined manner on the nights of the 16th and 18th.
The enemy lost heavily on both occasions, but inflicted
considerable loss upon our troops. On the 17th all
the force was engaged in destroying the towers of
villages belonging to Kandahari Safis and Halimzais ;
and on the next day the 2nd Brigade proceeded up
the Bohai Dag to destroy the headquarters of the
Hazrat Mullah, and met with strong opposition from
the Khwaezais, Baizais and others near Zarawar China,
the hills on both sides of the valley being held. The
enemy were dislodged, with heavy loss, by the 28th
and 55th. This brigade returned to Nahaki on the
20th, and the 1st moved north towards Lakarai, and
found the enemy holding in considerable strength the
village of Umra Kilai, with a deep and very intricate
nullah behind and hills beyond. They were driven
off after a stubborn resistance, during which their
leaders repeatedly led charges with swords. The
Mohmand losses were consequently very heavy, but
none the less they made some half-hearted attacks on
the bivouac during the night. Our casualties were
five killed and seventeen wounded.

During the next day several towers between

Nahaki and Lakarai were destroyed, a measure which resulted in some of the clans beginning to come in and submit.

On the 23rd the 1st Brigade moved from Lakarai to Shato Khel with only slight opposition, and on the day following to Kargha; the enemy had prepared and held a strong position at the entrance to Ambahar, but on their left flank being turned they fled, pursued by the cavalry, and heavily punished by the fire of the infantry. On the 27th General Willcocks returned, via Mulla Kilai, to Nahaki, and by this day the recalcitrant Utmanzai, Dawezai and Khwaezai had sent in jirgahs and submitted. There only remained the Khuda Khel Baizais, and their country was visited by the 2nd Brigade from Nahaki on the 28th, and this division was severely punished.

The force began its retirement to India on this date, and on the 1st June the last troops of the Mohmand Field Force had recrossed the border. Our casualties had been rather heavy for so short a campaign— 38 killed or died of wounds and 184 wounded; 51 succumbed to disease.

There does not appear to be any reason to believe that the continuation of the work on the Loi-Shilman railway had any connection with the Mohmand rising of 1908. The Tarakzai Mohmands are the only clan whose country abuts on the proposed line, and these do not seem to have taken any part in the fighting of that year.

CHAPTER XI.

AFRIDIS.[1]

THE Afridis are a large tribe, inhabiting the lower and easternmost spurs of the Safed Koh Range, to the west and south of the Peshawar district, including the Bazar and Bara Valleys. On the east they are bounded by British territory; on their north they have the Mohmands; west, the Shinwaris; and south, the Orakzais and Bangash.

Their origin is very obscure; Bellew identifies them with one of the peoples referred to by Herodotus; their traditions, however, says James, would lead us to believe that, in common with other Pathan tribes, they are the descendants of Khalid-ibn-Walid, a Jew, who embraced Islamism, and whose descendants had possession of great tracts in the western portion of Afghanistan during the tenth century. At this time, upon the convulsions in the country owing to the advance of Mahmud of Ghazni, a chief named Afrid was obliged, owing to his enormities and feuds, to fly from his country and seek refuge with a kindred spirit, by name Wazir, in the wilds of Shir-i-Talla. Here he seems to have settled and to have remained

[1] See Map VII.

with his family for a considerable time. Turner gives
something of the same story, viz. that Afrid, an individual of unknown country and parentage, came to
Ghor, and there had an intrigue with a woman of the
Karerai tribe, the eventual result of which was the
tribe of Afridis. Cavagnari says of their origin that
they are supposed to have been descended from a
woman named Maimana, who had two sons, Afrid
and Adam. But it is probably sufficient to surmise
that they are a tribe of Pactiyan stock, who have
been established in their present country for many
centuries—far longer than the majority of Pathan
tribes—and that living as they do on the high road
from Central Asia to India, it is likely that they have
a large admixture of Turkish and Scythian blood.

The Afridi country being bleak and sterile, and
the rainfall but small, agriculture is only scantily
pursued, although they raise a coarse kind of rice
in the Bara Valley, a considerable amount of which
finds its way to the Peshawar market. Some of the
tribe also gain a precarious living by cutting and
selling timber for firewood, but many of the clans
possess great stock in cattle, cows, sheep and goats,
and go in for breeding mules and donkeys, which are
much thought of locally. Their chief manufactures
are coarse mats and cloth, while in Maidan, at Ilmgudar near Fort Bara, and in the Kohat Pass there
are factories which annually turn out a certain
number of rifles.

The Afridi in appearance is generally a fine, tall,
athletic highlander, whose springy step at once denotes

his mountain origin. They are lean but muscular men, with long, gaunt faces, high noses and cheekbones, and rather fair complexions. Brave and hardy, they make good soldiers, but are apt to be somewhat homesick in the hot weather, and they have gained a greater reputation for fidelity as soldiers than in any other way. The Afridi has uniformly shown himself ready to enlist in our army, and at the present moment there are probably 4000 of this tribe serving in the ranks of the Indian army or in the Khyber Rifles. But since the Pathan is notoriously restless and dislikes expatriation, the average length of service is shorter than in the case of our other Indian soldiers; the result being that a greater number of trained soldiers from Pathan squadrons and companies annually pass back to their homes, than is the case with a proportionately larger establishment of any other race. While, therefore, their loyalty, while actually in our service and even during frontier expeditions against their own kinsmen, has been all that could be wished, it is not perhaps saying much—considering their normal family relations—that they should cheerfully fight for us against them. But, on the other hand, it can hardly be expected that men who have become again merged in their tribe, and who, according to their own ideas, are no longer bound to us by any obligation, should maintain an attitude of complete aloofness from any tribal movement prompted by racial feeling, or by that fanaticism which, on the border, has been defined as "a sentiment of religious intolerance excited into reckless action." During the Tirah Campaign the number of pensioners and reservists who fought against our troops is believed to have been very large. As long ago as 1884 it was stated of the Afridis that "almost every fighting man possesses a gun or pistol, besides other arms; many of the fire-arms are rifled, and some have percussion locks." To-day the armament of these tribesmen is far more complete and up-to-date,[1] and there can be no doubt that the fighting powers of the Afridis have increased during recent years to a very formidable extent. At the same time our powers of effectively dealing with them have increased in a still greater ratio. Our soldiers are more suitably trained for the particular warfare waged in these border hills; they are infinitely better armed; the services of transport and supply are more efficiently organised; the country of the independent tribesmen is more thoroughly known; the moral effect of uniformly successful expeditions— are all factors which more than counterbalance any accession of strength which the last twenty-five years have brought to the Afridis.

As to the measures to be taken effectually to coerce them, Oliver, writing twenty-two years ago, said that "strong as are the natural positions they hold among the spurs and defiles of the Safed Koh and the bare, rugged, inhospitable ranges of the Khyber; difficult of approach the passes which might have to be forced, and unanimous as the clans may be to defend them at the signal of a common danger, the people are so

[1] Particulars of the sources of supply of rifles will be found in Appendix A.

dependent on the plains, their position—secure though it may sound—is really their weakest point, and makes it easy to shut them up in their own hills. Peshawar, the great field for their plundering operations, is also the market for their produce and the source of supply for their many domestic wants. Exclusion from Peshawar is to many clans a severe form of punishment; and an effectual blockade that will cut them off from the outer world, would probably bring them to terms sooner than an expedition." But Holdich again reminds us that "across those wild break-neck passes over the Safed Koh into Ningrahar . . . the hard-pressed Afridi can constantly find refuge for his family, and sanctuary for himself, amongst the Durani tribes who dwell on the northern slopes of the Safed Koh." That there is always that back-door, "the keys of which are in their own pockets," and that "at the worst they could shift across the hills into Afghanistan, and there was the prospect . . . that something more than mere shelter would be accorded by the ruler of Kabul."

Of the moral attributes of the Afridis few people have found much to say in praise. Mackeson wrote of them: "The Afridis are a most avaricious race, desperately fond of money. Their fidelity is measured by the length of the purse of the seducer, and they transfer their obedience and support from one party to another of their own clansmen, according to the comparative liberality of the donation." Elphinstone, generally ready enough to record anything good of Afghans, said of the Afridis: "On the whole they are the greatest robbers among the Afghans, and, I imagine, have no faith or sense of honour; for I never heard of anybody hiring an escort of Khaiberis to secure his passage through their country—a step which always ensures a traveller's safety in the lands of any other tribe." MacGregor considers this estimate harsh, but that furnished by the same authority is hardly more flattering: "A ruthless, cowardly robber—a cold-blooded treacherous murderer; brought up from his earliest childhood amid scenes of appalling treachery and merciless revenge, nothing has changed him; as he has lived—a shameless, cruel savage—so he dies. And it would seem that, notwithstanding his long intercourse with us, and the fact that large numbers have been and are in our service, and must have learnt in some way what faith, justice and mercy mean, yet the Afridi is no better than in the days of his father." Against these adverse testimonies, however, there is the opinion of Sir Robert Warburton, who spent eighteen years in their midst and who wrote of them: "The Afridi lad from his earliest childhood is taught by the circumstances of his existence and life to distrust all mankind, and very often his near relations, heirs to his small plot of land by inheritance, are his deadliest enemies. Distrust of all mankind, and readiness to strike the first blow for the safety of his own life, have therefore become the maxims of the Afridi. If you can overcome this mistrust, and be kind in words to him, he will repay you by great devotion, and he will put up with any punishment you like to give him except abuse. It took me years to get through this thick crust of mistrust, but what was the after-result? For upwards of fifteen years I went about unarmed amongst these people. My camp, wherever it happened to be pitched, was always guarded and protected by them. The deadliest enemies of the Khyber range, with a long record of blood-feuds, dropped those feuds for the time being when in my camp. Property was always safe. . . . Time after time have the Afridi elders and jirgahs supported me even against their own Maliks."

Notwithstanding all that has been said against the Afridi he is, on the whole, one of the finest of the Pathan races on our border. His appearance is greatly in his favour, and he is really braver, more open, and not more treacherous than many other Pathans. This much is certain, that he has the power of prejudicing Englishmen in his favour, and there are few brought into contact with him who do not at least begin with an enthusiastic admiration for his manliness. Again, with a tight hand over him, many of his faults remain dormant, and he soon develops into a valuable soldier.

Though eternally at feud among themselves, they seldom quarrel with neighbouring tribes; that is, the Afridis do not care to waste their energies in fighting with their neighbours, but reserve the luxury for home consumption—a feud to an Afridi is the salt of life, the one pleasure that makes existence tolerable. On occasion, in the face of common danger, they are capable of concerted action, as was shown in the Tirah Campaign of 1897, but even then one clan held entirely aloof. Though nominally under the control of their Maliks, the Afridis have very little respect for their authority and are thoroughly democratic. They are all of the Sunni persuasion of the Muhammadan faith.

The following are the eight clans into which the Afridi tribe is divided, and of these the first six are known collectively as the "Khyber Afridis" :

1. Kuki Khel.
2. Malikdin Khel.
3. Kambar Khel.
4. Kamrai or Kamar Khel.
5. Zakha Khel.
6. Sipah.
7. Aka Khel.
8. Adam Khel.

The *Aka Khels* have no connection with the Khyber and are located to the south of the Bara River. The *Adam Khels* inhabit the hills between the districts of Kohat and Peshawar, and cannot be regarded, except ethnologically, as a part of the Afridi tribe; for whether they are viewed with reference to their position, their interests or their habits, they are a distinct community.

The area of the country inhabited by the Afridis is about nine hundred square miles. The principal streams draining their hills are the northern branch of the Bara River, or Bara proper, the Bazar or Chora River, and the Khyber stream, all flowing into the Peshawar Valley. The valleys lying near the sources of the Bara River are included in the general name of Tirah, which comprises an area of 600 to 700 square miles. The greater part of Tirah is inhabited by different clans of the Orakzai tribe, but the valleys known as Rajgal and Maidan are occupied by the Afridis. The Rajgal Valley is drained by one main stream, into which fall some lesser streams from the surrounding hills. Its length is about ten miles, and the breadth of the open country about four to five miles. The elevation is over 5000. Maidan lies to the south of Rajgal, and is a circular valley about ten miles across, watered by several large watercourses. The streams from Rajgal and Maidan unite and form the Bara River, flowing down the valley of the same name to the Kajurai Plain, shortly before entering which the Bara is joined by the Mastura River.

The *Kuki Khel* number some 5600 fighting men, and occupy the Rajgal valley and the eastern end of the Khyber Pass, as far as the Rohtas Hill, which overhangs the fort at Ali Musjid, and also the Bezai Spur—a long underfeature which flanks, but at a considerable distance, the latter part of the railway and road from Peshawar to Fort Jumrud. This clan has a bitter feud with the Zakha Khel, and is Gar in politics.

The *Malikdin Khel* is the Khan Khel or head clan of the Afridis, and is closely connected with the Kambar Khel, their settlements in Maidan, Chora and Kajurai lying together. In Maidan they occupy the central and northern portion of the valley— Bagh, the recognised meeting place of the Afridi Jirgahs, " where the Khyber raid and Afridi rebellion of 1897-98 were planned, and where fanaticism, intrigue and sedition have always been hot-bedded and nourished," being in their country. The Malikdin Khels number some 6000 fighting men, and are Samil in politics.

The *Kambar Khel* is numerically the most powerful of all the Afridi clans, being able on emergency to put 10,000 armed men in the field; they belong to the Gar political faction. This clan is very migratory, occupying in the hot weather the Kahu Darra and the valley of the Shalobar River, which joins the Bara River at Dwatoi, and moving in the winter to the Kajurai Plain and to other minor settlements. This clan is very strongly represented in the Indian Army and Border Militia.

The *Kamrai* or *Kumar Khel* form but a small clan, Samil in politics, having its settlements in the extreme west of the Bara Valley, and also moving down to the Kajurai Valley to the west of Peshawar in the winter months. Their fighting men number no more than about 800.

The *Zakha Khel* owe their undoubted importance to their geographical position in Afridi-land, rather than to the number of armed men they can turn out— probably not less than 6000. Their holdings stretch diagonally across the Afridi country from the southeast corner of Maidan to the Khyber Pass; they are the wildest and most turbulent amongst their tribe, and their land being unproductive they depend a good deal upon raiding and blackmail for their livelihood, are "the wolves of the community," and since— at any rate up to recent times—"they lent no soldiers

to the ranks of the British army and had no pensions
to lose," the Zakha Khels have always been more
ready to give trouble than the rest of their fellow-
tribesmen.   They hold, moreover, some five miles of
the country lying on either side of the road in what
Warburton calls "the real Khyber proper," from the
Shrine of Gurgurra (the sloe-tree)—where a small
post is held by the Khyber Rifles—to Loargai in the
Shinwari country.   Of this shrine Warburton tells
the following story of the manner in which the Zakha
Khels managed to remove the reproach which had
been levelled against them, *i.e.* that their country
possessed none of the ziarats, or sacred shrines, to
the memory of saints or martyrs.   "The Zakha Khel
Afridis," writes Warburton, "bear a most unenviable
name as being the greatest thieves, housebreakers,
robbers and raiders amongst all the Khyber clans,
their word or promise never being believed or trusted
by their Afridi brethren without a substantial security
being taken for its fulfilment.   Naturally a race so
little trusted were not fortunate enough to possess a
holy man whose tomb would have served as a sanctuary to swear by, and thus save the necessity of the
substantial security.   One day, however, a Kaka Khel
Mia came into their limits with the object of seeking
safe conduct through their territory to the next tribe.
They received him with all politeness, but finding in
the course of conversation that he was of saintly
character—a holy Kaka Khel Mia—they came to the
conclusion that he was just the individual wanted to
put their character for truthfulness on a better footing.

They therefore killed him and buried him, making his tomb a shrine for all true believers to reverence, and a security for themselves to swear by."

Oliver caps this story with another of the same character : "A Mullah was caught copying the Koran. 'You tell us these books come from God, and here you are making them yourself. It is not good for a Mullah to tell lies'; so the indignant Afridis made another ziarat for him."

It is only quite within recent years that the Zakha Khels have taken to military service, and even now the number enlisted in the regular Indian army is relatively small, the majority preferring service near their homes and joining the Khyber Rifles. In politics the Zakha Khels are Samil.

The *Sipah* is only a small clan, Samil in politics, and cherishing a standing feud with the Aka Khels. Their main settlements are in the upper portion of the Bara Valley, with the Zakha Khel bordering them on one side and the Kambar Khel on the other, while they also have settlements in the Kajurai plain, where is their notorious rifle factory at Ilmgudar.

Ranken defines the tribal limits in the Khyber Pass as follows : "The Kuki Khels from Jumrud to where the Mackeson road begins ; the Sipah Afridis from the beginning of the Mackeson road to Shagai ; the Kambar Khel from Sultan Tarra to the white mosque of Ali Musjid ; the Malikdin Khel from the mosque to Gurgurra ; the Zakha Khel from Gurgurra to the Kandar ravine near Garhi Lalabeg ; and the Shinwaris westward of Torkhan."

The above-mentioned six clans are known collectively, as already mentioned, as the "Khyber Pass Afridis." British connection with them commenced as far back as 1839, when a Sikh force under Colonel Wade, and Shah Shuja's contingent with British officers, forced the Khyber—of which the actual defile may be said to be in the hands of these half-dozen clans. "In our earlier Afghan campaigns they fully maintained their ancient fame," writes Oliver, "as bold and faithless robbers, but from the time the Punjab was annexed, up to the second Afghan War, their behaviour was, for Afridis, fairly good. In 1878 some of the clans took sides with us, and some with the Amir, necessitating a couple of expeditions into the Bazar Valley," and during the two phases of the campaign not less than 15,000 fighting men were required to keep open our communications with India by the Khyber route, despite the arrangement which had been come to with the clans bordering on the Khyber, and which will now be described.

When, in 1878, the Government of India called upon the Commander-in-Chief to put forward proposals for the conduct of a campaign in Afghanistan, Sir Frederick Haines offered the suggestion, *inter alia*, that "a demonstration should be made early in the operations of an advance by the Khyber, by encamping out a certain proportion of the Peshawar troops, making arrangements with the Khyberis for their passage through the pass." [1]   In consequence of the

[1] *The Second Afghan War, abridged official account.*

8

above, Major Cavagnari was instructed to come to a
friendly understanding with the Khyber Pass Afridis,
and to arrange for the passage of troops through the
defiles at certain rates. Major Cavagnari based his
estimate of the money payments to be made to the
headmen of the clans, on the sums paid by Colonel
Mackeson for the same purpose during the latter
period of the first Afghan War; and he finally com-
pounded with the six clans of Khyber Afridis for a
payment of Rs.5950 per mensem, which sum was
willingly accepted. When, in September 1880, northern Afghanistan was finally evacuated by our troops,
the Indian Government, recognising the undesirability
of maintaining any regular force in the Khyber, expressed a wish to hand the pass over entirely to the
independent charge of the neighbouring clans, provided some wholly satisfactory arrangement could be
come to for keeping the road open, and for safeguarding
the caravans passing to and fro between Afghanistan
and India. Early in 1881 a complete jirgah of all
the Khyber clans assembled in Peshawar, and an
agreement was arrived at whereby the independence
of the Afridis was recognised, and they engaged, in
consideration of certain allowances, to maintain order
throughout the Khyber; the Government of India
reserved the right of re-occupation of the pass, and
was to take all tolls; the Afridis providing a force of
Jazailchis paid for by the Indian Government, and
were to deal by a general jirgah with all offences
committed on the road. The allowances were fixed
at Rs.85,860 per annum for the six clans immediately

concerned with the policing of the pass, and for the
Shinwaris of Loargai ; and a further sum of approximately the same amount was guaranteed by the
Government of India for the upkeep of the Jazailchis
—since improved into the Khyber Rifles—a body
about 550 strong. As a set-off against these money
grants the tolls on caravans amounted to some 60,000
rupees per annum. The allowances then granted are
to-day substantially the same ; the pass is again in
charge of the Khyber Afridis, and is again guarded,
from Jumrud to Lundi Kotal, by the Khyber Rifles,
who have, however, been completely reorganised, and
are now a body 1700 strong, with six British officers.

Of that portion of the Khyber which is under our
own control the following description is given by
Warburton : " The main road from Peshawar to
Kabul passes through Jumrud, going almost due east
to west. After leaving Jumrud it passes through
an easy country, having low hills on the left hand
side, and about the third mile it enters the hills
at an opening called Shadi Bagiar. A ridge from
the lofty Ghund-ghar on the left runs down to the
road, and faces a similar ridge coming down from a
prolongation of the Rhotas Range. The highway runs
for a short distance through the bed of a ravine, and
then joins the road made by Colonel Mackeson in
1839-42, until it ascends to the Shagai Plateau on the
left hand side, and here Ali Musjid is seen for the first
time. Still going westward the road turns to the
right, and by an easy zigzag descends to the stream
and runs along its side, and below Ali Musjid goes up

the waterway. The new road along the cliff was made by us in 1879-80, and here is the narrowest part of the Khyber, not more than fifteen feet broad with the Rhotas hill on the right hand fully 2000 feet overhead. Still progressing, at about 400 yards from Ali Musjid, on the left hand side, three or four large springs issuing from the rock give the whole water supply to this quarter. Between two and three miles comes the Malikdin Khel hamlet of Katta Kushtia; soon after Gurgurra is reached, and then we are in Zakha Khel limits in the real Khyber proper, until we come to the Shinwaris of Lundi Kotal, or more properly Loargai. The valley now widens out, and on either side lie the hamlets and some sixty forts of the Zakha Khel Afridis. Here, there is no stream, and the residents have to depend on rainwater collected in tanks. The Loargai Shinwari Plateau is some seven miles in length, and there is its widest part. Just here above Lundi Khana, the old road was a very nasty bit. . . . From Shadi Bagiar to Lundi Khana the pass cannot be more than twenty miles in a direct line. When the first detachment of our troops returned from Kabul,[1] they marched from Ali Musjid along the bed of the stream, by Lala China, Jabagai, Gagri, Kaddam, 'the real gate,' and Jam, villages of the Kuki Khel Afridis, to Jumrud; but Colonel Mackeson, finding this way extremely difficult and unsuitable for guns and wheeled traffic, made an excellent road from Ali Musjid to Fort Jumrud through the hills, the same that we now use."

The trans-frontier portion of the Khyber route to

[1] During the first Afghan War.

Kabul is described by Oliver as follows : " Over the
Lundi Khana Pass, called the Kotal,[1] the road rises
by a steep ascent between steep cliffs less than 150
feet apart, and down again till the Valley of the
Kabul River is reached at Dakka. . . .   At Jalalabad
—ninety miles from Peshawar—the cross ranges of
hills are, for a change, replaced by a well-watered
fertile stretch of country, a score of miles long by a
dozen wide, dotted with towers, villages and trees ;
and where the Kabul River—that has all along had
to struggle through mere cracks—becomes a broad
clear stream 100 yards wide.   Thence the route lies
through a thoroughly unattractive country again,
over long stony ridges, across rocky river-beds, varied
with an occasional fine valley like Fathabad, or an
oasis like Nimlah, to Gandamak, which, by way of
comparison with what is beyond again, is a land flowing with milk and honey ; for on by Jagdalak and
the Lataband Pass, or Tezin and the Khurd Kabul, is
a wild waste of bare hills, surrounded by still more
lofty and forbidding mountains.   The teeth become
more closely set together ; the road narrower ; the
stony ridges change to bleak heights from 7000 to
8000 feet high, the river beds, deep valleys, or narrow
defiles, like the fatal Jagdalak, almost devoid of
verdure, and into whose gloomy ravines the winter
sun can hardly penetrate—these are the outworks
that have to be negotiated before the gardens and
orchards, the bazaars and forts of Kabul, can be
approached."

[1] On the frontier, the word " Kandao " is frequently used for Pass.

The *Aka Khel* clan occupies the hills to the south-west of Peshawar between the Bara River and the country of the Adam Khels, also the Bara and the Waran Valleys. It was in the Waran Valley and in the house of that firebrand among the border clergy, Saiyid Akbar, that there was found, during the course of the Tirah expedition, the whole of the inflammatory correspondence which had passed between the Afridi maliks and mullahs prior to and during the Pathan revolt of 1897. This clan is Samil in politics and can put 4000 armed men in the field.

The *Adam Khel* clan is located in the hills between Peshawar and Kohat, being bounded on the north and east by the Khattaks, on the south by the Bangash, and on the west by the Aka Khels (their deadly enemies), and by the Orakzais. They are one of the most powerful and numerous of the Afridi clans, have a great reputation for bravery, and can bring into the field 6500 fighting men, who, moreover, are unusually well-armed, with rifles stolen from our cantonments and with those they manufacture themselves at their factories in the Kohat Pass. They are to a small extent cultivators, but their chief occupation is carrying salt from the mines; while the allowance they receive from the Indian Government for keeping open the Kohat-Peshawar road is an assistance to their revenues, an allowance which has been paid them since the days of the Sikh governors of Peshawar. The Adam Khels do not belong to either of the two great political factions. From the situation of the Adam Khel country, and owing to the fact that

their very existence is dependent upon their trade
with British territory, this particular clan is very
susceptible to a blockade and can consequently be
easily brought to terms. Nearly all the trouble we
have had with the Adam Khels in the past has been
due to disputes about the salt tax, or about the maintenance of a practicable road through the Kohat Pass.
This short cut from Peshawar to Kohat has a certain
strategic value; by this road the two frontier garrisons
are no more than thirty-seven miles apart, and only
ten of these are in independent territory, while round
by railway, via Khushalgarh on the Indus, the distance
is 200 miles. Two divisions of the Adam Khels are
the actual keepers of the pass, and though we pay,
and have paid for years, a considerable subsidy, until
comparatively lately we were not allowed to make a
road, or even to remove the boulders that obstructed
the path. From about 1865 onwards the question of
the construction of a road practicable for wheeled
traffic was continually raised, and was as often dropped
in face of tribal opposition. It was one of the main
objects of the expedition of 1877, but was given up
by Lord Lytton to avoid "breaking the spirit of the
clan," who evinced their gratitude the year following
—that of the Afghan War—by threatening to close
the road to us. This threat came, however, to nothing,
and the pass formed, throughout the campaign, an
unmolested and important means of communication
between Peshawar and Kohat. Water is very scarce
in the pass, the supply being dependent mainly upon
tanks.

During the risings of 1897-98 the Adam Khels remained perfectly quiet, and troops constantly used the pass, through which at last, in 1901, a metalled cart-road was made.

CHAPTER XII.

AFRIDIS: OPERATIONS.[1]

ADAM KHELS.

As has been already mentioned, British connection with the Afridis as a tribe commenced in 1839, when Colonel Wade, with a contingent of Sikh troops, forced the Khyber Pass. The first occasion, however, after the annexation of the Peshawar Valley, upon which we came into actual conflict with any of the clan, was in 1850. In the previous year, following the example of former governors of Peshawar, the British entered into an agreement with the Adam Khel, or Kohat Pass Afridis, to pay them Rs. 5700 per annum, in consideration of which they were to protect and keep open the road through the pass connecting Peshawar and Kohat. The agreement had not, however, been in force a year, when a party of our Sappers, road-making in British territory on the Kohat side of the pass, were surprised by a body of 1000 tribesmen, and sustained eighteen casualties before they were able even to take to their arms. It was found that the assailants belonged to the Galai and Hassan Khel

[1] See Map VII.

divisions of the Adam Khel Afridis; and while the reputed reason for their act of aggression was the raising of the rates at which salt had hitherto been sold at the Kohat Mines, the chief cause was undoubtedly the construction of the Kohat road, now recognised as increasing the accessibility of the hill fastnesses of the neighbouring clans.

Expedition against the Kohat Pass Afridis, February 1850.—Sir Charles Napier, then Commander-in-Chief in India, happened at this time to be visiting Peshawar, and within a week of the outrage orders had been issued for the advance of a force through the Kohat Pass. The column, which was accompanied by the Commander-in-Chief, was under Brigadier Sir Colin Campbell, K.C.B., and consisted of one troop Horse Artillery with elephant transport (25½-inch mortars carried on one elephant), two companies each of the 60th Rifles, 61st and 98th Foot, the 15th Irregular and 1st Punjab Cavalry, the 23rd and 31st Native Infantry, and the 1st Punjab Infantry. The object was to escort the 1st Punjab Cavalry and 1st Punjab Infantry to Kohat, and to punish the offenders of the Adam Khel Afridis. The advance commenced on the 9th February, 1850, and the troops were back in Peshawar by the 14th, but in the interval they had fought their way through the Kohat Pass and back again. Strong opposition was offered at Akhor, at the northern entrance to the pass, which was taken and destroyed, and the tribesmen had then to be driven from positions they had occupied on the heights above the village of Zargun Khel,

which was also burnt. Here the column camped for
the night, but sniping was carried on from the surrounding hills, and several casualties occurred in the
force. When next day the advance was resumed, the
village of Khui had in like manner to be attacked,
while the rearguard was throughout the day's march
exposed to considerable annoyance from large bodies
of the enemy who pressed heavily on rear and flanks,
occupying each height as it was vacated by our
troops. The force encamped for the night of the 11th
at the foot of the Kohat Kotal, and the regiments
intended to garrison Kohat were passed on. During
the night the picquets in front of the camp were
attacked by the enemy, who were driven off without
difficulty. Early the next morning, however, as some
of the picquets furnished by the 23rd and 31st were
withdrawing from their positions, they were suddenly
and heavily attacked by the Afridis, and sustained
several casualties before the enemy was dispersed.
During this day the village of Bosti Khel, to the
west of the pass, was destroyed, and early on the
13th Brigadier Campbell's force started on its return
march to Peshawar; but from Sharaki to Akhor,
nearly the whole length of the defile, the Afridis contested the ground, opposing the force in front and
hanging on its flanks and rear with even greater
perseverance than they had manifested during the
advance. No transport animals or baggage, however, were lost throughout these operations, but our
casualties amounted to nineteen killed, seventy-four
wounded and one missing.

Within a fortnight of the return of the troops from this expedition hostilities broke out afresh. On the 28th February a jirgah of the neighbouring clans agreed to attack the police post in the tower on the summit of the pass, and next day the Pass Afridis, assisted by Bizoti and Utman Khel Orakzais, surrounded the tower, held the road, and drove back a police reinforcement arriving upon the scene. The defenders of the tower were nearly out of ammunition when Captain Coke reached the Kotal from Kohat, with a squadron of cavalry, two guns, and 450 bayonets, and found himself opposed to a force of from 1500 to 2000 Afridis and Orakzais. He attacked at once, drove off the enemy, and placed reinforcements, supplies and ammunition in the post. Of his party eleven were killed and fourteen wounded.

On the night of the 2nd-3rd March the tower was again attacked by a mixed band of Kohat Pass and Khyber Afridis and Orakzais, to the number of 2000, who cut off the water supply and erected breastworks close up to the post, which was defended with great spirit by a subadar of the 1st Punjab Infantry. Coke moved out from Kohat again with 450 of his regiment and some Bangash levies, and withdrew the garrison of the tower, which was thereupon destroyed by the enemy, who now dispersed to their homes.

For some months individual outrages continued, and it appeared that, while certain maliks were willing to submit to our terms, the body of the clan was still recalcitrant. A blockade of the offending divisions was therefore established, and men belonging to them who happened to be in British territory were seized. The reply of the tribesmen to these measures was an incursion into our border and the raiding of one of our villages in July.

For some time after this negotiations were carried on with the Afridis in regard to safe-guarding the pass, and temporary arrangements were made whereby, up to 1853, the pass remained generally open—occasional robberies only being committed. These arrangements thereafter broke down, and towards the end of this year the Bangash were asked if they would undertake to hold the pass against other tribesmen. They agreed, but they had hardly occupied the position on the Kotal and commenced the reconstruction of its defences, when they were attacked by the Afridis in force. There was a general panic among the Bangash, who hurriedly evacuated their position and retired, covered by a small force under Captain Coke.

Subsequently an arrangement was come to by which the defence of the Kotal was entrusted, on payment, to divisions of the Orakzais, Afridis and Bangash; and the Galai and Hassan Khel divisions of the Adam Khel Afridis having offered their submission, the blockade was removed and the pass might now again be said to be open.

The total allowances at this time paid to all the Pass tribesmen amounted to an annual payment of Rs. 14,600.

While the shortest and easiest route between Peshawar and Kohat traverses the Kohat Pass, there is an alternative, though tortuous, connection between these two outposts by way of the Jamu and Bori[1] Passes through the country of the Jawaki division of the Adam Khel Afridis; and when the early disturbances which have been above described made communication difficult and hazardous by way of the Kohat Pass, the Jawaki Afridis offered to carry the mails by their route, which for a short time was in actual use. But the misbehaviour of the Jawakis was soon found to be at least equal to that of their fellow tribesmen, and during 1851-53 they committed serious raids in the Kohat, Khushalgarh and Peshawar districts, the Bori villages especially becoming the refuge for every robber and murderer of that part of the Border. The amount of plunder taken by the men of Bori in 1852-53 was said to have surpassed that of any former period, and Captain Coke reported that there were half a dozen stolen cattle in every house. Every effort was made to persuade the Jawaki Afridis to see the error of their ways, to avoid the committal of crimes in British territory, to refuse passage through their lands to outlaws and criminals, and to come to terms with the Punjab Government, but they rejected all propositions and nothing therefore remained but to send a military force against them.

Expedition against the Jawaki Afridis, November 1853.—The Bori Valley is about twelve miles long and has an entrance at each extremity; but as they are both very narrow and very defensible defiles, it

---

[1] Not to be confused with a pass of the same name between the Khyber and the Bazar Valley.

was determined to cross the outer range at the most favourable point, and the Sarghasha Pass, crossing the outer range between Kandao and Taruni and believed to be the most practicable road, was chosen. The force—a squadron 7th Irregular Cavalry, a mountain battery, two nine pounders, 22nd Foot, Corps of Guides, 20th Native Infantry,[1] 66th Gurkhas, and a company of Sappers and Miners—under Colonel Boileau, advanced very early on the 29th November from Bazid Khel where it had been covering the construction of Fort Mackeson. The Sarghasha Pass was found to be steep, winding, narrow and long, but fortunately it was not held, and the Bori villages were not occupied in any strength, the Afridis inhabiting them having taken to the spurs commanding them. From these they had to be dislodged by the Guides and Gurkhas, led by Lieutenant W. S. R. Hodson of the former regiment, who had a hot struggle with the enemy in holding the heights, while the villages were being destroyed, and in withdrawing when the retirement commenced. The valley was left by the Taruni exit, up to which point the rearguard was as usual hotly pressed. Camp at Bazid Khel was regained at 8 p.m., the force having suffered a loss of eight killed and twenty-nine wounded. The effect of the expedition was apparent—not in the losses of the tribesmen, which were actually rather fewer than our own—but in the fact that within a few days the men of Bori made overtures of submission, and, after somewhat protracted negotiations, they agreed to our

[1] Mutinied in 1857.

terms and gave hostages for their future good
behaviour.

After the settlement of 1853 with the Kohat Pass
Afridis, the Pass remained open until 1866, when the
Basl Khel and Hassan Khel divisions seemed inclined
to give trouble, endeavouring to interfere with the
Pass arrangements, plundering the mail, kidnapping
our subjects and firing on our posts. The assembly,
however, of a punitive force soon changed the aspect
of affairs, the tribesmen at once submitted to our
terms, gave hostages, and for another ten years free
passage through the pass was assured.

In 1876 the question of the construction of a cart
road through the pass was re-opened ; the majority of
the Pass Afridis appeared to raise no objection, but
the Sharaki men absolutely refused to listen to the
proposal, and by placing obstructions on the road, ill-
using travellers, and insulting the Government
messenger sent to summon them to a meeting, they
necessitated the closing of the pass to Afridi trade.
Reprisals immediately commenced ; raids were made
in British territory, cattle were carried off, and the
towers on the crest of the pass and which were in
charge of the levies were burnt. In these outrages
the Galai Khel alone were at first implicated, but ere
long the Hassan Khel and Ashu Khel divisions were
included in the blockade which had been established.
By March 1877, however, all the offenders had submitted and the pass was again opened.

In this year a consideration of the re-allotment of
the pass allowances was rendered necessary, as it was

found that in some cases these were paid to divisions which rendered no appreciable service, while others received more than their dues. The Jawakis had hitherto been paid a sum of Rs. 2000 per annum, despite the fact that their settlements did not abut on the pass, and that they had in the past proved themselves incapable of assisting in the safeguarding of the road. It was proposed by Government to withdraw this Kohat Pass allowance from the Jawakis, but to give them an equivalent sum for guarding the Khushalgarh road and telegraph line, which, running close to the hills of independent tribes, were always liable to attack. Without, however, awaiting the decision of the Government, the Jawakis began, in July 1877, to give trouble; on the 15th they cut the Kohat-Khushalgarh telegraph line in several places; on the 24th they attacked a police escort on the Kohat road and rescued a couple of Afridi prisoners; on the 17th August they carried off a number of Government mules from near Khushalgarh; on the 19th they attacked and burnt a village; on two other occasions bodies of Jawaki Afridis attacked small armed parties moving along the road; villages in our territory were constantly raided; and finally, on the 27th August, a bridge on the Khushalgarh road was burnt. At the end of August it was decided to make a sudden dash into the Jawaki country with the object of quickly effecting as much damage as possible, and so bring them to terms, the season of the year being unfavourable for protracted operations.

Expedition against the Jawaki Afridis in August

T

1877.—Brigadier-General C. P. Keyes, C.B., commanding the Punjab Frontier Force, was to have had charge of the proposed operations, but in his absence through illness the command devolved upon Colonel Mocatta, commanding the 3rd Sikhs. The force employed was divided into three small columns, of which the first, consisting of a mountain battery, 45 sabres, and 625 bayonets, was to enter the Jawaki country by the Tortang defile, thence pushing forward, as rapidly as possible, until arrival at a central point at the northern end of the Gandiali ravine, so as to cut off the retreat in that direction of the enemy's main body, which, it was anticipated, would be opposed to No. 2 Column in the Gandiali defile. The second column—621 bayonets—was to advance up the Gandiali Pass at daylight, and keep the enemy in play until the first column should be in position. The third column—201 bayonets of the Guides—advancing from Shadipur on the Indus, via Sheikh Aladad Ziarat, was to cut off the enemy's retreat along the Tambal Hills, thereafter effecting a junction with the other two columns, the whole force retiring to British territory by the Gandiali Pass.

The operations were carried out as arranged, the junction with No. 3 Column being effected at the village of Lashkari Banda; but, owing to the difficulties of the road and the pressure of the enemy on the rear guard, the original intention of retiring by the Gandiali Pass had to be abandoned, and the whole force was withdrawn by the Kuka China Pass to the border village of Talanj, and thence to Gumbat on the Kohat—

Khushalgarh road. The men had been under arm in a burning sun for twenty hours, had marched nearly thirty miles, and had sustained eleven casualties— one killed and ten wounded.

These operations did not have the quieting effect which had been anticipated, chiefly because the loss of the Jawakis in killed and wounded had been but trifling, while the actual destruction of property had fallen upon one small section of the division alone. Their hostile attitude consequently remained unchanged, and aggressions upon British territory did not cease. Outrages of all kinds continued throughout September and October, and another expedition into the Jawaki country became imperative.

Expedition against the Jawaki Afridis, November 1877 to January 1878.—The arrangements made followed the procedure adopted earlier in the year— that is to say, three columns were formed which entered the Jawaki country at the same points as had the columns under command of Colonel Mocatta, but the strength of each had been slightly increased. Brig.-Gen. Keyes was in command.

No. 1 COLUMN.

Colonel Mocatta.

No. 1 Mountain Battery.[1]
  25 sabres, 2nd Punjab Cavalry.
380 bayonets, Corps of Guides.
225 bayonets, 1st Sikh Infantry.
225 bayonets, 3rd Sikh Infantry.

[1] Now the 21st Kohat Mountain Battery.

No. 2 COLUMN.

Major Williams.

25 sabres, 2nd Punjab Cavalry.
350 bayonets, 4th Punjab Infantry.
300 bayonets, 6th Punjab Infantry.

No. 3 COLUMN.

Colonel Gardiner.

2 guns, No. 2 Mountain Battery.[1]
280 bayonets, 5th Punjab Infantry.
280 bayonets, 5th Gurkhas.

The first and second columns, advancing on the 9th November from Kohat and Gumbat and by Tortang and Gandiali respectively, met at Turki, and moved in combination upon Paia, which was occupied after but insignificant opposition. Meanwhile, the third column had pushed forward from Shadipur through the Namung Pass, finding the enemy holding the ridges on the right of the exit from the defile ; these were quickly driven off, and the column moved on to Kakhto and there entrenched. On the 12th the third column was again engaged, and the 13th and 15th were occupied in the destruction of towers about Zal-Beg and in the Paia Valley, the main body then moving to Shindih and Turki. There was very heavy rain between the 16th and 25th, but a good deal of reconnaissance and survey work was carried out. No further military operations were, however, possible until the 1st December, when an advance on Jamu had been decided upon. As it

[1] Now the 22nd Derajat Mountain Battery.

appeared that heavy loss must accompany any retirement from Jamu after its capture, Brigadier-General
Keyes suggested that his operations should be assisted
by the advance of a force from Peshawar upon Bori :
this was agreed to.

On the 1st December the force under General Keyes,
divided into three columns, left camp at 4 a.m. The
right column moved to the plateau to the north-east
of the camp in the direction of Paia ; the centre
column advanced towards Bagh and Saparai ; while
the third, or left, moved by a high ridge to a point
to the north-west of the camp. The general advance
commenced at 6.30 a.m. ; the enemy were completely
surprised and, although they had constructed breastworks, did not in any place attempt to make a stand.
They were driven into and beyond the two villages of
Shahi Khel, close to the Nara Khula defile, where the
Jamu Valley is very narrow, and these villages were
then occupied by our troops and finally burnt. The
force then fell back and bivouacked at Saparai and
Bagh. On the 2nd and 3rd the Jamu Valley was
surveyed and the Bazid Khel Kotal reconnoitred, and
on the 4th the village of Bagh was burnt, the whole
force now bivouacking in its vicinity.

Meanwhile, the operations from the Peshawar side
had been delayed and hampered by the weather.
Heavy rain caused a flood on the Indus, the bridge
of boats at Attock was destroyed and communications
with Rawal Pindi were interrupted, so that it was not
until the 3rd December that the Peshawar column
was concentrated and ready to move forward into

the Jawaki country.   This force was under Brigadier-
General C. C. G. Ross, C.B., and was composed as
under :

FIRST BRIGADE.

Colonel J. Doran, C.B.

Three guns, I/C R.H.A.
51st Regiment.
Two Companies Sappers and Miners.
22nd Punjab Native Infantry.
27th Punjab Native Infantry.

SECOND BRIGADE.

Colonel H. Buchanan.

Three guns, I/C R.H.A.
13/ 9th R.A. (40-pounders).
9th Regiment.
4th Battalion Rifle Brigade.
14th Native Infantry.[1]
20th Punjab Native Infantry.

The Bori Valley is separated from the plain to the
south of the Mackeson–Sham Shatu road by a rocky
range of hills, as already described in the account
of the operations against the Bori villages in 1853.
This range is crossed by a comparatively low pass at
Kandao, and by a second, more direct pass, known
as the Sarghasha, over a higher part of the ridge.
The plan of operations was to occupy the crest of
the ridge with artillery and infantry, and from this
position—completely commanding the Bori Valley—

[1] Now the 14th Ferozepore Sikhs.

to take such measures as should be found most suitable
for attacking the villages and destroying their towers
and other defences.

The first brigade advanced via Kandao with orders
to proceed to the top of the ridge, turning the Sarghasha Pass, while the other brigade made a direct
attack upon it.   By these arrangements the crest of
the pass became untenable, and the enemy abandoned
the position and retired firing, partly towards the Bori
Valley and partly along the ridge towards Khui.   The
whole force bivouacked on the ridge.   For the next
few days the troops were employed in destroying the
towers and villages in the Bori Valley under a brisk
but ineffective fire from the tribesmen.   While these
operations were in progress, the force under command
of Brigadier-General Keyes had advanced upon and
destroyed the towers of the village of Ghariba, a place
which had long been considered the Alsatia of Jawaki
thieves, and, from the difficult nature of its approaches,
secure from attack.   This operation was effected by
a rapid and combined movement of two columns of
attack, without any casualties on our side.

Although the chief places of the Jawakis had now
been occupied and destroyed, and the blockade satisfactorily maintained by our forces, yet the enemy
showed no signs of surrender.   A further advance,
therefore, by both forces in combination, into the
Pustawani Valley was decided upon.   The strategic
value of this valley to any force operating against the
Adam Khel Afridis had long been recognised, and
it was known that this part of the country was

considered impregnable by the Jawakis, while its careful survey was very desirable. On the Peshawar side, the road from the Bori Valley to Pustawani leads through the Bori China Pass, which a reconnaissance, conducted on the 25th December, proved to be just practicable for mules. The actual advance to Pustawani was to have been made on the 27th, but heavy rain, with the probable consequent floods in the pass, delayed forward movement until the 31st, and it was hoped that the troops of both the Peshawar and Kohat columns would arrive on the same day in the Pustawani Valley.

Both forces effected their purposes successfully and with but small loss. Brigadier-General Ross moved almost entirely unopposed through the Bori China Pass to Pustawani, and thence to Walai, where he met Brigadier-General Keyes. The Peshawar force bivouacked unmolested in or about Pustawani, which was destroyed on the 2nd January, when General Ross retraced his steps, and, meeting with but very slight opposition, regained the Bori Valley early that afternoon, and reached the Sarghasha camp without any casualties.

Early on the 31st December Brigadier-General Keyes left his camp in front of Bagh, debouched on the Paia Plain, and having reached Ghariba, moved to the left up the spur of the Dargai Sar, and sent troops through the Dargai Pass. Thence the General rode on to Walai, where he met General Ross, and it was agreed that nothing was to be gained by further operations or a prolonged occupation of the

Pustawani Valley.   On the next day the whole force
commenced its retirement, the rear guard being
followed up by the enemy, who had collected in
some strength.   The retirement was, however, admirably covered by the Pathan company of the 5th
Punjab Infantry, and from Paia the troops marched
back unmolested to camp.

The remaining operations carried out by the troops
under Generals Keyes and Ross were mainly of topo-
graphical importance.   On the morning of the 15th
January both columns occupied the positions they
had held on the 31st December, and thence they
moved towards Jamu for the purpose of exploring
the Nara Khula defile and the valley to the west of
it, now the only remaining strongholds of the Jawakis.
Despite a certain amount of opposition, this country
was traversed by our troops, and by the 23rd January
the bulk of the force employed had been withdrawn
to Peshawar and Kohat, a small body of the three
arms only remaining temporarily on the Sarghasha
ridge as a force of observation.   During the whole
operations, from November 1877 to January 1878,
our casualties had amounted to eleven killed and
fifty-one wounded.

Almost immediately upon the withdrawal of our
troops the Jawakis had begun to show signs of submission, and after negotiations, protracted until March,
a settlement was effected, the tribesmen agreeing to
make complete submission in full durbar at Peshawar,
to pay a fine of Rs.5000, to expel certain ringleaders
of recent raids, to surrender a number of English

rifles and native matchlocks, and to give hostages for
future good conduct.

After the conclusion of the Jawaki expedition, the
Adam Khel Afridis continued to behave well as a
clan.   During the Afghan War it was rumoured that
they intended to close the Peshawar–Kohat road, and
that they had offered help to the Amir of Kabul;
but not only was the pass never closed for a single
hour during the campaign, but it was freely used by
us for the passage of troops and convoys, while the
Adam Khels hired themselves and their camels out
to us for transport purposes.

There have been disagreements since then—
notably in 1883—and chiefly connected with the
salt duties, but these differences, like "the quarrels
of lovers, are the renewal of love"—the pass has
remained open, the Adam Khels continue in the
undisturbed enjoyment of their pass allowances, few
important offences have of late years been committed,
and—most significant of all—the Adam Khels remained quiescent throughout the troubles of 1897,
in spite of many endeavours made by the other
clans to induce them to join in the risings of that
year.

Aka Khels.—The first occasion upon which, after
our arrival in the Peshawar Valley, we came in collision with the Aka Khel Afridis was in 1854.   The
Aka Khel settlements lie, some of them, to the west
of the country of the Adam Khels; and in 1854 the
Basi Khel section of the Aka Khel, not finding themselves admitted to any share in the Kohat Pass

allowances, began to give trouble on the Peshawar border, murdering British subjects, threatening the village of Matanni close to Peshawar, and attacking the camp of the Assistant Civil Engineer.

The operations which, during 1855, were carried out against the Aka Khels can hardly, even collectively, be dignified by the name of an "expedition," and consisted for the most part in a blockade of the clan, and in the carrying out of sudden raids into their winter settlements, the surprise of their border villages, and the seizure of their cattle from their grazing grounds. Since during the hot weather the Aka Khel migrate to their summer settlements in Tirah, any blockade to be effective must be long sustained, and the Commissioner of Peshawar, Lieutenant-Colonel H. B. Edwardes, obtained sanction to keep up the blockade until the clan surrendered at discretion. When, therefore, the Aka Khels returned in the winter to the low country, not a man of them could venture into Peshawar, their wood trade fell into other hands, and finally—after a determined but fruitless attempt to induce the other tribesmen to make common cause and take the field with them—the Aka Khel gave in about the middle of December, and agreed to the terms imposed upon them. They estimated their losses during the blockade at more than seventy-seven thousand rupees.

"Thus," said Lieutenant-Colonel Edwardes, "ended the struggle of the Aka Khel Afridis with a settled government. Instead of haughtily exacting blackmail from the British for the safety of the Kohat road, they paid a judicial fine for a highway robbery."

Since then the Aka Khels as an individual clan have given little or no trouble on our border.

CHAPTER XIII.

AFRIDIS: OPERATIONS CONTINUED.[1]

KHYBER PASS AFRIDIS.

FROM the year 1857 onwards the Khyber Pass Afridis have given the Punjab Government a good deal of trouble, and it has been necessary to carry out many raids and expeditions against one or other of the clans, and, at times, against all of them. Just before the outbreak of the Mutiny, when the Amir Dost Muhammad was encamped at Jamrud after his interview with Sir John Lawrence, a party of Kuki Khels fired upon some British officers near the mouth of the Khyber, and mortally wounded one of them. The blockade then established was maintained throughout that troublous year, and was so injurious to the interests of the clan that they paid up a fine and agreed to other terms proposed by us. The Zakha Khels were at the same time under blockade for innumerable highway robberies, but they also early made their submission.

They broke out again in 1861, and raided British territory in the neighbourhood of Kajurai—a tract of country occupied during the winter by the remainder

[1] See Map VII.

of the clans of the Khyber Pass Afridis, and it was
found necessary to put the usual pressure on these to
induce them for the future to refuse passage through
their lands at Kajurai to Zakha Khel and other robbers.

The Zakha Khel and Kuki Khel continued to give
trouble, and maintained their reputation as the most
inveterate and audacious of robbers, whose depredations up to the very walls of Peshawar, and even
within the city and cantonments, have been notorious
since the days of Sikh rule.   In those days, moreover,
the Sikh governors cultivated methods of repression
and punishment such as we have never practised.   In
General Thackwell's diary, dated Peshawar, 23rd
November, 1839, he writes, "Called on General
Avitabili to take leave.   They say Avitabili is a
tiger in this government, he has been known to flay
criminals alive and to break the bones of poor
wretches on the wheel previous to hanging them in
chains, and at our conference to-day very gravely
wondered we did not put poison in sugar to send in
traffic among the Khyberees."

In December 1874, the bandmaster[1] of the 72nd
Highlanders, stationed at Peshawar, was carried off
by some Zakha Khel raiders and taken to the Khyber,
being subsequently released uninjured ; and during
the operations against the Jawakis in 1877-78 the
Zakha Khels sent to their aid a contingent of from
300-400 men, who fired on some British troops in the
Kohat Pass and then turned back.

[1] For further details of this abduction see Warburton's *Eighteen
Years in the Khyber*.

Expedition against the Zakha Khels of the Bazar Valley, December 1878.—From the very commencement of the second Afghan war in 1878, the Afridis of the Khyber Pass began to give trouble. At the end of November a signalling party on the Shagai Heights, east of Ali Musjid in the Khyber, was attacked by some Kuki Khels from the village of Kadam, two men being killed and one wounded, but for this outrage punishment was inflicted by the tribal jirgah. Annoyance did not, however, cease ; our communications in the Khyber were continually harassed, and the camp at Ali Musjid was fired into regularly every night, the culprits belonging chiefly to the Zakha Khel clan. One or two small raids upon tribal villages proving ineffectual, a punitive expedition into the Bazar Valley was decided upon, the troops composing it being drawn from the 2nd Division of the Peshawar Valley Field Force, the headquarters of which were then at Jamrud, and from the 2nd Brigade of the 1st Division then at Dakka. The following composed the two columns :

JAMRUD COLUMN.

3 guns, D/A. R.H.A.
300 bayonets, 1/5th Fusiliers.
200 bayonets, 51st Foot.
1 troop, 11th Bengal Lancers.
1 troop, 13th Bengal Lancers.
500 bayonets, 2nd Gurkhas.
400 bayonets, Mhairwara Battalion.

DAKKA COLUMN.

2 guns, 11/9th R.A.

300 bayonets, 1/17th Foot.

41 bayonets, 8th Company Bengal Sappers and Miners.

263 bayonets, 27th Punjab Native Infantry

114 bayonets, 45th Sikhs.

The Jamrud column, starting at 5 p.m. on the 19th December, and moving by Chora, a village inhabited by friendly Malikdin Khels, reached Walai in the Bazar Valley by midday on the 20th, and from here communication was established with the Dakka column, which had then reached the Sisobi Pass [1]— about three miles to the east—and expected to effect a junction with the Jamrud Column next day.

On the 21st the Jamrud Column marched to China, and visited every village of any importance in the valley, destroying all the towers, returning that night to Walai, and withdrawing thence unopposed to Ali Musjid on the 22nd.

The Dakka troops destroyed the towers in the vicinity of their bivouac, marching later to Nikai, which was also burnt. It being then too late to arrive at the Sisobi Pass on the return march before

[1] The villages in the Sisobi Glen are inhabited by Mullagoria, a comparatively insignificant tribe of doubtful origin, and therefore rather despised by their neighbours. They number about 900 fighting men, and the bulk of the tribe live north of the Kabul river and to the west of the Peshawar border, owning the Tartara mountain, 7000 feet high, valuable as a sanatorium and as a position of considerable strategic importance. For further information about the Mullagoria see Chapter IX.

nightfall, the General (Tytler) halted, owing to difficulties as to water, in the Thabai Pass, with the intention of retiring on Dakka by this route. During the night the tribesmen assembled in strength about the camp, and when the march was resumed at daybreak it was seen that the enemy meant disputing every foot of it. The Afridis notoriously attack the baggage guard in preference to any other part of a force, and it was therefore determined to change the usual order of march. Orders were consequently issued for each corps to take its own baggage with it; the artillery and sappers, being most encumbered with mules, followed close to the advanced guard; while a very strong rearguard was left behind, which, being wholly relieved from the charge of baggage, was able to resist the pressure from the rear.

The road was winding, steep, and very difficult for mules, and from the moment the force started a lively but ineffective fusillade was opened on the column. The heights were taken and held by flanking parties; the rearguard was hotly engaged; the enemy seized the positions of the rearguard and of the flanking parties as soon as they were abandoned; and Dakka was not reached by the whole column until 11.30 p.m., when the force had marched 22 miles, and had lost two men killed and twenty wounded.

Second Expedition against the Zakha Khels of the Bazar Valley, January 1879.—After the expedition of December 1878, the Khyber Pass Afridis continuing to give trouble, every effort was made to break up the tribal combination, and the Kuki Khels and Kambar Khels came in and tendered their submission. The attitude of the Zakha Khels was, however, so unsatisfactory that the political officer, Major Cavagnari, recommended a temporary occupation of the Bazar Valley, coupled with visits to all the recusant villages in that and the Bara Valley. In consequence, Lieutenant-General Maude, commanding the 2nd Division, Peshawar Valley Field Force, applied on the 16th January for sanction for the proposed operations, in concert with a force furnished from the 1st Division. Sanction was accorded by the Commander-in-Chief, but a time-limit of ten days was laid down within which the operations were to be concluded. The following troops were placed at the disposal of Lieutenant-General Maude :

JAMRUD COLUMN.

2 guns, D/A Royal Horse Artillery.
2 guns, 11/9th Royal Field Artillery.
315 bayonets, 5th Fusiliers.
316 bayonets, 25th Foot.
145 sabres, 13th Bengal Lancers.
55 bayonets, Madras Sappers and Miners.
356 bayonets, 24th Punjab Native Infantry.

BASAWAL COLUMN.

2 guns, 11/9th Royal Artillery.
361 bayonets, 1/17th Foot.
210 bayonets, 4th Battalion Rifle Brigade.
32 sabres, Guides Cavalry.
43 bayonets, Bengal Sappers and Miners.
201 bayonets, 4th Gurkhas.

2 guns, 11/9th Royal Artillery.

213 bayonets, 51st Foot.

31 bayonets, Madras Sappers and Miners.

312 bayonets, 2nd Gurkhas.

320 bayonets, Mhairwara Battalion.

311 bayonets, 6th Native Infantry.[1]

DAKKA COLUMN.

52 bayonets, 1/17th Foot.

104 bayonets, 27th Punjab Native Infantry.

257 bayonets, 45th Sikhs.

Leaving Jamrud on the 24th January, the Jamrud Column marched by way of the Khyber Stream and the Chora Pass to Berar Kats, arriving there late on the following afternoon. There was some firing at the baggage escort *en route* and at the camp after dark, but it soon ceased.

The Ali Musjid Column started on the 25th, and, moving by Alachi, reached Karamna the same afternoon, being there joined by the 6th Native Infantry, which had marched thither from Lundi Kotal by way of the Bori Pass, the southern foot of which is in the north-west corner of the Karamna Valley. On this day the towers of the Karamna villages were destroyed, as were those of Barg, to which place the column marched on the 27th.

The Basawal Column reached China on the afternoon of the 25th January, and was here joined by the Dakka force, the united columns moving on to

[1] Now the 6th Jat Light Infantry.

Kasaba and Sisobi on the 26th; the Sisobi Pass was occupied on the 27th, and made practicable.   Here a junction was effected with the Jamrud force, and on the afternoon of this day all the columns were united in the Bazar Valley under Lieutenant-General Maude, who early that morning had secured possession of the China hill.

During all these movements the Zakha Khel had shown great hostility; the force had been fired on night and day from the moment of entry into the country, while the inhabitants had deserted their villages and had, in many instances, themselves set fire to them.   In a reconnaissance on the 28th of the Bukar Pass leading to the Bara Valley a good deal of opposition was experienced, and in the destruction on the 29th of the towers of Halwai the enemy disclosed their presence in large numbers.   It was now clear that any invasion of the Bara Valley would bring on an Afridi war, and it subsequently transpired that other tribes, as well as other clans of Afridis, were assembling to oppose our further advance —detachments from the Shinwaris and Orakzais, as well as from the Kuki Khel, Aka Khel, Kambar Khel, Malikdin Khel, and Sipah Afridis, gathering together and holding the passes over the Bara hills.

The responsibility of Lieutenant-General Maude as to further operations was not lightened by the receipt on the 29th January of a circular letter from Army Headquarters, reminding column commanders in Afghanistan that the operations then in progress were directed against the Amir and his troops alone,

and that unnecessary collisions with the tribes were
to be as far as possible avoided. Lieutenant-General
Maude therefore telegraphed for more explicit instructions, especially as to whether he should force
an entrance to the Bara Valley.

Before any reply could be expected, an urgent
demand was received from the General Officer commanding First Division, Peshawar Valley Field Force,
for the immediate return of his troops, in view
of an expected attack upon Jalalabad and Dakka by
Mohmands and Bajauris; but the awkwardness of such
a request in the middle of operations was smoothed
by the Afridis of the Bazar Valley now evincing a
disposition to open negotiations, while a deputation
from all divisions of the Bara Valley Zakha Khels
actually arrived in camp. On the 2nd February the
Political Officer reported that he had made satisfactory terms with the jirgah; and although the same
evening General Maude was informed that the words
of the circular above referred to did not preclude his
carrying out an expedition into the Bara Valley
should he consider such to be necessary, he decided
that the whole force under his command should
commence its withdrawal on the 3rd; and on that
date accordingly the different columns left the Bazar
Valley, the Dakka force by the Sisobi Pass and the
troops of the Second Division via Chora for Jamrud
and Ali Musjid. There was no molestation by the
Afridis during the retirement of any of the columns,
which, during the operations described, had sustained
a loss of five killed and thirteen wounded.

The effect of this expedition did not last more than a few weeks, for by the end of March the Zakha Khels had again begun to give trouble, continuing to do so until the termination in May of the first phase of the second Afghan war. On the withdrawal from Afghanistan in June, the Khyber Afridis made only one insignificant attempt to molest our troops ; and, fortunately for us, the trials of what has been called "the Death March"[1] were not aggravated by the attacks of fanatical tribesmen, during the retirement India-wards through the Khyber of the Peshawar Valley Field Force.

After the close of the first phase of the campaign in Afghanistan, arrangements, which worked generally satisfactorily, were made with the Afridis for the safety of the Khyber ; while the agreement come to in 1881, and honourably kept on both sides for sixteen years, will be found in Chapter XI.

It has been said that the Afridis of the Khyber kept faithfully to their treaty engagements during the sixteen years which followed the events which have been just described, but in 1892 there was one comparatively minor case of misconduct, when a Kuki Khel malik, smarting under a grievance connected with the deprivation for misbehaviour of a portion of his allowances, collected a body of 500 or 600 men and attacked three of the Khyber posts. The Tirah mullahs made an unsuccessful attempt to persuade other Afridi clans to join, and the prompt despatch

[1] For details of this march, see the narrative of Surgeon-General Ker-Innes.

of troops to Jamrud was sufficient to cause the dispersal of the lashkar.

Five years afterwards there was a sudden, unaccountable, and widespread display of hostility towards the government, in which almost all the border tribes from the Malakand to the Tochi were concerned; and it seems necessary to make something of the nature of a statement of the causes which have been put forward, at various times and by different persons, for an outbreak so serious and so wholly unexpected. It must, however, from the outset be borne in mind that, when we made our agreement for the safeguarding of the pass with and by the Khyber Afridis, they put the recognition upon record of the independence of their responsibility for the security of the road from any government aid in the matter of troops; while it was further by them admitted that "it lies with the Indian Government to retain its troops within the pass or withdraw them and to re-occupy it at pleasure." In face of this admission it is not easy to see how the Afridis can justify their complaint (made to the Amir of Afghanistan), that our hold on the Khyber was an infringement of treaty rights.

It may be admitted that a strong case is presented by those who hold that the real cause of the general Pathan revolt of 1897 is traceable to the policy which dictated the Afghan Boundary agreement of 1893. It is indisputable that one of the results of this measure—imperatively demanded by the difficulty, always present and ever increasing, of controlling the

tribes immediately beyond our border—aroused a
sense of distrust and uneasiness among the Pathans
of the frontier. 'They watched in impotent wrath the
erection of the long line of demarcation pillars; they
were told that henceforth all to the east of that line
practically belonged to the British, and that the
allegiance of all who dwelt within it must be to us;
they saw their country mapped and measured; they
witnessed the establishment of military posts, not
merely on their borders, but in their very midst, as at
Wana; and they came to a conclusion, not unnatural
to an ignorant people ever hostile to any form of
settled and civilised government, that their country
was annexed and their independence menaced.' The
tribesmen themselves put forward many pretexts for
their action—after the event; but religious fanaticism
undoubtedly furnished the actual incentive, while
there are not wanting indications that the discom-
fiture of the infidel (the Greek) at the hands of the
followers of Islam (the Turk), furnished the spur
which incited the tribesmen to try and throw off the
yoke of the unbeliever.

Then, again, there seems no doubt that the men of
the border believed that they might safely rely upon
the support, moral and material, of the Amir of
Afghanistan. It was known that the Durand Boundary Agreement was not particularly palatable to the
Ruler of the Unruly; he had lately written a book on
Jehad; he had recently assumed a title [1] which seemed
to include all Muhammadans under his sovereignty;

[1] King of Islam.

for years he had been a personal friend of the Hadda
Mullah, one of the chief apostles of insurrection. As
a matter of fact, however, subsequent revelations
proved that the Amir's attitude towards his ally had
been perfectly correct, throughout a situation which
for him was both difficult and dangerous; he issued
proclamations enjoining neutrality; he caused Afghan
reinforcements moving eastward to be stopped and
dispersed; the Afridis themselves admitted that "His
Highness advised us not to fight with the British
Government;" but the Amir was not able effectively
to control the active sympathies with the insurrec-
tionary movement of some of his people in general,
and of Ghulam Haidar, his Commander-in-Chief, in
particular.

The initial outbreaks, preceding that of the Afridis,
occurred on the 10th June, 1897, in the Tochi Valley,
on the 26th July at the Malakand, and on the 7th
August at Shabkadar in the Peshawar Valley; and
shortly after this latter date the possibility of the
rising, already sufficiently formidable, spreading to
the Afridis and Orakzais, caused the concentration at
Rawal Pindi of two brigades, in addition to those
which had already been formed for service against
other tribes on the frontier. At the same time a
movable column, composed of the three arms, was
formed at Peshawar, intended for the protection of
the frontier immediately adjacent to that cantonment,
but *not* intended to carry on operations in the Khyber;
the garrison of Jamrud was doubled, and regular
troops occupied the frontier forts at Michni and

Abazai. For some reason, not readily apparent, the authorities on the spot, military and civil, do not seem to have felt any real apprehension for the safety of the Khyber; and, as has been said elsewhere, reports sent from Kohat, emphasising the serious and widespread character of the rising, and pointing out the extent to which Afridis and Orakzais seemed to be implicated, appear to have been discredited or were considered to be exaggerated.

On the 17th August, definite information reached Peshawar from the Khyber that an Afridi force, reported 10,000 strong, had left Bagh in Tirah on the 16th, with the intention of attacking the Khyber posts on the 18th. Both the General Officer commanding and the Commissioner of Peshawar decided against any occupation of the Khyber forts by regular troops, for the reason that such a course would imply distrust of the tribesmen holding to their treaty obligations. This decision, and the resultant abandonment of the Khyber, and the failure to support the Khyber Rifles holding its different posts, have been widely criticised and greatly condemned. Holdich says : " But, alas ! whilst the Afridi fought for us, we failed to fight for ourselves ; 9500 troops about the Peshawar frontier looked on, whilst 500 Afridis maintained British honour in the Khyber." And those who were present at a lecture given at Simla in 1898, on " the Campaign in Tirah," will not have forgotten the general chorus of approval which there greeted the remarks of a prominent Punjab civilian, that " the 23rd of August was a day of pain and humiliation for every Englishman in India. We had 12,000 troops at the mouth of the Pass or within easy reach of Ali Musjid, marking time as it were, or held in leash, and we allowed these forts to fall one after the other."

But whatever opinion may be held in regard to the reasons of policy which held back the troops of the regular army, there seems no question that at the time any forward movement on anything like a large scale was practically out of the question; pack transport especially was very scarce, all immediately and locally available having already been requisitioned for military operations elsewhere in progress. At the same time, it cannot be denied that the military authorities in Peshawar had been in receipt of at least a fortnight's definite notice of what might be expected, while, for any operations in the Khyber Pass itself, wheeled transport, contrary to ordinary frontier experience, could have been utilised practically throughout.

The following precautionary measures were taken: Ali Musjid and Fort Maude were reinforced by 100 tribesmen each; the Zakha Khel and Shinwari maliks were reminded of their obligations; additional troops were sent to Fort Bara, and a column of all arms to Jamrud; while—a step which aroused, perhaps, more adverse comment than any other—the British commandant of the Khyber Rifles was recalled from Lundi Kotal to Peshawar, the Commissioner considering that his presence at the former place might hamper the action of the Indian Government.

On the 23rd August, when the storm finally broke over the Khyber, the distribution of the Khyber Rifles was as under :

Jamrud,	- -	271.
Bagiar, -	- -	13.
Jehangira,	- -	7.
Fort Maude, -	-	42 + 100 tribesmen.
Ali Musjid,	- -	80 + 100 tribesmen

(of whom only 40 were present on the 23rd).

Katta Kushtia,	-	7.
Gurgurra,	- -	10.
Lundi Kotal, -	-	374.
Fort Tytler, -	-	20.

Fort Maude was attacked at 10 in the morning, but in the afternoon Brigadier-General Westmacott, commanding at Jamrud, moved out to the entrance to the Khyber, and thence shelled the enemy about Fort Maude.

The attackers thereupon dispersed, and, on General Westmacott withdrawing again to Jamrud, Fort Maude, Bagiar and Jehangira were evacuated by their garrisons and then destroyed by the enemy. The Afridi lashkar then attacked Ali Musjid, and by evening the garrison, short of ammunition and hearing of the fall of the three posts above mentioned, escaped to Jamrud, having lost three of their number killed and wounded.   From Ali Musjid the tribesmen marched on the morning of the 24th for Lundi Kotal, their numbers being swelled *en route*, and being un-molested in their passage, since the garrisons of Katta Kushtia and Gurgurra early abandoned their posts

and took to the hills. The attack on the fortified
serai at Lundi Kotal began at 8 a.m., and during the
whole of that day and the night that followed, the
defence was resolutely maintained under Subadar
Mursil Khan, who had two sons in the attacking
force and one with him in the Khyber Rifles. The
garrison consisted of five native officers, and 369 men
of the Khyber Rifles. Of these, 120 belonged to
miscellaneous clans—Shilmani Mohmands, Peshawaris,
and Kohat Pass Afridis; of the remaining 249, 70
were Loargai Shinwaris, 50 were Mullagoris, the remainder being Zakha Khel and Malikdin Khel Afridis.
During the 24th the fire from the walls kept the attack
at a distance; but on the morning of the 25th, a
Shinwari jemadar being wounded, his men seemed to
think they had done enough for honour, scaled the
north wall, and deserted to their homes—the Afridis
of the garrison, it is said, sending a volley after them.
It is not clear exactly what proportion of the besieged
gave friendly admittance to the besiegers and what
proportion remained true to their salt; but negotiations were opened, Mursil Khan was killed, and
about 11 a.m. the gate was opened from inside by
treacherous hands and the tribesmen swarmed in. The
Mullagori and Shilmani sepoys fought their way out
and escaped—the Native Officer of the Mullagori company eventually bringing his little command back to
Jamrud without the loss of a rifle. It was estimated
that in the attacks on the Khyber posts the enemy
had sustained some 250 casualties, and immediately
after the fall of Lundi Kotal they dispersed to

their homes, promising to reassemble on the 15th September.

One of the most serious results of the capture of the Lundi Kotal serai was that fifty thousand rounds of ammunition fell into the hands of the enemy.

The Tirah Expedition of 1897-98 *against the Khyber Pass and Aka Khel Afridis.*—On the 3rd September the necessary orders were issued for the formation and concentration of the Tirah Expeditionary Force, the actual date for the expedition to start being fixed as the 12th October. By this date it was hoped that the operations, then in progress in other parts of the frontier and elsewhere described, would have ceased, and that both troops and transport there in use would be available for the larger expedition now projected. These anticipations, however, were not altogether justified by events, only one brigade with its accompanying transport being set free for employment under Sir William Lockhart, who was recalled from leave in England to command the Tirah Field Force, consisting of some 44,000 men. (For composition of the force see note at end of chapter.)

Kohat was made the base of operations, with an advanced base at Shinawari, thirty miles from Maidan. This route was on the whole considered an easier and shorter one into Tirah than those from Peshawar by the Bara and Mastura valleys, or from Kohat via the Khanki, despite, too, the fact that the nearest railway terminus was at Khushalgarh on the left bank of the Indus, and thirty miles to the east of Kohat.

The troops were divided into a main column of two

divisions, each of two brigades of infantry with divisional troops; two subsidiary columns; line of communication troops; and a reserve mixed brigade at Rawal Pindi.

The main column, operating from Kohat and Shinawari, was to move on Tirah via the Chagru Kotal, Sampagha and Arhanga Passes; while of the two subsidiary columns one was to operate from Peshawar, and the other from the Miranzai and Kurram Valleys, as circumstances might require. From railhead at Khushalgarh to Shinawari, the advanced base, the road was practicable for carts, thence onwards the troops could only be served by pack animals, and of these some 60,000 were required for the use of the Tirah Expeditionary Force alone, not counting those already engaged with other frontier expeditions still in progress.[1] The collection of so vast an amount of transport naturally caused delay, and it was not until the 20th October that any forward movement could take place.

With the arrival of troops at Shinawari a commencement had been made at improving the road from thence over the Chagru Kotal to Kharappa, and by the 15th October it was fit for transport animals as far as the top of the pass. In order, however, to work on the north side of the kotal, and so complete the road construction in readiness for the

[1] The requirements of expeditionary carriage always weigh with especial hardship on the Punjab; during the summer of 1897 the Deputy Commissioners in that Province impressed about 100,000 animals and 25,000 owners, and of these numbers not one in five was actually required and sent to the front.

advance on the 20th, it was necessary to drive the enemy from the vicinity so as to prevent them from disturbing our working parties.

On the 18th, then, Lieutenant-General Sir A. P. Palmer, temporarily commanding at Shinawari, moved out with troops of the 2nd Division, distributed in two columns. The main column was composed of Brigadier-General Kempster's 1st Brigade of the 2nd Division :

    1st Battalion Gordon Highlanders.
    1st Battalion Dorsetshire Regiment.
    1st Battalion 2nd Gurkhas.
    15th Sikhs.

To which were added

    No. 4 Company Madras Sappers and Miners.
    No. 8 Mountain Battery.
    Machine Gun Detachment, 16th Lancers.
    Scouts, 5th Gurkhas.

The second column was under Brigadier-General Westmacott, who had either with him, or was joined by on reaching the Chagru Kotal, three of the battalions of his own, the 2nd Brigade of the 2nd Division, viz. :

    2nd Battalion King's Own Scottish Borderers.
    1st Battalion Northamptonshire Regiment.
    1st Battalion 3rd Gurkhas,

supplemented for this day by

    No. 5 Mountain Battery.
    No. 9 Mountain Battery.
    Rocket Detachment Royal Artillery.

The two columns left camp at Shinawari, the one
at 4.30 a.m., the other half an hour later. The main
column moved along the foothills to the north-west
of camp and, then, making a wide circle to the east,
was to operate against the right flank and right rear
of the enemy occupying the cliffs about Dargai. The
second column was to make a frontal attack upon
Dargai from the Chagru Kotal; and on its arrival
here about 8.30, and seeing few of the enemy on the
Dargai position, it was decided to at once attack
without awaiting the turning movement of the main
column. Some description of the famous position
must now be given.

[1] "The Chagru Kotal is at the top of the hill, 5525
feet high, between the plain on the southern or
Shinawari side of the Samana Range and the Khanki
Valley, but at the lowest point of the gap between
the Samana Sukh, or western extremity of that part
of the Samana Range on which stand Forts Gulistan,
Saraghari and Lockhart, and the heights above
Dargai. These heights, continued to the north
beyond the village of Dargai, form what is called the
Narikh Sukh, from which a rough track drops down
into the Narikh Darra a short distance above its
junction with the Chagru defile, which again meets
the Khanki River almost at right angles some two
miles further on. The road from Shinawari to the
Khanki Valley runs very nearly due north. At

[1] For much of the following I am indebted to Captain A. K. Slessor's
Tirah Campaign—being No. 5 of the "Derbyshire Campaign Series,"
printed for regimental circulation.

the Chagru Kotal it is overlooked on the east by the
Samana Sukh, a steep cliff rising precipitously to a
height of some 700 feet above it, at a distance of from
700 to 800 yards. Opposite and nearly parallel to this
on the western side of the kotal, but 1000 yards
from it, are the Dargai heights, which attain an
elevation of slightly over 6600 feet, 1100 feet above
the Chagru Kotal. Although the range from the
kotal to the enemy's sangars on the top of the
heights was only 1800 yards, the distance to be
traversed on foot was about a couple of miles. For
the first mile or more the track followed a more or
less level course, until, passing through the village of
Mamu Khan, it took a sharp turn to the right and
began to zig-zag up a very steep watercourse, which
became gradually narrower as it neared the top of a
small wooded, rocky ridge running roughly parallel
to the enemy's position and connected with it by a
narrow col or saddle. This ridge was 400 feet lower
than the crest of the position, and some 350 yards
from the foot of it. The angle of descent from the
position to the top of the ridge, or rather to the
narrow gap at which alone it was possible to cross
the ridge—which elsewhere was precipitous on the
side nearest the position—was less steep than the slope
from the gap downwards—or rearwards. Consequently,
except at a point not far beyond the village of Mamu
Khan, which was too distant from the position to be
of any importance, the attacking force was not exposed
to the enemy's fire until it reached the gap. The
approach to the gap was, as has been already stated,

up a water-course which narrowed at the top until it
formed a sort of funnel, not wide enough to admit of
the passage of more than two or three men abreast,
who, as they issued from it, found themselves at the
edge of a narrow ledge, 350 yards long to the foot of
the position, exposed every inch of the way to a fire
from half a mile of sangared crest."

The cliffs of Dargai are everywhere almost sheer,
the final ascent being made by a rough track, which
climbs up at a point where the cliff is rather more
broken and shelving than elsewhere.

The advance commenced about 9 a.m., the 3rd
Gurkhas leading, followed by the King's Own Scottish
Borderers and Northamptons; and just before midday the position had been taken, the enemy, chiefly
Orakzai Ali Khels, at the last only offering a comparatively feeble resistance, as they were beginning to
feel the pressure of the main column. These fled
towards the Khanki Valley, leaving twenty dead
behind them. The attacking force had sustained but
fifteen casualties—two killed and thirteen wounded.
The advance of the main column had been greatly
delayed by the impracticable character of the ground,
which had necessitated the return of the mountain
battery and all other pack animals; and it was after
3 p.m. before the junction of the two columns was
effected at Dargai, by which time parties of the enemy
had commenced to harass the rear of the main column,
and some 4000 Afridis appeared to be advancing from
the direction of the Khanki Valley, with the intention
of attempting a re-occupation of the position.

No operation of this campaign has been more criticised, either by those who took part in it or by
historians, than the evacuation on the 18th October of
the Dargai position and its recapture thereby necessitated only two days later. The matter is barely
touched upon in Sir William Lockhart's despatch,
appearing in the *Gazette of India* of January 22nd,
1898, beyond a remark that "the track to the water-
supply was afterwards found to be about three miles
in length, so commanded from the adjacent heights
that water could not have been obtained in the
presence of an enemy unless these heights as well
as Dargai itself had been held." The inference is that,
to hold the position won on the 18th, and safeguard
the water-supply, a far larger force would have been
required than could at the time be spared.   "Colonel
(now Lieutenant-General) Hutchinson in his book,
the *Campaign in Tirah*, states [1] as the principal
excuse for the failure to hold the Dargai heights
when they had once been captured, that 'the water-
supply of Dargai was at a place called Khand Talao,
nearly three miles away to the west, and the road to
it was commanded throughout by adjacent heights,
so that, in the presence of an enemy, water could not
have been obtained for the troops, unless these heights,
as well as the village of Dargai, had been held in
force.' This statement is all the more remarkable
in view of the fact that, on the excellent map of the
position which he gives three pages before, are clearly
marked both the small Talao (or tank), 100 yards

[1] Quotation is here again made from Captain Slessor's book.

below the village, containing muddy but not undrinkable water, which we used at first on the morning of the 21st, but also the larger tank some 500 yards further to the east.... The summit of the Narikh Sukh completely dominates the village of Dargai and the reverse slope of the enemy's position, and commands an extensive view of the country for miles round. It is strewn with large rocks, very much like a Dartmoor Tor, and abounds in natural cover. A battalion left there on the 18th could have set at defiance any number of tribesmen, and, supported by another battalion on the kotal to connect it with the base and furnish it with supplies, could with little difficulty, in conjunction with the troops already in possession of the Samana across the valley, have effectually prevented any attempt of the Afridis to come up to meet us from the Khanki Valley."

Immediately the junction of the two columns had been effected the retirement to camp commenced; a mountain battery was posted at the Chagru Kotal, and another, with a battalion, on the Samana Sukh, to cover the withdrawal—a difficult operation and attended with considerable loss, for the path was very steep and broken, and the enemy pressed the rearguard closely. They do not, however, appear to have pursued beyond the heights, and the further retirement of Sir Power Palmer's force to Shinawari via the Chagru Kotal was unmolested. Our total casualties this day amounted to one officer and seven men killed, five officers and twenty-nine men wounded.

The reports which he had received, as to the

relation of the Dargai position in occupation by the
enemy to the use of the road over the Chagru Kotal,
seem to have convinced General Yeatman-Biggs,
now again commanding his division, that passage
could not safely be attempted unless the tribesmen
were dislodged from the heights on the left flank.
He, therefore, proposed to Sir William Lockhart on
the 19th, that the advance be made by way of
Gulistan, the Samana Sukh, and the Talai Spur;[1]
but this suggestion was negatived, and the previous
arrangement for the advance to Kharappa over the
Chagru Kotal was to stand, Sir William considering
that the well-known anxiety of the enemy as to
their flanks, would cause them to evacuate the Dargai
position on our troops arriving at the junction of
the Narikh and Chagru ravines; at the same time
the G.O.C.-in-Chief admitted that "it would be
necessary to clear the Dargai heights overlooking
the road to the west." It seems, then, that what
Sir William Lockhart suggested was a frontal attack
on the Dargai position, combined with a threatening
of the flanks by continuing the advance towards
Kharappa.

The force placed at the disposal of General
Yeatman-Biggs on the 20th, was composed of the
troops of his own division, which had already taken
the Dargai position on the 18th, *less* the 36th Sikhs,
but strengthened by the inclusion of the 21st Madras
Pioneers (divisional troops) and by the loan of two

---

[1] This was afterwards found to be a mere goat-track, quite unsuited
to the movement of any large force—still less for its transport.
   "Talai" is sometimes called "Tsalai."

infantry battalions (2nd Battalion Derbyshire Regiment and 3rd Sikhs) from the 1st Division. The
whole force left camp at Shinawari at 4.30 a.m. on
the 20th by the direct road to the Chagru Kotal:
no flank attack was attempted as on the previous
occasion, but, fortunately, the expectation of such a
movement kept a large contingent of the enemy from
the actual point of attack during the whole day. As
might have been expected with the passage by a
single narrow road of so large a body of troops and
transport, the block, inevitable under ordinary conditions, was accentuated by the opposition experienced;
and, while some of the baggage was unable even to
leave the Shinawari camp that day, late on the
21st the Shinawari–Chagru Kotal road was for quite
half its length still absolutely choked with transport
of all kinds—many of the animals had been standing
loaded up for upwards of thirty-six hours.

The Dargai position, which on the 18th had been
held by a limited number of Orakzais, was now
occupied by a gathering of tribesmen estimated to
number 12,000, partly Orakzais, but more than half
consisting of Afridis from the Malikdin Khel, Kambar
Khel, Kamar Khel, Zakha Khel, Kuki Khel, and
Sipah clans.

The advanced troops, under Brigadier-General
Kempster, reached the kotal about 8 a.m., and, on
being joined there by Major-General Yeatman-Biggs,
were at once ordered to take the position; the remainder of the force being halted on the summit or
the south side of the pass, and no attempt being

made to threaten the enemy's flanks by continuing
the advance. The assault on Dargai was led by
the Gurkha Scouts and 1st Battalion 2nd Gurkhas,
with the Dorsets in support and the Derbyshire
Regiment in reserve, covered by the long-range
fire of the Gordons and Maxim gun from a ridge
immediately west of the kotal, of three mountain
batteries on the pass, and of another on the Samana
Sukh. The whole of the infantry of the attack was
able to mass, without loss and under cover, within
less than 500 yards of the position, and from
here the Gurkhas dashed out, and, with something
over fifty casualties, succeeded in establishing themselves in shelter in the broken and dead ground
immediately under the cliffs. The enemy now concentrated a rapid, accurate, and well-sustained fire
upon the narrow col or saddle described on page 322.
The remainder of the Gurkhas were unable to get
across, and attempts made, first by the Dorsets and
then by the Derbyshires, to rush forward in driblets
(necessitated both by the narrow exit from the
" funnel " and the congested state of the ground
whereon these regiments were massed) were beaten
back with considerable loss. About 2.30 p.m. the
colonel of the Dorsets, the senior officer on the spot,
signalled for reinforcements. The Gordon Highlanders
and 3rd Sikhs were then sent up, and, under a rapid
concentrated fire from all the batteries, the Gordons
led a dash, which was joined by all the other troops
in the position, and the enemy, not waiting for the
final assault, fled towards the Khanki Valley.

By this time it was too late to continue the advance ;
consequently, while the bulk of the force bivouacked
about the Chagru Kotal, the Narikh Sukh was held
by the Derbyshires, the position at Dargai by the
Gurkhas and Dorsets, with the Gordon Highlanders
lower down the hill. The total casualties sustained
in this, the second assault on Dargai, amounted to four
officers and thirty-four men killed, fourteen officers
and 147 men wounded. It may here be mentioned
that the troops now holding these heights remained
wholly unmolested, even when, after the 23rd, the
position was occupied by no more than one battalion
—the 30th Punjab Infantry.

On the 21st the Second Division resumed its march ;
on the 24th the First Division began to move from
Shinawari ; and by the evening of the 27th the whole
of the main force under Sir William Lockhart's command, was, with its supplies and transport, concentrated at Kharappa ready for a further advance.
During this time the Sampagha Pass to the north
was reconnoitred, foraging parties were sent out,
camps were strengthened and communications improved ; the enemy was always active, following up
reconnoitring and foraging parties, and " sniping "
nightly into camp, whereby several casualties were
sustained.

By the 28th a force of some 17,600 fighting men,
nearly as many followers, and 24,000 animals, was
concentrated in camp, and marched out this day to
Ghandaki, a short four miles from Kharappa, proceeding by two roads ; and in the afternoon a

reconnaissance by the 1st Brigade of the First Division was pushed to the foot of the Sampagha Pass. On the following day the same brigade moved out while it was still dark; the Devons seized a village and some spurs on the right of the road to the pass, the Derbyshire Regiment occupied a mass of small brown hills in the centre—afterwards the first artillery position, and the 1st Gurkhas moved against the Kandi Mishti villages on the left. The Sampagha was captured by direct attack, the opposition not being very serious, and by 11.30 a.m. was in our hands, at a cost of two killed and thirty wounded. Three brigades were that same day pushed forward into the Mastura Valley, where up to this date no European had ever penetrated, the 1st Brigade remaining on the south of the Sampagha to help forward the transport, and eventually joining the main body on the night of the 30th.

On the 31st the force moved against the Arhanga Pass leading into Afridi Tirah, but the general expectation that the tribesmen would here make a real stand proved unfounded. The pass was captured practically by a single brigade—General Westmacott's —at the expense of only three casualties, and the 2nd Brigade, First Division, with the whole of the Second Division, hurried on to Maidan, leaving the 1st Brigade of the First Division in the Mastura Valley.

Arrived in Maidan, expeditions were now made into the settlements of the different tribesmen in arms against us. As a preliminary, Bagh was visited

on the 1st November. This was about three miles to
the west of the Maidan camp, is the political centre
of Tirah, and the meeting place of the Afridi jirgahs.
On the 9th, a reconnaissance was made of Saran Sar,
a pass into the Bara Valley, a number of defensive
villages of the Zakha Khel were destroyed, and grain
and forage supplies were removed; we sustained a
considerable number of casualties in the retirement,
the Northampton Regiment especially losing heavily.
On the 13th, a force under General Kempster visited
the Waran Valley to overawe and punish the Aka
Khels, and the house of the notorious mullah, Saiyid
Akbar, was destroyed. In the retirement our rearguard was again heavily handled, over 70 casualties
being sustained at the hands of the Aka Khel, Zakha
Khel, Kamar Khel and Sipah Afridis who took part
in the action.

On the 18th November, the main force moved from
Maidan to Bagh, which was considered a better political and strategical centre; and on the 22nd, Sir
William Lockhart accompanied thence a force which,
under General Westmacott, started on a three days'
reconnaissance to Dwa Toi to explore the approaches
to the Bara Valley and to punish the Kuki Khels.
In all these expeditions our losses were not light, the
rearguard being invariably followed up and harassed;
the clans in general, and the Zakha Khel in particular,
appeared irreconcilably hostile; and skirmishes and
attacks on convoys were of almost daily occurrence.
Foraging parties from Mastura camp were also attacked
by the Orakzais, but it was evident that the back of

the resistance of this tribe had been broken at Dargai, and, indeed, by the 20th November they had accepted our terms and paid their fines in full, both in rifles and in money. The greater part of Afridi Tirah had now been traversed and surveyed; the Chamkannis and westerly Orakzais were visited and punished as mentioned in Chapter XVI., and Sir William Lockhart now resolved to evacuate Tirah and attack the Afridis in their winter settlements near Peshawar.

Heavy baggage was now sent back from Bagh and Mastura to Shinawari, the base was changed from Khushalgarh to Peshawar, and on the 7th December the Maidan and Mastura Valleys were evacuated, the 2nd Brigade of the First Division rejoining its division detailed to march down the Mastura Valley. The Second Division withdrew by the Bara Valley, and experienced some of the heaviest rearguard fighting ever encountered in an Indian frontier campaign.

The march of the First Division was but little opposed throughout. On the 9th the 1st Brigade marched from Haidar Khel into the Waran Valley, destroyed a large number of fortified houses, and also the house of Saiyid Akbar, which had been partially repaired since destroyed by General Kempster's brigade. In its retirement the Aka Khel and Zakha Khel pressed upon our rearguard, but the losses were not heavy. The remainder of the march down the valley was practically unmolested, and the division was concentrated at Ilmgudar near Peshawar on the 17th November.

General Westmacott's brigade of the Second Division

marched from Bagh on the 7th, through the Shaloba
Pass to Dwa Toi, where it was joined on the 9th by
General Kempster's troops, whose march had been
delayed, at the outset, by the necessity for destroying
the defences of the Kambar Khel and Malikdin Khel,
and, during its execution, by the state of the road
rendered slippery by rain and congested by the
baggage of the advanced brigade. On the 10th, the
march of the two brigades was unopposed, but on
the 11th, movement and communication were rendered
difficult by a thick mist, touch was lost between the
two brigades, and the Afridis following up closely,
favoured by the mist and abundant cover, inflicted
great loss among the transport and followers. Part
of the rearguard did not get into camp at all that
night, and, seizing some houses, the commander defended his rearguard and a large amount of transport
against the attacks of the tribesmen, who kept up a
fire all night. On the 12th the Second Division
closed up and remained halted. On the 13th the
march was resumed, and the tribesmen attacking with
great boldness as soon as the rearguard of the rear
brigade (General Westmacott's) left camp, the fighting
was continuous throughout the day. The enemy
suffered heavily in his attacks on the baggage column
and rearguard, but, nothing daunted, came on again
and again, making most determined rushes. Firing
was incessant throughout the night into the bivouac
of Westmacott's brigade, which encamped where darkness found it, and the brigade was again attacked at
daybreak, but the enemy did not on this day follow

the column very far or for very long. On the 17th
December the two brigades of the Second Division
had reached respectively Bara and Mamanai; here
they remained for the present guarding the Bara
Valley line, while the Peshawar Column and First
Division advanced into the Khyber Pass and Bazar
Valley.

On the 18th December the Peshawar Column reconnoitred the Khyber Pass as far as Fort Maude; on
the 23rd Ali Musjid was occupied; and on the 26th
the column marched to Lundi Kotal, finding villages
deserted, barracks destroyed, and everywhere damage
done to Government property. The Shinwaris living
about Lundi Kotal, who had assisted in the early
attacks on the Khyber posts, had by now paid up
their fines and submitted, and proved their repentance
by assisting in picqueting the hills and keeping off
Zakha Khel raiders, and even restored some of the
property taken away when the serai at Lundi Kotal
was looted.

The Bazar Valley, which is one of a series of
parallel valleys running almost due east and west,
is only about twenty miles long, with an average
breadth of between eight and twelve miles from
watershed to watershed, and lies at an elevation of
3000 feet. On the north the Alachi Mountains
separate it from the Khyber, and on the south the
Sur Ghar Range divides it from the Bara Valley.
Through the valley the Bazar stream runs almost due
east till it joins the Khyber stream at Jabagai. The
east end of the valley is narrow, and just before its

final debouchure into the Peshawar Plain it contracts
into an almost impassable defile. The west end, on
the other hand, is comparatively wide and open, and
climbs gradually up to the snow-capped range of the
Safed Koh, the lower ridges of which form the boundary of the Bazar Valley. The Zakha Khel own this
upper portion of the valley. It consists of two main
branches, each about two miles broad, enclosing between them an irregular spur. This spur, running
out from the main watershed in a series of relatively
small hills, ends in an abrupt peak just above China.
About two and a half miles east of China the two
branch valleys unite, and in the apex of their junction,
closing the mouth of the China plain, is an isolated
hill known as Khar Ghundai.

Through the circle of mountains to the south-west
and west go four main passes—Mangal Bagh and
Bukar leading into the Bara Valley, and the Thabai
and Sisobi, or Tsatsobi, into Afghanistan. The former
give communication to neighbours, the latter form
back-doors or " bolt-holes " into Afghanistan, and the
existence of these back-doors constitutes the real
difficulty of dealing effectively with the Zakha Khels.
The " front-door " is over the Alachi Range, crossed
by the Chora, Alachi, Bori, and Bazar Passes, and of
these the first named is the easiest, but it leads, as has
been already stated, through Malikdin Khel territory.

On the 25th the First Division entered the Bazar
Valley in two columns from the immediate vicinity
of Ali Musjid, where it had concentrated the day
previous. The 1st Brigade moved by the Alachi Pass

to Karamna, and the 2nd by way of the Chora Pass to Chora; neither was seriously opposed, but the roads were found to be very difficult. On the 26th the 1st Brigade was only able to march as far as Barg, no more than two and a half miles, but a road presenting extraordinary difficulties to the progress of troops and almost impassable to transport. The same day the 2nd Brigade was advancing to China, with its rearguard harassed all the way; it returned next day to Chora, followed up on both flanks, and reached the Khyber on the 28th and Jamrud on the 29th. The 1st Brigade supported, on the 27th, the retirement of the 2nd Brigade from China, moved back to Karamna on the 28th, and on the next day returned to the Khyber, the rearguard, furnished by the Derbyshire Regiment, being persistently followed up nearly to Lala China in the Khyber.

During the latter part of December and beginning of January 1898, the Peshawar column was frequently engaged with the Zakha Khels about Lundi Kotal, and on all sides punitive measures, accompanied by desultory and indecisive fighting, continued as before. Many of the Afridi clans—the Malikdin Khels, Kambar Khels, Sipah and Kamar Khels—had sent in asking for peace, while bewailing the severity of our terms; but the Aka Khels were obdurate, and the Zakha Khels as defiant as at the very commencement of the campaign, their two most recalcitrant maliks, Khwas Khan and Wali Muhammad Khan, from the secure haven of Afghanistan, exhorting them to stand firm and to continue to resist.

The last action of the campaign took place at the Shinkamar Pass on the 29th January, when all the four brigades combined to endeavour to surround the Kajurai plain, where the Afridis were reported to be again grazing their cattle. Few of the columns employed experienced any opposition, but one operating from Mamanai, and belonging to General Westmacott's brigade, when about to retire was hotly engaged by the enemy, and sustained some seventy casualties; these were chiefly among the Yorkshire Light Infantry and the 36th Sikhs, the last named regiment losing a splendid frontier soldier in their commanding officer, Colonel John Haughton.

Before the end of February nearly all the Afridi clans had submitted or were making advances towards a settlement; the Khyber Pass had been reopened to kafilas, but the Zakha Khels evinced no real intention of giving in. On the 17th March, therefore, preparations were made for a spring campaign; Sir William Lockhart returned to Jamrud, fresh transport was distributed among the troops, and one of the brigades of the Second Division made a short advance towards the Bara Valley. The effect upon the Zakha Khels was immediate. By the 3rd April all the clans had definitely submitted and given hostages for fines still due; hostilities then ceased and demobilisation commenced, but for some months regular troops were retained in occupation of the Khyber posts.

By November 1898 the arrangements for the

Y

government of the Khyber previously in force were practically re-established.

The total casualties during the campaign amounted to 287 killed, 853 wounded and ten missing.

It was hoped that the settlement effected, coupled with the knowledge the Afridis now possessed that no part of their country was inaccessible to British troops, would have proved satisfactory to both sides ; and it was noticed as a favourable sign that the enlistment of Pathans, and especially of Afridis, into the regiments of the Indian Army, had never been brisker than during the months immediately succeeding the close of hostilities. It was hardly to be expected that individual raids and outrages would cease, and had any such expectations been cherished they would have speedily been disappointed ; but at any rate for a brief term of years it was not considered necessary to undertake military operations against any of the Afridis. But among these tribesmen the mullahs appear to be specially inimical to the British Government—as they probably would be to any civilised administration—while there is also always present in Afghanistan a faction opposed to British interests, and from this faction disaffected tribesmen can safely reckon upon a large measure of support. In 1904 a number of Afridis visited Kabul—whether by invitation or not is not certain—were accorded a very friendly reception, and seem to have returned determined—especially the Zakha Khel members of the deputation—upon a policy of opposition to the British authorities. During the next four years raids, ever increasing in audacity, were committed on and within our border by the Zakha Khels, culminating on the 28th January, 1908, in a raid carried out by some seventy or eighty men upon the city of Peshawar, whence property valued at a lakh of rupees was carried off, the raiders getting clear away. Tribal allowances were stopped in the endeavour to force the more well-behaved tribesmen to undertake the coercion of the Zakha Khel, but they declared their inability to restrain the clan—and their impotence was recognised—while suggesting to the British authorities the occupation of the Bazar Valley, as the only means of dealing effectively with a situation which was rapidly becoming intolerable, since security of life and property on the Kohat and Peshawar borders was seriously menaced.

By the beginning of 1908 the Government of India saw that military operations must inevitably be undertaken, and proposed that three brigades (one in reserve) should be mobilised in view of an expedition into the Bazar Valley; and on the 13th February Major-General Sir J. Willcocks, who had been appointed to command, moved out from Peshawar.

The three brigades were thus constituted:

FIRST BRIGADE.

Brigadier-General Anderson.

1st Battalion Royal Warwickshire Regiment.
53rd Sikhs.
59th Scinde Rifles.
2nd Battalion 5th Gurkhas.

SECOND BRIGADE.

Major-General Barrett.

1st Battalion Seaforth Highlanders.
28th Punjabis.
45th Sikhs.
54th Sikhs.

THIRD (RESERVE) BRIGADE.

Major-General Watkis.

1st Battalion Royal Munster Fusiliers.
1st Battalion 5th Gurkhas.
1st Battalion 6th Gurkhas.
55th Coke's Rifles.
No. 9 Company 2nd Sappers and Miners.
23rd Peshawar Mountain Battery.

DIVISIONAL TROOPS.

Two Squadrons 19th Lancers.
Two Squadrons 37th Lancers.
23rd Sikh Pioneers.
25th Punjabis.
No. 3 Mountain Battery.
Four Guns, 22nd Derajat Mountain Battery.
No. 6 Company 1st Sappers and Miners.
800 Khyber Rifles.

The main force, under General Willcocks, left Peshawar on the 13th February, and on the 15th, marching by the Chora Pass, entered the Bazar Valley. The Second Brigade, with some divisional troops, pushed on rapidly through Malikdin Khel country, accompanied by little or no transport and all ranks carrying three days rations on the person, and bivouacked that night near Walai. The latter part of the march was opposed. The First Brigade followed more leisurely, escorting the baggage and supply columns of both brigades, and halted for the night at Chora, sending forward next day the Second Brigade baggage and supplies. On the same day a small column under Colonel Roos-Keppel, political adviser with the force, and composed of a wing of the 2nd Battalion 5th Gurkhas and the Khyber Rifles, left Lundi Kotal, and, marching by the Bazar Pass, arrived that evening at China. There was no opposition en route, but the camps, both here and at Walai, were subjected to the usual " sniping " after nightfall.

The Walai camp was particularly well chosen; it was well covered, was surrounded by a circle of hills admitting of effective picqueting, had a secure line of communication with Chora, and, commanding as it did the whole valley, was especially well placed for carrying out punitive operations among the Zakha Khels.

From the 17th to the 24th the troops were engaged in destroying towers and defensive enclosures, and in collecting wood and fodder; the columns were always followed up by the enemy, who, however, usually suffered heavily; the whole of the Bazar Valley was visited and important surveys were completed; sniping occurred on most nights; but already by the 23rd the resistance offered was no more than half-hearted, and that afternoon a tolerably representative jirgah came in professing anxiety to effect a settlement. An agreement was rendered difficult by the presence about the Thabai Pass of a gathering of Shinwaris and Mohmands, who had come to offer their services to the Zakha Khels, but these were prevailed upon to withdraw; and after protracted negotiations, lasting from the 25th to the 27th, a satisfactory settlement was arrived at. On the 29th the force withdrew wholly unmolested to the Khyber and Peshawar, the Afridi jirgah having undertaken the punishment of raiders, responsibility for future good behaviour, and restitution, as far as possible, of stolen property.

The casualties in this short and successful campaign amounted to three killed and thirty-seven wounded.

NOTE.

COMPOSITION OF THE TIRAH EXPEDITIONARY FORCE.

THE MAIN COLUMN.

FIRST DIVISION.

COMMANDING—BRIGADIER-GENERAL W. P. SYMONS, C.B.

FIRST BRIGADE.

COMMANDING—BRIGADIER-GENERAL R. C. HART, V.C., C.B.

1st Battalion, the Devonshire Regiment.
2nd Battalion, the Derbyshire Regiment.
2nd Battalion, 1st Gurkha (Rifle) Regiment.
30th (Punjab) Regiment of Bengal Infantry.

SECOND BRIGADE.

COMMANDING—BRIGADIER-GENERAL A. GASELEE, A.D.C., C.B.

1st Battalion, Royal West Surrey Regiment.
2nd Battalion, the Yorkshire Regiment.
2nd Battalion, 4th Gurkha (Rifle) Regiment.
3rd Regiment of Sikh Infantry, Punjab Frontier Force.

DIVISIONAL TROOPS.

No. 1 Mountain Battery, Royal Artillery.
No. 2 (Derajat) Mountain Battery.
No. 1 (Kohat) Mountain Battery.
Two Squadrons, 18th Regiment of Bengal Lancers.
28th Regiment of Bombay Infantry (Pioneers).[1]
No. 3 Company, Bombay Sappers and Miners.

[1] Now the 128th Pioneers.

No. 4 Company, Bombay Sappers and Miners.
The Nabha Regiment of Imperial Service Infantry.
The Maler Kotla Imperial Service Sappers.

SECOND DIVISION.

COMMANDING—MAJOR-GENERAL A. G. YEATMAN-BIGGS, C.B.

THIRD BRIGADE.

COMMANDING—COLONEL F. J. KEMPSTER, A.D.C., D.S.O.

1st Battalion, the Dorsetshire Regiment.
1st Battalion, the Gordon Highlanders.
1st Battalion, 2nd Gurkha (Rifle) Regiment.
15th (the Ludhiana Sikh) Regiment of Bengal Infantry.

FOURTH BRIGADE.

COMMANDING—BRIGADIER-GENERAL R. WESTMACOTT, C.B., D.S.O.

2nd Battalion, the King's Own Scottish Borderers.
1st Battalion, the Northamptonshire Regiment.
1st Battalion, 3rd Gurkha (Rifle) Regiment.
36th (Sikh) Regiment of Bengal Infantry.

DIVISIONAL TROOPS.

No. 8 Mountain Battery, Royal Artillery.
No. 9 Mountain Battery, Royal Artillery.
No. 5 (Bombay) Mountain Battery.
Machine Gun Detachment, 16th Lancers.
Two Squadrons, 18th Regiment of Bengal Lancers.
21st Regiment of Madras Infantry (Pioneers).
No. 4 Company, Madras Sappers and Miners.
The Jhind Regiment of Imperial Service Infantry.
The Sirmur Imperial Service Sappers.

LINE OF COMMUNICATIONS.

COMMANDING—LIEUTENANT-GENERAL SIR A. P. PALMER, K.C.B.

3rd Regiment of Bengal Cavalry.
18th Regiment of Bengal Lancers.
No. 1 Kashmir Mountain Battery.
22nd (Punjab) Regiment of Bengal Infantry.

2nd Battalion, 2nd Gurkha (Rifle) Regiment.
39th Garhwal (Rifle) Regiment of Bengal Infantry.
2nd Regiment Punjab Infantry, Punjab Frontier Force.
No. 1 Company Bengal Sappers and Miners.
The Jeypore Imperial Service Transport Corps.
The Gwalior Imperial Service Transport Corps.

THE PESHAWAR COLUMN.
COMMANDING—BRIGADIER-GENERAL A. G. HAMMOND, V.C.,
C.B., D.S.O., A.D.C.

57th Field Battery, Royal Artillery.
No. 3 Mountain Battery, Royal Artillery.
2nd Battalion, the Royal Inniskilling Fusiliers.
2nd Battalion, the Oxfordshire Light Infantry.
9th Regiment of Bengal Lancers.
No. 5 Company, Bengal Sappers and Miners.
9th Gurkha (Rifle) Regiment of Bengal Infantry.
34th Pioneers.
45th (Rattray's Sikh) Regiment of Bengal Infantry.

THE KURRAM MOVABLE COLUMN.
COMMANDING—COLONEL W. HILL.

3rd Field Battery, Royal Artillery.
6th Regiment of Bengal Cavalry.
2nd Regiment of Central India Horse.[1]
12th (Khelat-i-Ghilzie) Regiment of Bengal Infantry.
1st Battalion, 5th Gurkha Rifles.
The Kapurthala Regiment of Imperial Service Infantry.

THE RAWAL PINDI RESERVE BRIGADE.
COMMANDING—BRIGADIER-GENERAL C. R. MACGREGOR, D.S.O.

1st Battalion, the Duke of Cornwall's Light Infantry.
2nd Battalion, the King's Own Yorkshire Light Infantry.
27th Regiment (1st Baluch Battalion) of Bombay (Light) Infantry.[2]
2nd Regiment of Infantry, Hyderabad Contingent.[3]
Jodhpur Imperial Service Lancers.

[1] Now the 39th King George's Own Central India Horse.
[2] Now the 127th L.I.   [3] Now the 95th Russell's Infantry.

CHAPTER XIV.

ORAKZAIS.[1]

THE tract of country inhabited by this tribe is some sixty miles long by about twenty broad. It is bounded on the north by the Shinwaris and Afridis, on the east by the Bangash and Afridis, on the south by the Bangash and the Zaimukhts, and on the west by the Kharmana River and by the country of the Chamkannis. The Orakzais also possess some settlements in British territory in the Kohat district. The Orakzai country proper is generally termed Orakzai Tirah, and it contains four principal valleys—the Khanki, the Mastura, the Kharmana and the Bara; but Holdich lays due stress upon the peculiarities of its position, when he says that "the Orakzai geographical position differs from that of the Afridis in some essential particulars. . . . It is through their country that the way to the heart of the Afridi mountains lies. They keep the front door to Maidan (which is near the Dargai Pass across the Samana), whilst the back door is open to Afghanistan, but they possess no back door themselves, so that once their valleys (Khanki and Mastura) are held, they are in the power of the enemy and they must submit."

[1] See Map VII.

The origin of the tribe is rather obscure, and local traditions vary greatly. One version is that three brothers—Pridi, Wazir, and Warak—came from Afghanistan to the Orakzai Hills, where they quarrelled over some trifle—as their descendants have continued to do down to present times—and Pridi then went north, Wazir to the south, while Warak remained where he was. Another tradition is that they are descended from a Persian prince who was exiled ("Wrukzai" in Pushtu) and who settled in the Kohat district, marrying a daughter of the King of Kohat. Others, again, say that the original home of the Orakzais was on the slopes of the Suleiman Mountains; that they and the Bangash settled in the Zaimukht country during the invasions of Sabuktagin and Timur, and were driven thence into the Kurram, and from there, again, into the Miranzai Valley. The occupation of the Kurram by the Turis, and their gradual encroachment into the lower part of that valley, then held by the Bangash, forced these in their turn to press the Orakzais. The struggle came to an end with a great battle at Muhammadzai, near Kohat, towards the end of the sixteenth century. The story goes that after three days' fighting the victory remained with the Bangash, the actual issue being materially assisted by the intervention of a supernatural figure garbed in spotless white raiment, which appeared between the contending forces, crying out—"the plains for the Bangash and the hills for the Orakzai."

The Orakzais thereupon retired to their present

holdings, while the Bangash have ever since occupied the Miranzai Valley. Historically, however, it is more than probable that the Orakzais are of an ancient Indian stock, and that in process of time successive emigrations from the west have brought to them an infusion of Turkish blood.

These tribesmen are wiry-looking mountaineers, but they are not such fine men physically, their reputation for courage does not stand so high, nor are they as formidable as their northern neighbours, the Afridis, while they are prone to be influenced by fanaticism to a far greater extent. Their mountains are barren, and they themselves are often ragged, poverty-stricken and underfed in appearance, distinguishable from their neighbours—and, incidentally, wholly *indistinguishable* when skirmishing on their hill-sides—by reason of the peculiar pearl-grey tint of their dress, dyed from an earth found in the Tirah hills. Their chief source of wealth lies in their flocks and herds, and they do a considerable trade with Peshawar, especially in the *mazarai*, or dwarf palm, which is cut during August and September, and which has a certain commercial value for the manufacture of ropes, grass-sandals, bed-strings, nets, matting, baskets and grain-bins. Many of the Orakzais are weavers by trade.

Of their moral character the usual contradictory evidence is forthcoming. It was against the Orakzais that Macgregor brought the indictment already quoted, that "there is no doubt that, like other Pathans, they would not shrink from any falsehood, however

atrocious, to gain an end. Money would buy their
services for the foulest deed; cruelty of the most
revolting kind would mark their actions to a wounded
or helpless foe, as much as cowardice would stamp
them against determined resistance." And Oliver,
after saying that, if not better, they are probably not
much worse than their neighbours in the Pathan
qualities of deceit, avarice and cruelty, reminds us
that "it must not be forgotten that they have been
embittered by centuries of bitter religious feuds and
the influence of fanatical teachers; they have never
had a government of any decent sort, its place being
supplied by superstition; and they do not understand
our theory of tolerance or non-interference." On the
other hand, it is said that as soldiers they are, in
general, quiet, well-behaved and intelligent, respond-
ing easily to discipline. At home they are given,
even more than other Pathans, to internecine feuds,
due to the fact that part of the tribe are Samil and
Sunnis, and part Gar and Shiahs. Their fighting men
number, all told, some 24,000, all tolerably well
armed.

Of two out of their four main valleys the following
descriptions are given by Holdich: "The Khanki
Valley offers no special attractions in the matter of
scenery. The flanking mountains are rugged and
rough, and unbroken by the craggy peaks and fan-
tastic outlines which generally give a weird sort of
charm to frontier hills. The long slopes of the
mountain spurs gradually shape themselves downwards into terraced flats, bounded by steep-sided

ravines, along which meander a few insignificant
streams, and the whole scene, under the waning sun
of late October, is a dreary expanse of misty dust
colour, unrelieved by the brilliant patchwork which
enlivens the landscape elsewhere.   On a terraced
slope between the Khanki and the Kandi Mishti
ravines, under the Pass of Sampagha, stands a mud-
built village with an enclosure of trees, called Ghandaki ; and it is through this village that the road
to Sampagha runs after crossing the Kandi Mishti
declivities, ere it winds its devious course up a long
spur to the pass.... Beyond the Sampagha lay the
elevated Valley of Mastura (some 1500 feet higher
than the Khanki, itself 4300 feet above sea-level),
and 700 feet below, the pass. The difference in
elevation was at once apparent in the general appearance of the landscape. Six thousand feet of
altitude lifts Mastura above the dust-begrimed and
heat-riddled atmosphere of Khanki or Miranzai, and
gives it all the clear, soft beauty of an Alpine climate.
Mastura is one of the prettiest valleys of the frontier.
In spite of the lateness of the season, apricot and
mulberry trees had not yet parted with scarlet
and yellow of the waning year. Each little hamlet
clinging to the grey cliffs, or perched on the flat
spaces of the bordering plateau below, was set in its
own surrounding of autumn's gold-tinted jewellery ;
and in the blue haze born of the first breath of clear
October frost, the crowded villages and the graceful
watch-towers keeping ward over them were mistily
visible across the breadth of the valleys, tier above

tier, on the far slopes of the mountains, till lost in the vagueness of the shadows of the hills."

The Kharmana Valley has been described as dotted with hamlets and towers, well-wooded and cultivated, and abundantly watered. It is entered from the south by the Kharmana defile, some seven miles in length, the hills on either side being very steep and covered with scrub jungle; and from the east over the Durbi Khel Kotal, a rough and difficult pass, and by way of the Lozaka defile, a narrow ravine with precipitous hills on either side.

Of such part of the Bara Valley as is occupied by the Orakzai, it may be said to be that portion between the right bank of the Bara River and the Mastura—formerly known as the Orakzai Bara—and enclosed between Bar And Khel, where the Mastura makes a sharp bend to the south, and Mamanai, where it joins the Bara on its entry into the Kajurai plain. From this part of the Bara Valley the upper reaches of the Mastura are arrived at by a very narrow, rocky gorge to Sapri and Kwaja Khidda, thence over the Sapri Pass—an ascent of some 2000 feet—and thence by the stream bed or over the Sangra Pass to Mishti Bazar and the upper Mastura.

The Orakzais are now usually considered to be divided into six clans, since, of the original seven, one is practically extinct; these six clans are again sub-divided into many divisions; the six clans are as under:

1. Ismailzai.	4. Daulatzai.
2. Lashkarzai.	5. Muhammad Khel.
3. Massuzai.	6. Sturi Khel or Alizai.

In addition, however, to the Orakzai clans, there are four hamsaya clans :

1. Ali Khel.   3. Mishtia.
2. Malla Khel.   4. Sheikhans.

The *Ismailzai* are divided into six divisions ; all of them are Sunnis by faith, and the majority are Samil in politics. The clan is very disunited, but can turn out some 1800 fighting men, chiefly from two of the divisions, which are rather increasing in power and numbers at the expense ef the remaining four. One of these divisions, the Rabia Khel, is remarkable for the fair hair, fair complexions and blue eyes of those belonging to it. The Ismailzai, residing as they do rather nearer to our territory than the rest of the Orakzais, have hitherto given us considerably more than their share of tribal trouble.

Commencing from the east, the settlements of the Ismailzai extend along the right bank of the Khanki River to near Shahu Khel, and include the northern slopes of the Samana Range. This tract belongs to the Rabia Khel and Akhel divisions, and they also own a small strip of ground on the left bank of the river, while both have also settlements in the British portion of the Miranzai Valley. Another division, the Mamazai, live in the Daradar Glen, which drains into the Khanki on the left bank, and here is the village of Arkhi, of more than local reputation for the manufacture of rifles. The remaining three divisions of this clan are scattered about in small settlements on the left bank of the Khanki River, the Khadizais at Sadarai and Tutgarhi, the Sadakhel at Ghandaki,

at the foot of the Sampagha Pass leading to the
Mastura Valley, and the Isa Khel in hamlets on
either side of the pass itself. The Isa Khel are
considered inviolable and are hamsayas of the Rabia
Khel, Ali Khel and Mishtis—the two last themselves
hamsaya clans—while the curse of an Isa Khel is said
to possess particular potency, and is in consequence
dreaded by the neighbouring tribesmen.

The *Lashkarzai* consist of two divisions only,
Alisherzais and Mamuzais, the former Gar and the
latter Samil, both being of the Sunni sect, and each
being at feud with the other. The clan can muster
some 5800 fighting men, of which number the
Alisherzais contribute the larger half—all are fairly
well armed. The country of the Alisherzai is divided
—like the seats at a Spanish bull-fight—into the
"sunny" and the "shady"—the former title applying
to the country lying on the southern slopes of the
Tor Ghar, towards the Kurram Valley, and the latter
to that on the northern slopes at the head of the
Khanki Valley. The Alisherzais have a great reputation for bravery, and it is said that at one time in
their military history they employed mounted men in
battle; but if this was ever the case their taste for
cavalry service would appear to have weakened, since
barely a dozen Orakzais all told are at the present
moment to be found serving in our regular regiments
of the Indian cavalry. In this division the Khan-ship
is hereditary, being vested in a family living at
Tatang; in the year 1897 the then holder of the office
was greatly implicated in the risings on the Samana.

z

The Mamuzais live at the head of the Khanki Valley,
to the north of the Minjan Darra, in a tract called
Sama, Khanki Bazar, a rich trading centre, being
the tribal headquarters. There is, perhaps, no other
clan between the Kabul and the Kurram Rivers, so
much under the influence of their mullahs and so
fanatical as are these people; they also rather take
the lead among the Orakzais.

The *Massuzais* are contained in three divisions, of
which one is Gar and the other two are Samil, while
all three are Sunnis. They can put 2000 men in the
field, but have not a great reputation for courage.
Their holdings are in the Kharmana Valley—the
Kharmana River flows into the Kurram near our
frontier post at Sadda—and they have a number of
Afridi hamsayas settled amongst them.

The *Daulatzai* clan consists of the Firoz Khel, the
Bizotis, and the Utman Khel,[1] all Sunnis and all
Samil, but the Firoz Khel hold aloof from the other
two, who are leagued together against them. The
three divisions can turn out 1600 men between them,
the Firoz Khel being the most powerful, and the
Bizotis the worst armed. The Bizotis and the Utman
Khel have given us a good deal of trouble since our
first occupation of the Miranzai Valley, while the Firoz
Khel on the other hand have been generally well-
behaved, the reason no doubt being that living further from our territory they have had less temptation
to transgress. The Firoz Khel, from which division

---

[1] Not to be confused with a tribe of the same name in the Yusafzai
country.

the reigning family of Bhopal is said to be descended,
inhabit the Upper Mastura Valley and the north-
eastern slopes of the Mola Ghar as far west as the
Sapri Pass; the Utman Khel live in portions of the
Upper and Lower Mastura Valley, as far as the junction of that river with the Bara; while the Bizotis
are intermixed with them in the Upper Mastura,
living in the lower reaches of the river between the
Ublan Pass and the Asman Darra.

The *Muhammad Khel* comprise four divisions, all
of which are Gar in politics, and being of the Shiah
sect, set in the midst of Sunni neighbours, they are
inclined to separate themselves to some extent from
the rest of the Orakzais and to turn to the British;
they have always been well-behaved and favourably
disposed towards us. They number 2500 well-armed
fighting men, and are accounted among the bravest
of the Orakzais. Their country is in the centre of the
Mastura Valley, of which it commands either end and
turns the greater part of the Khanki Valley; it is
also easy of access from Kohat, and would furnish a
convenient advanced base for operations against the
Afridi country directed from the south. It was the
Khan of one of the sections of the Muhammad
Khel who led the Orakzai lashkar which, in 1587,
defeated, in a battle at the Sampagha Pass, a Mogul
army under Ghairat Khan which had attempted to
penetrate into Tirah.

The *Sturi Khel* or *Alizai* are divided into Tirah
and Bara Sturi Khel, who are at mortal feud with
one another, half being Shiahs and half Sunnis. The

clan is only a small one, its fighting men numbering no more than 500 all told, and but indifferently armed. The Tirah division occupies both sides of the Mastura River from Shiraz Garhi to the Gudar Tangi, while the Bara Sturi Khel inhabit the lower Bara Valley from Galli Khel to Mamanai, thus commanding the approach to the Mastura Valley by the way of the Sapri, or Walnut Tree, Pass.

Hamsaya: Ali Khel.—This is by far the most important of these alien clans, is very united, with a high reputation for courage, and mustering from 2800-3000 fighting men. They are said to be descended from Yusafzai emigrants, and being thus of the same origin as the Mishtis they form a coalition with them, despite the fact that they belong to different political factions, the Ali Khel being Gar while the Mishtis are Samil. In religion the Ali Khel are partly Shiahs and partly Sunnis. Their country extends from the Tor Ghar Range on the north, to the Khanki River on the south, with summer settlements near the source of the Mastura River and on either bank. This clan thus occupies in the Orakzai country much the same position of command as do the Zakha Khels in Afridi-land. They are consequently, by right of position, very troublesome neighbours, both to their fellow tribesmen and to the Indian Government.

Hamsaya: Malla Khel.—A clan of Ghilzai origin, Sunni by persuasion and Samil in politics. They occupy a strip of country in the Mastura Valley between the Sampagha and Arhanga Passes. In the cold weather they migrate to Darband in the Miranzai

Valley, which they hold as a perpetual gift from the
Khan of Hangu—a family formerly possessing great
local influence—for having aided him in the eighteenth
century against the Khan of Kohat.   They hold also,
on a lease, the village of Turki in British territory.
The Malla Khel have a considerable reputation for
bravery, and their fighting men number 800, but the
clan is much divided against itself, and, as a clan, is
to a great extent swayed by the counsels of the
Mishtis, who command the routes to and from the
summer quarters of the Malla Khel.

Hamsaya: Mishtis.—These are, as already stated,
of Yusafzai descent, Samil in politics, and of the
Sunni sect.   They are rather a scattered clan, living
in the Upper Mastura south of the Waran Valley, in
the Upper Khanki south of the Sampagha Range, and
also in the Lower Khanki Valley, while in the winter
months many of them migrate to the Miranzai Valley.
The Mishtis rather take the lead among the Samil
faction of the Orakzai; they have 3000 warriors, are
well off, and engage a good deal in trade with British
territory.   One division of this clan is known among
the remainder as " the Dirty Ones "—their want of
cleanliness must consequently be something quite
abnormal to render them thus conspicuous among
Pathans.

Hamsaya: Sheikhan.—These are believed to have
been originally Wazirs; they are Sunnis and Samil in
politics.   Their possessions form a compact tract, extending from the Mastura River on the north to the
Khanki on the south, and from Khangabur on the

west to Talai on the border of the Kohat district on the east. They trade but little, and come down to the neighbourhood of Kohat to pasture their flocks in the winter. They can muster from 2750-3000 fighting men of no great repute for courage, but are a clan of some importance and not easy to control, though susceptible to blockade.

As regards the question of the southern boundaries of the Orakzai territory, it may be mentioned that as far back as 1865, the Rabia Khel division of the Ismailzai clan formally acknowledged that the crest of the Samana Range was the northern boundary of British territory; but the strip of country in question does not then appear to have been marked on our maps as British, although it was assessed as such, and was always acknowledged by the clans as being within our borders. It was not, however, until 1889 that the Government of India agreed to the proposals of the Punjab Government that "the country up to the *foot* of the Samana Range should be declared to be British territory and dealt with accordingly," and not until two years later that posts were established upon the Samana Range itself.

This chapter may fittingly be closed by a brief account of the circumstances under which certain Orakzai clans and divisions petitioned to be taken under British administration, and of the decision which was then come to on the matter.

As has already been mentioned, the Orakzai tribe is partly Sunni and partly Shiah by persuasion, the

Sunnis predominating, and between these two religious communities there exists a long-standing and bitter animosity.   In the summer of 1894 the Bar Muhammad Khel division of the Muhammad Khel clan of Orakzais made a request through the Assistant Political Officer, Kohat, that they might be allowed to come under British rule, on the grounds that they could not much longer defend themselves against their Sunni fellow-tribesmen, as they found themselves cut off from local supplies of arms and ammunition by the influence of Sunni mullahs.   To some of the frontier officials the idea of such voluntary annexation had a good deal to recommend it, but the Government of India declined to meet the desire of the division concerned that they or their country should be put under the control or the protection of the British Government.

In the following year the Shiahs of the Ali Khel (hamsaya) clan of Orakzais preferred a similar petition, but the annexation of their country did not present advantages equal to that which had accompanied the request put forward in the preceding year. The tract of country offered us by the Bar Muhammad Khel was an undivided stretch of hills with no inhabitants save Shiahs; while in the case of the Ali Khel, although some of the villages concerned were large and powerful, yet they were so mixed up with Sunni communities that annexation would have been impracticable, even if desirable.   The request of the Ali Khel was consequently also refused, the Governments of the Punjab and of India being very strongly against any extension of our responsibilities in the tribal tracts beyond the Kohat district. So matters remained until the frontier disturbances of 1897-98, during which these Shiah clans maintained a uniformly friendly attitude towards us, as they had also during the Miranzai expeditions, when they gave us material assistance. In January 1898 the then Secretary of State for India laid down certain principles for the conduct of frontier policy, whereby his successors seem in the main to have since been guided. These were : (1) That no fresh responsibility should be accepted unless absolutely required by actual strategic necessities and for the protection of the British border.; (2) that interference with the tribes must when possible be avoided ; (3) that no countenance should be given to the idea that Government intended to administer or enclose the tribal country ; and, finally, (4) that in view of the suspicion which the Durand demarcation had aroused, one of the primary objects of our future actions should be gradually to allay such doubts and misgivings.

In 1904, however, an even more extended offer of annexation was made to the Government of India, under circumstances differing from those of 1895. In the summer of 1903 a fakir from Ghazni created disturbances in the Orakzai country, preached a jehad, and made an organised attack against the Shiahs. The fakir's Sunni forces were, however, twice defeated, the fakir left the country, and hostilities came to an end. But even while the fighting was still in progress, the Chappar Mishtis, a Sunni division, applied to be taken over by the British Government, but were informed that we could not interfere in a purely religious war, and that no petition from them could be entertained until peace was restored.   When the war had come to an end, all the four Shiah divisions of the Muhammad Khel clan—the Mani Khel, Bar Muhammad Khel, Sipaia and Abdul Aziz Khel—with the Ibrahimzai and the Chappar Mishtis, at once made overtures to be taken over, expressing their desire to come under Government control somewhat on the same lines as the Kurram clans.   The fighting strength of these tribes represented approximately 2710 men, the tract occupied by them containing some seventy villages, and being about thirty miles in length with a maximum breadth of some fourteen miles.   The territory formed a complete block, bounded on the north by the Mastura river, running down on the south to the broken and undulating country within the limits of Kachai and Marai in British territory ; on the east it extended to within four miles of Kohat ; while on the west the boundary stopped just short of the point where the road, made during the expedition of 1897, crosses the Sampagha Pass.   The strategical advantages conferred by the possession of this tract of country are especially great in the event of the Afridi tribe being ever again arrayed against us. These Shiah clans command one of the shortest routes from the Kohat side to the centre of Tirah by the Landuki Pass ; there is access to the Bara Valley by the Maturi or the Uchpal Pass, and by Waran to the Khyber Afridi settlements in Rajgal and Maidan.

They also overlook the territory of three of the hamsaya clans, and are in rear of the country of some of the Ismailzai divisions.

On the 28th October, 1904, the Secretary of State for India expressed himself as unwilling to take any steps which he was of opinion might add appreciably to our frontier responsibilities, and therefore declined to authorise any serious departure from the general policy laid down by his predecessor in January 1898, or to incur the risk attaching to the suggested extension of the tribal area under our control.

CHAPTER XV.

ORAKZAIS: OPERATIONS.[1]

Up to the year 1855 the Orakzais, though occasionally committing petty depredations on the border, and known to be capable of mischief if so inclined, gave no positive trouble to the British authorities; but in the spring of that year many of the tribe were concerned in the demonstrations and attacks upon posts and parties in the Miranzai Valley, mention of which will be found in Chapter XVI. Divisions of the Ismailzai clan had been especially aggressive; the Akhel division had attacked a village (Baliamin) in British territory and carried off 156 head of cattle; and on the 30th April of that year the Orakzais, made up by Afridis and Zaimukhts to a strength of between 1500 and 2000 men, attacked our camp, but were driven off with heavy loss.

After the withdrawal of the troops, the Orakzais continued to commit depredations upon the Bangash living in the Kohat district, making no fewer than fifteen raids, carrying off many hundred head of cattle and killing several British subjects. In these affairs the tribesmen of the two hamsaya clans, the

[1] See Map VII.

Sheikhan and the Mishti, were concerned, but the Rabia Khel division of the Ismailzai was also conspicuous; and finally, a feud having commenced between the Orakzais and the people of Hangu, a village in the neighbourhood was raided and 660 head of cattle were carried off. At this Major J. Coke, commanding the 1st Punjab Infantry, and also Deputy-Commissioner of Kohat, reinforced Hangu with two guns and 300 bayonets, and, the raids continuing, reported that he proposed to attack the Rabia Khel village of Nasin,[1] assisted by Bangash and other levies. Coke's proposals were, however, vetoed both by the Brigadier-General commanding the Punjab Frontier Force, and by Mr. John Lawrence, the Chief Commissioner—chiefly on the ground of the difficulty and danger of moving troops at that season of the year—July—and defensive measures only were for the present sanctioned. During the next few weeks the tribesmen became more unsettled; the Rabia Khel, Mamazai and Ali Khel held a jirgah, at which it was agreed that, provided the Ali Khel and Akhel would join, the combined four divisions should make an attack upon British territory somewhere about the date of the Eed (the 25th August). There was, moreover, no doubt that the rest of the hill clans were in a most excited state, and were trying to foment a jehad. Brigadier Chamberlain, commanding the Frontier Force, had by this time arrived at Kohat, reinforcements were called up, the border villages were put in a state of defence, communications were

___
[1] No longer in existence.

improved, supplies collected, and friendly chiefs were called upon to collect armed levies.

Expedition against the Rabia Khel (Ismailzai), 1855.—By the 25th August a force of nine guns, one regiment of cavalry, and three battalions of Punjab Infantry had been assembled at Hangu, and on the 1st September arrangements were made to attack early the following morning the villages of Nasin and Sangar, the one on the summit, the other on the slopes of the Samana Range, and that of Katsa on the northern side of the Samana and on the left bank of the Khanki River. The two first-named villages were so situated, both in regard to position and approach, that any attack, during daylight and with the tribesmen prepared to meet our troops, would have entailed serious loss of life. Success depended almost entirely upon the simultaneous surprise of both Nasin and Sangar; and since any preliminary approach would have excited suspicion, it was necessary to start from Hangu, thus involving a march of fourteen miles before the commencement of the ascent of the Samana; while even if the range were ascended opposite camp, the same distance would have to be marched along the ridge before reaching Sangar. It was determined to attack the villages both from above and below, and the following dispositions were made. The 1st Punjab Infantry and three companies of the 2nd Punjab Infantry were detailed, under Major Coke, to attack the village of Sangar, leaving camp at 10 p.m., climbing the range near Hangu, and, moving along

the crest, to reach and rush Sangar before daybreak.

The second column, composed of three companies of
the 3rd Punjab Infantry, was to move at 9 p.m. on
Nasin, taking up such a position above and near the
village as to command it. If in difficulties, this column
was to be reinforced by Major Coke, who was further,
after capturing and destroying Sangar, to move the
whole of his party down the hill to aid in the attack on
Nasin. Katsa, with its rice crops and mills, and
which was reported to be almost undefended, was to
be attacked and destroyed by a party of levies, who
were to move in rear of Major Coke's column. The
remainder of the force, under the Brigadier, was to
leave camp shortly after 10 p.m. and, climbing the
same spur as the second party, was to move on Nasin
in readiness to support any one of the three columns.
A reserve, with field guns, came behind the main body,
timed to reach the foot of the spur by dawn, so as to
cover the retirement.

The troops were warned only one hour before
starting.

Each of the three columns effected its purpose without loss, the enemy being completely surprised and
making no stand ; a large number of sheep and cattle
was seized, the towers of the villages were blown up
and the crops destroyed ; but, on the retirement commencing, the enemy followed up with great determination, and, as the skirmishers of the 2nd Punjab
Infantry evacuated a commanding position, they were
attacked and driven back by a sudden rush of swords-

men, when a native doctor and seven men were hacked
to pieces. The enemy did not leave the hill in pursuit,
and the whole force reached the camp, one mile south-
west of Hangu, by sunset, having suffered a loss of
eleven men killed and four wounded. The enemy
sustained casualties to the number of twenty-four
killed and wounded, among the former being four
maliks. The troops had been under arms for over
seventeen hours, had marched some twenty-eight
miles, and had ascended and descended a rugged
mountain nearly 4000 feet in height.

Within a few days of the close of these operations
the Mishtis came to terms and gave hostages; the
Rabia Khel then came in and submitted, bringing
back many of the plundered cattle and promising
payment for those not forthcoming; the Sheikhans
also made submission, and the force was back in
Kohat by the 7th October, when it was broken
up.

After this the Orakzais did not again trouble our
border until 1868, when complications arose with the
Bizoti division of the Daulatzais. This being a small
and insignificant branch with its chief settlements in
Tirah, its members had hitherto been able to avoid
punishment for any misdeeds of which they had been
guilty. From the commencement of British rule
beyond the Indus, the Bizotis were constantly engaged
in cattle-lifting on our border, and had attacked and
robbed travellers and others at every opportunity.
In 1865-67 they continued to give trouble, plundered
cattle, and made demonstrations against our police

posts in the Ublan Pass, about six miles from Kohat. The representatives of the offending divisions—Bizotis, Utman Khels and Sipaias (the last of the Muhammad Khel clan) were summoned to Kohat, were informed that they were debarred from trade with British territory, and the Bizotis were further deprived of certain allowances which had been granted them some years previously. Finally, in March 1868, it was reported that the Bizotis intended attacking the village of Muhammadzai, at the southern foot of the Ublan Pass, and accordingly, during the night of the 10th and early morning of the 11th, Lieutenant Cavagnari, Deputy-Commissioner, occupied the hills on the left of the gorge with police and levies.

Operations against the Bizotis (Daulatzai), 1868. —There appearing to be no doubt that a raid was intended, 100 bayonets were sent out from Kohat to reinforce the levies at Muhammadzai, and about 11.30 a.m. the enemy collected to the number of some 200 about the Ublan Kotal, beating drums, and occupying the right of the Pass. Major Jones, 3rd Punjab Cavalry, commanding at Kohat, now ordered out two guns, eighty sabres, and 480 infantry, and the enemy were at once driven from the positions they had first taken up, and fell back upon a high peak where they had erected a breast-work. Three attempts to take this position were defeated, and as it was then 4.30 p.m., it was decided to retire, covered by the guns. Our retirement was in no way pressed, from which it may be assumed that the enemy had suffered considerably, but our own casualties were not slight—

eleven killed (one British officer), and forty-four wounded.

After this affair the blockade against the Bizotis and other offending divisions was made more stringent, but this measure was comparatively ineffective, as these tribesmen soon departed to their summer quarters in Tirah. As the time again approached when they would return to their winter settlements, it was determined to put pressure on the Orakzais generally by extending the blockade so as to include the whole clan; there seemed some prospect of this measure resulting in the submission of the Daulatzais, when, on the 13th February, 1869, a raiding party of the Utman Khel surprised our police post at the foot of the Kohat Kotal, killed one policeman and carried off three others. As it seemed certain that the well-disposed divisions did not possess the power necessary to coerce the offending parties, it was determined by Lieutenant-Colonel Keyes, then commanding at Kohat, and by Lieutenant Cavagnari, Deputy-Commissioner, to make a counter-raid into the territory of the Bizotis and Utman Khels. This raid is admirably described in Chapter XIX., "A Pathan Surprise," in Oliver's *Across the Border*, and appears, in all the preliminary arrangements and the actual conduct of the operations, to be a model of how a petty border expedition of this kind should be projected and carried out.

The plan was to cross the Ublan Pass, and if not opposed at the village of Gara to pass on to and destroy that of Dana Khula; if, however, opposed at

Gara, then no further advance was to be made, as the delay would preclude the surprise of Dana Khula, where the enemy would be able to make preparations, while to reach it the troops would have to fight their way for two miles. The jirgah of the Kohat Pass Afridis happened then to be in Kohat, and to prevent any information leaking out through them to the Daulatzais, the jirgah was detained in Kohat on some pretext while the troops were absent. It was clear that the complete success of the whole operation depended upon the sudden and surprise seizure of the Ublan Kotal, and, consequently, not even commanding officers were informed of what was in view until a few hours prior to a start being made. At midnight on the 24th February, the 4th Punjab Cavalry [1] moved out and formed a complete cordon round the town of Kohat, so as to prevent anybody from entering, and, still more, from leaving it; police picquets were posted also at all places where a footman might seek to enter the hills. At the same hour the mountain guns were got ready for service, half an hour later the native gunners were warned, and the 1st and 4th Punjab Infantry were turned out; at 1 a.m. the 2nd Punjab Infantry was paraded, and at that hour two guns and two infantry battalions left Kohat; all without bugle sound.

The Kotal was found undefended, but the enemy made some stand at Gara, which was taken with a loss on our side of one killed and nineteen wounded, and the surprise of Dana Khula was consequently im-

[1] Disbanded in 1882.

practicable. Gara, however, was completely destroyed, cattle and other live stock were driven off, and the retirement commenced. The descent was steep and difficult, and the retreat, harassed by the enemy, was necessarily slow, but the troops were withdrawn from the hill with great coolness and steadiness, incurring, however, a further loss of two killed and fourteen wounded.

While these operations were being carried on from Kohat, a strong column had moved out from Peshawar, and had materially assisted the movements of Colonel Keyes' force by distracting the attention of the Utman Khel Orakzais and a division of the Aka Khel Afridis.

The Bizotis and their neighbours had learnt a lesson, and early in April the jirgahs of the Bizotis, Utman Khels and Sipaia (Muhammad Khel) divisions came into Kohat, made submission, paid a fine of Rs. 1200, and gave up nine of their principal headmen as hostages for their future good behaviour; the long-standing blockade was then removed.

For the next three years this part of our border remained tolerably quiet, but thereafter there was a constant succession of petty raids and disturbances— not individually, perhaps, of much account, but forming, in the aggregate, sufficient reason for undertaking at no distant date punitive measures against the Orakzais as a whole. In 1873 the Sipaia division of the Muhammad Khel gave trouble on the Kohat border. In 1878 the Massuzai and Lashkarzai evinced hostility towards us, both in Upper Miranzai and in the Kurram; during the Afghan War emissaries from the Amir, aided by the preachings of the mullahs, disquieted all the Sunni Orakzai clans; and although there was no concerted action undertaken by these tribesmen, the Ali Khels, and the Alisherzai and Mamuzai divisions of the Lashkarzai, committed many outrages and raids between Hangu and Thal, attacking posts, carrying off cattle, cutting up unarmed parties and coolies, and increasing generally the difficulties of our communications between India and Afghanistan. Despite, too, the fact that only two clans of Orakzais were actively engaged in these raids, the men appeared to have been accorded free passage through the country of the Ismailzai and Malla Khel, both in proceeding to the scenes of their outrages, and when returning home with the plunder obtained. Fines had been imposed by Government, whose hands were at the time too full for embarking upon the military expedition necessary for their collection, and already by the end of 1880 the indebtedness of the Orakzais in fines amounted to upwards of Rs. 15,000.

From 1884 until the end of 1890 increased and increasing trouble was given by parties belonging to divisions of almost every clan of Orakzais whose settlements are nearest to our frontier—Ismailzai, Sturi Khel, Mishtis and Malla Khel—fines remained unpaid, and new scores, though marked up, were ignored. The necessity for strong measures was urged by the Deputy-Commissioner again and again; one division committed forty-eight fresh offences in one year; the Sturi Khel made a partial payment of fines for past misconduct, and then commenced a fresh indebtedness by new outrages; the Samana boundary line, acknowledged and acquiesced in since 1865, was repudiated in 1888. A new frontier post was established at Shinawari, at the southern exit of the Chagru defile, and was promptly attacked by a mixed band of Malla Khel and Rabia Khel; and on the main road between Kai and Hangu, a police guard was attacked in open day, prisoners were rescued, and arms carried off. This lawless condition of the border abated somewhat at the beginning of 1890, when a punitive expedition appeared to the tribe to be imminent, and a portion of the outstanding fines was paid up; but the Rabia Khel continued to be aggressive, and in December of this year sent an insolent message to the Deputy-Commissioner, that they had no intention whatever of paying up any of the heavy arrears of fines due from them—an example which was promptly followed by the Sturi Khel.

First Miranzai Expedition, 1891.—The patience of the Lieutenant-Governor of the Punjab and of the Government of India was now exhausted, and an expedition was decided upon, having for its special object the punishment of the Rabia Khel (Ismailzai), Mamuzai (Lashkarzai), Sheikhan and Mishti divisions and clans, and also of the Sturi Khel, should these not submit on the occupation by our troops of the Khanki Valley.

The expeditionary force, under command of Brigadier-General Sir William Lockhart, K.C.B., C.S.I., was assembled at Kohat by the 12th January, the advance being arranged for the 19th, and on the

former date a proclamation was issued to the four
Samil clans, whose punishment was about to be
undertaken, warning them not to resist, and to the
remainder of the Orakzais informing them that they
would be in no way interfered with provided they
did not oppose us. The force was composed of—

    Two Squadrons of Cavalry.

    Two Mountain Batteries.

    One Company Bengal Sappers and Miners.

    Seven Infantry Battalions, each of a strength
       of 600.

No British troops formed part of the force, which was
divided into three columns, rendezvousing respectively
at Shahu Khel, Togh and Hangu. The start was
delayed by heavy rain and snow, and the troops were
not in position until the 21st January. On the
advance commencing practically no opposition was
experienced; the country of each one of the offending
clans was visited by the different columns; and
within a very short space of time each division had
made its submission—the Rabia Khel standing out to
the last. The Khanki Valley was traversed as far
west as Ghuzghor; a reconnaissance was pushed up
the Daradar Valley through Star Khel to the Kharai
Kotal overlooking the Sheikhan country; Dran was
visited; and a column marched from Shahu Khel and
reached the Zera Pass via Bar Marai, sending reconnaissances through the Gudar defile to Sultanzai and
Shirazgarhi on the Lower Mastura. The casualties
were *nil*, but the troops suffered severely from the
extreme cold. The following terms imposed were

agreed upon : the establishment of three posts on the Samana connected by mule road with each other, and with Baliamin, Darband and Hangu; payment of outstanding fines ; undesirables and outlaws not to be harboured by the tribes. The tribes had not agreed to the construction of the Samana forts—at Gulistan on the west, near Sangar, and on the east at Lakka—with an especially good grace, but their submission had been so complete that no further immediate trouble was anticipated.

The field force had barely broken up when it was rumoured that the clans concerned, egged on by the taunts of those tribesmen who had not been proceeded against, were trying to form a combination to prevent the construction of the Samana posts, and that the Rabia Khel were particularly truculent. Kohat was, as a precautionary measure, reinforced by a battery and a battalion, but nothing of the nature of an actual outbreak occurred until the 4th April. On this date an attack was made upon our working parties on the Samana by men of the Rabia Khel, who, having been taken on as labourers on the road, suddenly turned upon the covering party, and were then at once reinforced by large numbers of tribesmen who had been awaiting events on the north side of the Samana. Our troops were obliged to abandon the crest of the range and to fall back upon Baliamin, having suffered a loss of fourteen killed and seven wounded.

From subsequent enquiry it was elicited that the Rabia Khel had been joined in this outbreak by the

Mamuzai, Sheikhans and Mishtis, and the temporary
success of the movement at once swelled the numbers
of the enemy, until it was computed that many thousand men were under arms ; these included not only
all the Orakzais of the Khanki Valley, but a certain
number of Afridis under one Mir Bashar, a Malikdin
Khel, who, during the Afghan War, had assumed the
title of " King of Tirah," and had received a pension
from the Amir. Mir Bashar was reported to be
preaching a jehad, aided by Aka Khel and Mamuzai
mullahs. It seemed evident that the work commenced on the Samana posts, and on the roads connecting them, had aroused the suspicions of all the
Orakzais, and enlisted the sympathies of many of the
more fanatical of the Afridis. Both from the Kohat
and the Khyber side proclamations were issued, assur-
ing the tribesmen that we had no designs on their
independence, and that the posts on the Samana were
being erected purely as a defensive measure against
the Rabia Khel ; but in view of the threatening state
of affairs in the district troops were at once pushed
up to Kohat, Darband and Baliamin. The tribesmen
now forthwith commenced hostilities ; on the 8th
April they attacked a small party of the 1st Punjab
Infantry at Hangu, and two days later a lashkar of
about 1000 men attacked our camp at Darband, but
was beaten off without loss to us. On this date a
reply was received to the proclamation above mentioned, demanding our abandonment of the Samana
and the release of certain notoriously troublesome
characters then in our custody.

Second Miranzai Expedition, 1891.—The troops
detailed for this, the second, Miranzai Expedition, consisted of six squadrons of cavalry, fifteen mountain and
three heavy guns, one company of Bengal Sappers, and
ten and a half battalions of infantry (one and a half
British), and were divided into three columns, concentrating the one at Hangu, the other two at
Darband. The whole numbered something under
8000 men, and Sir William Lockhart was again in
command.

The enemy—Mishtis, Sheikhans, Mamuzais, and
Rabia Khel—were reported to be on the Samana to
the number of about a thousand men, while several
thousand others were in support in the Khanki
Valley.

The advance was made on the 17th April, No. 1
Column moving up on to the Samana, reaching Lakka
without opposition, and assaulting and carrying Tsalai,
Gogra and Sangar in succession, and with only trifling
loss. Meanwhile Nos. 2 and 3 Columns left Darband,
No. 2 advancing to the Darband Kotal, and thence,
with some opposition, to Gwada, and No. 3 from
Darband to Sangar, where it joined No. 1 Column.
On the 18th No. 2 remained halted, while Nos. 1 and
3 attacked Sartop, and cleared and held the plateau
between it and Gulistan—at the western end of the
range—leaving No. 3 Column there in position. Next
day No. 2 moved up to Sangar, joining there the first
column ; and throughout the whole of this day and
the greater part of the 20th, No. 3 Column was
fired upon from three sides. Having been reinforced

after midday on the 20th, No. 3 Column moved out, attacked and captured Saragarhi and Gustang, whence most of the fire was proceeding, burnt these villages and drove the Orakzais off the mountain down into the Khanki Valley. On the 22nd No. 2 Column advanced to the extreme western end of the Samana, overlooking the Chagru Valley, where a large assemblage of armed men was visible. On these moving forward in a threatening manner they were attacked and driven back, as was also another body some 1500 strong, advancing from the Khanki Valley, and the British force retired to camp practically unmolested, although our picquets were threatened later on in the evening. On the same day another column had attacked and destroyed several villages of the Rabia Khel, experiencing but slight opposition. Tribesmen again collecting in large numbers on the 23rd, No. 2 Column moved out in full strength, dispersed them and then burnt the village of Tsalai, where they appeared to have rendezvoused. From the 24th to 29th jirgahs began to come in with offers of submission ; and while negotiations were in progress, the General Officer commanding took the opportunity of visiting the Sheikhans and of levelling their towers.

By the beginning of May most of the opposing divisions had come in and had submitted, but were told that all stolen government property must be restored before negotiations could really be opened. With the Rabia Khel, Akhel and Sheikhan, matters were speedily settled, but it was felt that a special punishment must be meted out to the Mishtis, who

had been equally troublesome with the others, but
whose villages, lying at a considerable distance from
our frontier, had not suffered to anything like the
same extent as those of other tribesmen, who had
taken a no more prominent part in the recent disturbances. It was, therefore, decided to destroy the
towers of the large villages about Kandi Mishti, in
the Khanki Valley, and lying at the foot of the
Sampagha Pass. Sir William Lockhart, then, taking
No. 2 Column, marched from Gulistan on the Samana
by the Tsalai Spur and the Chagru Kotal to Kharappa,
blew up three of the Kandi Mishti towers in the
presence of the jirgahs, and from Kharappa marched
through the country of some of the more westerly
clans, sections of which had been concerned in the
risings, and who had hitherto imagined that their
position rendered them inaccessible. The Khanki
Valley was, therefore, traversed from end to end,
and the Kharmana Valley was overlooked and
overawed.

The result of these operations was that all the
clans concerned agreed to our occupation of the
Samana; adequate punishment had been dealt out
to offenders; practically the whole of the Orakzai
country had now been traversed by our troops; and
for the next six years this part of the border was
at peace.

Our casualties in this expedition amounted to
twenty-eight killed and seventy-three wounded.

From the date of the conclusion of these operations
up to the general "Pathan Revolt" of 1897, the

behaviour of the Orakzais as a tribe may almost be described as irreproachable—although, of course, isolated cases of misbehaviour were not uncommon. It was known, too, that our actual presence in occupation of posts on the Samana Range rankled in the minds of the tribesmen. Although the crest of the Samana had for more than thirty years been acknowledged as our boundary, and had been assessed as such, the outward and visible sign of our occupation appeared to be a source of continual offence, and early in 1892 a deputation of the Orakzais asked the assistance of the Amir of Afghanistan in inducing us to abandon the range. The Amir, however, very properly replied that he did not see his way to take any action in the matter.

In May 1897 the Orakzais appear, in conjunction with the Afridis, to have again solicited the intervention of the Amir, and it was felt that the situation on the frontier generally, and particularly on this section of it, was becoming serious. The actual causes which may be said to have led to the outbreak along four hundred miles of border have been given at more length in Chapter XIII., and it is not proposed here to recapitulate them; it is sufficient to state that the first definite news of unrest amongst the Afridis and Orakzais was contained in a telegram from the Deputy-Commissioner of Kohat, stating that the Mullah Saiyid Akbar, Aka Khel, had succeeded in persuading the Orakzais to unite against the British Government, and was in Tirah trying to persuade the Afridis to do the same. This information appears, however, to have been discredited by the Commissioner of Peshawar (Sir Richard Udny), even when followed by another telegram from Kohat announcing the actual assembly of hostile tribesmen ; and all that was done —so far as precautionary measures against the Orakzais were concerned—was the reinforcement of Kohat on 20th August by a force of the three arms—the 9th Field Battery, 18th Bengal Lancers, and 15th Sikhs.

Information was now received that the tribal jirgahs had decided that, of the Orakzais, the Massuzais, assisted by the Chamkannis, should move against the Kurram, the Daulatzais against Kohat, and the remainder of the tribe against the forts on the Samana ; whereupon the following measures were taken for the security of the district generally by Major-General Yeatman-Biggs, who had now, on the 21st August, assumed command of the troops on the Kohat–Kurram border.

A flying column—four mountain guns, six squadrons cavalry, and one battalion infantry, under Colonel Richardson—was formed for action in the Kurram, and moved out to Hangu ; Kohat was reinforced by the 3rd Gurkhas and four companies Royal Scots Fusiliers, while rifles were issued to friendly villagers on the border. On the 25th Colonel Richardson was able to put supplies and ammunition, bringing up the number of rounds per rifle to 400, into the Samana posts ; and that this was accomplished none too soon was made clear by the news which now came in, that 12,000 tribesmen were concentrating at Kharappa in the Khanki Valley—chiefly Ali Khels, Malla Khels, and the Alisherzai and Mamuzai divisions of the Lashkarzai. So far it was reported that neither Mishtis nor Akhels (Ismailzai) had joined the gathering, but at the same time their headmen sent in to say that public opinion and tribal pressure would oblige them, sooner or later, to take the field also. A force, composed of fighting men from all three divisions of the Daulatzai, had occupied the Ublan Pass, whence they sent into Kohat a statement of the terms upon which they would be willing to vacate it and disperse ; and in the Kurram Valley, too, matters looked threatening, and anxiety was felt in regard to the posts at Sadda and Parachinar, which could not be relieved from Hangu until some, at least, of the Orakzai lashkars had been driven off.

The Orakzais now themselves began to take the offensive. The Daulatzais descended from the Ublan Pass and attacked and captured the old police post, held by twenty-five border police, at Muhammadzai. Against them the Major-General moved out on the 27th August with a field battery, a squadron, two companies Royal Scots Fusiliers, and 487 rifles of the 2nd Punjab Infantry, drove the enemy from the pass and towards the Bara Valley. Our casualties were only two killed and nine wounded, but the heat was intense, twenty British soldiers were prostrated with sunstroke, of whom one died, and eighty-six of the Fusiliers had to be carried back to Kohat in ambulance tongas.

On the same day the Orakzais had been active all

along the Samana Range. The levy-posts at Lakka and Saifaldara, further west, had been surrounded and attacked, but Colonel Richardson sent out a force under Lieutenant-Colonel Abbott (two mountain guns, half a squadron of cavalry, one and a half battalions), and the garrisons were successfully relieved and withdrawn, the posts being burnt by the enemy the same evening. The eastern end of the Samana about Gulistan was threatened by large gatherings; the border police post at Shinawari was attacked three nights running, and finally captured and destroyed on the night of the 28th August; and on the night following the tribesmen, intoxicated with their success, raided down into the valley south of Shinawari, plundered Mariab and Kai, and fired into the camp at Hangu.

By this time, however, troops had been pushed up to Kohat from Rawal Pindi, and from Peshawar through the Kohat Pass, and the advanced force at Hangu had now been strengthened. Lieutenant-Colonel Abbott was sent on from Hangu to Doaba, twenty-two miles further west, with two mountain guns, a squadron of cavalry, the 15th Sikhs, and half a company Bombay Sappers; and on the 31st Major-General Yeatman-Biggs left Kohat for Hangu, and formed the troops there into two brigades. One of these, now commanded by Colonel Richardson, was ordered to proceed at once to the relief of the posts at Sadda and Parachinar—distant seventy and ninety-two miles respectively—which expected to be attacked in force on the 3rd September. The rapid advance of

this brigade—Sadda was reached on the night of the
3rd—staved off actual attack; but Thal had been
fired into, Torawari post had been burnt, while Balish
Khel, a post on the border three miles from Sadda,
had been fiercely attacked, and its defence by twenty
men of the Kurram Militia, under an Afridi havildar,
was particularly fine.   Its relief was effected by the
arrival of some fifty armed Turi villagers from Sadda,
and 200 militia from Hasan Ali.   With the appearance in the neighbourhood of Colonel Richardson's
brigade, matters quieted down for a time, but on the
16th a determined attack was made upon the camp
about 10.30 p.m. by 2000 of the Massuzais, who were
not finally beaten off until 1 a.m.

While these operations were in progress in the
Kurram desperate fighting had taken place on the
Samana.

The posts of Lakka and Saifaldara, at the western
end of the range, had, as we have seen, been abandoned, and thereupon destroyed, and in addition two
other small police posts, Gogra and Tsalai, had been
evacuated and burnt.   There remained on the hill
two large posts—Fort Lockhart, on the centre of the
range, and Gulistan (Fort Cavagnari), at the western
end overlooking the Chagru Kotal—and several
smaller ones—Saraghari, the Crag Picquet, the Sangar Picquet, Sartop and Dhar.   Each of the two
larger posts was capable of accommodating two companies, though at Gulistan one company had to be
placed in a small hornwork to the west, while the
smaller posts could hold from twenty-five to fifty

rifles. Of these small posts, Saraghari was by reason of its situation the most important, being on high ground and in signalling communication with the different posts on the range.

On the nights of the 3rd and 4th September Gulistan was attacked in force, and the enemy came on so determinedly that they succeeded in setting fire to the abattis outside the hornwork, but the fire was extinguished by volunteers rushing out from the fort. In these attacks the Orakzais lost so heavily that they withdrew entirely from the Samana for some days, and indeed made up their minds to leave the posts alone unless the Afridis should come to their assistance. Raids continued, however, but as the Tirah Expeditionary Force was now being assembled, Government refused to permit of any reprisals against the Orakzais on a large scale; but the Mishtis, who were easily accessible in the Lower Khanki Valley, were proceeded against, several of their fortified villages being destroyed by a small column sent out from Hangu.

Between the 7th and 12th September Major-General Yeatman-Biggs was able to throw a month's supplies into the Samana forts, and on the last-named date his column came in contact with the combined force of the enemy, estimated at a total of 10,000 men, for the Afridis had now thrown in their lot with the Orakzais. As the column was, however, short both of water and supplies, it was unable to remain on the hill, and was forced to descend to Hangu, when the whole strength of the tribesmen

was pitted against the Samana forts, held by the
36th Sikhs, distributed as follows :

Fort Lockhart   -   168, and 2 British officers.
   (Headquarters),
Crag Picquet,   -   22.
Sartop,   -   -   21.
Sangar,   -   -   44.
Dhar, -   -   -   38.
Saraghari,   -   -   21.
Gulistan,   -   -   175, and 4 British officers.

On the night of the 11-12th September the post of
Sangar was first attacked, but being well situated and
with no cover in the vicinity, the enemy were repulsed
without serious difficulty.   They then, on the morning of the 12th, vigorously assailed Saraghari, one of
the smallest posts in regard to garrison, and being
further weakly constructed and badly placed for prolonged resistance to overwhelming numbers.   The
whole course of the attack could be seen from both
Fort Lockhart and Gulistan, whence no effective
assistance could be rendered, for these garrisons were
themselves small, the villages between Fort Lockhart
and Saraghari were full of the enemy, and Gulistan
was itself being vigorously attacked.   None the less
two attempts were made from Fort Lockhart to effect
relief, but they were unsuccessful.   During one of the
rushes upon the post, some men established themselves
under the wall where there was a dead angle, and
managed there to effect a breach, when the enemy
rushed in in overwhelming numbers, and the garrison,
fighting manfully to the last, were killed to a man.

The twenty-one heroes had, however, inflicted heavy loss upon the enemy, who owned to a death-roll of 180; the last of the Sikhs killed twenty men before he was overpowered. Truly of these twenty-one men of the 36th Sikhs may be said, as was recorded of the Guides at Kabul: "By their deeds they have conferred undying honour, not only on the regiment to which they belong, but on the whole British Army."

Gulistan had been closely invested since noon, all was over at Saraghari by 4 p.m., and the tribesmen now put out their whole strength against the first-named post. The attack was pressed throughout the whole of the night, a hot fire being maintained upon the post from the closest quarters. When the morning of the 13th dawned the enemy were found to be entrenched within twenty yards of the walls, but the Sikhs under Major Des Vœux, not only maintained their ground throughout the day and the night that followed, but carried out two most successful sorties, capturing three standards and striking terror into the tribesmen as much as they heartened themselves.

At midnight on the 13th General Yeatman-Biggs had moved out from Hangu with a relieving force.[1] Advancing up the Samana via Lakka, the column met and drove off a body of the enemy, estimated at 4000, holding Gogra hill and the ruined Tsalai post; and, continuing its progress, put to a hurried flight into the Khanki Valley a second force, numbering several thousand, entrenched on the Saraghari ridge.

[1] 4 mountain guns, 300 rifles Royal Irish Regiment, 500 1st Battalion 2nd Gurkhas, 500 1st Battalion 3rd Gurkhas, 500 2nd Punjab Infantry, half a company Bombay Sappers and Miners, and departmental details,

Continuing westward, Gulistan was seen to be surrounded by swarms of tribesmen, but, declining attack,
these also drew off hurriedly into the Khanki Valley,
and by 1 p.m. Gulistan was relieved. Our losses were :
Saraghari, twenty-one killed ; Gulistan, two killed,
thirty-nine wounded ; relieving force, one killed, six
wounded ; while the total losses of the enemy on the
Samana were found later to have amounted to about
400 killed and 600 seriously wounded.

The subsequent operations of this year, wherein the
Orakzais were concerned, will be found described in
Chapter XIII., " Afridis : operations," and in Chapter
XVI., " Chamkannis," but the moral effect of the
heavy losses incurred in the attacks on the Samana
forts was undoubtedly responsible for the feeble
character of the resistance thereafter offered to us
by the Orakzais, and for the readiness they evinced
in coming to terms, and making a complete and unconditional submission.

Since 1897 the Orakzais, as a tribe, have given us
no trouble.

CHAPTER XVI.

BANGASH—ZAIMUKHTS—CHAMKANNIS—TURIS.[1]

SINCE the territories of the above-mentioned tribes are either situated in, or are most easily approached from, the Miranzai and Kurram, the account of these peoples had better be prefaced by some description of those valleys.

During the days of Sikh rule on the frontier, Miranzai remained under the Governor of Kohat, but not much interference was attempted. On the annexation of the Punjab by the Government of India, Miranzai, being an outlying territory, was over-looked when possession was taken of the rest of Kohat; the Kabul Government, accordingly, made arrangements to occupy Miranzai, the Amir's son, Sirdar Muhammad Azim, who was then Governor of Kurram, sending in 1851 some cavalry to hold the villages of Bilandkhel, Thal and Torawari. The people of Miranzai, thereupon, appealed to the Indian Government, and petitioned that their country might be included in British territory, offering to pay a yearly revenue of Rs. 7500. Their request was acceded to, and in August 1861, a proclamation was issued

[1] See Map VII.

declaring Miranzai to be a portion of the Kohat
district.

This country has been thus described by Oliver in
his book *Across the Border*: "The Miranzai Valley,
perhaps the pleasantest part of the Kohat district, has
been arbitrarily divided into an Upper and a Lower,
though the river which runs east, down the latter, is
a feeder of the Kohat *toi*, or stream, and goes thence
to the Indus, while the Ishkali, which runs west along
the Upper, is a branch of the Kurram. Both Upper
and Lower Miranzai, equally with the Kurram, lie
along the base of the great Safed Koh Range, the white
peaks of which tower over everything else, a gigantic
barrier between this and the still more famous Khyber
route to Kabul. . . . It is a land of mountains, small
and great, of rocks and of stones. The rivers that
rush down the steep slopes are at one time dangerous
torrents, at others yielding with difficulty a little
water from the holes dug in their beds, with small
and circumscribed, but well-cultivated valleys, where
grain and fruit flourish abundantly, varied with
raviney wastes, growing little beyond the dwarf
palm which affords materials for one of the few
staple industries the country possesses. These, again,
are interspersed by grassy tracts, on which are pastured
abnormally small cattle and exceptionally fat-tailed
sheep." The Miranzai Valley is about forty miles in
length, and its width varies from three to seven miles;
it extends from Thal to Raisan—where the Khanki
River breaks through the hills into the valley—and from
the Zaimukht and Orakzai hills to those of the Khattaks.

Up to the time of the second Afghan war the
Kurram Valley was ruled by the Afghans, but it came
under our influence during the campaign, and was
finally occupied by us in the autumn of 1893. The
country is now administered by the Indian Government, and is ruled by a political officer, the valley
being to all intents and purposes British territory.

"Once past Thal," says Oliver, "and the banks of
the Kurram River reached—more or less all along are
cornfields and fruit gardens, mulberry groves and
fertile glades, passing up to ridges crested by oak
and olive, yew trees and pines; the range behind
again culminating in the snow-capped peak of Sika
Ram, which rises over 15,000 feet high. Some parts
of the valley have the reputation of being unhealthy,
for the same reason as Bannu, but there are few more
fertile spots along the Afghan Border than the
Kurram." The valley is about sixty miles long and
in some parts not more than ten miles broad; it is
bounded on the west by Afghanistan, on the east
by the country of the Chamkannis, Zaimukhts and
Orakzais, on the south by Waziristan, while on the
north Kurram is separated from the country of the
Shinwaris by the Safed Koh Range. "Dark pine
forests cover the lower ranges, and naked cliffs and
snowy peaks rise high above them. The chain is so
situated that the rays of the setting sun fall full upon
it, and the effect on a chill winter evening, when
the pale snows flush scarlet and crimson, while darkness is already gathering in the valley below, is very
fine."

Enriquez, from whose work, *The Pathan Borderland*, quotation has already been made, tells us that
"Lower Kurram,[1] that is as far as Alizai, differs very
essentially from the Upper Kurram and in appearance
resembles the Miranzai. The villages are built of rough
and irregular blocks of stone interspersed with layers
of brushwood. Towers and defensive walls are the
exception, and the inhabitants are but poorly armed.
The fodder is collected in ricks inside the hamlets,
and great stacks of hay and 'johwar' are also
grouped together in large numbers on rising ground
near by. The valley is narrow, and there is little
room for cultivation. The trees are few and stunted,
and the general appearance of the country is of low
hills and broken nullahs, where the usual 'palosa,'
bera, seneta and mazarai form a thin scrub jungle.
Upper Kurram, on the other hand, is wider, and the
mountains containing it are more imposing. There
is a good deal of cultivation ; the villages are larger
and far more prosperous looking, and are built chiefly
of mud. The more important ones have from eight
to ten fortified towers, and are besides protected by
high loop-holed walls. A very successful attempt is
made to decorate these forts by means of patterns
in the brickwork and of crenelations along the upper
parapets. They are, moreover, neatly built and kept
in good repair. Chenar trees abound and grow to as
fine a size as they do in Kashmir. To judge by their
girth, many of them must be very old. There are

[1] Above Sadda is Upper Kurram, between Sadda and Thal is Lower
Kurram.

willows, mulberries and 'palosa' in the valley and
the walnuts of Kurram rival those of Tirah." The
valley is said, with pride, to produce four remarkable
and marketable commodities—the stone of Malana,
the rice of Karman, the wood of Peiwar, and the women
of Shalozan—the last a village from which ladies have
always been supplied for the Royal zenana in Kabul.
The grandmother of the late Amir, Abdur Rahman
Khan, was a daughter of the Turi Malik of Shalozan
in Kurram.

The Miranzai and Kurram Valleys are of importance
as providing an alternative route, practically wholly
through friendly territory, from our frontiers to the
borders of Afghanistan. A narrow-gauge railway runs
from Kohat to Thal, and is eventually, it is stated, to
be extended to Parachinar—fifty-six miles further up
the Kurram Valley. The Peiwar Kotal is only fifteen
miles further west from Parachinar, and is of an
elevation of 9200 feet, the onward road then crossing
the Shutargardan, or Camel's Neck Pass, at a height
of 11,900 feet, into the Logar Valley leading to Kabul.
The route affords a subsidiary line for part of the
year, but its closing by snow, and the great altitudes
at which the several passes have to be crossed, forbid
its being classed as a principal line of communication.
During the second Afghan war it was used as a line
of advance mainly because Lord Lytton firmly believed
in the value of Kurram, being influenced in this, as
in many other matters, by his Military Secretary,
Colonel, afterwards Sir George, Colley; who wrote:
" Personally my hobby is the Kurram—I had long

ago come to the conclusion that the possession of the Peiwar held the most commanding military position, short of Kabul, in Afghanistan. . . . The Kurram Valley is mainly fairly open and inhabited by a peaceful agricultural population, so that our communications there will never be troublesome or uncertain."

Lord Roberts, however, has on the other hand described the Kurram route as no more than a "by-road"; and on its final evacuation at the close of the last phase of the second Afghan war, Sir Frederick Haines, who was then Commander-in-Chief in India, wrote that: "As a line of military communication experience has condemned it, and I abandon it as such without the slightest regret."

The Bangash.—Of this tribe something has already been said—of their battle near Kohat with the Orakzais, and of the final issue resulting in their holding to the plain country, while the Orakzais remained in the hills. Tradition has it that the Bangash are of Arab origin, and that, pressed by the Ghilzais, they moved eastward about the end of the fourteenth century. Settling then in the Kurram Valley, and expanding further eastward, they drove the Orakzais into the mountains. Dr. Bellew, however, is inclined to think that they are in the main of Scythian origin, and that they came into India with the Central Asian hordes which followed Sabuktagin and Timur. But at the present day it will probably be enough to describe them as a tribe of Pathans who inhabit the

Kurram and Miranzai Valleys down to Kohat. Bangash families are also settled in Persia and in some parts of India, notably in Farakhabad, the Nawab of which place, who was banished from India for his conduct during the Mutiny, being descended from a Bangash family. They are Gar in politics and partly Shiah and partly Sunni. They enlist readily in the Indian Army and Border Militia, and are thought well of, being quieter than most Pathans.

"The Kohat, Miranzai and southern part of the Kurram Valley," Oliver tells us, "are mainly Bangash; those towards Kohat mostly Sunnis, the bulk of the remainder Shiahs. The Westerns wear their beards long, with a few short Jewish ringlets on either side of the face, shaving the rest of the head; the Easterns clip them short; otherwise there is not much difference. Physically they are quite up to the average Pathans, though they are not generally credited with great fighting qualities. A few deal in salt, but they are eminently an agricultural rather than a pastoral people. Reported hospitable, many of them are undoubtedly treacherous and cruel, not specially disposed to wanton violence, but much addicted to thieving. They are rather the victims of raids by their neighbours than raiders themselves"—the Orakzais, in their barren mountains, regretting their old-time homes and occasionally indulging in a foray into Miranzai—"and have generally behaved well from an administrative point of view. Their situation is such, they have had the good sense to see that in this lay their best chance of security."

The three main clans of the tribe, now recognised, are as under :

1. Miranzai.
2. Samilzai.
3. Baizai.

The first-named live for the most part in Upper Miranzai—that is to say, west of Kai, but some of them inhabit villages nearer to Kohat, and a few, again, live in the Kurram. The Samilzai are to be found some in the Kurram and some in Lower Miranzai; while the Baizai live chiefly in the Kohat Valley proper. The Baizai claim that in the days of the Mogul emperors they received an allowance for holding the crest of the Kotal of the Kohat Pass; and as a solution of the difficulties about the pass in 1853, to which allusion is made elsewhere, they petitioned to be allowed to resume their ancient responsibilities. Their request was granted, but they proved unable to hold the position against Afridi attack, and an arrangement was come to under which four different clans, the Baizai Bangash included, received grants for keeping open the pass. These they still retain, and up to 1882, when the management of the pass was transferred to the Deputy-Commissioner, the chief of the Baizai was in charge of the Kohat Pass arrangements. The Bangash have themselves given us little or no trouble, but have suffered much by being unusually exposed to the raids of neighbouring tribes.

The Zaimukhts.—This tribe are also known as Zwaimukht and Zaimusht; they are of Afghan stock

and live on the southern slopes of the Zawa Ghar
Range, having for their neighbours, on the north-west
the Turis, on the north and east the Orakzais, and on
the south and south-west the Bangash.   With every
one of these the Zaimukhts are at feud.   Their
country is very fertile, and they own, too, a number
of villages in the Kurram and Miranzai valleys in
British territory.   They are strong, well-built men
with pleasing features, and can muster some 2300
armed men, who appear to possess good fighting
qualities, but so far none of the tribesmen have taken
service either in the Indian Army or in the local
militia.   They are all Sunni in religion and Samil in
politics.

The country of the Zaimukhts may be described as
a triangle, with the Zawa Ghar Range as its base, and
the village of Thal as the apex; this includes a tract
of country on its western side, occupied by the
Alisherzai Orakzais.   The northern range rises to a
height of over 9000 feet above the village of Zawo,
and from 7000 to 8000 feet elsewhere.   The crest is
in some parts covered with pine forests, in others it
is bare of trees.   From this main range several streams
run southward between precipitous and rocky spurs
whose sides are quite inaccessible; from the crests,
here and there, rise steep, craggy peaks, which render
the ridges also very difficult, if not impracticable.
Among these glens lie many hamlets of small size,
the village of Zawo being composed of several hamlets.
This village was considered the chief stronghold of
the Zaimukhts, and, from its position, impregnable,

nestling close under the mountain range, and from the
south only approachable up a ravine several miles in
length, hemmed in by precipitous spurs rising to
8000 feet in elevation.   The spurs of the Zawa Ghar
Range are steep and rugged for about six to seven
miles ; as they run southward they fall away, and
form a succession of small plateaux, intersected by
ravines, 4000 to 5000 feet in elevation.   Across these
runs the route from Torawari, in Upper Miranzai, to
Balish Khel, near the junction of the Kharmana River
with the Kurram—a route formerly used by kafilas.
The drainage divides into three parts—one running
westward into the Kharmana and Kurram, near
Balish Khel and Sadda ; a second, collecting below
Chinarak, forms the Sangroba, which falls into the
Kurram near Thal ; while the remainder runs eastward into the Ishkali which drains into the Kurram
River.   Dividing these are two passes at the villages
of Manatu (5200 feet) and Urmegi (4300 feet), which
also form the connecting links between the Zawa Ghar
hill, and a second series of hills, that rise abruptly
from 4000 feet to 8000 feet in two groups—one round
the peak of Dingsar west of the Sangroba, the other
round Dondo Ghar, east of that stream.   The crests
and spurs of these two groups are rugged, rocky and
almost treeless.   Amongst them lie several secluded
glens, in which are other hamlets of the Zaimukhts,
very difficult of access.   The country is, as a rule,
devoid of timber trees ; water is plentiful ; the soil is
fertile and there are large numbers of cattle, sheep,
goats and poultry.

The tribe is divided into two main branches, each at bitter feud with the other :

1. The Mamuzai or Western Zaimukhts.
2. The Khoidad Khel or Eastern Zaimukhts.

In the early days of the annexation of Miranzai the Zaimukhts gave little trouble to the Indian Government, but in the year 1855 they assumed a hostile attitude, and, among other acts of hostility, they took part in the affair near Darsamand (see Turis). From 1856 to 1878 the Zaimukhts kept quiet. The outbreak of the second Afghan war, and the long British line of communications through Miranzai and Kurram, provided an opportunity of raiding which the Zaimukhts found it impossible to resist. From December 1878, to August of the year following, the Zaimukhts, chiefly of the Khoidad Khel clan of the tribe, committed a number of offences, cutting off grazing pack animals, kidnapping British subjects, raiding the post, culminating in the murder of two British officers passing along the road. Besides these, there were also a number of petty thefts and such offences as cutting the telegraph wire; and in October 1879, the bill for damages against the tribe amounting to Rs. 25,000, a force under Brigadier-General Tytler, V.C., C.B., was ordered into the Zaimukht country. The objects of the expedition were :

1. To punish the tribe.
2. To punish, if convenient and desirable, the Lashkarzai Orakzais, who had equally been guilty of misbehaviour.

3. To secure a right-of-way through the Zaimukht
country, between Torawari and Balish Khel.

4. To secure the safety of communications on the
Thal–Kurram road.

The expedition was delayed owing to the renewal
of active operations in Afghanistan, consequent upon
the murder at Kabul of Sir Louis Cavagnari and the
members of his Mission, and it was not until the end
of November that General Tytler was able to commence operations.   In the interval, however, the
tribesmen had continued their raids upon a larger
scale than before, 3000 of the Lashkarzai Orakzais
having concentrated for that purpose at Balish Khel,
and a mixed force of Zaimukhts and Orakzais, in
numbers about 1000, having assembled close to the
post at Chupri in the Kurram Valley.   Both these
hostile concentrations were dispersed by small British
columns collected on the spot, and which suffered but
small loss.

While General Tytler was pushing on his preparations, several reconnaissances were made into Zaimukht
country from Balish Khel, where the headquarters of
the expedition was established on the 28th November.
A party, numbering 500 infantry and two mountain
guns, under Colonel J. J. H. Gordon, C.B., 29th
Punjab Infantry, ascended the Drabzai Mountain,
7300 feet high, seven miles from Balish Khel, and
commanding the whole southern Alisherzai (Lashkarzai Orakzai) Valley, with the passes leading to the
northern Alisherzai and Massuzai country.

Lieutenant-Colonel R. C. Low, 13th Bengal Lancers,

taking with him 400 infantry, 100 cavalry and two mountain guns, passed round the foot of the Drabzai Mountain, through Tindoh, as far as the entrance to the Krumb defile.

400 infantry, 50 cavalry and two mountain guns under Lieutenant-Colonel R. G. Rogers, C.B., 20th Punjab Infantry, explored the Tatang defile and the Abasikor Pass, the latter about thirteen miles from camp and 7700 feet in height. A mile beyond Tatang village, the road enters the Tatang defile, narrow, about forty or fifty yards long, and with precipitous, rocky sides overhanging the roadway. The road was rough and difficult for any but lightly laden baggage animals. From the crest of the pass a good view was obtained of the Massuzai (Orakzai) Valley.

A small party of the 13th Bengal Lancers, under Major C. R. Pennington, reconnoitred the country in the direction of the old Kafila road from Durani to Gawakki, which was found to be fairly good, and was consequently selected as that by which the main force should advance. The party under Colonel Rogers was the only one of the four which experienced any, and that but an altogether insignificant, opposition.

On the 8th December, Brigadier-General Tytler moved to Gawakki, in the Zaimukht country, with the undermentioned force :

Total strength.

1-8th Royal Artillery, four guns (screw),   195
No. 1 Kohat Mountain Battery, two guns,   78
2nd Battalion 8th Regiment,   -   -   41

2 c

	Total strength.
85th Regiment, - - - - -	733
1st Bengal Cavalry, - - - -	57
13th Bengal Cavalry, - - - -	155
18th Bengal Cavalry, - - - -	55
8th Company Sappers and Miners, -	57
13th Native Infantry, - - - -	323
4th Punjab Infantry, - - - -	557
20th Punjab Native Infantry, - -	399
29th Punjab Native Infantry, - -	568

During the next ten days the country was thoroughly explored, and every village of any importance was visited. On the 9th, Manatu was reached without opposition, and from here three columns were despatched into the Wattizai Valley, the inhabitants of which had been largely implicated in the offences on the Thal–Kurram road, and there, in spite of some opposition, the villages of Kandali and Katokomela were burnt to the ground; at the same time some other villages in this valley were attacked from Kurram by a party of Turi levies and were also destroyed. The Wattizai Valley is about six miles long, well cultivated and watered. On the 12th the column marched five miles to Chinarak, distant about eight miles from the stronghold of Zawo, the objective of the expedition. Chinarak is situated on a fairly open and level plateau, surrounded by terraced fields, through which ran numerous water channels, and was almost at the foot of the defile leading to Zawo. At Chinarak the three main routes into the Zaimukht country converge, viz. from Balish Khel, from Tora-

wari, and from Thal by the Sangroba defile, and it
may therefore be looked upon as the most important
strategical point of the whole valley.

On the 13th, the force, less a small party remaining
to guard the camp at Chinarak, moved out to attack
Zawo; to this fastness there are three approaches—
one by a difficult ravine about seven miles long and
ten feet wide, one to the left over a steep spur on the
west of the ravine, one to the right over high hills
west of the valley of Surmai. The plan adopted was
to hold the commanding ground on the right, while
the main advance was made by the ravine. There
was a certain amount of opposition—the enemy at
one place fighting hand-to-hand with the 29th—the
advance was much delayed by the ground, and the
bed of the defile was found to be excessively difficult;
so that when by 4 p.m. the Brigadier-General found
himself in possession of the village of Bagh, three and
a half miles from Chinarak and four and a half from
Zawo, he decided to postpone any further advance
till the following day and bivouac at Bagh for the
night. Early on the 14th, while Colonel Gordon,
with three companies of the 85th, three companies of
his own regiment, and two guns, occupied the high
ground to the north, flanking the approach to Zawo
from Bagh, the main force under General Tytler
advanced up the gorge, over increasing difficulties for
about a mile, and gained, under a heavy fire, the
summit of the pass overlooking the village, or cluster
of eight or ten villages, of Zawo, situated amongst
terraced fields in a horse-shoe shaped valley. The

villages were destroyed, and the force returned that night to Bagh, and thence on the 15th to Chinarak, the retirement having been entirely unmolested.

In these operations the loss of the enemy was estimated at over forty killed and one hundred wounded, the British casualties being one officer and one sepoy killed, one native officer and one non-commissioned officer wounded. The result of the Zawo expedition was the complete destruction of the settlements of the Khudu Khel subdivision. The Zaimukhts had for this occasion been aided by from 2000 to 3000 of the Lashkarzai Orakzais, and so confident were they of the natural strength of the position and of their capability to defend it with the numbers at their disposal, that they hardly commenced to desert the village until the ridge above Zawo had been taken by our troops. Their losses in retirement were consequently unusually heavy, and may account for the unmolested withdrawal of Brigadier-General Tytler's force.

The subsequent operations were of the nature of a military promenade, portions of the force visiting Nawakila and Sparkhwait; the latter place is a small open valley at the foot of the Mandatti Pass, the mouth of which is in Zaimukht country, but which leads into the settlements of the Alisherzais (Lashkarzai Orakzais). Yasta was also visited, as was the village of Sangroba, through the difficult and narrow defile of the same name. Sangroba is at the head of a valley containing three other villages.

The operations were happily concluded, and all

the offending tribesmen brought to terms, just as orders were received that all movements against the Zaimukhts were to cease, with a view of releasing General Tytler's column for a demonstration in the direction of the Shutargardan, so as to assist Lieutenant-General Sir F. Roberts, reported hard pressed at Kabul. Fortunately, no news from Afghanistan had reached the enemy, and it was possible at once to bring the expedition to a satisfactory conclusion. All the four objects mentioned on p. 399 had been fulfilled; the Zaimukhts had been severely punished, their country traversed from end to end, and their strong places had been captured. They paid up their fines in full, surrendered 500 matchlocks and an equal number of swords, and gave hostages for the fulfilment of these terms. The Lashkarzai Orakzais had also made their submission and paid their fines. The construction of the Torawari–Balish Khel road was assured, should such be necessary, but it was found that the line of country it would traverse was extremely difficult, the saving in actual length was only seven miles, while it would be much exposed to raiders. The last object of the expedition was fully obtained, and the Thal–Kurram road henceforth enjoyed an immunity from outrages which it had not previously known since the commencement of the operations in Afghanistan.

Since 1879 the Zaimukhts have given no trouble on our border.

The Chamkannis.—This tribe—known also as Chakmannis—is traditionally supposed to belong to the Ghoria Khel section of the Sarbani Pathans—one of the two divisions of the Gandhari section of the Pactiyan nation, said by Herodotus to have been in existence when Alexander invaded India in B.C. 327.

Other authorities assign them a Persian origin. By their Sarbani descent they are related to the Mohmands, Daudzais and Khalils; the major portion of the tribe appears to have joined forces with the Khattaks, who were settled on our western border in the fourteenth century; and when these moved into the Kohat district, the Chamkannis remained in Waziristan, going later into the Kharmana Valley to the north-east of the Kurram Valley. The tribe is at present located in the Thabai and Awi Darras, in the Kharmana Valley, and in the Karman Darra on the northern slopes of the Sika Ram Range. Their neighbours are the Afridis on the east, the Orakzais on the east and south-east, the Turis on the west and south-west, while the Safed Koh Range is the boundary on the north, beyond which lies the country of the Shinwaris.

With few exceptions the Chamkannis are all Sunnis; the tribe is poor, but fairly united, can turn out rather over 3000 fighting men, and is at feud with the Turis, and with the Massuzai clan of Orakzais who border them on the east.

Dr. Bellew describes the Chamkannis as originating in a heretical sect of Persian Islamites, who were driven out of their own country by constant persecution on account of their peculiar religious ceremonies and immoral proceedings. "One of the stories

against them is not altogether without a savour of
the 'Love Feast' of more modern sects in England,"
says Oliver, "and consisted in putting out the lights
at a stage of the religious performances, in which
both sexes joined indiscriminately, and which was the
signal for possible improprieties. The Persians called
it *Chiragh-kush* or lamp-extinguisher,' and the
Pathans *Or-mur* or fire-extinguisher'; the Chamkannis, however, have turned over a new leaf and
become orthodox Muhammadans."

The tribe is divided into four main clans—
exclusive of a small band called also Chamkannis,
who, however, claim to be Ghilzais, and who live at
the head of the Kurram Valley above Karlachi:

1. Bada Khel.   3. Khwajak Khel.
2. Haji or Para Khel.   4. Khani Khel.

Up to 1897 the Chamkannis had never been conspicuously troublesome, or what seems more probable
is that while they may on occasion have leagued with
their more powerful neighbours against us, their own
comparative insignificance has helped to preserve
them against the consequences. When, however, in
1897 the long line of north-west frontier broke into
flames, and the several tribes evinced a quality of
cohesion which had not been expected of them, and
the several points of our border had been portioned
out for attack, the general jirgah held on the 20th
August had arranged that the Chamkannis and their
neighbours, the Massuzai Orakzais, should move
against the Kurram.

The Chamkannis remained, however, tolerably

quiescent until the 16th September, when a proportion of their fighting men are believed to have been concerned in a sudden and hotly-pressed attack by night upon Colonel Richardson's camp at Sadda, at the junction of the Kharmana and Kurram Rivers. To Sir William Lockhart's proclamation of the 6th October they returned insolent and defiant replies, offering peace upon their own terms; they built a barrier right across the Kharmana Darra; and it was probably only the presence in the neighbourhood of the Kurram Moveable Column under Colonel Hill, which kept from other open acts of hostility the large concentration of tribesmen known to be in this neighbourhood. But even then it did not appear certain that the Chamkannis *as a tribe* had thrown in their lot with the remaining firebrands of the frontier; and their complete and final implication was probably due to the unfortunate result of a reconnaissance undertaken by our troops on the 7th November. On that date the Commander of the Kurram Moveable Column, taking advantage of a temporary suspension of hostilities in the neighbourhood of Sadda, moved out into the Kharmana defile. The resulting reconnaissance, successful enough in itself, was marred by a heavy loss of life. The defile is seven miles long, and the river bed is throughout commanded from both sides within short rifle range, but the enemy was evidently taken by surprise by our advance, which was undisputed, even the barrier erected across the defile not being held. The villages of Hissar and Janikot were reached, and although the

final retirement to Sadda was followed up as usual,
our casualties were but few, while the enemy suffered
heavy losses.   It was not until some time after arrival
in camp, that a havildar and thirty-five men of the
Kapurthala Infantry were found to be missing.   Subsequent inquiries revealed the fact that this body had,
during retirement from a position, taken the wrong
road, and being surrounded in a ravine with further
retreat cut off by a jungle fire, had there been shot
down by the Chamkannis.   This comparative success
of the tribesmen naturally inflamed afresh the spirit
of revolt on the northern side of the Kurram Valley,
the Chamkannis and Orakzais being reinforced by
other tribesmen who had hitherto held more or less
aloof, and the strength of the concentration near the
village of Hissar, which Colonel Hill had destroyed,
being continually augmented.

As a punishment for their complicity in this resistance the Chamkannis were ordered to pay a fine of
Rs. 1000, to surrender thirty breech-loading rifles, and
to restore all Government property ; but as these
demands were treated with contempt, it became necessary to march through their country and inflict other
punishment.

On the 26th November, therefore, the Kurram
Moveable Column took part in the operations alluded
to on p. 388, entering the Khani Khel country of
the Chamkannis in two bodies, destroying Thabai
and other villages, and inflicting heavy loss upon
them.   In these operations another of the famous
family of the Battyes was killed ; hardly a single

frontier expedition has closed but that a Battye has died for his country, and has always fallen foremost in the fight.

Unlike the rest of the tribes in 1898, the Chamkannis failed to make formal submission, and thus encouraged, they broke out again in 1899, raiding two villages in the Kurram Valley, killing and wounding several villagers, and carrying off a large number of cattle. A counter-raid, however, quickly organised by Captain Roos-Keppel, and directed against Chamkanni villages in the Kurram Darra, soon brought these tribesmen to terms. Over a hundred prisoners were taken, several villages burned, and large numbers of cattle and firearms were seized. Upon this the Chamkannis at once paid up their fines, and since then have remained tolerably quiet.

The Turis.—The Turis, or Torizais as they are sometimes called, are a tribe of whose origin little definite is known, but all authorities are agreed that if Afghans at all they are not Afghans of pure descent. Muhammad Hyat Khan says they are Karlanrai Afghans; Lumsden says they are of Mogul extraction; Ibbetson regards them as being probably Tartar tribes which accompanied Chengis Khan and Timur in their Indian raids; Bonarjee calls them a tribe of mixed blood—Indian stock with a Tartar admixture; while Edwardes and others say that they are a Hindki race, some sixty families of whom, about four or five hundred years ago, because of drought, migrated from their native country in the Punjab (opposite Nilab on the Indus in the Kohat district)

to the Kurram Valley, or, as it was then called, the
Bangash Valley, and became hamsayas of its inhabi-
tants. They themselves support this last tradition,
but say that the ancestor who originally settled at
Nilab was one Torghani Turk, who came from Persia.
In his diary of the year 1506 the Emperor Baber
mentions the presence of Turis in the Kurram Valley.
About the year 1700, owing to a quarrel arising out
of insults offered to Turi women, the Turis and Jajis,
who were then united, attacked the Bangash, and the
Turis gradually made themselves masters of the
Kurram Valley, the Bangash remaining on in their
turn as hamsayas. The Turis were in the course of
time conquered by the Afghans, though the exact
date is not known ; but there was no actual attempt at
occupation of their country until 1850, the Afghans
satisfying themselves with periodical expeditions every
five or six years to collect the revenue, the soldiers
living on the people. About 1850, however, the districts both of Khost and Kurram, were occupied, and
an Afghan governor was appointed, a fort being built
at Ahmadzai and a strong garrison maintained in the
valley. Until the outbreak of the second Afghan
war in 1879, the Kurram Valley was ruled by a succession of Afghan governors, and the Turis were so
heavily oppressed at times that they rose in rebellion,
and on one occasion attacked the Afghan camp and
slew 500 men.

Of the Turis, Oliver writes : "They are not very
big nor very good-looking, and have somewhat of the
look of the savage about them, but they are strong,

hardy and compact, and are essentially horsemen, as
the Wazirs, in spite of their well-known breed of
horses, are essentially footmen. The Turi is a model
moss-trooper. Profusely armed, he has probably a
couple of brass-bound carbines at his back, two or
three pistols in front, knives of many sizes and sorts
in his waist-belt, and a sword by his side. His mount,
often a small, sorry jade, is necessarily wiry and active;
for, in addition to the Turi and his armoury, it has to
carry his entire wardrobe packed under the saddle,
certain wallets containing food for man and beast,
some spare shoes, nails and a hammer, an iron peg
and a picket rope, all the requisites to enable this
distinguished highwayman to carry on distant and
daring raids, which is the Turi road to distinction.
The local Dick Turpin is honoured with the title of
Khlak, a hard man, the Turi equivalent for the hero
of the hour. The newly-born Turi is introduced to
ordinary life by a number of shots fired over his head,
to accustom him to the sound and prevent him shrink-
ing when his turn comes to be shot at. Nor does he
usually have to wait long for this, for he is at feud
with pretty well all his neighbours, Wazirs, Zaimukhts
and Mangals, and most bitterly with the Jajis; even
a Bangash has to attach to himself a Turi *badraga*, or
safe-conduct—an excellent word for a most ragged
but faithful little ruffian, who protects him from all
other Turis.

" And to violate a safe-conduct once given, whatever form it takes, is as exceptional on the Pathan
border, as in the Scotch Highlands; no greater insult

could be put on the Khan or the clan giving it. Plowden tells of a Turi Malik who gave his cap as a badraga to an Afridi Kafila, which was plundered, and fell himself in avenging it. He is hospitable, this moss-trooper, even to allowing the women of the house to wait upon strangers, and in a way he is religious. He divides mankind into straight and crooked. The Shiahs—and all Turis are Shiahs—are straight, the rest are crooked. To a stranger the question takes a masonic form ; the Turi salute is a finger placed perpendicularly on the forehead for a straight man, and a contorted one for a crooked man. If the stranger is well-advised, he will give the countersign with a perpendicular finger."

Enriquez says, " The Turis are on the most friendly terms with the Englishmen who live among them ; and the heartiness of their salutation when they meet a Sahib is quite refreshing to listen to. The Turis look upon the British Government as their deliverer from the oppression of their rapacious Sunni neighbours, and even consider that their Shiah religion resembles, to a certain extent, Christianity. They are not forgetful that Christians fought and died for them in their wars against the Sunnis, and are even in a few cases buried in the most sacred Shiah shrines. . . . Their dress is very distinctive. . . . The sleeves of their shirts have blue cuffs, and there is a thin red piping, or an ornamental border round the neck. In the cold weather they wear a coat made out of a cloth called ' sharai,' which is woven from sheep's wool."

On their eastern border the Turis have the Chamkannis, Orakzais and Zaimukhts; on the south the Wazirs, and on the west Afghanistan, or the tribes within the sphere of influence of the Amir of that country. The total male population of the Turi country is about 6000. Every Turi considers himself to be the spiritual disciple (murid) of some Saiyid (pir), and from this practice of pir-muridi four great families of Saiyids have arisen. Of these one family composes one faction, the Mian Murid, while the remaining three compose the Drewandi faction. The first, while the weaker, is the most united, the other the more patriotic, but since besides these there are also two political factions, it results that there is no tribal combination, each Turi being an absolute democrat who thinks himself as good as his neighbour, and cannot bear to see anybody in authority over him.

In the middle of the last century the Kurram, and especially the Miranzai Valley, was to the Deputy Commissioner of Kohat a source of endless trouble. Wazirs, Turis, Zaimukhts and Orakzais were constantly assembling, either as tribal parties or in combination, to raid the well-disposed villages on the Hangu and Khattak frontiers, and, yet, whenever trouble threatened them from without, the people of Miranzai were loud in their calls for aid. Small punitive expeditions were sent into the valley in 1851, 1855 and 1856 to deal with these raiders, and especially with the Turis, who, since the first annexation of the Kohat district, had given much trouble—leaguing with other tribesmen to raid the Miranzai

Valley, harbouring fugitives, encouraging all to resist, and frequently attacking Bangash and Khattak villages. In 1855 Darsamand was thus raided. In 1856 the Kurram Valley was traversed right up to the Peiwar Kotal, and the Turis, who had intended to refuse compliance with our demands, thinking they could prevail on the surrounding tribes to make common cause with them, very soon changed their language and policy, and came to terms. Since those days the Turis have not merely given no trouble, but have helped us on several occasions.

The universal detestation of Afghan rule has, no doubt, greatly assisted us to gain the confidence of the Turis. Our advance into the Kurram Valley was hailed with delight. "There can be no doubt," wrote Major Collett, "that the people in the Kurram Valley were glad to see us, and that, smarting, as they then were, under Sher Ali's late exactions, they regarded General Roberts' troops as deliverers from an oppressive Government." During the operations in the valley the Turis furnished transport and supplies, and a levy was raised among them of from 350 to 400 men under their own Maliks. Prior to our withdrawal in 1880 the tribe made a formal petition to the Indian Government that they should for the future be independent of Kabul. This request was granted, but the experiment then instituted of managing, unaided, their own affairs did not prove a success. Faction fighting broke out, and for a long period complete anarchy prevailed, and, finally, in 1893 we occupied the Kurram Valley. In the Turis

we now possess a true and loyal race occupying a
country of great strategical advantages.

The Turis helped our troops against the Zaimukhts
in 1879, and against the Chamkannis, twenty years
later. They stood by us, too, in the troublous year
of 1897, and their eagerness for the fray when
hostilities first broke out, is thus described in an
Indian newspaper of that date: "The road into
Sadda, on the 3rd and 4th September, presented a
most extraordinary sight. On the 3rd, before the
news of the advance of reinforcements had been confirmed by letter, bands upon bands of friendly Turis,
horse and foot, could be seen making their way from
Upper Kurram to Sadda, and other points likely to
be attacked in Lower Kurram. The big attack was
expected on the night of the 3rd September; all
these men were going down to help to beat off the
common enemy; they all gladly responded to the call
of the Political Officer, and every village sent a contingent, just as they would have done in the old days
before we took over the safe custody of the valley.
Many an old raider's heart must have beat quicker as
he thought of the past, when he had ridden forth in
just the same way on some foray far across the border.
Breech-loaders were very scarce, but two-thirds of the
men had jazails, and all of them had the long Pathan
knife stuck through their kummerbunds, while here
and there was a revolver or pistol, the latter generally
of native workmanship. To look at their merry faces,
one would have imagined they were off to a wedding
or other tamasha, and not going to fight against odds

for hearth and home. The Turi cavalry, especially, took things with evident lightness of heart. Here and there a grass *chupli* would be stuck up in the middle of the road, and the next minute it was to be seen at the end of a lance, high in the air. . . . The following day they were to be seen returning to their homes ; the arrival of reinforcements in the very nick of time had made their presence no longer necessary in Lower Kurram."

. There are, at this date, some nine hundred Turis in the Kurram Militia. So assured is their loyalty that a systematic effort is now being made to arm them better. Their weapons are all registered, and means are available on the spot for arming the Turi lashkar on emergency.

CHAPTER XVII.

WAZIRISTAN AND ITS TRIBES.[1]

ON the annexation of the Punjab in 1849 by the Indian Government, and our consequent occupation of Kohat, the inhabitants of Waziristan became our neighbours for one hundred and forty miles along the boundary line—from the north-west corner of the Kohat district to the Gomal Pass west of. Dera Ismail Khan. Waziristan, the frontier Switzerland, is in shape a rough parallelogram, averaging one hundred miles in length from north to south, with a general breadth of sixty miles from east to west; at the north-west corner a wedge of hilly country juts into the Kohat and Bannu districts. It is bounded on the west and north-west by Afghanistan; on the north-east and east by the British districts of Kurram, Kohat, Bannu and Dera Ismail Khan; and on the south by Baluchistan.

The chief inhabitants of Waziristan are :

    1. The Darwesh Khels.
    2. The Mahsuds.
    3. The Batannis.
    4. The Dawaris.

[1] See Map VIII.

The two first named are the only Wazirs proper, and all four have but little in common with each other, and for many generations have been in a perpetual state of feud.

Bellew and Ibbetson are inclined to think that the Wazirs are a tribe of Rajput origin, and it is probable that ethnologically they are an Indian race with a large admixture of Scythian or Tartar blood. Their own traditions, however, represent them to be the descendants of Wazir, who was the son of Suleiman, who was the son of Kakai, himself the son of Karlan and grandson of Ghurghusht, so that they are usually described as being a tribe of Karlanri or Ghurghusht Pathans. From this common origin come the Wazirs, a title which properly includes both Darwesh Khel and Mahsuds, but the name Wazir has now been practically appropriated by the former. The ancient home of the Wazirs appears to have been in Birmal, in Afghanistan, whence they began to move eastward at the close of the fourteenth century, ousting the Khattaks from Shawal and the Kohat border north of the Tochi. In process of time they took possession of the mountainous region about Shuidar, and the whole country as far as the Gomal River, south of which but few of their settlements are to be found. The Darwesh Khel and Mahsuds differ greatly in habits and characteristics, and are practically separate tribes; but despite the enmity existing between them, their villages are much mixed up, and many of the leading men of each are connected by marriage.

Waziristan has been described by Oliver as "a land

of high and difficult hills, deep and rugged defiles,
brave and hardy people, in their way as independent
and patriotic, and, in the presence of the common
enemy, hardly less united, than the famous com-
patriots of Tell. Geographically and politically the
two have several points in common; and as regards
the mass of hills that lie between the Gomal and the
Tochi, or Dawar Valley, of which Kaniguram is about
the centre, this is more especially true. The east
front is protected by the bare hills, held by the
Batannis; beyond which are ravines, flanked by precipitous cliffs, which occasionally widen out to enclose
small valleys fairly fertile, from one hundred to one
thousand yards wide, but narrowing again as they
ascend. Not unfrequently the mouth is a mere gorge
or tangi (waist), where the water forces its way
through a range crossing it at right angles and forming a colossal natural barrier. In these valleys, and
the small strips of alluvial land which border the
base of the higher mountains, locally called *Kaches*—
which are quite a distinctive feature of the whole
range—there is often a good deal of cultivation, the
whole carefully terraced, and irrigated by means of
channels cut out of the hill sides, a great deal of
ingenuity and skill being expended in leading the
water from field to field."

The principal rivers in Waziristan are the Kurram,
Kaitu, Tochi and Gomal; the valley of the last-
named is particularly barren, there being hardly any
cultivation to be seen between Murtaza and Khajuri
Kach, and no villages along the river itself. The

tributaries of the Gomal in southern Waziristan flow through the wide and open, but stony and barren plains of Wana, Spin and Zarmelan. Indeed, Waziristan answers to the description Pathans give of their country when they tell us, that "when God made the world there were a lot of stones and rocks and lumber left over, which were all dumped down on this frontier, and that this accounts for its unattractive appearance."

"Waziristan," writes Holdich, "the land of the Waziris or Wazirs, constitutes a little independent mountain state, geographically apart from the larger mountain systems to the north and south. No roads through Waziristan lead to Afghanistan—at least no roads that are better than mere mountain footpaths. Of these there is no lack at any part of the frontier. North of Waziristan the Tochi Valley affords a through route about which we know little; and south of it the Gomal Valley leads to Ghazni; but at the back of Waziristan, between it and the plateau or high-land of Afghanistan, there is a band of rough hills packed in more or less parallel lines across the path from India, which shuts off the head of the Tochi from the Ghazni plains, and forms the barrier through which the Gomal breaks ere it reaches the open stony plain of Wana. Wana lies to the south-west of Waziristan. From the Gomal River southward commences the true Suleimani mountain system, presenting a band of rugged, serrated ridges, facing the Indus, and preserving the attitude of an impenetrable barrier (an attitude which is, after all, only a magnificent assumption) between the plains of the Indus and Afghanistan.... Waziristan is sufficiently far north to partake rather of the characteristics of the mountains of the Kurram and Safed Koh than of the Suleiman Hills to the south. There are pine trees and grand deodars on the far slopes of Waziristan to the west; there are magnificent ilex (oak) trees, which throw broad square spaces of solid shade. The young ilex sprouts all over the lower slopes of the hills, imitating holly in its early stages. The spreading poplar is the glory of many a village, and the ubiquitous bher, or jujube, is in every low-lying nullah. And Waziristan possesses a glorious group of mountains, culminating in two giant peaks—Shuidar, or Sheikh Haidar, to the north, Pirghal to the south—each of them rising 11,000 feet above the plains of the Indus, and standing like twin sentinels, guardians of the western passes of the country. From Shuidar, looking northward, one may see the flat, white back of the Safed Koh, which divides the Khyber from the Kurram, culminating in Sika Ram (16,000 feet), and from Pirghal, the craggy outline of Kaisarghar, the highest peak of the mountain called the Takht-i-Suleiman, bars further view to the south. From both peaks westward there stretches a boundless vista of ridge and hazy plain, a diapason of tender distances fainting to lighter tints of blue, till it is only against the yellowing evening sky that the pale silhouette of the hills that stand about Ghazni can be detected.... The wide cultivated ramp formed by the valley of the Tochi to the north of Waziristan, as well as the more

restricted valley of the Gomal to the south, are both
of them highroads to Ghazni. They figure in history,
though no modern force has ever made use of them.
Tradition points to the former as the route sometimes
selected by that arch-raider of the Indian frontier,
Mahmud of Ghazni, early in the eleventh century,
who is said to have swept down with hordes of
irregular cavalry through the band of hills which
heads the Tochi Valley with a rapidity that seems
incredible in these days, and to have laid waste the
Indus Valley from Bannu to Multan. . . . The Tochi,[1]
moreover, dominates much of the northern hills of
Waziristan. We have not yet shut off Waziristan
from Afghanistan, and the Wazirs will be as ripe
for mischief in the future as in the past. But Waziristan is now dovetailed in between the Gomal and
the Tochi, and the influence of our military pressure
north and south, as well as east, cannot fail to make
for peace and good order. . . . If there is so much to
be said for the occupation of the Tochi (a more or less
isolated valley) surely there is yet more to be said for
the occupation of the Gomal. The Tochi Valley leads
nowhere, so far as we are concerned at present. . . .
The Gomal is the most important pass between the
Khyber and the Bolan. It gives access to the very
centre of Afghanistan from India. It is the regular
highway for thousands of trading and fighting people
who bring their Kafilas yearly to India. . . . From
Wana we not only dominate the southern Waziri
valleys, but we round off the line of frontier outposts

[1] The Tochi Valley is sixty-three miles in length.

which hold all the wild people of the Suleiman mountains in check from Quetta to Waziristan. It secures
the end of the chain, and can itself be supported and
fed either from India by the Gomal Pass, or from
Quetta by the Zhob Valley."

Some explanation of this last sentence is necessary;
at Khajuri Kach—"the plain of palms," trees which,
by the way, are here said to be conspicuous by their
absence—the Zhob River flows into the Gomal, and
here the road bifurcates, that along the Zhob Valley
leading to Quetta, the other continuing north-west
along the Gomal to Ghazni. Further on again, at
Domandi, the Gomal is joined by a river called the
Kundar, the valley route of which leads directly to
Kandahar.

Of the approach to Ghazni by the Tochi we know
that it is easy enough, for we have made it so, as far
as Sheranni, and thence onward to the Katanni Kotal
very difficult, steep and broken; but we know practically nothing of the road between the head of the
Katanni Pass and Ghazni. Of the Gomal route, so
far as Domandi and Wana is familiar enough, but we
would give much to know more than we do of the
country beyond.

Physically the Wazirs are tall and muscular, and
they are also courageous, while, though poor, they are
hospitable. They raise a good breed of horses, said
to have Arab blood in them, derived from horses left
behind him by Nadir Shah, but they are themselves
bad riders for the most part, and are essentially footmen. They are a pastoral rather than an agricultural

race, and possess herds of small black cattle and sheep in abundance. Unlike most other independent border tribes, the Wazirs have had the good sense to avoid, to a large extent, internal feuds, and their unity as a tribe is proverbial. Their blood feuds are consequently not so indiscriminate as those of some of their neighbours, it being ruled that the slaying of the actual murderer is sufficient. They are satisfied also with what they call "make-up money," the price of a male adult being Rs. 1300; a woman is only half-price, while the tariff for sword-cuts is on a graduated scale—some twelve rupees for the first half inch!

The Wazirs are Muhammadans of the Sunni sect, but, like any other Pathan tribe, they are not particularly strict in the performance of their religious duties. The mullahs have influence only so far as the observances of religion go, and are powerless in political matters, but the Wazirs are an especially democratic and independent people, and even their own Maliks have little real control over them.

Of the Wazirs, Enriquez tells us that they "are held in abomination by all their Pathan neighbours, who have a common saying to the effect that 'a Wazir will murder you for the sake of your pugaree.' ... To the poor of their own community they are said to be charitable, and they do not offer violence to the wives and children of their personal foes. Their barbarity to all strangers, however, is such that every Pathan sepoy in the Indian Army longs for nothing so keenly as a Wazir war."

"Of the Wazir," said Edwardes, "it is literally true that his hand is against every man, and every man's hand against him."

The *Darwesh Khel* are divided into two main clans :

1. The Utmanzais.
2. The Ahmadzais.

The Utmanzais live in the Tochi Valley, in Shawal, and on the Khaisora, Kaitu and Kurram Rivers.

The Ahmadzais live for the most part round Wana, in Shakai, and in the western part of the Bannu district along the border.

Thus the Darwesh Khel occupy by far the larger portion of Waziristan—the southern, western and northern part of the country. The approximate fighting strength of the Darwesh Khel Wazirs is rather over 25,000 ; there are barely one hundred of them serving in the regular Indian Army, but probably not far short of 800 are at the present moment in the Border Militia.

The *Mahsuds* are equally Wazirs with the Darwesh Khel, but are only so described by strangers to their country ; they pronounce their name "Mahsit."

They inhabit the very centre of Waziristan, being hemmed in on three sides by the Darwesh Khel, and being shut off by the Batannis on the east from the Derajat and Bannu districts. Chamberlain says of the Mahsuds that it was their boast that, while kingdoms and dynasties had passed away, they alone, of all the Afghan tribes, had remained free ; that the armies of kings had never penetrated their strongholds ; that in their intercourse with the rest of mankind they knew no law nor will but their own; and, lastly, that from generation to generation the plain country, within a night's run to the hills, had been their hunting ground from which to enrich themselves.

Under the Sikh rule this state of things was even worse, for, through misgovernment, the chief of Tank became a refugee in the mountains of Waziristan, and his country was farmed out to Multani or Tiwana mercenaries, according as either class was for the time being in favour at the Lahore court. The chief being expelled from his territory, his course was naturally to ally himself with the Mahsuds (which he did by marriage), and to keep the country in so distracted a state that it became almost uninhabited; the town of Tank at last contained nothing but its garrison and a few bunnias. On one occasion it was attacked and plundered by the Mahsuds, who retained possession of it for three days. After the first Sikh war the rightful owner was restored, and matters returned to pretty much their usual state, the Mahsuds not causing uneasiness as a tribe, but raids being of constant occurrence.

The principal villages of the Mahsuds are Makin and Kaniguram, the majority of the population being pastoral and living in tents, but caves are also used as habitations. During the winter the Mahsuds move down to the lower valleys. Kaniguram is inhabited principally by a people called *Urmar*, whose origin is not thoroughly known, but who are believed to be of Indian descent. They have a language of their

own, muster about 1000 fighting men, and identify
themselves with the Mahsuds in all their quarrels.
The Mahsuds are said to be even more superstitious
and under the influence of mullahs than are the
Darwesh Khel. They are also more democratic, and
any man who distinguishes himself in bravery or
wisdom may rise to the position of malik. Their
physique and stamina are good, and judged from the
limited extent to which they have hitherto enlisted
with us, some rate their soldierly qualities even higher
than those of the Afridis.

The Mahsuds are divided into three clans, all very
much mixed as to locality; they number some 11,400
fighting men :

    1. The Alizai.
    2. The Bahlolzai.
    3. The Shaman Khel.

The *Batannis* claim descent from Baitan, the third
son of Kais, who was the founder of the Pathan race.
They live in the hill country on the borders of Tank
and Bannu, from the Gabar Mountain on the north
to the Gomal Valley on the south. They are the
hereditary enemies of the Mahsuds, but have on
occasion aided and abetted them in their attacks
upon and raids into British territory; usually, however, on these occasions they have played the part of
jackal to their more powerful neighbours. Though
an insignificant tribe, numbering only 6000 fighting
men, they have always been troublesome. They
resemble the Mahsuds in physique and appearance,
but are cleaner and more civilised, and within com-

paratively recent years have practically identified themselves as a tribe with British interests; they are now responsible for the control of the passes through their country whereby alone the Mahsuds can reach the plains.

The Batannis comprise three clans:

1. Tatta, living at Jandola and Siraghar and in the Dera Ismail Khan district.
2. Dhana, on the Gabar Mountain and the Bannu border.
3. Uraspan, living in the Dera Ismail Khan district and in the valleys between the first and second ranges of hills.

The Batannis have only once been accorded an expedition to themselves—in 1880, when it was necessary to punish them for permitting the Mahsuds passage through their country when proceeding to raid our border.

The *Dawaris* or *Daurs* are Ghurghusht Pathans of the Kakai Karlanri branch, descendants of Shitak, and thus closely allied to the Bannuchis. Traditionally, however, they are not classed as true Pathans, being supposed to be descended from one Shah Husain, who reigned in Ghor at the commencement of the eighth century, by a mirasi wife. The original home of the Dawaris appears to have been in Shawal, whence they, in company with the Bannuchis, were driven to their present holdings by the Wazirs in the fourteenth century. These holdings comprise the open valleys—watered by the Tochi River—called Upper and Lower Dawar, which are surrounded on

all sides by the Darwesh Khel, who also divide Upper
from Lower Dawar, one section of that tribe having
villages in the Taghrai Tangi, a narrow pass some
three miles in length.

They are a fanatical, priest-ridden race, numbering
about 8000 fighting men, but with a very poor reputation for courage, and are not now enlisted in the
local militia.

They still appear to suffer from the evil reputation
they bore for many years. "The very name Dawari,"
says Oliver, "is a byword of reproach. . . . An object
of supreme contempt to his warlike neighbours, the
Wazirs, he is even looked upon as a bad character by
a Bannuchi. Worse, probably, could not be said of
him. To call him dirty would be almost a compli-
ment; his clothes, usually black cotton to start with,
are worn till they would be considered malodorous by
a Ghilzai. . . . His complexion naturally inclines to
yellow. He is essentially a non-fighting man and an
unenterprising man; he is ready for any robbery and
to back up any villainy, but he has not energy or
pluck enough to venture out of his valley to attempt
it. . . . The fringe of warlike tribes by which the
valley is surrounded has, however, really been its
protection from annexation over and over again. It
seems to have been included in the Mogul Empire
during the time of Aurangzebe, whose son, Bahadur
Shah, is said to have levied in person some heavy
arrears from the wealthy inhabitants. The Durani
lieutenants occasionally used their armies from Khost
to extort revenue; and there are stories of a shadowy

Sikh jurisdiction, but which really relate to mere forays. Though Dawar has at different times been nominally subject to the Kabul authorities, practically it has been perfectly independent. In 1855 the Government of India renounced any rights in favour of the Amir, Dost Muhammad, though neither he nor his successors were ever strong enough to enter into possession, and the sovereign rights of Kabul remained just as imaginary as before."

The Dawar country is entered from British territory by the valleys of the Tochi, Baran and Khaisora Rivers.

The tribe has the following clans :

1. The Tappizad.
2. The Idak.
3. The Mallizad.

After the annexation of the Punjab, the first occasion on which we came into collision with the Dawaris was in 1851, when they attacked a police guard in charge of camels belonging to the Latammar post. They were quiet for twenty years, and then in 1870 they gave shelter and assistance to the Muhammad Khel Wazirs, then in open rebellion against the British Government; and subsequent inquiry revealed the fact that, while outwardly aiding the local civil authorities, they were advising the Wazirs to oppose us. There was a general settlement in September 1871, when all those tribes who had assisted the Muhammad Khels were fined. The men of Upper Dawar paid their share of the tribal fine, but the men of Lower Dawar declined to do so, and insulted

and assaulted our messengers. Subsequently they
sent a specially insulting letter to the district officer.

Such conduct from a petty tribe could not, of course,
be tolerated, and Brigadier-General C. P. Keyes, C.B.,
commanding the Punjab Frontier Force, was directed
to march to the Tochi Pass on the 6th March, 1872,
taking with him all the troops available in garrison
at Bannu. The operations were not to be protracted
over twenty-four hours. On the 6th, then, General
Keyes moved out towards the Tochi Pass with a force
of two guns, 149 sabres and 1412 bayonets, having
previously sent on 1000 friendly levies to seize and
hold the Shinkai Kotal at the western end of the
pass. These levies were, however, but indifferently
armed, and being attacked by the hostile tribesmen,
they abandoned the position before General Keyes
could send them any support. It was now expected
that the Dawaris would hold the pass against us, and
the alternative of advancing by the longer route
through the Khaisora Pass was considered; but fortunately it was resolved to keep to the original plan,
for, when the advance was resumed, the crest of the
pass was found to be unoccupied, and the Shinkai
Kotal was gained on the morning of the 7th without
opposition.

The guns were with difficulty dragged up the ascent,
and then the General, pushing on with the cavalry,
found himself, at the end of an hour's ride up the
rocky bed of the stream, at the edge of a broad
plateau with the three refractory Dawari villages—
Haidar Khel, Hassu Khel and Aipi—in front. Some

of the Hassu Khel maliks came forward to beg for
terms, the nature of which was communicated to
them; they agreed to our demands but asked for
time; but while the amount of the fines was being
collected, the men of Haidar Khel became very
defiant in their demeanour and were evidently preparing for an attack upon the advanced troops. The
infantry and guns now arrived and assurances of
submission were repeated, but on the force advancing
to destroy some of the towers—the destruction of
which was part of our conditions of peace—the
enemy suddenly opened fire on the troops from
behind walls and houses. The 1st Sikhs at once
stormed the closed gates of the village of Haidar
Khel, the 4th Sikhs and 1st Punjab Infantry took
the defenders on either flank, while the cavalry,
moving round in rear, sabred the men who were now
evacuating the village. The rest then surrendered,
and all three villages yielded unconditionally to our
demands, when the force retired, no opposition of any
kind being encountered during the return march.

After this punishment the conduct of the Dawaris
was satisfactory up to 1876, when several serious
offences were committed, and the Dawaris evading
surrender of the offenders, a blockade of Lower
Dawar was instituted, and was kept up until the
tribe submitted in June 1878. During the Afghan
war, the men of both Upper and Lower Dawar were
concerned in raids on the Thal–Bannu and Thal–
Kurram roads. In April 1880 Dawaris joined with
the Wazirs in an attack upon the Baran militia post,

and on the Chapri post in the following month ; and
it was suggested that opportunity should be taken
of the operations of 1881 against the Mahsud Wazirs,
to visit the Dawar Valley and inflict punishment on
its inhabitants.   Eventually these measures were not
sanctioned by the Government of India ; the mere
threat of coercion, however, appears to have been
sufficient, and the conduct of the Dawaris at once
improved and has since remained very fairly satisfactory.

CHAPTER XVIII.

WAZIRS: OPERATIONS.[1]

Darwesh Khels:—Immediately after the annexation
of the Punjab, the Umarzai subdivision of the Ahmadzai
Wazirs began and continued to give trouble on our
border. A dispute which commenced with a disagreement with a Bannuchi chief, responsible for the
collection of the revenue from Wazir villages in our
territory, gradually developed into a grievance against
the local British authority, and finally, early in 1850,
men from several divisions of the Ahmadzai, to the
number of 1500, attacked our post at Gumatti,
immediately north of Bannu, but were repulsed.
Later in the same year the Umarzais, joined by
the Mahsud Wazirs, collected a force of several
thousand men, intending to make an attack upon
Bannu itself, but finding it too strongly defended,
they dispersed. During the next two years the
outposts of Bannu were constantly engaged in
skirmishes with the Wazirs, who came down almost
daily, occupying the foothills and firing at long range
into Gumatti. Attempts were made to effect a settlement with them, but they resisted all overtures, and

[1] See Map VIII.

operations were then decided upon against them. Before, however, these could be undertaken, the southern Umarzais, living between the Tochi River and the Gabar Mountain, made a raid towards the Kurram, but were headed off by Major John Nicholson, then Deputy-Commissioner of Bannu, who at once made arrangements for the punishment of this particular section.

Expedition against the Umarzai Wazirs, 1852.— The punitive force was divided into three columns. One column, composed of the 2nd Punjab Infantry, was to leave Bannu at 10 p.m. on the 20th December, and march through the Gumatti Pass upon Derabina and Garang, distant respectively fourteen and seventeen miles, attacking both places simultaneously at daybreak. Garang was at the foot of a narrow precipitous chasm in the Kafirkot Range, through which ran the road to Sappari, near the summit of the ridge. The Gumatti Pass was entered at midnight, the valley and a low range of hills were crossed, and Derabina was reached and destroyed. The hills above the Garang ravine were occupied just as the head of the second column was seen emerging from the village of Garang.

This force—two companies 1st Punjab Infantry and 350 men 4th Punjab Infantry, and accompanied by Major Nicholson—had moved from Latammar on Sappari by the Barganatu Pass, which was entered at midnight, the crest of the Kafirkot Range being reached about daybreak. Sappari was taken by surprise and destroyed, as were other encampments of

the Umarzais in the Garang Pass. The surprise had
been complete and but small resistance was made, but
none the less the force suffered a loss of twenty-three
men killed and wounded.

The third column—forty sabres, 2nd Punjab
Cavalry, fifty Mounted Police, and 400 of the 6th
Punjab Police Battalion—moved on the Umarzai
settlements at the north of the Khaisora and Sein
Passes, and these were destroyed and the cattle
captured, the whole force returning to Bannu on the
22nd by the Kurram Pass. The Umarzais now
appeared thoroughly humbled, and made complete
submission.

Expedition against the Kabul Khel Wazirs, 1859-
1860.—The Ahmadzai were not the only clan of the
Darwesh Khel Wazirs which gave trouble in those early
days, for in 1850 the Kabul Khel subdivision of the
Utmanzai clan made an audacious attack—in conjunction with some of the Khattaks—upon Bahadur Khel
and the salt mines. Our troops being quickly brought
up they dispersed, but they did not fail to collect again
for the harassment of the working parties engaged in
building a fort at Bahadur Khel. They joined the
Umarzais in 1851 in their various raids against our
posts, and gave some annoyance to our troops during
Captain Coke's Miranzai expedition of 1851. During
the next two years they were particularly aggressive,
committing nineteen raids and carrying off cattle, but
on Captain Coke commencing reprisals they made
terms, and for a time were more careful in their behaviour. They, however, cut up some of our cavalry

grasscutters near Thal during the Miranzai expedition
of 1855-6, and in 1859 some of the Hathi Khel sub-
division of the Ahmadzais, having murdered a British
officer near Latammar, took refuge with the Kabul
Khels.   As was only to be expected, these refused to
hand over the murderers, and a force of nearly 4000 men
was assembled in December of this year at Kohat and
marched to Thal, where, on the 19th, it was joined by
Bangash and Khattak levies, raising the strength of
the force to some 5400 men: the whole was under the
command of Brigadier-General N. B. Chamberlain, C.B.
On the 20th December the force crossed the Kurram
River and encamped at Biland Khel, then in Afghan
territory, the ruler of which had sanctioned our movements; and it was found that the main body of the
Kabul Khels had taken their stand on a high range
of hills called Maidani, whither they had removed
their belongings, and where they had stored grain,
and raised defences.   Maidani is about eight miles
south-west of Biland Khel, near Zakha Narai, and
consists of two parallel ranges contiguous to each
other, terminating at either end in a gorge and
enclosing a long, narrow valley ; the inward slopes of
both mountains are tolerably easy, and covered with
grass and bushes, but the outward sides or faces are
rugged and precipitous.   The two gorges, forming the
water channels, were the entrances to the valley—the
one facing east being called Gandiob, the one to
the south Zakha.   The enemy were believed to be
from 2000-3000 strong.

It was resolved to attack before other clans could

join the enemy, or before the tribesmen should be led
to evacuate the position by seeing the preparations
made to assault it.

At 6 a.m. on the 22nd the following marched upon
Gandiob :

> Four guns, Peshawar Mountain Battery.
> Three guns, Hazara Mountain Battery.
> Guides Infantry.
> 4th Sikh Infantry.
> 1st Punjab Infantry.
> 3rd Punjab Infantry.
> 4th Punjab Infantry.

The enemy had evidently expected the advance
upon Maidani by the Zakha gorge, where most of the
defenders had taken post, and the defences at Gandiob
were incomplete, consequently the resistance was
comparatively feeble; the heights were taken with
but small loss, and after destroying the defences, the
force returned unmolested to its camp at Gandiob.
Next day the advantage gained was followed up; the
bulk of the force returned to Maidani, marched down
the valley near to the Zakha exit, and crossed over
the range into the Durnani Valley, where the night
was passed; a large amount of Kabul Khel stock was
captured, and on the return to Shiwa, whither the
camp had been moved from Gandiob, representatives
of the clans came in asking for terms. The Utmanzais were directed to give up two of the murderers or
the actual leader of the gang. On the 29th the main
body moved to Spinwam, whence the tribesmen could
more easily be coerced, while the remainder marched

up the river nearer to Biland Khel. The tribesmen now brought in a man who had harboured the murderers, and on the 2nd January the troops moved back to Karera in the Kurram, having now satisfactorily settled with the Wazirs on the left bank of that river.

On the 4th January, while two battalions and a mountain battery remained on the right bank of the Kurram to keep open communications, the Brigadier-General marched to Sappari with the Hazara Mountain Battery, a detachment of Sappers and Miners, the 3rd and 6th Punjab Infantry, and one company 24th Punjab Infantry. There was no opposition, the Ahmadzai maliks were told they must assist in the capture of the murderers, and the force was then broken up. As might, however, have been expected, the dispersal of the troops did not facilitate the attainment of the object for which the expedition had mainly been undertaken; but eventually, through the personal influence of Lieutenant-Colonel Reynell Taylor, the Commissioner, the tribesmen were induced themselves to assemble a force, and capture and bring in one of the murderers, who was ultimately hanged on the very spot where he had committed the crime.

The next occasion when we came in contact with the Darwesh Khels was in 1869, when in retaliation for an attack made upon a party of them by the Turis, they came down upon the village of Thal, and carried off about 7000 head of cattle. They refused restitution, but on Lieutenant-Colonel Keyes, commanding the Kohat district, collecting and moving a strong force out to Thal in April, the chief men of the division implicated tendered their submission and paid up the fines demanded. In the year following, the Muhammad Khel section of the Ahmadzai, hitherto a well-behaved community, began to give a good deal of trouble. Beginning with a grievance about a fine, and a judgment against them in regard to water-rights —Oliver tells us that across the border more than half the trouble arises about women, money, land or water—it culminated in ambuscading and shooting down seven sepoys of a party marching from Bannu for the relief of the Kurram outpost, by a raiding party of 140 Muhammad Khels. The section concerned was at once outlawed; all members found in British territory were arrested, and their lands in the Bannu district were sequestered until the whole clan submitted, and gave up the men who had committed this last outrage. This they refused to do, and for some fifteen months they lived among other clans, who sympathised with, and befriended them in their exile. They committed several further raids, but eventually expressed their anxiety to come to terms and surrendered unconditionally. Their six headmen were sentenced to various terms of imprisonment, and the fines inflicted on the section had to be paid up before they were permitted to return to their holdings in British territory. Nor did the lesson taught end here; every division which had harboured or befriended the Muhammad Khels was called to account, and punishments suitable to the degree of their offences were inflicted.

For some years after this the Darwesh Khel Wazirs
gave but little trouble, but this unusual abstinence was
not due to any consideration for the British Government, but was necessitated by the tedious war they
were engaged in against the Mahsuds, and which
endured—to the general disadvantage of the Darwesh
Khels—until September 1878, when the feud was
patched up.

On the outbreak of the war in Afghanistan a convoy
route was opened between Thal and Bannu, and which,
following for the most part the line of the Kurram
River, passed through the independent territory of
the Utmanzais and Ahmadzais ; it had been traversed
during the Kabul Khel expedition of 1859, but had
not since been used by us.   Many detachments and
contingents of all arms marched by this route during
the winter of 1878-79, and Wazir camels were extensively used in the carriage of supplies for the Kurram
Valley Field Force.   For assisting in these arrangements, allowances amounting to Rs. 1000 per mensem
were made to the more important Utmanzai and
Ahmadzai chiefs, and the route remained open until
the latter part of March 1880, when, in view of a
fanatical excitement fanned by the Mullah Adkar, the
road was closed.

 During the time the Thal-Bannu route was in use,
the number of offences or raids committed was particularly small, considering the number of valuable
convoys passed through ; but almost immediately the
road was closed, a serious raid was committed on a
Turi caravan near Thal by a mixed band of Darwesh

Khels, Mahsuds and Dawaris, and on a Khattak labour camp on the Thal–Kurram road. A few weeks later—on the night of the 1st–2nd May—a determined attack was made on the military post at Chupri, eight miles to the north-west of Thal, garrisoned by fifty bayonets and thirty sabres. The raiders were some 200 men of the Darwesh Khels, Mahsuds and Dawaris; and forty of these, having by some means gained access to the enclosure of the post, inflicted upon our troops a loss of eleven killed (including a British officer), and sixteen wounded before they were beaten off. No reparation for this outrage ever appears to have been exacted.

Expedition against the Malik Shahi Wazirs, October 1880.—By October 1880, the fines due from the Kabul Khel and Malik Shahi Wazirs had amounted to a considerable sum, chiefly on account of thefts committed by them in the Kurram and near Thal during the Afghan war; and there appearing to be some difficulty in collecting the amount, a force, under Brigadier-General J. J. H. Gordon, C.B., entered the Kabul Khel Hills on the evening of the 27th October. The force was composed of:

Two guns, 1/8th Royal Artillery.
250, 85th King's Own Light Infantry.
250, 18th Bengal Cavalry.
250, 20th Punjab Infantry.

The object of the expedition was to seize men and cattle of the Malik Shahi section as security for their share of the fine. These people are almost entirely nomadic, spending the summer on the slopes of the

Siah Koh Mountains, and wintering on both banks of the Kurram River between the ninth and sixteenth milestones on the Thal–Bannu road. In order to reach them it was necessary to traverse the whole of the Kabul Khel settlements; and the difficulty, therefore, of the enterprise lay in moving through Kabul Khel country without warning reaching the Malik Shahi section, and so giving them time to escape from the comparatively open country watered by the Kurram River, into the more intricate hill country to the west in the direction of the Siah Koh.

The force left Thal at 9.30 p.m.; the advance party surrounded the Malik Shahi encampment at the south-west of the valley, another party, detached to the left, surrounded other settlements on the Charkhanai plateau; while a third small party went to the right to try and capture some noted Wazir thieves; the supports remained at Drozanda on the Thal–Bannu road. The surprise was complete, 2000 head of cattle and 109 prisoners were taken, and the force returned to Thal on the 28th, where, two days later, the jirgahs came in, and within a few weeks the whole of the fines due had been realised from the Malik Shahi and Kabul Khels; their conduct did not, however, materially improve, despite the punishment they had received and the knowledge they had acquired of our ability to exact reparation from them whenever it should suit us to do so.

Our later dealings with the Darwesh Khel Wazirs will be described further on in this chapter.

Mahsud Wazirs.—The reputation of the Mahsuds

has never been good; they have from the earliest days been notorious robbers, and their raids upon British territory have been frequent and serious. The Powindah caravans of the warrior traders, mostly Ghilzais, which pass to and fro by the Gomal Pass between Afghanistan and India, bringing Central Asian merchandise as far as the markets of Benares and Patna, have ever been the objects of constant attack and harassment by the Mahsuds, whose country commands the Gomal; and both in 1855 and 1857 John Lawrence, the Chief Commissioner, urged the Government to undertake retributive measures against them. Again, in 1859 and 1860, Brigadier-General Chamberlain, Commanding the Punjab Frontier Force, made similar appeals, but Lord Canning, to whom the matter was then referred, decided against an expedition as not being actually urgent at the moment.

In March 1860, however, the Mahsuds committed a most serious and unprovoked act of aggression. This was nothing less than the arrival before Tank of some 3000 Wazirs, under one Jangi Khan, with the intention of sacking the town, which stands on the plains some five miles from the foot of the hills. Warning of the intended attack had, however, been received, and Ressaldar Saadat Khan, of the 5th Punjab Cavalry, commanding the post, had taken the necessary steps to oppose the tribesmen. He had called in mounted men from other posts in the neighbourhood, and had collected levies and horsemen in the service of the Nawab of Tank, and on the 13th March he moved out towards the hills at the head of 158 sabres of his regiment and thirty-seven mounted levies. He found the Wazir lashkar drawn up near the mouth of the Tank Pass, and, feigning retreat, he drew the enemy after him into the plains. The cavalry then turned and, having cut off the enemy's retreat, Saadat Khan charged in the most dashing manner. The Wazirs were cut down, ridden over and put to flight, leaving 300 dead on the ground, including six leading maliks, and having many more wounded. The Ressaldar's force had only one man killed and sixteen wounded.[1]

Expedition against the Mahsud Wazirs, 1860.— It was now felt that operations must be undertaken against the Mahsuds, and Brigadier-General Chamberlain was accordingly ordered to take a force into their hills. The general decided to advance by way of Tank; this line was better known than that via Bannu, and it led more directly to the country of the tribesmen concerned in the recent outrage; he intended, moreover, should the Mahsuds not early come to terms, to advance to their chief places, Kani-

---

[1] "The family history of Badshah Khan shows the extraordinary conditions which obtain across the frontier, and how seldom men of any note die in their beds. His grandfather, Jangi Khan, was a well-known raider, and he met his death in 1860 at the hands of the 5th Punjab Cavalry when leading a force of Mahsuds to attack Tank. His father, Umar Khan, sacked Tank in 1879, but was killed in a blood-feud in the following year. Badshah Khan was always a prominent figure in the Mahsud jirgahs which came in to discuss matters with our political officers, and he occasionally exerted his authority to keep the more lawless spirits of the tribe in check, but he had to join in the general resistance when punitive expeditions entered the country. His eldest son, Jehan Khan, was killed during the blockade of 1901. He has left two other sons, and these will doubtless maintain the reputation of the family."—*Pioneer Mail*, August 11th, 1911.

guram and Makin, returning to British territory by
the Khaisora defile debouching near Bannu. It was
expected that the Mahsuds would probably make a
stand, either at an advanced position at Hinis Tangi
or at the more retired Shingi Kot, protecting the
actual entrance to their country. As a matter of fact,
however, they did not seriously defend either position,
and as this was the first occasion upon which operations in the Mahsud country had been undertaken,
there was no precedent to guide the commander and
troops as to the amount of resistance which was to be
expected, or where it would most probably be met.

A large number of levies—about 1600,—chiefly
drawn from the hereditary enemies of the Mahsuds,
were called up to take part in the expedition, while
the regular portion of the force, assembled on the
16th April at Tank, was composed as under :

> Three guns, No. 2 Punjab Light Field Battery.[1]
> Three guns, No. 3 Punjab Light Field Battery.[2]
> Four guns, Peshawar Mountain Battery.
> Three guns, Hazara Mountain Battery.
> 108 sabres, Guides Cavalry.
> 131 sabres, 3rd Punjab Cavalry.
> 100 sabres, Multani Cavalry.[3]
> 60 bayonets, 1st Company Sappers and Miners.
> 407 bayonets, Guides Infantry.
> 427 bayonets, 4th Sikh Infantry.

[1] Now the 21st Kohat Mountain Battery.

[2] Now the 22nd Derajat Mountain Battery.

[3] Now the 15th Cavalry, at that time attached to the Punjab
Frontier Force.

397 bayonets, 1st Punjab Infantry.
684 bayonets, 2nd Punjab Infantry.
373 bayonets, 3rd Punjab Infantry.
381 bayonets, 4th Punjab Infantry.
400 bayonets, 6th Punjab Infantry.
207 bayonets, 14th Punjab Infantry.[1]
418 bayonets, 24th Punjab Infantry (Pioneers).[2]
464 bayonets, Hazara Gurkha Battalion.[3]
394 bayonets, 6th Police Battalion.

The force started on the 17th, and arrived unopposed at Palosin Kach next day, a party being detached to destroy Shingi Kot. A halt was made during the 20th to give the Mahsuds an opportunity for submission; but nothing resulting, the Headquarters and main column moved on the 20th to Haidari Kach, so as to survey the country and punish certain especially troublesome sections, leaving a small force at Palosin and at Jandola (the latter a Batanni village) to keep open communications with the plains. From Haidari Kach the Brigadier advanced as far as Barwand, meeting with no opposition and seeing few of the enemy; and on the morning of the 24th returned to Palosin, where in the meantime the camp under Colonel Lumsden, with six guns, some 200 sabres and about 1400-1500 bayonets, had been very seriously attacked.

The camp had been placed on the Kach[4] land, on the left bank of the Tank stream, with its right resting

---

[1] Afterwards disbanded.   [2] Now the 32nd Pioneers.
[3] Now 5th Gurkhas.
[4] *Kach*, a stretch of alluvial land subject to inundation, in a valley or in the broad bed of a nullah.

on an old tower (distant some 800 yards) overlooking the stream; the left was protected by a picquet on an abrupt peak to the south-east, having the scarped bank of the river in its front and the edge of the high table-land immediately in the rear. On the night of the 22nd, the outlying picquets were at their posts on the ridge behind the camp; a complete company occupied the tower, three other parties, each of a havildar and eight sepoys, were posted along the rear, while one of thirty men was on the high peak above mentioned. Each picquet had a support of equal strength close in rear.

No information as to any tribal gathering had been received, and the night had passed quietly enough, when just at *reveille* the rear picquet fired a volley, and a rush of 3000 Wazirs overpowered and nearly destroyed the picquets holding the high bank. Fortunately the whole body did not come on; some 500 swordsmen stormed into the camp, while the remainder kept up a heavy fire from the ridge. For some little time confusion reigned in the camp, but then discipline prevailed, and the Guides, 4th Sikhs and Gurkhas drove out the enemy at the point of the bayonet, pursuing them for three miles and punishing them heavily. Our losses had been serious —63 killed and 166 wounded—but those of the enemy were even more so. The attack had been a complete surprise, and was carried out with great gallantry and determination: we shall see another instance of such an attack further on in this chapter.

2 F

It had been intended to commence the march on
Kaniguram on the 2nd May, forcing *en route* the
position at the Ahnai Tangi, which the Wazirs were
said to have occupied; but on the 1st some Mahsud
maliks arrived in camp, purporting to represent the
whole tribe, and expressing their anxiety to make
terms. They were offered the option of a heavy fine,
with security for its payment and hostages for good
behaviour, or the unopposed passage of the force to
their capital, Kaniguram. Neither alternative recommended itself to the maliks, who asked for a day to
consider the matter, and the General decided to move
the camp on to Shingi Kot for greater convenience
of supply, and here the maliks were to bring their
decision on the 2nd. Nothing, however, was heard
from them this day, and on the 3rd the onward march
was resumed, the Ahnai gorge being found abandoned,
and the force encamped at Zeriwam, where another,
and an unsuccessful, attempt was made to effect a
peaceful settlement with the Mahsuds. Next day
the troops moved on, the defile becoming narrower
and the Barari gorge turning out to be the most
difficult of any that had been yet seen, being a narrow
cleft cut by the Tank stream through a chain of
mountains crossing its course at right angles. Both
sides of the passage are perpendicular cliffs of forty
or fifty feet in height, from which the mountains slope
upwards at a considerable incline, while the actual
mouth of the pass was hidden by a thick grove of
trees.

It was soon abundantly evident that here the enemy

had made every preparation for defence, while the position itself was one of great natural strength. Both sides of the pass-mouth were very steep, while everywhere sangars had been placed in terraces, and there was a safe line of retreat, but the ground to the north seemed just practicable for infantry and mules. There was, however, a ravine which joined the Tank stream at the mouth of the pass on this side, and there was no means of knowing whether, after the northern heights had been seized, the actual position might not still be inaccessible owing to the presence of this ravine.

General Chamberlain decided to attack on both sides, and formed two columns for this purpose, the left under Colonel Lumsden, the right or northern under Colonel Green. On the right the attack was at first conducted without loss, but thereafter the advance became difficult, the ground was much cut up by ravines, the fire was very heavy, and the men attacking became a good deal exposed and dispersed. There was something of a check, and the Wazirs, leaping out of their sangars, charged down upon the 3rd Punjab Infantry sword in hand. These gave way and fell back upon the support, which also retired, and the Mahsuds prepared to charge the guns and the reserve. The 1st Punjab Infantry, under Captain Keyes, now stemmed the tide; the enemy, met by these men and by the fire of the guns, fell back in their turn hotly pursued. The 1st Punjab Infantry followed them into the breastworks, the other troops rallied, and the right of the position was now taken.

Colonel Lumsden's party had an easier task; disheartened at seeing the northern part of their position in our hands, and fired on by Colonel Green's guns, the Mahsuds on this flank offered but a feeble resistance, and the force marched through the gorge and camped three miles beyond it. Our losses in this affair were thirty killed and eighty-six wounded.

On the 5th the force arrived, unopposed, at Kaniguram, remaining there until the 8th, and receiving the expression of a desire for peace from the Mahsud maliks, but nothing satisfactory was arranged. On the 9th a move was then made to Makin, which was reached with but little opposition on the following day. Next to Kaniguram, Makin is the most important and best built town in the Mahsud country, the seat of their iron trade ; it is situated at the point where the mountains of Shuidar and Pirghal close in upon each other, a spur from each forming its northern and southern face. As the Mahsuds still failed to come to terms, towers were destroyed and villages burnt; but the state of the supplies rendering it impossible for the force to remain longer in the country, the General directed the return march on Bannu to commence on the 12th. Moving by Razmak, Razani and Saroba, on the 20th Bannu was reached, and the force was broken up.

Although the operations had been successful, they had not resulted in the submission of the Mahsud Wazirs; the tribe was therefore put under blockade, thus inflicting increased financial loss on them, and at last in June 1862 they gave in, agreed to the principle of sectional responsibility for outrages committed, and gave hostages, but they had hardly concluded this treaty before they broke it.

The next sixteen years form a continuous record of raids on the Bannu and Dera Ismail Khan borders ; attacks on posts, cattle-lifting, highway robbery, abduction, murder and wounding. The offenders were punished when they could be met with, and the divisions and sections to which they belonged were made to suffer for their misdeeds ; blockades were imposed, additional posts were built for the overawing of the Mahsud Wazirs, service was offered to them in the frontier militia, and at last, in 1878, it was reported that the Tank border had never before been in so settled a condition, or life and property so secure. Within a year, however, the peace of this part of the frontier was rudely broken by a raid on a large scale and of a particularly audacious character.

About Christmas 1878 rumours of an intended attack upon Tank reached the local authorities, and precautions were accordingly taken. All the posts on this border were doubled, and in some of the more important the strength of the garrison had been trebled, so that when, on New Year's Day 1879, the attack, instigated by emissaries of the Amir Sher Ali, actually commenced, nearly half the available force in the district was concentrated in the Tank Valley. All the villages had also been warned.

On the 1st January, however, the Mahsuds descended from their hills to the number of between 2000

and 3000, brushed aside the opposition met with
from the post at the mouth of the pass, and, descending upon Tank, burnt the bazaar and many houses,
and finally regained the hills before they could be
intercepted, carrying off a considerable amount of
property with them.

The Mahsuds engaged in this affair belonged chiefly
to the Alizai clan; but men from all the country
round, within and without our border, joined the
marauders, being unable to resist so unusually favourable an opportunity for fomenting disorder and
obtaining plunder, and lawless and predatory bands
destroyed and robbed several border villages.

The news of the outrage did not reach Dera Ismail
Khan until the morning of the 2nd, when a force of
cavalry and infantry at once moved out to Tank,
came up with some clansmen about four miles from
that place, took a number of prisoners, recovered a
certain amount of plunder, and reached Tank the
following night, having marched nearly fifty miles.
During the next fortnight minor operations were
carried out from Tank and from the border posts
with the comparatively small force available, and the
enemy were everywhere driven from the positions
they took up and suffered considerable loss, order
being eventually restored on this border.   All the local
tribesmen implicated in the recent attacks had now
been punished, with the exception of the Mahsuds,
and these were offered certain terms for acceptance,
failing which a punitive expedition was to be sent
into their country so soon as a favourable oppor-

tunity should occur. Meanwhile a strict blockade was enforced.

In March 1880 the Mahsuds, stirred up by the preachings of a fanatical mullah, commenced hostilities against the British Government, and collected up the Tank stream within ten miles of our border. A force was at once—on 5th April—moved out from Dera Ismail Khan (3 guns, 50 sabres, 300 bayonets) and marched to Tank. The Mahsuds could not make up their minds where their blow should fall, and many consequently returned to their homes, while the remainder, moving south, attacked the town of Gomal, but, being driven off, dispersed. As it was apparent that the Batannis of Jandola had given passage to this raiding party, the Dera Ismail Khan force advanced on Jandola from Kot Khirgi on the morning of the 12th, forced the Hinis Tangi and, having destroyed Jandola, returned unopposed to Tank.

During 1880 the Mahsuds, associated with the Darwesh Khels and Dawaris, committed several serious outrages on our border, and, with the termination of the operations in Afghanistan, the Government now found itself able to send the long contemplated expedition into the Mahsud country. Accordingly, early in 1881 arrangements were put in hand for coercing that tribe. While the force was in process of assembly, the Mahsuds, who had been offered a final opportunity of peaceful submission, sent in certain headmen to make terms and thus avoid punishment; but these belonged almost exclusively to clans living immediately without our borders, while those sections among the more inaccessible hills, and which had for long been opposed to peace with the British Government, were still entirely unrepresented among those suing for peace.

During the third week in April, after a great council at Kaniguram, our terms were to some extent complied with, but the submission of the tribe generally was still incomplete. Several important subdivisions, notably the Nana Khel division of the Bahlolzais, were still defiant, and it was decided that this division must be coerced. The force assembled at Tank, composed entirely of troops of the Punjab Frontier Force with some additions, was placed under command of Brigadier-General T. G. Kennedy, C.B., and consisted of twelve guns, 290 sabres and 3662 bayonets; while a reserve brigade—eight guns, 326 sabres and 3380 bayonets—under Brigadier-General J. J. H. Gordon, C.B., was formed at Bannu.

Expedition against the Mahsud Wazirs, 1881.— The main force moved from Tank by Kot Khirgi to Jandola, which was reached on the 23rd April, when the pass leading to the Shahur Valley was reconnoitred without opposition. The column then moved on by Haidari Kach and Turam China to Barwand, and so far, although the rearguard was always fired on, there had been no casualties and nothing in the way of serious opposition had been experienced, while some of the headmen had already submitted. The force now moved on towards the Khaisora Valley, and on arrival in this neighbour-

hood the Alizais made terms, but the troops were
now in the country of the Nana Khels, who showed
a good deal of hostility.   On the 5th May General
Kennedy arrived at Kaniguram via Kundiwan, having
had a sharp affair with some 500 Bahlolzais holding
the densely wooded slopes about Shah Alum.   Makin
was reached on the 10th, by which date the Bannu
column was encamped at Razmak, only seven miles
distant.

On the 16th April this brigade had moved from
Bannu and had taken up a position on the right
bank of the Tochi River near Miriam, commanding
the entrances of the Khaisora, Tochi and Shakto
valleys.   General Gordon, in compliance with instructions received from General Kennedy, marched
up the Khaisora Valley to Razmak via Saroba and
Razani practically unopposed, being accompanied by
representatives of the sections inhabiting the valley.
A convoy of supplies was passed from here to Makin,
and on the 12th May the Bannu column began to
retire, visiting the Shakto Valley *en route* and
having only one casualty in the force.   On the next
day General Kennedy marched from Makin via
Janjal to Jandola, and arrived on the 18th unmolested at Tank, where the column was broken up.
The total British casualties during these operations
only amounted to thirty-two killed and wounded.

The Mahsuds seemed now ready and eager to make
peace, but still our terms remained uncomplied with,
and the blockade consequently was reimposed; and
it was not until September of this year, and after

several fruitless attempts to play off the Amir against
the British Government, that the Mahsuds finally
gave in. They surrendered the remaining ones
among the proscribed ringleaders in the 1879 outrages, but since the aggregate of the fines accumulated
against them now appeared quite beyond their powers
of payment, it was agreed that the amount should
gradually be liquidated by a tax imposed on all
Mahsud goods imported into our territory, and for
a breathing space at least quiet reigned on this
portion of the border.

Mahsud and Darwesh Khels.—The behaviour of
all the Wazirs, Mahsuds and Darwesh Khels, may be
said to have been uniformly good for a further period
of ten years, dating from the conclusion of the
expedition of 1881. In 1883 the Mahsuds gave
facilities for the survey of the country about Khajuri
Kach ; in 1889 the Zhob Valley was traversed by us ;
the Gomal Pass was opened up, and our protectorate
extended over the Zhob Valley and the country
between the Gomal and Pishin ; a railway survey
was carried out in the Gomal ; and our influence was
strengthened among the Mahsuds and the Wazirs
of Wana by the granting of new or increased allowances. There had, of course, been periods of disquiet,
occasioned and accentuated by the fact that at this
time there was no definite boundary line demarcating
British and Afghan spheres of influence. The difficulty of restraining the tribesmen within limits and
of inflicting punishment for outrages was increased,
and a delicate situation thereby created, owing to

the fact that it was often impossible to determine whether offenders were subjects of the Amir of Afghanistan, or came within the pale of British influence. It was then, in October 1893, that, after long negotiations, Sir Mortimer Durand went to Kabul and returned with an agreement signed by the Amir. By this settlement the respective spheres of influence of the British Government and of the ruler of Afghanistan were carefully defined. The Amir agreed to retire from Chageh in Baluchistan, and withdrew his objections to the extension of the railway to New Chaman, west of the Kwaja Amran Range, and to the establishment of a British cantonment at that place; the Bajauris, Afridis and Wazirs were left outside the limits of his influence, but Asmar, and the Kunar valley above it as far as Chanak, and the tract of Birmal, bordering on the Wazir country, were included within his territory; on the other hand, a somewhat clumsy arrangement, and one almost certain to be fruitful of future trouble, had been come to, whereby the country of the Mohmands had been arbitrarily divided by the watershed of the Kunar and Panjkhora rivers.

Early in 1894 the Government of India began to make preparations for the demarcation, in co-operation with the Commissioners appointed by the Amir, of the western boundaries of Waziristan; and the attitude of the Wazirs being, as ever, uncertain, it was decided to maintain a considerable force on the frontier. Work was to commence at Domandi on the 15th October, and some weeks prior to this a proclamation was

issued to the tribesmen, fully explaining the objects
and limitations of the expedition; the news seemed to
be generally received in Waziristan in a friendly spirit.

The following troops under Brigadier-General
Turner were detailed to form the escort :

129 sabres, 1st Punjab Cavalry.

6 guns, No. 3 Punjab Mountain Battery.

189 bayonets, No. 2 Company Sappers and Miners.

748 bayonets, 1st Battalion 1st Gurkhas.

744 bayonets, 3rd Sikh Infantry.

741 bayonets, 20th Punjab Infantry,

while, in addition, the following units were held in
readiness at Multan and Dera Ismail Khan to form a
reserve brigade, viz.:

2nd Battalion Border Regiment.

One squadron 1st Punjab Cavalry.

No. 8 Mountain Battery.

4th Punjab Infantry.

38th Dogras.

On the 1st October the escort was concentrated at
Dera Ismail Khan, and within ten days the Ahmadzai
clan of the Darwesh Khels from Wana had sent in
their jirgah, *unanimously repeating a previous invitation to the British Government to take over their
country and permit them to become British subjects.*

Operations of the Waziristan Field Force, 1894.—
The escort finally left Dera Ismail Khan on the 13th
October, concentrating again at Khajuri Kach and
reaching Wana—via Spin and Karab Kot—on the
25th. A jirgah of the Wana Ahmadzai came in here

and expressed pleasure at the arrival of the troops, but none the less the camp was fired into two nights in succession, and it was reported that the mullahs were endeavouring to stir up strife and to prevent a really representative jirgah from coming in.

The plain of Wana is about 13 miles long, 11 broad, and very stony; the camp was placed at the eastern end of it, the ground in the vicinity being much cut up by ravines. The position, moreover, which had been chosen for the camp of the British Joint Commissioner, was a source of weakness and of anxiety to the General in command of the escort, having been pitched some 210 yards from the south-east corner of the military camp, so as to afford the jirgahs free access to the Political Officers. Up to the end of October there was no reason to anticipate an attack upon the escort by any large body of Mahsuds; but on the 1st November it became known that the Mullah Powindah, a noted firebrand, was in the neighbourhood with not less than 1000 followers, and that he had expressed his intention of attacking the Wana camp. Picquets were accordingly doubled, the defences were strengthened, and the troops ordered to be under arms at 4 a.m. every day.

The camp was surrounded by some thirteen picquets, furnished by the 3rd Sikhs, 20th Punjab Infantry and 1st Gurkhas, in addition to an old Darwesh Khel fort held by 100 rifles of the last-named regiment; but, contrary to the procedure usually followed in frontier warfare, the majority of these picquets were no more than observation posts, and were not intended to hold their own in any serious attack, but were to fall back, in some cases on their supports, in others on their regiments in camp.

At 5.30 a.m. on the 2nd November, while it was still dark, the camp was suddenly aroused by three shots, and a desperate rush of some 500 fanatics, supported by fire from the left front, was made on the left flank and left rear of the camp, held by the 1st Gurkhas. It appears that the enemy—consisting for the most part of Mahsuds, with a few Darwesh Khels —had crept up two large ravines on the west, overwhelmed the picquets there posted, from one of which the three warning shots had issued, and came on so rapidly that the leading assailants had climbed the camp defences and penetrated into the middle of the camp, before the defenders had turned out of their tents. Another party, swinging round to the right, made their way into the camp by the rear or south, did much damage among the transport animals, and cut loose some of the cavalry horses.

By this time the troops had turned out and got to work. The Gurkhas stopped the main rush down the centre of the camp; reinforced then by two companies of the 20th and one of the 3rd Sikhs, the men swept through the camp, clearing it with the bayonet; and though two further but less determined attacks were made, no second rush followed the first, and soon after 6 a.m. the enemy were in full retreat. They were followed by a small column for six miles, and were charged into again and again by the cavalry, who inflicted serious loss upon them. Our casualties were forty-five killed and seventy-five wounded, while the enemy carried off many rifles and much loot, but left some 350 killed behind them in camp or on the line of their retreat, out of 3000 who were present, but not all of whom joined in the actual attack on the camp.

On the 18th a jirgah came into camp but nothing resulted, and on the 27th a large tribal meeting, attended by the Mullah and some 2000 or 3000 men, took place in Shakai, where the Government terms were fruitlessly discussed. The maliks then returned to our camp at Wana, stating they could not carry our terms out at once, but that if given until the 12th December all demands would be met. The extension was sanctioned, but the headmen were informed that on that date our troops would move forward unless all claims had been satisfied. All preparations were also made for the prosecution of further operations.

On the 2nd December the formation was ordered of a punitive force, under the command of Lieutenant-General Sir William Lockhart, K.C.B., consisting of three brigades, the first being composed of the original escort, strengthened by the inclusion of the 2nd Battalion Border Regiment, and later by the arrival of the 1st Battalion 4th Gurkhas.

The composition of the Second Brigade, under Brigadier-General W. P. Symons, was as under ;

No. 8 Mountain Battery.
One Squadron 1st Punjab Cavalry.
One Squadron 2nd Punjab Cavalry.
33rd Punjab Infantry.[1]

[1] Now the 33rd Punjabis.

38th Dogras.

4th Punjab Infantry.

1st Battalion 5th Gurkhas.

No. 5 Company Bengal Sappers and Miners.

One Maxim Gun.

This brigade concentrated at Tank for Jandola.

The Third Brigade was under the command of Colonel C. C. Egerton, C.B., and assembled at Miriam, near Bannu ; it was made up as follows :

No. 1 Kohat Mountain Battery.

3rd Punjab Cavalry.[1]

1st Sikh Infantry.

2nd Punjab Infantry.

6th Punjab Infantry.

In the meantime the Mahsuds had added to their already long list of offences, and finally, on the 12th December, the jirgah came in and admitted that there appeared no hope of the tribe complying with our terms.   Consequently, on the 16th, Sir William Lockhart was ordered to advance, when the following instructions were issued by him : The First Brigade to move from Wana by the Tiarza Pass and the Sharawangi Kotal on Kaniguram; the Second Brigade to advance on Makin from Jandola by the Tank stream ; the Third to proceed by the Khaisora Valley, in Darwesh Khel limits, to Razmak. Each column to arrive at its destination on the 21st December.

Before leaving Wana the Officer commanding First Brigade established there a military post in a fortified

[1] Now the 23rd Cavalry.

village, occupying it with two guns, twenty sabres and a battalion of infantry. Moving then by the Tiarza Pass, the column arrived at Kaniguram on the 21st, encountering only slight opposition *en route*, but the road was found to be very bad, and the rearguard never reached camp before midnight. Meanwhile the Second Brigade, accompanied by Sir William Lockhart, marched from Jandola via Marghaband, Shilmanzai Kach and Janjal, and reached Makin on the 21st, having *en route* destroyed the Mullah's village at Marobi. The camp was fired into every night, but no really active opposition was met with, and the mullah was reported to have fled to the Darra Valley, north of Pirghal.

The Third Brigade, marching on the 17th, was at Razmak on the 23rd—the rearguard having been fired at from one village only—and arrived on the following day at Makin. The force was now split up into a number of smaller columns, and all parts of the country were visited—the Baddar, Shakto, Sheranna, Shinkai, Nargao, Tangai and Janjara Valleys—and only in the first of these was opposition experienced. Cattle were driven in, forage collected, and towers destroyed ; nearly all the divisions implicated in the attack on Wana camp had been punished, our terms had to some extent been complied with, and by the last week in January the delimitation party was able to commence work. On the 4th March the last of the Mahsud hostages required were surrendered, and the force was then gradually reduced, troops remaining in occupation of Jandola, Barwand, Wana, and in the

Tochi Valley—this last offering the means for maintaining a hold over the Darwesh Khels.   By the end
of the operations all concerned in the attack on Wana
had been punished, our terms had been fully complied
with, and the boundary from Domandi to Laram had
been demarcated.

In 1895 there were several murderous attacks upon
individuals, chiefly in the Tochi Valley, and it was
evident that the establishment of military posts, and
the permanent military occupation of the Tochi Valley,
had done little to counteract the natural lawlessness
of the inhabitants.

In the summer of 1896 a British subject had
been murdered at Sheranni in the Tochi, and the
Madda Khel, who inhabit Maizar in the lower part
of the Shawal Valley, considered they had been
unfairly treated in the apportionment of the blood
money, levied according to tribal custom for the
murdered man.   The matter was still unsettled in
June of the following year, when the Political Officer
gave notice that he would visit Maizar to discuss the
case, and further to select a site for a new levy post,
the construction of which had been decided upon.
On the 10th June, then, Mr. Gee, the Political Officer,
left Datta Khel, which since the autumn of the year
previous had been the civil and military headquarters
of the district, with an escort of two mountain guns,
twelve sabres, and 300 rifles under Lieutenant-Colonel
Bunny, 1st Sikhs.   On arrival at Maizar the maliks
evinced every sign of friendship, pointing out a halting
place, and, with an excess of treachery unusual even

among Pathans, provided food for the Muhammadan soldiers of the escort. The halting place chosen was close to a Madda Khel village and commanded by other villages from 100 to 400 yards distant, but, so far as the position admitted, all possible precautions were taken. The meal promised was produced and partaken of, and then, while the pipers of the 1st Sikhs were playing for the benefit of the villagers, a hubbub suddenly arose in the village, from the top of a tower in which a man was seen to wave a sword. The villagers quickly drew off, and firing at once commenced on the escort from the houses on three sides.

Colonel Bunny and three officers were hit almost immediately, and the baggage animals, carrying most of the reserve ammunition, stampeded; but the guns at once came into action, driving back into the village the men who seemed upon the point of charging, and giving time for preparations for the retirement of the escort, now inevitable. The circumstances were trying in the extreme for the troops, and their staunchness is worthy of the highest praise. By this time every one of the British officers had been hit, two of them mortally, but the native officers of the 1st Punjab Infantry and 1st Sikhs nobly filled their places. Getting together a party of men, a most determined stand was made by a garden wall, whereby the first withdrawal was covered, the wounded were helped away, and the guns were able to retire to a fresh position, whence they fired "blank" to check the enemy, the small number of service rounds brought out having now been exhausted. The retirement was continued, the enemy coming on and enveloping the flanks, until the Sheranni plain was reached ; and about 5.30 p.m., reinforcements coming out from Datta Khel, the enemy were at last beaten off, and the further withdrawal to camp was unmolested.

Operations of the Tochi Field Force, 1897-98.— The decision to send a punitive expedition into the Tochi was arrived at on the 17th June, and by the 8th July the concentration at Bannu was completed. The force was placed under command of Major-General Corrie-Bird, C.B., and comprised two brigades.

FIRST BRIGADE.

Colonel C. C. Egerton, C.B.

2nd Battalion Argyll and Sutherland Highlanders.
1st Sikh Infantry.
1st Punjab Infantry.
33rd Punjab Infantry.
One squadron 1st Punjab Cavalry.
No. 3 Peshawar Mountain Battery.
No. 2 Company Bengal Sappers and Miners.

SECOND BRIGADE.

Brigadier-General W. P. Symons, C.B.

3rd Battalion Rifle Brigade.
14th Sikhs.
6th Jats.
25th Punjab Infantry.
One squadron 1st Punjab Cavalry.
Four guns No. 6 Bombay Mountain Battery.

The field force concentrated at Datta Khel on the 19th July, and on the next day the First Brigade marched to Sheranni, finding that place and Maizar deserted, the Madda Khel being reported to have fled to the hills preliminary to seeking a refuge in Afghanistan. All the defences in the neighbourhood were destroyed, and a proclamation embodying our terms was issued, but to these the Maizar and Sheranni maliks on the 3rd September definitely refused to agree. The Kazha, Shawal and Khina Valleys were visited by columns, and strong places were destroyed, but with the exception of some sniping into camp there was no sign of opposition. It was not, however, until the 31st October that the head of the Madda Khel gave himself up, and a fortnight later the whole tribe formally submitted, paid up a first instalment of all fines, including the overdue blood-money which had occasioned the outrage, and early in 1898 the field force began to be gradually broken up.

The total casualties at Maizar and in the subsequent operations amounted to twenty-nine killed and forty wounded; but during this expedition the troops suffered to an altogether unusual extent from sickness, chiefly diarrhoea and dysentery. The climate of the Tochi Valley is always trying, while the forced march in the hot weather from Khushalgarh to Bannu had no doubt affected the men's constitutions.

Operations against the Mahsuds in 1900-1901.— No sooner were operations concluded in the Tochi Valley than the Mahsuds began again to be troublesome. During 1898 and 1899 raids were of frequent

occurrence, and in the year following a levy post at
Zam and a police post near Tank were attacked. The
maliks seemed quite unable to restrain, still less to
coerce, the tribesmen. The fines for past offences
now amounted to no less a sum than Rs. 100,000, and,
no portion of it being forthcoming, a blockade was
declared, which came into operation on the 1st December, 1900. To ensure its effectiveness movable
columns were mobilised from Bannu and Dera Ismail
Khan, and by their means cordons were drawn on
the east and south of the Mahsud country. These
measures were so far effectual that the Mahsuds made
a commencement with the payment of their fine, but
in January 1901, fresh offences were committed,
raids continued, and more serious attacks were not
infrequent.

A new procedure was now introduced into the
ordinary measures of a purely passive blockade.
Hitherto the tribesmen had invariably received notice
prior to the commencement of active operations—
they had always been afforded an opportunity of
coming belatedly to terms—but it was now decided
that, while the blockade should continue, it should be
varied and accompanied by sharp attacks, carried on
during three or four days by small mobile columns
acting simultaneously and by surprise. The first series
of such operations, for which preparations had been
made in secret, commenced on the 23rd November,
and was directed against the Mahsuds of the Khaisora
and Shahur Valleys, combined with demonstrations
from Jandola into the Takhi Zam, and from Datta

Khel against the north-west portion of the Mahsud country; the general object being to demolish all defences, capture prisoners and cattle, and destroy grain and fodder. Four columns, each consisting almost exclusively of infantry, and varying in strength from 900 to 1250 men, started from Datta Khel, Jandola, Sarwekai and Wana; all were opposed, and each suffered some loss, but the combined operations were very successful. Moreover, no sooner were these at an end than a further series was projected. On the 4th December Brigadier-General Dening left Jandola with 2500 rifles and four guns and moved to Shingi Kot, where he divided his force into two columns. Marching north-west up the Tazar Tang, Dwe Shinkai and Guri Khel were visited, and the force returned by way of Marghaband to Jandola. The enemy fought fiercely, following up the columns and driving home their attacks with great determination; their losses were consequently very severe.

The third series of operations began on the 19th December, and was undertaken by two columns starting from Jandola and Sarwekai converging on Dwe Shinkai, where, as well as in the Spli Toi Algad, there were now known to be many Mahsud settlements. The Jandola column under General Dening (four guns, thirteen sabres, and 2052 rifles, exclusive of the South Waziristan Militia), marched via Shingi Kot and Umar Ragzha to Paridai up the Tre Algad, destroyed all defences, and joined the other columns at Dwe Shinkai on the 21st. The Sarwekai column under Colonel Hogge (two guns and three battalions) had marched

to Dwe Shinkai by way of the Shahur Nala, Badshah
Khan, Nanu Narai and the Spli Toi Algad. On the
22nd the whole combined force, told off into three
columns, raided up the Dwe Shinkai, and, after
destroying a number of fortified towers and other
defences, returned on the 24th to Jandola.

The Mahsuds still, however, evinced no inclination
to submit, and a fourth series of operations was consequently planned against them, the object of these
being the punishment of the sections living in the
Shakto, Sheranna and Shuza Algads. For this three
columns were formed, based respectively on Jandola,
Jani Khel and Datta Khel, and varying in strength from
2500 to 1400 men, and their operations were uniformly
successful, resulting in the capture of a large number
of cattle and the destruction of many fortified places.
Standing camps were now formed at Zam, Miramshah
and Baran, whence it was intended that punitive
measures should be resumed so soon as the troops had
enjoyed a much needed rest. The Mahsuds had by
this, however, lost heavily in men and cattle, and had
throughly realised that the innermost parts of their
country could be reached and traversed by our troops.
They consequently opened negotiations for peace and
for the removal of the blockade, and after the usual
delays they paid up their fines in full, restored all the
rifles they had captured, and gave hostages for the
return of all plundered cattle.

Our casualties during these operations had amounted
to thirty-two killed and 114 wounded.

The punishment inflicted on the Mahsuds did not,

however, appear to have had any particular effect upon all Wazirs, and before the end of 1901 another expedition became necessary against the Kabul Khel sub-division of the Utmanzai Darwesh Khels, who inhabit the wedge of hilly country lying between the Kohat and Bannu districts and east of the Kurram River.

Expedition against the Kabul Khels (Darwesh Khels) in 1901-1902.—During the years between 1896 to 1899 many outrages were committed upon our border by men living at the village of Gumatti, some eight miles north of Bannu.   In February of the latter year this village was surrounded by our troops and the surrender of all outlaws demanded.   This was refused, and some of the men "wanted" shut themselves up in two strong towers, from which, owing to the short time available, it was not found possible to dislodge them.   The force had consequently to withdraw with its object only partially accomplished, and its retirement was harassed by the tribesmen all the way back to Bannu.   Crimes of all kinds continued to be committed on this part of the border, and it was finally decided to send an expedition into the district.   Four small columns directed by Major-General Egerton were accordingly formed, comprising all three arms, and varying from 600 to 1000 men in numbers.   These concentrated at Thal, Idak, Barganatu and Bannu, and started, the Idak column on the 17th November and the others on the next day.   By these forces the Kabul Khel country was traversed in all directions, many of the outlaws were killed or captured, over 5000 head of cattle were carried off by us, and a large number of fortified towers were destroyed. Since the close of this expedition the Darwesh Khels have given us but little trouble, the Mahsuds continuing, however, to be almost as turbulent as ever.

APPENDIX A.

THE ARMS TRADE AND THE TRIBESMEN.

No book dealing with the military relations, now and in the past, of the Indian Government and the frontier tribes, can be said to be complete, which does not contain some allusion to the armament of these men. In the matter of small arms we have not invariably possessed the conspicuous superiority which might have been expected of a highly-civilised nation warring against a semi-savage people. Readers of Kaye's *History of the War in Afghanistan* will not need to be reminded how frequently both the Afghans, and the tribes which followed our columns, proved that their firearms were better in range and in man-killing power than were the weapons with which in those days, and even for some years after, our soldiers were armed. We read of our muskets: "Little could they do against the far-reaching Afghan matchlocks. . . . The muskets of our infantry could not reach the assailants. . . . The two forces were at a distance from each other, which gave all the advantage to the enemy, who shot down our men with ease, and laughed at the musket balls, which never reached their position. . . . But, again, the British muskets were found no match for the Afghan jazails...the Afghan marksmen mowed down our men like grass." [1]

At the time of the second Afghan war we had completely re-established the superiority of our armament; but since then arms factories have been set up in many places within and without our border, and by this means and by a well-organised, large-scale system of rifle-stealing—not only from regiments in our frontier garrisons, but from others far down country—the tribesmen, who could pay the prices asked, gradually became well equipped with modern rifles and the necessary ammunition. At the time of the Tirah Expedition of 1897-98 the old-fashioned, home-made jazail had practically been everywhere replaced by the breech-loader, many of which, if not actually made at Enfield, had probably been manufactured in the Kohat Pass with all the Government "marks" carefully reproduced. Such confidence had their improved armament inspired in the men of the border, that the feeling found expression in an offer made from more than one clansman at the close of the Tirah campaign : "if we would only leave our artillery behind, they would fight us all over again."

But the improvement noticed in 1897 in the armament of the tribes, seemed to point to the existence of other and more open markets for the supply of modern rifles, than those known to exist to the west of our border; and the Government of India now set inquiries on foot relative to statements, of late years

[1] Vol. III., pp. 86 and 89, 1851 edition.

often repeated and as persistently disregarded, of the existence of a well-established and flourishing trade in arms carried on in the Persian Gulf. There can be no doubt that the arms traffic both at Bushire and at Muscat was originally begun and maintained by British subjects; but the demand for modern rifles in Southern Persia, in Afghanistan, and on the north-west frontier was now so great, that other nations quickly went into the business, and it has been computed that in 1906 four European nations between them imported £278,000 worth of rifles into Muscat alone. The traffic at Bushire does not appear to have exercised any perceptible influence on the arming of the north-west frontier tribes; but that which originated at Muscat in the early nineties soon grew and flourished exceedingly, "parcels" of rifles and ammunition being shipped in native craft from Muscat to the Mekran coast, where they were met by the caravans of the Afghan traders, and being taken thence along the Perso-Baluch frontier into Southern Afghanistan, were distributed among the tribes on our border. This trade was permitted to flourish for fully ten years before any adequate steps were taken to stop it.

In the reports of the Baluchistan Agency during the last five years, so far as these have appeared up to the time of writing, it is possible in some degree to trace the growth of the traffic, and to note the steps belatedly taken for its suppression. Thus, in the Report for 1906-07 we read: "During the months of October to December over a thousand rifles imported from Muscat are reported to have been landed and distributed throughout Persian Baluchistan."

Report for 1907-08 : " Not so satisfactory to record is the enormous increase in the arms trade between the Persian Gulf and Afghanistan. A very large number of rifles and a vast amount of ammunition are reported to have been landed on the Persian coast during the year under report. Arrangements were being made at the close of the year under report to reinforce the military garrison at Robat, with a view to preventing these arms being taken through British territory. The Afghan arms traders have since successfully brought all their large consignments of arms into Afghanistan through Persian territory."

Report for 1908-09 : " In the year under review very large numbers of rifles, with great quantities of ammunition, were again imported into Afghanistan and into Persian Baluchistan from the Persian Gulf. A force of 500 infantry, with two machine guns, was sent to Robat in April to reinforce the military detachment already there, and to assist in intercepting any caravans which might attempt to reach Afghanistan through the Chagai District. This additional force returned in August at the close of the arms-running season. Though no captures were made, the traffic by this route was effectively checked. In the absence of any effective measures on the Persian side, however, this was of little advantage, and the trade through Persia, being practically completely unchecked, increased considerably in volume."

In 1909 the Admiral of the East Indian station took the matter seriously in hand, and the result of the efforts of the Navy is recorded in the Report of the Baluchistan Agency for 1909-10. After making some complaint of the increase in the number of raids from across the border, and stating that "owing to the possession of modern rifles and abundant ammunition these outlaws have been more daring and difficult to deal with," the Report goes on to say : "Throughout the year under review reports continued to be received regarding the landing of arms and ammunition on the Persian Gulf coast. It is estimated that over 16,500 rifles, 352 revolvers and pistols, 1,079,000 rounds, as well as 137 boxes of ammunition, were landed between the 31st March, 1909, and 1st April, 1910. Owing to the frequency of these reports regarding the landing of arms, the Government of India, in September 1909, decided to resume naval operations on the Persian Gulf coast. It is satisfactory to note that these operations proved far more successful than previous ones, some 6307 rifles and 619,700 rounds of ammunition being captured between July 1909 and April 1910, and 4260 rifles with 520,000 rounds being accounted for after the close of the year. As a result of a conference held at Simla in July 1909, Mr. Gregson, Superintendent of Police, North-West Frontier Police, was placed on special duty in November, with a view of preventing Ghilzais and other trans-frontier tribesmen from getting to the Gulf through India. This measure resulted in some 152 Afghans with about Rs. 73,000 in their possession being detained, and it has been proved that another Rs. 26,000 was returned from Muscat.

"Half a battalion of Native Infantry, with a maxim gun section, left Quetta for Robat on the 3rd January, 1910, with a view to protecting the trade-route and closing the road leading through British territory to arms-runners. No attempts were made by the Afghans to make use of these routes, but as the Persian authorities made no attempt to close the routes leading through Persian Baluchistan, the Afghans experienced no difficulty in entering Afghanistan by skirting Robat and travelling a few miles to the west of that place. It is, however, satisfactory to note that several of the caravans are reported to have had to return empty owing to the naval operations referred to above. . . . One attempt was made during the year to land arms on the coast on the British side of the Persian boundary. A consignment, estimated at from 9500–15,000 rifles, was landed at Pishukan, near Gwadar, which is a Muscat possession within British territory. It is, however, satisfactory to note that the fate of this consignment should act as a warning to arms-runners not to make the attempt again; for 850 of these rifles were captured by a party landed by H.M.S. *Perseus*. . . . But for the active steps taken to check the arms traffic, the trade during the year would have attained abnormal proportions. Very large numbers of Afghans went down to the coast, and with them large numbers of Afridis and men of the north-west border tribes. Very great discouragement was caused to them by the failure of their ventures, and how far the success of our operations will diminish the number of those who will make similar ventures next year remains to be seen."

The Report of the Baluchistan Agency for 1910-11 hardly does sufficient justice to the success met with by the naval operations of the twelve months under review. "The combined naval and military operations in the Persian Gulf," we read, "were continued during the year. Several large consignments of arms and ammunition were captured by His Majesty's ships, and the landing of arms on the Mekran coast was rendered more difficult than ever. Notwithstanding the difficulties experienced by arms-runners last season, large numbers of Afghans and tribesmen again proceeded to the Gulf for the purpose of obtaining arms, but it is satisfactory to note that a large proportion of these are said to have returned either with unladen camels or with ordinary merchandise. Those that managed to procure arms are reported to have purchased them mostly from the local Baluch, with the result that prices have risen and very few arms are now obtainable even at the high prices offered by the arms-runners. Half a battalion of Native Infantry, with a maxim gun detachment, was maintained at Robat throughout the year, and prevented any attempts being made to use the routes leading through British territory. The routes followed by the Afghans, both when proceeding to and returning from the coast, were those to the west of Robat, which the Persian Government

2 H

is incapable of closing. Reports from all sides show
that the active measures again taken to stop the
arms traffic are keenly felt both in Afghanistan and
among the gun-running community generally. The
trade is now looked upon as an extremely difficult
and hazardous undertaking."

It was, of course, hardly to be expected that so
independent a people as these border folk would take
"lying down" this interference with their supply of
arms and ammunition—the less that the business
appears to have been conducted on the " payment-in-
advance" principle, and, the money being already in
the hands of the traders for the rifles seized by
British ships, whole communities were not merely
disappointed but ruined. Much ill-feeling and disaffection was aroused on the frontier; and the Kohat
Pass Afridis actually put in a claim against the Indian
Government for compensation—a demand which was
not entertained.

Thanks to the energy of the naval authorities, the
Muscat gun-trade would appear to have been scotched,
but it is very far from being killed, while the operations in the Gulf have cost something like £100,000
each season. How, too, can any preventive service,
however well organised, deal with cases such as that
reported in August 1911 in the Indian papers—
of a steamer of the Hansa Line which arrived in
Bombay, having among its cargo a number of cases
labelled "Loaf Sugar"—shipped at Hamburg, through
Antwerp, for Koweit via Bombay? Unfortunately
for the consignees, one of these cases was damaged

in trans-shipment, when the "loaf sugar" was found to be magazine rifles, fifty in number, of ·203 bore, and with a quantity of ammunition to match.

Mr. Lovat Fraser has told us that when he was on the north-west frontier in 1909, he tried to ascertain what proportion of the tribesmen were then armed with modern rifles. The lowest estimate was 80,000, and many frontier officers seemed of the opinion that there were probably 150,000 good rifles in possession of men of the border. "Not only," says Mr. Lovat Fraser, "does this great influx of arms affect the character of our relations with the tribesmen, by giving them greater confidence in their offensive capacity, but it may also have very grave results should it ever be necessary for us to advance again into Afghanistan."[1]

But coincident with the departure from Indian waters of Rear-Admiral Sir Edward Slade, whose vigorous measures have done so much during the last three years for the suppression of the arms traffic between Muscat and Mekran, comes the opportune announcement that the Sultan of Oman has happily decided to control the trade himself—hitherto protected by a treaty, dating back to the Second Empire, between the Sultan and the Government of the French Republic. The Sultan of Oman has come to the decision to store all arms and ammunition imported into his dominions in a bonded warehouse, from which they are not to be released except upon production of certificates of destination, while no such

[1] *Proceedings of the Central Asian Society*, May 1911.

certificates are to be issued for the Mekran coast.
If the supervision · of the bonded warehouse is
thorough, the traffic in arms should be effectively
controlled, and a considerable relaxation of British
naval activities should be possible; unfortunately,
however, the continued existence of the trade benefits
many others besides the men of the "Bloody Border"
—Oriental officials and European manufacturers and
exporters—and it is possible that, though the traffic
is to all appearance dead, it may ere long be surrep-
titiously revived.

APPENDIX B.

TABLE OF EXPEDITIONS AGAINST THE FRONTIER TRIBES MENTIONED IN THE PRECEDING CHAPTERS.

Year.	Tribe.	Commander.	Number Employed.[1]	Casualties. K.	W.
1847	Baizais,	Lt.-Col. Bradshaw, C.B.,	Mixed Brigade	1	13
1849	Do.,	Do.,	2300	7	40
1850	Afridis, Kohat Pass,	Brig. Sir C. Campbell, K.C.B.,	3800	19	74
1851	Miranzai Tribes,	Capt. J. Coke,	2050, including levies	2	3
1851-2	Mohmands,	Brig. Sir C. Campbell, K.C.B.,	1597	4	5
1852	Do.,	Do.,	600	2	8
„	Ranizais,	Do.,	3270	11	29
„	Utman Khels,	Do.,	2300	3	15
„	Wazirs, Darweah Khel,	Major J. Nicholson,	1500	24	7
1852-3	Hassanzais,	Lt.-Col. Mackeson, C.B.,	3800, including levies, etc.	5	10
1853	Hindustani Fanatics,	Do.,	9000	Nil	
„	Afridis, Adam Khel,	Col. Boileau,	1740	8	29
1854	Mohmands,	Col. Cotton,	1782	1	16
1855	Afridis, Aka Khel,	Lt.-Col. Craigie, C.B.,	1500	9	25

[1] These figures are in many cases only approximate.

APPENDIX B.—continued.

Year.	Tribe.	Commander.	Numbers Employed.	K.	W.
1855	Miranzai Tribes, -	Brig. Chamberlain, -	3766	—	14
"	Orakzais, Rabia Khel, -	Do.,	2457	11	4
1856	Turis, -	Do.,	4896, including levies	5	3
1857	Yusafzais, -	Major Vaughan, -	400	2	3
			990	5	21
1858	Khudu Khels, etc., -	M.-Gen. Sir S. Cotton, K.C.B.,	1625, including levies	1	8
1859-60	Wazirs, Darwesh Khel, -	Brig.-Gen. Chamberlain, C.B.,	4877	6	29
1860	Wazirs, Mahsuds, -	Do.,	5372, including levies	1	19
1863	Ambela Expedition (Hindustani Fanatics, etc.),	Do., (later M.-Gen. Garvock),	6796, including levies	100	261
			9000	238	670
1864	Mohmands, -	Col. Macdonell, C.B., -	1801	2	17
1868	Orakzais, -	Major Jones, -	970, including levies, etc.	11	44
"	Black Mountain Tribes,	M.-Gen. Wilde, C.B., C.S.I.,	12,544	5	29
1869	Orakzais, -	Lt.-Col. Keyes, C.B., -	2080, including levies	3	23
1872	Dawaris, -	Brig.-Gen. Keyes, C.B., -	1896		6
1877	Afridis, Jowaki; -	Col. Mocatta, -	1750	1	10
1877-8	Do.,	Brig.-Gen. Keyes and Ross,	7400	11	51
1878	Utman Khels, -	Capt. Battye, -	280	—	8

APPENDIX B.—*continued.*

Year	Tribe	Commander	Numbers Employed	Casualties K.	Casualties W.
1878	Ranizais,	Major Campbell,	860	Nil	
,,	Utman Khels,	Lt.-Col. Jenkins,	875	—	1
,,	Afridis, Zakha Khel,	Lt.-Gen. Maude, V.C., C.B.,	2500	2	9
1879	Do.,	Do.,	3750	5	13
,,	Mohmands,	Capt. Creagh and Major Dyce,	600	6	18
,,	Zaimukhts,	Brig.-Gen. Tytler, V.C., C.B.,	3226	2	2
1880	Mohmands,	Brig.-Gen. Doran, C.B.,	2300	2	3
,,	Batannis,	Lt.-Col. Rynd,	721	—	5
,,	Wazirs, Darwesh Khel,	Brig.-Gen. Gordon, C.B.,	800	Nil	
1881	Wazirs, Mahsuds,	Brig.-Gens. Gordon and Kennedy,	8531	8	24
1887	Bunerwals,	Col. Broome,	460	3	2
1888	Black Mountain Tribes,	B.-Gen. J. McQueen, C.B., A.D.C.,	9416	25	57
1891	Do.,	M.-Gen. W. K. Elles, C.B.,	7289	9	39
,,	Orakzais,	B.-Gen. Sir W. Lockhart, K.C.B.,	4600	Nil	
,,	Do.,	Do.,	8000	28	73
1894	Wazirs,	Brig.-Gen. Turner and Lt.-Gen. Sir W. Lockhart, K.C.B.	11,150	46	75
1895	Chitralis,	M.-Gen. Sir R. Low, K.C.B.,	15,249	21	101

APPENDIX B.—continued.

Year	Tribe	Commander	Numbers Employed	Casualties K	Casualties W
1895	Chitralis,	Col. Kelly,	1400[1]	165	88
1897	Wazirs, Darwesh Khel,	M.-Gen. Corrie-Bird, C.B.,	8000	29	61
"	Akozais (Swat),	Col. Meiklejohn, C.B., C.M.G., and M.-Gen. Sir B. Blood, K.C.B.,	12,650	97	386
"	Mohmands,	Brig.-Gen. E. Elles, C.B.,	8500	12	98
"	Akozais and Tarkanris (Dir and Bajaur)	M.-Gen. Sir B. Blood, K.C.B.,	12,200	61	218
"	Utman Khels,	Colonel A. Reid, C.B.,	2900	Nil	
"	Orakzais,	M.-Gen. Yeatman-Biggs, C.B.,	9600	26	54
"	Afridis,	Lt.-Gen. Sir W. Lockhart, K.C.B.,	34,550	287	853
"	Chamkannis,	Brig.-Gen. Gaselee, C.B., and Col. Hill, C.B.,	9700	46	35
1898	Bunerwals,	M.-Gen. Sir B. Blood, K.C.B.,	8800	—	1
1899	Chamkannis,	Capt. Ross-Keppel,	1200, including levies	—	1
1900-01	Wazirs, Mahsud,	Brig.-Gen. Dening,	Small Columns[2]	32	114
1901-02	Wazirs, Darwesh Khel,	M.-Gen. Egerton, C.B.,	Do.,[2]	4	15
1908	Afridis, Zakka Khel,	M.-Gen. Sir J. Willcocks, K.C.M.G.,	14,000	3	37
"	Mohmands,	Do.,	12,000	38	184

[1] Includes garrisons of Chitral Fort and Mastuj, and parties under Capt. Ross and Lieut. Edwardes.
[2] Four to six small columns employed, strength averaging 1000.

APPENDIX C.

TABLE SHOWING BY WHOM THE TRIBES ARE CONTROLLED.

Dep.-Commissioner, Hazara.	Cis-Indus Swatis — Allai, Tikari, Deshi, Nandihar and Thakot. Yusafzais — Trans-Indus Utmanzai, Mada Khel, Amazai, Hassanzai, Akazai and Cis-Indus Chagarzai.
Political Agent, Dir, Swat and Chitral.	Yusafzais—Trans-frontier Akozai. Sam Ranizais. Bajauris. Chitralis.
Dep.-Commissioner, Peshawar.	Yusafzais—Trans-Indus Chagarzai, Khudu Khel, Chamlawala, Sam Baizai and Cis-Indus Utmanzai. Utman Khel. Mohmands. Gaduns. Bunerwals. Afridis—Adam Khel of Janakor and Kandar.
Political Agent, Khyber.	Afridis—except Adam Khel. Mullagoris. Mohmands—Shilmani. Shinwaris.
Dep.-Commissioner, Kohat.	Orakzais—except Massuzai. Afridis—Adam Khel. Bangash.
Political Agent, Kurram.	Zaimukhts. Turis. Orakzais—Massuzai. Chamkannis.
Dep.-Commissioner, Bannu.	Bannuchis.
Political Agent, Tochi.	Dawaris. Wazirs—Darwesh Khel.
Political Agent, Wana.	Wazirs—Mahsuds.
Dep.-Commissioner, Dera Ismail Khan.	Batannis.

INDEX.

Printed in the United States
145317LV00003B/26/A